American Exceptionalism

American Exceptionalism

A New History of an Old Idea

IAN TYRRELL

The University of Chicago Press

Chicago and London

The University of Chicago Press, Chicago 60637
The University of Chicago Press, Ltd., London
© 2021 by The University of Chicago
Published 2021
Paperback edition 2024
Printed in the United States of America

33 32 31 30 29 28 27 26 25 24   1 2 3 4 5

ISBN-13: 978-0-226-81209-0 (cloth)
ISBN-13: 978-0-226-83342-2 (paper)
ISBN-13: 978-0-226-81212-0 (e-book)
DOI: https://doi.org/10.7208/chicago/9780226812120.001.0001

Library of Congress Cataloging-in-Publication Data

Names: Tyrrell, Ian, author.
Title: American exceptionalism : a new history of an old idea / Ian Tyrrell.
Description: Chicago : University of Chicago Press, 2021. |
    Includes bibliographical references and index.
Identifiers: LCCN 2021010982 | ISBN 9780226812090 (cloth) |
    ISBN 9780226812120 (ebook)
Subjects: LCSH: Exceptionalism—United States. | United States—
    Historiography. | United States—History—Philosophy.
Classification: LCC E169.1 .T97 2021 | DDC 973—dc23
LC record available at https://lccn.loc.gov/2021010982

♾ This paper meets the requirements of ANSI/NISO Z39.48-1992 (Permanence of Paper).

To Diane Olive Collins, 1948–2021
Writer, educator, and so much more

.

Contents

The Peculiar Tale of American Exceptionalism

American exceptionalism has had a strange history. Little known in public debate as late as 2007, the term *exceptionalism* proliferated in usage after Barack Obama's election as U.S. president. When Republicans denounced Obama as an enemy of "American Exceptionalism," television viewers scurried to their computers and smartphones to find out from the World Wide Web exactly what this obscure term meant. A graph of its usage in the American media shows it soaring from practically nothing in 2007 to a peak in 2011–12. In the 2012 presidential election, "American Exceptionalism" became for the first time an entire chapter in the platform of an American political organization, the Republican Party.[1]

The real spark was a Barack Obama news conference in 2009. On his first trip abroad as president, he averred in Istanbul that the United States, especially in foreign policy, had "like every other nation" made "mistakes" and exhibited "flaws," all admissions that raised American eyebrows. Then, in Strasbourg, France, Obama had the effrontery, in some eyes, to relativize American power and its mission in the world.[2] He believed in American exceptionalism, but in an apparently qualified way: "just as I suspect that the Brits believe in British exceptionalism and the Greeks believe in Greek exceptionalism." The logical conclusion was this: Either one nation was exceptional, or none. The idea of "many" exceptionalisms logically disqualified the notion of American exceptionalism as a national conceit.[3]

Republicans seized on Obama's words to condemn him, and that attack set the stage for the frontal assault on his presidency that culminated in the 2012 election. Ironically, a fuller reading of his Strasbourg conference showed that Obama did subscribe to American exceptionalism.[4] It is often forgotten that Obama was the first sitting president to use the term, and to do so affirmatively. No matter. Would-be Republican presidential and vice presidential candidates Newt Gingrich and Sarah Palin weighed in, with Palin declaring the United States "a nation of exceptionalism" in the wake of Obama's apparent apostasy. In the course of this fractious debate, exceptionalism ceased to be an obscure academic concept; adherence to its tenets became a measure of individual conformity to national patriotism.[5] Exceptionalism had morphed into an ideology reflecting and shaping a social and political worldview, and through which public policy would be refracted.

As with many terms and concepts, the election of Donald J. Trump as president in 2016 gave this American exceptionalism a strange turn, with a swag of articles declaring its end or its decline, or its "souring," as David Frum wrote in the *Atlantic*.[6] Trump himself disavowed exceptionalism. "I never liked the term," he proclaimed.[7] As if for emphasis, Trump openly dismissed the idea of national moral superiority, proclaiming that Vladimir Putin's Russia was not the only country with evil people implementing government policy. When TV personality Bill O'Reilly pressed Trump on his respect for Putin, saying, "But he's a killer. . . . Putin's a killer," Trump shrugged, "There are a lot of killers. We've got a lot of killers. What, do you think our country is so innocent?"[8] "Innocency," as famed American theologian Reinhold Niebuhr termed it decades before, has been a self-perceived feature of American exceptionalist thought in foreign policy.[9] In contrast, Trump showed contempt for the idea that the nation stood apart as a noble bearer of ideals above the grubby jockeying of geopolitics and militarism. His "America First" slogan did not equate with exceptionalism. Rather, Trump exuded ethnonational sentiment and stentorian patriotism, and he shared this disposition with more overtly authoritarian leaders in Europe, Asia, and Latin America.[10]

Though Trump had borrowed (unacknowledged) the "Make America Great Again" slogan from the successful 1980 presidential run of Ronald Reagan, it was clear that for Trump, "great again" meant something other than a singular status in the world. "Great" did not mean exceptional; it had connotations of scale—great, greater, greatest—or of a numerical grid, whether measured by the size of navies, armaments, gross domestic product, or any other aspect of quantitative national attainment. It did not mean a nation set in a separate category, with unique moral and political ideals. Trump never favored the "city upon a hill" concept of the United States as a model for the world, as Ronald Reagan did and as Barack Obama concurred.[11] Instead, Trump proclaimed "America First," a slogan with an etymological pedigree dating from 1930s fascist sympathizers. "America First" means treating the relations between nations as a zero-sum, geopolitical struggle, without reference to international norms or ideals. It is a program for retrieved national greatness, not exceptionalism.[12] If greatness were to be meaningful as exceptionalism, it must be as a "true" greatness distinguished by its values from mere quantitative superiority.

The difference between "great" and "exceptional" is foundational to the discussion in this book because greatness has a habit of altering over time. The United States is undoubtedly a great power, possibly the greatest yet in world history. But with China challenging American economic hegemony, and many conventional standards of exceptionalism in material life eroded—in educational achievement, equality of opportunity, economic growth, and governmental conduct—something other than greatness would be needed to back the exceptionality of the United States. More important, the idea of American exceptionalism posits the United States as exceptional from the start, at a time and in an imperial world when it clearly was not great as a military or economic power.

American exceptionalism seems to many U.S. historians to be a settled question. Some never did support the theory, others no longer do. The rest, perhaps still a majority, probably support it only in carefully qualified and limited intellectual contexts. But I'm inclined to think that the skeptics underestimate the resilience and the cultural sway of this concept for the American people. In other words, a gap remains between historical interpretation on the meaning of U.S. history on this issue and the wider public's conflation of patriotism with exceptionalism. It is this idea of American exceptionalism as a discursive practice that concerns me in this book. Just because something cannot be verified as fact or seems old-fashioned as an idea in cutting-edge scholarship doesn't mean its hold is diminished. American exceptionalism is especially important as a contested idea in the current political conjuncture, but I suspect that it will continue to be important for quite some time.

The kerfuffle over the ideological doctrine of exceptionalism during the Obama presidency generated much heat but little enlightenment. Yet the character of the debate did show two distinguishing marks: first, that the widespread and often belligerent use of American Exceptionalism as an ideological "ism" has been a recent phenomenon; and second, that the idea behind the term was shaped by political forces and subject to conflicting interpretation and shifting meanings. In this book, I capitalize *Exceptionalism* in the term only in reference to its current ideological and political iteration. Otherwise, I use "American exceptionalism" to refer to the more general and underlying set of ideas prominent in American society and politics long before the term itself came into being. American exceptionalism as a clearly articulated concept and term dates only from 1929, but it has since the beginning of the twenty-first century been used to describe an idealized version of the

American past.[13] There is every reason to suggest that there were earlier variations of the notion equally subject to human construction and manipulation. In other words, American exceptionalism is a historically contingent and slippery idea. No fixed or pure entity called "American exceptionalism" has ever existed. It is always buried in its historical context. This is both its strength as an ideological and political weapon and its weakness as a guide to interpret the world. This malleability does not make it unimportant, however, because the idea has deeply influenced behavior. It can even be argued that "America"—understood for the purpose of this book as the United States—has been exceptional only because so many have *believed* it to be so.[14] But the internal coherence of that belief and its changing valence over time require close inspection.

The idea of the United States as *exceptional* can be easily found in the early republic, though the term was not invented then. Other formulations were used, such as the "model" republic or "experiment." Applied mostly to the prosperity, wealth, or liberal institutions of the nation, the closest was the old and now unfamiliar English word *unexampled*, meaning "without peer or parallel."[15] On occasion, it was still found in Fourth of July orations around the turn of the twentieth century; but it is not clear how, why, and when Americans collectively began to set their country off as so distinctive that its history and destiny represented a different order of things. Investigating these origins will require us to look beyond the modern concept to the gestation of the idea that Americans saw their country as in some way special long before they embraced any particular phrase or gave clear meaning to the term *exceptionalism*.

Under the doctrines of exceptionalism, the United States is not simply unique, as all nations are in their peculiarities and particularities, but outside the historical path of other nations. The latter are assumed to follow historical laws or norms. While other nations have histories that may be studied empirically and contextually, in an important sense exceptionalism is a ahistorical doctrine. Indeed, much of eighteenth- and nineteenth-century American exceptionalism may even be termed *pre-historicist* because it preceded the emergence of historicist explanation as a way of interpreting change over time. Though twentieth-century exceptionalism has been modified by statistical and social scientific versions of the doctrine that are ahistorical and positivist, not technically pre-historicist, we can still see vestiges of that old-fashioned assumption that the origins and meaning of the United States fall outside the course of time itself.[16] Not only is the exceptional nation often thought to be literally incomparable but, typically, it is also treated as unchanging in core values and characteristics. The expansion of the republic is regarded therein as the equivalent of a train going along a single track. Once the main lines of development are laid down, the United States can only move in one direction—along the track. To deviate would risk a wreck. "America" may become a better, bigger, and greater nation, but its major ideational structure cannot be changed. This is what may be called a historical involution, rather than evolution, as it occurs within these parameters, constantly striving to improve upon itself.[17]

Exceptionalism as an overt and analytical concept was derived from Marxism. It arose from the attempt to explain why the United States appeared to have escaped the class conflict that was occurring with the formation of large socialist parties in Europe by 1900, and how the nation dodged social upheaval comparable to the Bolshevik (Communist) revolution in tsarist Russia in 1917. Marxists argued that the rise of industrial capitalism produced a proletariat, which, forming class interests and pursuing class actions, would inevitably overthrow the bourgeois state. This simple transformation from capitalist oppression to workers' paradise occurred nowhere, but a series of revolutions inspired by Karl Marx's ideas purported to do just that. Class consciousness may or may not have developed in the United States—social historians differ on that point—but an American socialist revolution has not occurred, and Marxists themselves deployed the concept of exceptionalism to explain why the most purely capitalist of countries did not appear to demonstrate the validity of Marx's ideas. "American exceptionalism" was the pejorative that foreign Marxists gave to this American deficiency.[18]

The explicit concept did not take hold quickly. Until very recent times, it was not a piece of self-congratulatory rhetoric but an analytical way for academics and progressive intellectuals to explain key features of American history and politics. It did not necessarily mean the history of the United States was perfect or superior in its achievements, or that its characteristics had to be understood as positive. To be exceptional was, above all, to be superior in intention and promise—and, in its purest formulations, to have a special place in the world's progress.[19]

The bearer of this particular ideology is ultimately the American people, but its concrete expression is the American nation-state. Modern U.S. exceptionalism is not a class ideology but a national one that frames how Americans judge their *nation* against "the world." All nations develop nationalist ideologies of one sort or another; the American variety is a version of *national* exceptionalism. Though some states and regions within the United States have also claimed an exceptional status (notably the South of the former

Confederacy, and California), only national exceptionalism has a continuous history back to the beginning of the republic. Only national exceptionalism addresses the meaning and teleology of "America" in world history.

Any search for what makes Americans self-identify with this ideology requires returning not only to the beginning of the republic but also to the colonial inheritance. To many adherents, the idea behind the concept can be dated from the time when the English sailed across the Atlantic to form colonies in the early seventeenth century. But this colonial experience has been seen too often through the lens of subsequent history. Contemporary Americans and even historians have often mistakenly assumed that British America was somehow like an acorn from which the great oak tree of the present-day United States has sprung. This cannot be, since several British colonies in North America did not join the revolution of 1776, and the present-day United States includes huge swaths of territory, people, and historical experience apart from the original Anglo-American base. Only with the coming of the republic from 1776 to 1789 could a national exceptionalism even be considered possible. What has changed since that time is the relationship between the state and the people. What was in the early nineteenth century a loose and grassroots feeling, heterogeneously grounded in (white male) democratic participation, has become a state-sponsored ideology and a patriotic necessity.

Themes and Theories

The idea of American exceptionalism has been articulated in a remarkable diversity of ways. Far from being a stable entity, exceptionalism has been subject to contradictions and alternative interpretations. Its efficacy has fluctuated. One must examine how exceptionalism was made in a concrete, social practice. This does not mean an elite imposing exceptionalism on a people, but it does entail studying exactly who "made" exceptionalism and how exceptionalist belief emerged out of experience.[20]

This process was an intensely political matter. The growth in exceptionalist doctrines to an intellectually dominant position occurred in response to political controversies and challenges generated by the American Revolution's aftermath. Apart from the external environment of wars, revolutions, and political upheaval, an ensemble of institutions became crucial to solidifying it. Schools, textbooks, churches, courts, and voluntary associations developed what amounted to the sustaining elements of an exceptionalist ideology. Its concrete expression was a creed of national beliefs, values, and ideals. (Some scholars have called this creed a "civil religion," transcending denominations and even faiths, though that term is not necessarily exceptionalist in implication since other countries have manifested civil religion).[21] The means for imparting exceptionalist ideas were as varied as creative literature, songs, hymns, anthems, and so on but especially Fourth of July and other patriotic orations in the period of the early republic, the sermons of clergy, and the addresses of historians and other literary people. The creation of American exceptionalism was not the property of—or under the control of—any one group. The processes involved both state and society; indeed, the boundaries between these two domains were fluid through much of American history, but Americans did not control all.

Americans shaped the doctrine of exceptionalism by comparing the United States with Europe, but the views of Europeans were also influential. The two cannot be disentangled. A succession of foreign travelers as well as incoming migrants observed the United States; so too did later social theorists. They all conveyed facts and opinions about the United States back home, but Americans were also interested in these views. The French liberal aristocrat Alexis de Tocqueville was to become the most famous of these observers, yet he was only one among a host of interested travelers in the nineteenth century.[22] European visitors such as Britons Charles Dickens and Harriet Martineau came and, whether they liked or hated what they saw, described the United States as a social and political experiment. Some of these sojourners could even be regarded as pioneer comparative sociologists. Their work has been drawn upon by historians for evidence of U.S. social, political, and cultural distinctiveness, and by post-1945 champions of American exceptionalism.[23] While South Asians and other non-Europeans also came and reported home, it was the Europeans whose observations circulated most widely in the United States, perhaps because they were more often written in English or rapidly translated.[24] It was in this way that American exceptionalism was enmeshed with transatlantic relations. In turn, this Europe/America, Old World/New World dichotomy reconceived and repackaged myths about the regeneration of the world through the history of the United States. The early Puritans treating their Massachusetts settlement as a site of a chosen people were Europeans by birth, upbringing, and heritage. They were not "Americans" in any meaningful sense. Only the indigenous tribes were "American" then.[25]

This transnational dialogue over American exceptionalism is illustrated in the work of a Frenchman. J. Hector St. John de Crèvecoeur published his much-quoted comments on the American colonies in *Letters from an American Farmer* in 1782, but the letters were mostly penned before the American Revolution began. Crèvecoeur emphasized the shaping of the American character under the impact of a favorable environment: "men are like plants," he wrote, and their "goodness" came from the "peculiar soil and exposition in which they grow."[26] Yet his account was by no means completely positive, as the role of slavery was discussed in a critical way. Moreover, the subject of the letters was the larger entity of British North America, not the United States, which did not exist when the bulk of the letters were written. First popular in Europe rather than in the fledgling United States, the *Letters* represented the transnational production of American exceptionalism as an idea, with its constituent parts reflecting European perceptions of the colonies.[27] Only in the twentieth century have U.S. advocates of exceptionalism found his work particularly interesting for their beliefs.[28]

Outsiders did not necessarily like the assertion of exceptionalism as a roseate doctrine of American superiority. Many gave negative accounts, whereas Americans tended to assimilate the positive ones, or to change the terms and misunderstand the points that foreigners were making. This was true of Tocqueville's reception, which was not as sanguine about American democracy as frequently thought. Tocqueville was an extraordinarily insightful visitor, but outsiders on the receiving end of U.S. exceptionalism in the nineteenth century often experienced American patriotic bombast and boastful exaggeration. British observers "found the American enthusiasm for such 'spread-eagle' oratory quite ridiculous."[29] Ironically, these foreign audiences helped make the young nation seem more exceptional by focusing on hyperbolic representations rather than on the more considered and variable content of American debate.

On this basis, one may posit a theory of American exceptionalism that uses both transnational analysis and comparative method. Adapting the ideas of Richard Pells, one can argue that exceptionalism was to a considerable degree conceived abroad or by recent arrivals or visitors, then continually modified, repackaged, and exported through American commodities, personnel who traveled overseas (such as tourists and missionaries), and media, literature, arts, music, and the like.[30] For example, the actual term *exceptionalism* was conceived by European socialists, adapted in the United States, mostly to have a more positive connotation, and then applied to the history of other countries in judgment as to how well they compared with the gold standard of exceptionalism set by the United States. As an insidious spin-off, other nations have begun in recent decades to depict themselves in explicitly exceptionalist language, even as this idea seems incompatible with the American intention.[31] Foreign influence must not be exaggerated, of course, but whether purveyed by outsiders or insiders, American exceptionalism was the product of a transnational dialogue over the meaning of what Europeans and other foreigners called the American republic.

The views of foreigners were important, but American nationals would pay attention to external claims only if the propositions fitted, to some degree, Americans' lived experience and their understanding of "Europe." That is why they modified European observations and picked and chose among foreign assessments. Americans made their own way in life, and many of them *made* exceptionalism as they went. Some did not succeed, or were not in a position to articulate the ideology, but enough did to keep the idea alive and to provide the public resonance with the notion to sustain it.

Not all Americans have seen their nation in exceptionalist terms. An anti-exceptionalist pushback against the overreach of American mission has been common enough. Anti-imperialism has been a recurrent example, parts of the abolitionist critique of American slavery another, and the economic and political upheavals of the 1970s a more recent case. Striking is the extent to which individual Americans have vacillated between the two positions. Depending on historical events and individual circumstance, the same Americans could be for or against exceptionalism. In part, this behavior reveals the complexity and variability of the ideology. But it has also reflected in many cases a call to reclaim the nation's exceptionality from the prospect of defeat. This raises the issue of the jeremiad.

Under the Puritan jeremiad, seventeenth-century New England clergy denounced the social, moral, and religious failures of their communities in a series of lamentations reflecting or threatening a break of the settlers' covenant with God, but these clerics offered the hope of a return to the true way of God through renunciation of sin. As the literary scholar Sacvan Bercovitch saw, both criticism and affirmation are contained here as a self-perpetuating discursive critique existing "only in the United States."[32] This type of critique may denounce American social and political institutions—yet reinforce belief in exceptionalism as reflective of history or future promise. Where the jeremiad ends and antiexceptionalism begins is often indeterminate, however.[33] That is because the critic may consider the response of Americans to the jeremiad against their behavior to be so inadequate as to require an entire departure from exceptionalist discourse.

In practice, we shall see how the jeremiad was only one form of prevalent critique. Antigovernment sentiment has also been present. Making "government" the cause of the nation's ills, rather than target the "sins" of the "people," has implications for the modern transformation of American exceptionalism into a political ideology. This antigovernmental attitude has roots in the so-called Court versus Country or "civic republican" tradition of seventeenth-century English politics, under which centralized power through the British Crown (the Court) provoked anxieties about aristocratic luxury and corruption. The Court was juxtaposed to the virtuous, common citizenry (the Country), which was considered the necessary foundation for a new republican social order. Transferred to the American colonies, the doctrine not only contributed to revolutionary ideology in the 1770s; civic republicanism was also a strain of thought that influenced the anti-Federalists' attempts to put curbs, through the Bill of Rights, on the power of the new federal government authorized in the U.S. Constitution of 1787.[34] The animus of Court versus Country thinking arguably continued in antigovernment rhetoric and practice long after that.[35]

★

Debates over contemporary American Exceptionalism have been the victim of both media overkill and frequent assumptions of a continuity in ideas. Finer distinctions need to be made, and a plethora of concepts commonly associated with exceptionalism requires close examination and historical perspective. What, for instance, are the relationships of the "American Idea," the "American Dream," the "American Creed," "Americanism," the "City upon a Hill," "Manifest Destiny," and so on, to one another and to American exceptionalism? Are they subsidiary myths or alternative ones? A second set of questions concerns the connection between the idea of American exceptionalism and the practice; that is, between what is believed to be true and what is. I argue that these two are not independent of each other but exist in a reciprocal and constantly changing relationship. A third point is the need to examine the means by which the idea was defined and transmitted. American exceptionalism did not spring into life fully grown in 1607, 1630, 1776, or 1861–65. It was made by Americans casting about to discover and affirm what they learned or experienced.

Three competing concepts must be singled out. They have helped support American exceptionalism but are conceptually distinct from it and have proven less useful than it in interpretive power. These three concepts are the American Way, the American Dream, and the American Creed.

American exceptionalism is not the same as the American Way (or the "American Way of Life"), which rose as an idea amid growing anxiety in the United States over national identity in the face of the Great Depression, and over the emergence of European (fascist) threats to American security. The American Way did not have a comparative dimension aside from its Cold War connotations. By the 1950s it became a covert means of expressing political consensus and religious interfaith cooperation in resisting "Godless" communism, rather than a key to explaining the nation's radical distinctiveness. The idea was bound to these mid-twentieth-century geopolitical crises and lacked the capacity of American exceptionalism to apply to the United States across time, irrespective of foreign ideological threats.[36]

Nor is American exceptionalism identical with the American Dream. A more durable concept than the American Way, the historian James Truslow Adams popularized the term *American Dream* in his *Epic of America* (1931), though he did not invent it.[37] For Adams the dream was not material satisfaction but the opportunity for all people to achieve their worth, irrespective of origins and station. This idea became, after World War II, almost interchangeable with modern American exceptionalism, but not quite. Instead, it served as a secondary support for exceptionalism, a tantalizing yet vague dream to inspire Americans to believe in the promise of the nation. Unlike exceptionalism, it was not an interpretation of American history's core values. The American Dream did not mean judging other countries as conforming to a common pattern from which the United States diverges; it did not require national comparisons, though those may have been implicit, nor did it prescribe patriotism focused on the nation-state. Finally, it did not have the quasi-religious content increasingly associated with exceptionalism since the 1980s. More ephemeral than American exceptionalism, and yet more materialist, the dream expressed connotations of happy homes and families with a high standard of living, rather than values or principles.[38]

If the American Dream is conceptually distinct from exceptionalism, the third concept, the American Creed, is clearly part of it. The American Creed expresses exceptionalism's specific ideological and political content of individualism, egalitarianism, and related liberal and democratic values. Popularized by the Swedish sociologist Gunnar Myrdal, who analyzed the "American dilemma" facing the liberal "creed" in incorporating African Americans into the body politic, the terminology has gained resonance; it is an offshoot of the cluster of ideas expressing and underpinning exceptionalism.[39] The historian John Higham wrote of this "cosmopolitan" ideal as a "universalist" nationalism of broadening diversity, liberalism, and inclusivity. Others have "scornfully" called it American exceptionalism, Higham added. In the self-image of the nation, American universalism is a positive quality; it holds out a model for American society, and for the human race as well, to strive for the better, but how emulation is to be accomplished is another matter. Universalism may be interpreted in two ways. Americans may seek to share their core values with others, or they may focus on extending the liberal and egalitarian tenets of the American Revolution within the United States, but universalism has not existed outside concrete historical circumstances in which many particularisms, such as ethnic or racial discrimination, have also operated.[40]

As an idea framing public debate, exceptionalism's meaning has changed repeatedly over time, sometimes stressing political issues, at other times material ones, and at still others religious ones. Great attention has been given to the religious and political content, but the theme of material abundance has been too often taken for granted. Whether conceived as a modern consumer society, the availability of resources, opportunity for social mobility, or the processes of frontier expansion, it underpinned the other values of freedom, democracy, and religious chosenness.

Over long periods of U.S. history, the "material" dimension and the "idea" of exceptional status were fairly well aligned or bent toward ultimate fulfillment. The connection between abundance and the notion of "futurity" is particularly relevant here. From the early republic through to the Civil War, exceptionalism was primarily associated with the coming greatness of the United States produced by the nation's rich endowment. As the nation prospered and grew to world prominence, assumptions of future material promise gave way to a conviction of present abundance underwriting the assumption of global power. Since the 1970s, that pattern has changed again. The idea of exceptionalism has been pushed more insistently, while certain material conditions seem less and less exceptional as globalization, urbanization, and modernization have reduced national differences among many countries. Inequality of opportunity and of condition have risen markedly while economic growth has lagged behind key competitor nations. The links between abundance, futurity, and exceptional status have been broken. While that circumstance would seem to weaken the whole notion of exceptionalism, strangely it has not, at least not yet. Exceptionalism's relevance must, therefore, stem from something other than the straightforward representation of material fact. Exceptionalism must be considered not as an account of American "reality," but as an ideology representing reality.

Whatever its theoretical, logical, and empirical weaknesses, exceptionalism is still a useful concept for political purposes, more so than others. It expresses a sense of the United States in which a noble ideal of human freedom is rendered coterminous with a specific place and nation-state, while not excluding any group within the nation. In contrast, Anglo-Saxonism, a prominent concept in the nineteenth century, was exclusionist in implication and had major difficulties in gaining public consensus after the immigration of Poles, Slavs, Mediterranean peoples, and Jews had reached a torrent. Anglo-Saxonism's successor term by World War I was *Americanism*, but that had its own limitations. No one agreed on its meaning, and it did not explicitly single out the United States as a model nation. Americanism was strongly patriotic but inward looking and often plainly xenophobic in implication at the high point of its influence in the 1920s. Exceptionalism sidesteps those negative connections and encapsulates the idea of a nation with a special destiny, while avoiding outright affinity with any particular racial group or religion. The latter point is important for a religiously diverse society with a strong tradition of church-state separation. For all these reasons, American exceptionalism deserves close study as a historical phenomenon.

Approaches

Two broad analytical approaches have been adopted for American exceptionalism.[41] The first asks how it could be objectively appraised as "fact." As a statement of radical difference from other nations, the idea is at least implicitly comparative and therefore open to empirical testing, which can be broken down into case studies manageable for serious research. However, the search for definitive answers has helped not to validate or discredit the idea empirically but to shape exceptionalism into a more powerful ideological tool. This comparative exceptionalism can be traced back to the political and economic rhetoric of statesmen and scholars in the era of the Enlightenment. Nevertheless, scholarly literature assessing the role of institutions and social circumstances in forming American singularity has been intensely influenced by the rise of twentieth-century social science in academia and public life. This type of exceptionalism considered as "science" I label "Lipsetian" because the modern scaffolding of the idea, as well as the use of the actual term *American exceptionalism*, derives to a considerable extent from the tireless work of the eminent political sociologist Seymour Martin Lipset, even as contemporary work of this kind has been more rigorous and qualified than Lipset's was.[42]

The (Lipsetian) social science approach has involved measuring differences between the United States and other countries across any number of individual characteristics. Nowadays, this research is more noticeable in political science, economics, and legal studies than in sociology and history, but it still covers many behavioral phenomena often made to stand for a wider exceptional status.[43] Lipset evaluated the United States against other countries to determine how different the nation was. He made serial comparisons of concrete phenomena, and he concluded that the differences amounted to a value system of "American exceptionalism," a term he popularized in academia from *The First New Nation* (1963) to *American Exceptionalism: A Double-Edged Sword* (1996). These exceptional values centered on an American "creed" of "liberty, egalitarianism, individualism, populism and laissez-faire."[44] But to display categories such as the level of philanthropy, higher education achievement, gun ownership, entrepreneurial crime, choice of sports, or anything else

of a measurable kind as markers of exceptionalist characteristics, as his followers and imitators have done, is flawed because it characterizes particular
manifestations of behavior as expressions of a deeper value system that is itself
beyond empirical measurement. Lipset himself saw the underlying values of
exceptionalism as in tension with one another, not fixed.[45]

There are further pitfalls. Because the data reveal that American behavior
patterns are sometimes similar to non-Western rather than "European" countries, Lipset limited the empirical testing of exceptionalism to "comparable"
cases, typically Western or "modern," on the ground that the United States
itself was a quintessentially "modern" country. Still present in contemporary
public discourse and media more than in current scholarship, this stance
begs the question whether the United States should be considered uniformly
"modern," and whether "modernization" as a concept can be objectively as-
sessed and compared as a historical phenomenon. Lipset's analysis reinforced
the existing dichotomy in social science of the 1950s between "tradition" and
"modernity."[46] However, his analysis did not require purely positive judgments about the United States. His comparative approach allowed for negative as well as positive characteristics to be associated with the elements of his
American Creed, though he believed the positive outweighed the negative.

Individual comparisons may show the United States to be different from
any another country in particular patterns of behavior or belief, but Lipsetian
research does not make the United States exceptional, only different. As political scientist Keith Dowding argues, speaking of Australia, "One must carefully describe the level of granularity at which comparison is to be made and
then accurately note differences" not only between that one country "and the
rest of the world, but between each country and the rest."[47] This approach is
too daunting ever to be effectual. Lipset's own comparisons were asymmetrical, using a variety of countries to establish a behavioral norm to compare
with the United States. Thereby, exceptionalism arises as an issue because
the United States has been arbitrarily made the fixed point of reference for
comparative research.[48]

The second analytical approach treats exceptionalism as a mythic belief
system with deep roots in European and American culture. The influential
Romanian historian and phenomenologist of religion Mircea Eliade regarded
myths as stories about origins revealing "an archetypal history" of "how the
world came to be"—at the beginning of time.[49] They provide a necessary
anchor for personal and group identity outside of everyday life. American
exceptionalism is such a creation story, but it is also more precisely a myth
rooted in the recorded history of national institutions. It requires reference to
personal and group experience, not simply the inherited knowledge of folk

stories. This does not mean that a myth constructed in the historical time of a modern state conforms more strictly to observable data than a so-called traditional one, but it must present plausible historical data for its origin stories. This type of American exceptionalism as mythic origins may be called Winthropian because it is often thought to be derived from the idea of a "city upon a hill" that the Puritan governor John Winthrop expressed for the Massachusetts Bay Colony in 1630.[50]

For religious exceptionalists, the United States has had a mythic beginning that was both Christian and chosen for a providential task in the eyes of God. The connection to "providence" is a tricky matter, however. One may carve up providentialism in a taxonomy of divine intentions, but the categories will overlap. The term can simply be a ritualistic reference or assumption about an inscrutable force present in the universe. It may also refer to the judgment of God as an interpretation of history's patterns or convey a belief in the direct intervention of God in history. The focus may be not only the idea of God's plan for the world but also the choice of a specific nation to carry forward that plan. Americans have used *providence*, often indiscriminately, in all of these meanings, but the latter is the most important as a signature of exceptionalism.[51] Though the Christian part of chosenness draws upon Puritan precedents, modern Christian nationalism has asserted the Christian character of the U.S. Constitution based on inference from the document's cultural context rather than (nonexistent) specific provisions.[52] It would be more plausible to acknowledge the "achievement of America's founders in creating the world's first secular republic," one critic of the Christian America argument has replied.[53]

Even if the United States could be regarded as a Christian nation by exaggerating the Puritan impact, that would not necessarily mean it is a chosen nation. There have been many nations in which a Christian profession has been state-endorsed or otherwise supported, but, under biblical teaching, there can be only one Chosen Nation: Israel. As respected modern authorities have argued, the analogy between the United States and Old Testament Israel on this point is nothing but "bad theology." Christian ethicist David Gushee put it this way: no "scriptural warrant" has existed "for believing that God's special relationship with biblical Israel could ever be, or has ever been, transferred to another nation." Under Christian theology, Christians belong to a "faith-community gathered around Jesus" that is "multiethnic and multinational," however compromised this universalistic stance might be in historical cases.[54] This theological rebuttal has not stopped exceptionalists from calling the United States chosen, and the complexities of that argument will be unveiled in the actual history of those claims as exceptionalism evolved.

There is an alternative to these two dichotomous approaches: settler colonialism. That idea focuses on the dynamics of the settler process. As an
international approach, settler colonial studies mostly examine European expansion in the Pacific, the Americas, and parts of Africa not as self-contained
national systems but as colonies with a shared underlying dynamic. Settlement processes dramatically altered the landscapes, ecologies, economies,
and cultures of places invaded. To one degree or another, settler empires sup-
pressed or oppressed indigenous people and marginalized or exterminated
them. All were products of what theorists have labeled settler colonialism.
The nation-states that inherited the mantle of sovereignty from these colonial
regimes depended on that prior expropriation and built their state structures
in the knowledge of the need to stake ownership of and legitimate the space
seized by colonists.[55]

Methodologically antiexceptionalist, such an approach would be not only
comparative but also transnational and interactive. It would see the histories of colonies and European empires in real time, influencing one another.
Work of this sort is found in modern accounts of British colonial America,
but far less so in histories of the American republic.[56] The underlying reason
is the entrenchment of exceptionalist ideas. In particular, seeing the United
States as a self-governing republic of citizens, not an empire of subjects, has
powerfully reinforced the commonplace assumption that Native American
incorporation in the polity transcends the history of dispossession and the
subsequent treatment of these people by the American state. A further reason is found in the myth of the "nation of immigrants," which for decades
discounted the indigenous claim to a unique and prior settlement by wrongly
asserting that U.S. history and the history of immigrants have been virtually
coterminous. To a considerable degree, exceptionalism's history as an idea is
the story of how Americans came to understand their past as an exception
to settler colonialism, not as a dispossessor but as an instrument of Manifest
Destiny. While settler colonialism does not provide a single or infallible key
to American history, it has the potential to go a fair way toward realizing
a more comprehensive alternative to exceptionalism as a national narrative,
when added to consideration of the United States as a form of empire. Settler
colonialism may be justly criticized for ignoring or homogenizing (tribal)
indigenous histories and indigenous agency, but the issue here is how settler
colonialism and its denial underpinned U.S. exceptionalism.[57]

This underutilized theory in U.S. history aside, the two versions of American exceptionalism—as empirical reality and as myth—may be set out sepa-
rately for analytical purposes. Yet there has usually been interplay between
these two. While the mythos of a chosen nation or country might seem less

vulnerable to purely empirical attack, the opportunity to critique exceptionalism as a modern mythos remains. The idea may be ahistorical in character, but not in origins, which are within time and subject to historical analysis.[58] Any story of the nation setting it apart from others, whether by a specific religion, an all-seeing God, or some mysterious but secular destiny, cannot simply be assumed, especially since other nations have claimed a similar status. Moreover, the elements of chosenness vary, from broadly secular ones to pious religious purposes connected to an actual Second Coming of Christ. The idea can be internally challenged too; examining the belief in a chosen nation and its meaning in history shows that the concepts contain contradictions and qualifications. The idea of chosenness has not, as often assumed, been "consistently strong and surprisingly uniform" in U.S. history, and the relationship between belief, a people, and a nation is not self-evident.[59]

For these reasons, the composition of American exceptionalism is best understood as a blend of myth and social experience. The result is not a single foundational story about the American past but rather a changing cluster of myths that reflect and refract historical experience. The collective content is flexible enough to withstand the empirical refutation to which a single modern myth might be vulnerable. American exceptionalism is founded not on one but on three central pillars, regarding religious, political, and material conditions. Not simply an amalgam of these three, the pattern is more like an experience in mix and match. At various times, particular aspects have been stressed or joined. Only by understanding this historical process can one be in a position either to discard the idea of exceptionalism entirely or to adapt it to contemporary circumstances. These matters will be discussed in relation to subsidiary myths that have waxed and waned, from Manifest Destiny to a "Nation of Immigrants" and many in between.[60] These variations collectively support a national ideology derived not from a creation moment or philosophical essence but from the accretion, over time, of myths concerning the nation's experience.

Traditionally, American exceptionalism has been seen as either a moral example to the world or a missionary intervention in it, but this division is simplistic. Setting an "example" may be passive or actively promoted—for example, by media and communications or cultural diplomacy. The active type tends to become missionary or interventionist, though intervention may not involve a material influence. On the other hand, the idea of a standoffish or passive "example" approaches the view of the United States as sui generis. At the extreme, the American "model" becomes pointless because the United States is taken as truly unique, and American precepts could not apply elsewhere. Modernization theorists have seen the possibility of the American example being generalized, but in practice, the historical experience of projecting the "example" or "model" abroad has tended to confirm an underlying incompatibility in the national ethos.[61] As the Norwegian political scientist Hilde Restad judiciously concludes, "the classic Janus-faced view of American identity as either exemplary or missionary is too clever by half."[62] Any attempt to divide exceptionalism into these dichotomies either restates the equally simplistic political alternatives of isolationism and internationalism or fails to account for contradictory impulses within the notion of exceptionalism. The contradictions are typically exposed in attempts to apply American exceptionalist ideas abroad. The case of the Arab world is one illustrating the damage that may occur.

Collateral Damage

American exceptionalism is not only important because it attempts to describe an American polity, society, and culture in the definite terms of social science, nor simply because exceptionalist myths are so important to American identity. Exceptionalism has also structured the way that American political figures and opinion makers have understood the world. The trope of exceptionalism has been adapted to fit numerous situations for which it was never intended. Social scientists have used it to conceive how other nations fit into American values, or not. They have developed social surveys to rank foreign countries on measures of freedom, equality, and belief in individualism and religion, but they have also used the language of exceptionalism to typecast these other nations as rigid, tradition-bound, and incapable of true progress. In these terms, the United States is the nation of modernity above all others. It has been able to advance as a modern nation because of its attributes of exceptionality, typically understood as markers distinguishing it from less desirable qualities manifest in countries that could not break the barrier into modernity. Perhaps the best example of this—although by no means the only one—is so-called Arab exceptionalism. During the 1970s to 1990s, the U.S. government-funded Freedom House devoted much of its energy to rating "democracies" and their freedoms. Its studies showed, for example, that Muslim and Arab states were "comparatively . . . exceptional in being resistant to democracy."[63]

Such scorecards of democratic achievement should not be seen in an academic vacuum, as they have had practical applications. Influential policy makers did adopt similar views of an "Arab exceptionalism" under the Project for a New American Century (PNAC). Certain advocates of American exceptionalism campaigned for a democratic revolution in the Middle East after PNAC's inception in 1997.[64] Some of these figures joined the George W. Bush administration in 2001. Although their presence does not prove influence on the specific policy behind the invasion of Iraq in 2003, that policy was directed at democratizing a region deemed deficient, with Iraq targeted as a potential model state, provided Saddam Hussein was overthrown.[65] The irony was the tendency for these exceptionalists to project an inverse version of exceptionalism on their "Arab" or "Muslim" adversaries. Though PNAC was discreetly dissolved in the wake of the Iraq War's disastrous outcomes for the people of Iraq, American veterans, and the careers of some American politicians, the idea of a peculiar Arab exceptionalism continued to guide certain opinion makers in foreign policy. It has influenced liberal figures in the Brookings Institution as much as conservatives. Tamara Cofman Wittes, a senior fellow in the Center for Middle East Policy, wrote, "Only the development of liberal democracies in the Arab world's major states will, in the long term, secure the advancement of American goals in the region." The Middle East was, "according to Freedom House," the "least democratic region on the globe." Despite the Iraq War to which PNAC had given support, Wittes argued that the United States must still overcome "Arab" distinctiveness. Ironically, the United States has sought to use its own exceptionalism to remake the Middle East and end "Arab exceptionalism." Wittes was aware of the irony that U.S. policy, if successful, might mean the demise of American exceptionalism too, underscoring the extent to which American exceptionalism is a contradictory ideology. The corollary of a special national status is that other countries never catch up with the United States, though they are expected to do so, and may be subject to coercive economic or military pressures to change.[66]

The outcome of foreign policies to project American power and values has raised fundamental questions about exceptionalism within the United States as well. Was a country seeking to impose its values on others exceptional? Or was the United States no longer exceptional because it seemed unable to achieve this imposition easily? Did the policy trajectory reflect the nation's failures in the period of perpetual war in Asia after 2001 to live up to higher ethical standards that American exceptionalism connoted? This discourse over the fate of American power underpinned the supercharging of exceptionalism as a guiding notion for U.S. nationalism after 2009. Whether this era presaged a decline of the United States or a perpetuation of exceptionalism as a doctrine, or both, will be canvassed in this book. Though Donald Trump scoffed at the exceptionalist idea, it quickly became central to the developing critique of Trump's presidential performance and, in another way, to some of his key backers. Exceptionalism's contemporary advocates, whether of the Left or the Right, are not about to give up, and the idea is not about to die.

The Puritans and American Chosenness

Democratic rights, individualism, and high levels of belief in a special religious destiny are all traits associated with American exceptionalism that,
to varying degrees, have been traced to the Puritan influence. Democracy
and individualism are the easiest to assess, and the verdict is largely negative.
This is not to deny the Puritan contribution to the foundational myths of the
United States. Rather, understanding those myths requires attention to the
subsequent history of the United States and its mythmaking processes.[1]

Political, Economic, and Religious Contributions of Puritanism

The term *Puritan* originally applied to the Massachusetts Bay Colony settled
in 1630, not the *Pilgrims* who arrived on the *Mayflower* at Plymouth Rock in
1620. Though these two colonies had distinct historical, doctrinal, and organizational origins, in the nineteenth century the two settlements and the
terms used to describe them became blurred in American memory as both
Puritan and *Pilgrim*. But the legacy of 1630 has been better placed to reso-
nate with American exceptionalism in the twentieth century because of that
colony's religious justification, especially as expressed in John Winthrop's "A
Modell of Christian Charity" address.

The Puritans brought with them to North America a decentralized idea
of church government. Authority was founded not on bishops and archbish-
ops, as in the Church of England, or on the papacy, as in the Roman Catholic Church, but on congregations that could select their own ministers and
conduct internal affairs. Alexis de Tocqueville noted these arrangements as
the forerunner of a democratic tradition: "Puritanism was not merely a religious doctrine, but it corresponded in many points with the most absolute

democratic and republican theories."[2] In modern America, particularly in the struggle with fascism in World War II, it was tempting to reach back to Puritan origins to find a compatibility though not a complete correlation with American ideals. This was the path of the Harvard University philosopher Ralph Barton Perry, who sought in *Puritanism and Democracy* (1944) the roots of American cohesion and purpose in the face of wartime threats. In more recent times, early Puritanism has even been invoked as the bedrock of a more vital and direct democracy than the constitutional liberalism prevalent after the American Revolution.[3]

Either way, a link between the growth of American democracy and early Puritan governance is far from clear, partly because seventeenth-century New England was more geographically, politically, and socially diverse than the old stereotypes of bigotry and killjoy behavior allow. Attributing Puritan contributions is also complicated by the development of comparable politico-economic features in other British North American colonies not founded on Calvinism.[4] With a stretch, the case for pioneer "democratic" status may be made for the Massachusetts Bay Colony, wherein a participatory religious society with an elective franchise was conceived as a self-governing entity. Yet that colony's religiopolitical hierarchy expelled dissenters and, as early as 1636–38, Puritan settlers began to exterminate or remove those Native Americans they found troublesome, essentially because these indigenous peoples took issue with the European concept of (private) land ownership entailing exclusive property rights.[5] As the colony developed in the second half of the seventeenth century, its legislative franchise was far from universal, let alone broadly accessed in practice by adult (white) males. At most, the Puritans could be described as "Godly republicans" rather than democrats in their early preference for a self-governing religious polity since freemen had to be church members to qualify for voting. Only if we include Roger Williams's protests on behalf of religious dissent leading to the founding of Rhode Island can we find a compatible pluralistic and "democratic" alternative within Puritanism, but Williams was concerned with nurturing religious rather than political freedom. Under the Rhode Island Royal Charter of 1663, voting was restricted to landowners, and that state was one of the last to enact (white) manhood suffrage in nineteenth-century America.[6]

The Puritans have been credited with pioneering still other features associated with American exceptionalism. Political sociologist Seymour Martin Lipset claimed that a deeply ingrained "Calvinistic Puritanism" was bequeathed to Americans as exceptional self-reliance, competitive individualism, and acquisitiveness.[7] Lipset's idea had foundations in Max Weber's thesis on the causal link between the rise of capitalism and Protestantism.[8] In contrast, American Puritan writers gave priority to theology, covenant, and community rather than individualism.[9] Yet religious and politicoeconomic ideas were part of the same intellectual and theological matrix.[10] None of the early colonies was precapitalist because they all depended on private property, markets, and capital accumulation. Puritanism alone can hardly account for individualism in American exceptionalist thought and politics and, even less, its later antistatist attitudes and laissez-faire practices that Lipset identified as exceptional. For one, acquisitive individualism was far from absent in the many British North American colonies outside Puritan New England. For another, the Puritans focused on a self-regulated duty of obedience to a community rather than the liberty to do what one liked. To the extent that the latter-day Protestantism of the nineteenth century could be held to underpin the capitalist market economy through doctrines of hard work and self-improvement, the dominant theology had been changed by non-Calvinist (Arminian) views stressing free will and individual conscience.[11]

Though the Puritan legacy to American religious culture has been more considerable, its contribution to exceptionalism has become too closely identified with the settlement of the Massachusetts Bay Colony. Since the 1960s, American politicians seeking the roots of exceptionalism have often referred to Winthrop's warning to the colonists in "A Modell of Christian Charity." In this lay "sermon," probably written before the colonists set foot in New England, Winthrop evoked the Christian symbolism of the "City upon a Hill," challenging his followers to serve as an inspiration to the churches of Christendom and invoking the authority of God as judge of their collective enterprise.[12]

Historians have convincingly debunked the common misconception that modern U.S. exceptionalism could be traced to Winthrop's address. They have shown how politicians and conservative clerics retrospectively revived and distorted Winthrop's idea of a City upon a Hill and turned it into a patriotic slogan in the late twentieth century. This idea thrived as a result of Christian fundamentalism's post-1945 turn to political activity and the emergence of the Moral Majority and its successor movements since the 1970s. The content of this special status in enacting God's plan for the world was not the same as for the Puritans of Winthrop's time, not least because of the simple fact that the United States did not exist in the seventeenth century. More important, Winthrop's now-famous address concerned the spiritual purpose of a covenant with God and the requirement of a this-worldly rectitude in a religious community. The text was not even published until 1838, and early republican thought did not single out Winthrop to legitimate expressions of the nation's special position and destiny.[13]

It is not surprising that interest was low at that time, because it was not the Puritans who made the first European settlements in North America. The Spanish had been in North America since 1519, and the English established the Jamestown colony in 1607. There the Church of England had a favored position as a state-supported church. Only by the 1820s did the focus, not on Winthrop's colony but generically on New England, become highlighted in the remembering of the young nation's colonial history. A marker of this shift was future Whig senator Daniel Webster's reference to the "Pilgrims" as the country's de facto founders and the model for its progress, recorded in his December 22, 1820, address for the Plymouth Colony's bicentennial. The idea's emergence reflected a move to shore up New England's political and cultural authority as the republic expanded west, and as the New England economy became far less important in American economic growth.[14]

Modern formulations of the City upon a Hill metaphor from Ronald Reagan's time onward have avoided these complexities and misapplied the label. Indeed, Reagan added the adjective *shining* to the image of the City, thus converting it from a provisional singularity and warning to remain true to God's covenant into a self-congratulatory endorsement of this-worldly success.[15] As historian Daniel Rodgers has related, this story of a spiritual city as the light of the world is complicated, and the concept is a malleable one.[16]

Conceptualizing Chosen Nations and Peoples

Despite the mistaken modern use, it remains true that the Puritans bequeathed to eighteenth-century Americans, particularly New Englanders, the idea of the North American colonies as chosen by God for a special task. For the Puritans this circumstance came to mean New England as the elect "nation." Puritan clergy even went so far as to contemplate the colonies as a successor "nation" to Israel in terms of God's favor. They derived the belief in a Protestant "elect" from Britain and took the idea of chosenness and the role of providence in history as their own with the failure of the Puritan revolution in Britain and the resumption of a monarchy in 1660 associated, under the Stuarts, with Roman Catholic sympathies. As early as 1674, the Reverend Thomas Thatcher of Boston exhorted the Congregational Church: "we are the people that do succeed Israel."[17] The Reverend Cotton Mather's *Magnalia Christi Americana*, first published in 1702, told the story of the early Pilgrim settlements and God's providential role in their development, while chastising the inhabitants for their collective failings before God.[18]

In the eighteenth century, the growing material prosperity of the North American colonies fueled the persistent idea that "America," however defined, was exceptionally endowed with resources, and the notion spread well beyond New England that the millennial kingdom prophesized in the Bible might find its critical center in that "America." The rise of Jonathan Edwards of Connecticut as a magnetic preacher in the First Great Awakening of the Calvinist churches in the 1740s encouraged these expectations, especially when he proclaimed, "The latter-day glory is probably to begin in America."[19] This was a religious prediction concerning Christ's return but, when the American Revolution broke out in 1775–76, the established churches in New England and dissenters across the American colonies appropriated the language of a new Israel to the fledgling United States. Biblical typology was used to justify and explain the revolution. Thereby the notion arose of the United States as the chosen instrument of God.

This idea of a chosen nation is important in American exceptionalism, but chosenness has been a broader concept than seeing the United States as merely Christian. A Christian status does not mean an exceptional one, because there were known to be other Christian nation-states in Europe at the time of the American Revolution. The chosen nation idea does not necessarily rely on Protestant evangelical belief, and it is compatible with the notion of a civil religion above sectarian disputes, or even non-Christian religions.[20] Unlike the idea of a Christian nation, chosenness cannot be refuted by resort to the absence of Christian provisions within the American state structure. In conception, the realm of the chosen nation is more theoretical, and more idealist; that is, chosenness becomes treated as immanent in history.[21]

On the other hand, from an empirical viewpoint, any number of cases can be enumerated to show that the idea of chosenness has been widely spread internationally, just as the idea of a Christian nation has. Ethiopia has perhaps as strong a claim as any to an enduring chosen status running back to biblical times. Its claim came with a Hebraic connection through the Old Testament and with early Christian conversion. One could also cite Protestant Britain of the seventeenth century, Israel, Armenia and Georgia (in the Caucuses), the nineteenth-century Boer states in southern Africa, and the early Dutch Republic, among others. Owing to their common derivation from Calvinism, Puritans and Boers staked a covenantal status, but some other "national" claims are not Christian at all.[22] Japanese exceptionalism has been often cast as uniqueness enhanced by an urge to express ethnic superiority over neighbor nations such as China and Korea, but the Japanese Empire also exhibited a chosen status. Japanese society was considered "like no other," and Japanese culture invoked "the protection of the deities" under a "divine nation," but without acceptance of a "universalistic mission."[23] Whether Christian or not, some groups have applied the old idea of chosenness to a modern nation-state, as Americans have done, while others, such as Rastafarians and Mennonites, have asserted a chosen *people* status without making the transition to nation. Within the United States, the idea of a chosen people has also applied to enslaved and emancipated African Americans in the nineteenth-century South.[24] Either as a people or as a nation, in no respect were Americans exceptional in claiming chosenness. Only the history of how the idea applied in practice could possibly rank as such.

Preachers and politicians in the early republic drew on the Puritan legacy of chosenness to assert a special status for the United States but applied it to political and ideological purposes. Some evocations stressed parallels in practical action. The legitimacy of the republic's legal foundations, like many other things, became the subject of biblical analogy in the new republic.[25] Second U.S. president John Adams noted that, like the United States, "the government of the Hebrews, instituted by God, had a judge, the great Sanhedrim, and general assemblies of the people." With this rhetorical flourish, Adams could assert a tendentious Hebraic parallel with the separation of powers under the U.S. Constitution. Others suggested deeper links indicating a divine providence. New England clergy and politicians found matches with the troubles of the Jewish people in "ancient Israel." Writers and sermonizers proclaimed that the situation of the American people in the Revolutionary War was similar to the delivery of the Jews out of Egyptian bondage in biblical times.[26] The Reverend John Cushing of Massachusetts made this point through a Fourth of July oration in 1796: "there is as great a similarity, perhaps, in the conduct of Providence to that of the Israelites" as in "the history of any people."[27] Three years later, the Rev. Abiel Abbot noted the wide use of the term, "Our American Israel," to summarize the correspondences. Such language encourages contemporary scholars to consider religious chosenness as foundational to American nationalism.[28]

Despite the biblical parallels, from the beginning of the republic, the evidence for American chosenness depended on the assumed superiority of the nation's new legal, political, and constitutional features, not the Puritan legacy. The founders and those who followed them in endorsing the exceptionalist nature of the American Revolution and the U.S. Constitution tended to think this way. Christianity intersected with the exceptionalist history of the republic in the constitutional prohibition on a religious status, not an inferred Christian status. Whereas the Christian nation concept necessarily exposed the imperfect nature of the existing American state from a Christian viewpoint, the advocates of chosenness believed that it was the constitutionally derived prohibition on an established church that underpinned their views. This position was well stated in the liberal Congregationalist and

Democratic-Republican Reverend Solomon Aiken's July 4, 1810, address in Newburyport, Massachusetts, where the revolution was valued because it opened the opportunity for delivering the dissenter sects from the tyranny of church establishments.[29] The Baptists and other religious dissenters were also keen on depicting the United States as exhibiting characteristics of chosenness because they gained so much in religious freedom from the Constitution. They drew favorable contrasts with the continued existence of an oppressive established church in many European countries.[30] But recognition that the United States was the bearer of religious freedom did not mean uniformity in the beliefs concerning a chosen status as a nation because freedom was interpreted in terms of the interests and social position of the various religious denominations toward religious liberty, on the content of which they often differed. These denominations were themselves undergoing changes, as they responded to the new environment of religious democratization in the former colonies that disestablished the state churches, mostly between 1776 and 1789.

The chosen nation idea always had its contradictions. Though Abiel Abbot found "traits of resemblance in the people of the United States of America to ancient Israel," a tension existed between a rising evangelical consciousness of the nation's material and moral possibilities, on the one hand, and the absence of any textual validation of the American position as a successor chosen nation, on the other.[31] Protestant clergy did use the biblical typology of Exodus, and other Old Testament stories, and saw Israel as "an important example" for mobilization of morale during the Revolutionary War and the early republic. But, they did not actually declare the United States a second Israel, assigning that honor instead to the universal Christian church, as was theologically orthodox.[32]

Chosen Status in Early Republican and Antebellum America

For this reason, the use of the biblical Israel in American thought from the revolution to the Civil War was common, but the language and impact require careful attention. In Abbot's much-cited text, he did not equate Israel with the United States. "Our American Israel" was a term commonly used, he stated, but he warned against "national vanity" and reminded his audience that, in God's eyes, ancient Israel's case "shall have a signal preeminence over the American." The "resemblance not inconsiderable" between the two peoples was derived from evidence of U.S. political and economic progress, which revealed a divine superintendence.[33] Abbot measured the United States not against ancient Israel, whose people had dispersed across the world, but against the world of his own time, stressing "our *distinction* from all other nations," not in every matter but in respect of good government.[34] The United States had "the wisest" government in the world, he averred, with "rapid growth, early independency and unexampled prosperity" the products of its governmental arrangements. From this evidence of national survival and material well-being he inferred that Americans were "in a sense like Israel, designed to be a religious people" with a place in God's plan for human salvation.[35] This was indeed taken as a material expression of God's favor, but not quite the exclusivist assumptions of the chosen nation idea.[36]

Parallels aside, no other document than Abbot's discloses more clearly a preoccupation not with the timeless truths of exceptionalism so much as with anxieties over the cultural, economic, and political position of New England.[37] Any resemblance to Israel applied "more particularly to the New England states," conceded Abbot.[38] The New England "pilgrims" were described in a telling phrase as "the acorn, from which has grown this noble oak"—the nation. Urging "pious caution" against national hubris, Abbot ended his sermon with a lamentation on the death of Massachusetts's Federalist governor, Increase Sumner, and made thinly veiled references of foreboding over the Jeffersonian-Republican alternative.[39] This was a warning against the secular and foreign "infidel philosophy" that Abbot believed was infecting the nation through the influences of the French Revolution and Thomas Jefferson. For this reason, his sermon embodied a partisan political jeremiad. The nation did not have an "indefeasible title" to divine favor, Abbot argued, and the standard of judgment for rectification was endorsement of the (political) Federalist case against the Jeffersonians.[40]

In this interpretation, the "American Israel" became less the United States than a metaphor for the attempted intellectual hegemony of the New England churches in the evangelical printed culture and its ensemble of moral institutions. These were the colleges, pulpits, and reform societies of the early republic identified with the antebellum "Benevolent Empire" ministering to the American West. The American Home Mission Society (and similar groups) perpetuated the usage; in 1838 the "American Israel" phrase expressed this sectional assumption of elite authority stemming from New England Congregationalism and the theologically allied Mid-Atlantic Presbyterianism, as the core of the republic's Christian community and its duties to the rest of the country. The sermons, Fourth of July orations, and Thanksgiving and other public addresses of the clergy on this issue came heavily from those same sources. It is uncertain to what extent they reflected the mood of the country as a whole. Even prominent southern-based clergy who used this language sometimes had a New England upbringing and education.[41]

The use of Old Testament ideas of chosenness enabled preachers, missionary boards, and politicians to communicate with the public through the Bible, the most widely known conceptual framework. A politician could appeal to the largely rural and little-educated masses by using their common idiom, but it is not immediately clear why that would privilege the Old Testament over the New. The evidence is stronger that the former provided convenient parallels with the *political* rather than religious history of the American people. As the Israeli historian Eran Shalev notes, "While the language of the Bible reiterated Americans' understanding of their collective mission, it also positioned politics as the new religion of the republic."[42]

After the American Revolution, the real font of the chosen nation (or "people") was as a register of a prosperous present and a sanguine future. It is hazardous to establish how many statesmen in the early republic regarded themselves as part of a chosen polity, but those who did stressed ideological and economic foundations. In his first inaugural address in 1801, President Jefferson made the most overt statement by singling out exceptional resources. Americans were "possessing" that "chosen country, with room enough for our descendants to the thousandth and thousandth generation."[43] In perceiving this largesse, Jefferson acknowledged "an overruling Providence, which by all its dispensations proves that it delights in the happiness of man here and his greater happiness hereafter." This assertion of progress drew explicitly on Old Testament language of the Exodus and the Promised Land "of milk and honey."[44] The nation's good fortune did not convey to it an assigned religious role as a nation. Rather, this was a thesis of American exceptionalism based on material abundance. Jefferson saw national identity as a synthesis of political individualism founded on liberty and the largesse of the land itself once cleared of indigenous tribes.[45] By "chosen country," Jefferson meant the United States of the 1783 settlement with Britain, east of the Mississippi. Farther west, he thought, there would develop like-minded but separate republics. These could, he hoped, join in concert to found a congenial world society as liberty spread universally.[46] Andrew Jackson was another prominent president who made similar claims for an increasingly secular focus of American chosenness, grounded in the material abundance of land presumed to be free for the taking; in 1837 Jackson singled out the United States as the bearer of liberty: "Providence has showered on this favored land blessings without number, and has chosen you as the guardians of freedom, to preserve it for the benefit of the human race."[47] From that point on, the older religious view of a chosen status became an expression of the new material reality of national progress.

Rooting chosenness in a specifically American space and time was also present in the history of the Church of Jesus Christ of Latter-day Saints. Whether consciously or not, the Mormon prophet Joseph Smith's revelations of 1827–29 offered a window on the tensions in American Protestantism over the cosmic purpose of the nation. In western New York, religious revivals and a plethora of cults spurred attempts to reconcile that Babel of voices. Smith's discovery of the golden plates and his tale of their contents, conveyed courtesy of the Angel Moroni at Hill Cumorah, near Palmyra, New York, served as an answer through the Book of Mormon to this antebellum religious and social confusion. Whether certain lost tribes of Israel had made it to the Americas was somewhat ambiguous in Smith's claims, but contemporaries took that migration to be his meaning. The tribal descendants' purported history in pre-Columbian North America linked God's Old World interventions to the New World. Smith not only mixed Old Testament religion, local stories, social reform, and American Indian legends in the Book of Mormon; he also drew on the existing Protestant discussion of a chosen country and distilled it into a singular form that made the Church of Jesus Christ of Latter-day Saints the expression of the material space of the nation. Smith's announcement of a sacred revelation broke new ground, supplying a new religion that placed American exceptionalism at the center of God's plans for the world.[48]

Unfortunately for Smith, who was killed in Illinois by an angry mob, identifying chosenness with a particular sect, worldview, or nation was highly fractious. Not only did Mormonism represent a tiny minority of the native-born U.S. population (of European ancestry); Americans also repeatedly criticized and persecuted it as un-American. Mainstream Christians did not accept the heterodox theology; in fact, many regarded its professions as a preposterous concoction and reviled the sect's polygamous practices—so much so that Smith's followers began to leave the country for what was then northern Mexico in 1846, only to find the United States annexing the territory that Mormons proposed as the State of Deseret. The assertion of the Mormons as a new chosen people did not make a new Israel out of the United States, which in this episode seemed to represent Pharaoh's Egypt. Rather, Mormonism demonstrated the common circulation of such notions of chosenness in American culture as well as intractable disagreement over their application.

Whatever its diverse allure in the early republican era, the concept of an American Israel began to lose purchase after the mid-nineteenth century.[49] The novelists Nathaniel Hawthorne and Herman Melville unsettled the chosen status, even as they admitted that the commonplace boasting of such claims concealed a brutal truth about American geographic expansion. In *White-Jacket* (1850), Melville backhandedly undermined chosenness by pointing to the violence with which Americans were taking possession of the continent and spreading their influence around the world. In regard to American exceptionalism, literary scholar Deborah Madsen has argued, Melville "shared his friend Hawthorne's sense of scepticism towards America's destiny."[50]

As education spread and literacy levels rose, the Old Testament's language of fire and brimstone had to compete with the Romantic perfectionism of the abolitionists and, in book sales, with the sentimentalism of *Uncle Tom's Cabin*, the nineteenth century's best-selling novel. Exacerbated by the Mexican War of 1846–48, the growing dispute over slavery played a crucial role in questioning chosenness. Antislavery advocates argued that the United States had sinfully abrogated its support of freedom. When Abraham Lincoln spoke in 1861 of Americans as God's "almost chosen people," the epithet betrayed a resigned spirit of chastisement over the nation's sectional conflict and the imminent threat to the Union from slavery's defenders. Lincoln's ambiguous phrase could be read as a critique that the nation had failed to seize the providential chance, where the American people had collectively demonstrated an all too human and sinful character.[51]

The idea of American chosenness did not die then; it remained a feature of religious discourse that spilled episodically into mainstream political speech. In the late nineteenth century, the emergence of the United States as a world power complicated chosenness once more (a story to be documented in chapter 8). Even in its antebellum ascendancy, the rhetoric and its values were closely tied to the fate of the American nation-state. The latter was a product not of the Puritans but of Enlightenment thinking, which raised new ideas about American exceptionalism, principally of a pioneering republican revolution that sowed the seeds for democracy, and to which we must turn next.

Looking Back, Looking Forward:
Remembering the Revolution

Like Puritanism, the American Revolution did not have a simple relationship with exceptionalism. On the one hand, the revolution was transnational and nonexceptional in character because it drew from European Enlightenment thought and became part of a set of transatlantic revolutions from 1776 to 1815. On the other hand, 1776 could be seen as the ignition point for those other republican and democratic revolutions. The first idea grounded the United States in history, the second took the new nation out of time, in line with cultural inclinations toward pre-historicism and millenarian thought linked to chosenness. These tendencies were reflected in the way the revolution was remembered.

The American Revolution indeed seemed something new under the sun in 1776, but it was not the first modern republic. In an era dominated by monarchies and empires, a more economically important republic already existed, the so-called Dutch Republic (formally the Republic of the Seven United Netherlands), which won independence from Spain in 1585. Through its trade networks under the Dutch East and West India Companies, the Dutch Republic exerted global economic influence and possessed a large navy to defend its maritime interests. This geographically small state was based on a strong middle class, and a degree of religious toleration jostled with a sense of chosenness. The revolt against Hapsburg Spain for independence was "seen as God's struggle" by Dutch Calvinists. To them, the Bible, especially the Old Testament, "was a source of inspiration." Feeling a "special kinship with the great biblical figures," they "drew parallels between the Jewish people and themselves."[1] Perhaps due to its urban centers and its prosperous merchants, a strong cultural influence of its painters and scientists also flourished. However, in the eighteenth century, the republic was weakened by interimperial rivalries and the rise of France as an adversary. By the time of the American Revolution, the Dutch Republic had vastly diminished in power under a de facto monarchy, but it did side with the American colonists in the Revolutionary War, and it existed formally as a republic until 1795.[2]

In republican terms, the United States might become exceptional, but it could only be considered such in 1776 by looking forward in time to an assumed chosenness and singularity. It took the first half of the nineteenth century to develop the material conditions for that status through geographic expansion. For this reason, the American Revolution had to be *imagined* as a unique break with the past. American exceptionalism became tied to the novelty of the justification for seeking independence from Britain, enunciated in the Declaration of Independence, and to the events of the subsequent revolution and their connection with democracy.

Historiographical Issues

The American Revolution and national identity have long been intertwined in public consciousness and academic scholarship. The presence of a "revolution" was one of the few historical experiences that, for the nineteenth century, appeared truly to distinguish the United States in qualitative terms from the otherwise highly comparable "Anglo" settler colonial societies of Australia, New Zealand, and Canada. None of these had an identifiable revolution, and Americans have typically seen their revolution as the exceptional element. This argument does not fairly apply, however, to Latin American independence movements against Spain. Republics such as Argentina and Chile had settler colonial histories similar in their displacement and even attempted extermination of indigenous peoples. Those comparisons were not taken seriously by many nineteenth-century Americans and later political commentators, who widely assumed that the combination of political development, stable constitutional government, and continued republican status was not present in Latin American history.[3]

As with Latin American republics and the heroic status of Simón Bolívar, the American Revolution bequeathed a sense of national identity sustained by the stirring stories of George Washington and other revolutionary-era "founders."[4] Because it has played such a strong part in national consciousness, the American Revolution and its value system became a major preoccupation of the modern social science approach to analyzing American exceptionalism. The theme of the revolution can be pursued in two ways: the historical interpretation of the events as actuality; or the memory of 1776. The former is relevant to American exceptionalism chiefly because the academic interpretation has turned on the significance of the revolution as qualitatively different from the bloody ground of European equivalents. Yet no agreement on this empirical question exists.

Two foundational theorists in the analysis of American exceptionalism from the social science perspective struck contrasting positions on the revolution's significance. For political scientist Louis Hartz in *The Liberal Tradition in America* (1955), "America" (meaning the United States) was born liberal, and this liberalism was present from the colonial beginnings because of the absence of feudalism. The revolution of 1776 thus expressed what already existed in essence: a liberal (and exceptionalist) nation. The role of the American Revolution was only to make manifest this essential difference. For political sociologist Seymour Martin Lipset, however, the revolution was crucial. It became the foundation of national identity and exceptionalism. It was the revolutionary experience that took the ideas of liberalism from their inchoate form in the colonial era and institutionalized them. These two interpretations did not intersect. Lipset paid little attention to Hartz other than to note in passing that he provided a "discussion of the predominant liberal ideology in America."[5] The neglect was reciprocated.

In actuality, the American Revolution as a political and social phenomenon did not conform to any one strand of exceptionalism.[6] If it was independence rather than a social revolution that marked those events, one could make the case for a full-blown national exceptionalism well before 1776. As a result, the revolution itself could be interpreted as merely consolidating the shift to a democratic system of government—unlike the violent trajectory of European counterparts, especially the French and Russian revolutions. Historians such as Jack Greene, who have emphasized the relative equality of most (white) colonials in the prerevolutionary period, have tended to play down the millenarian and religious elements of the American Revolution and have highlighted the colonies' material exceptionalism (in relation to Europe) and relative political and economic equality as underpinning an exceptionalist national identity.[7]

To stress the transformative nature of the American Revolution, on the other hand, might make it seem "generic." That approach has produced interpretations of the period from 1776 to 1789 as less exceptional and more comparable to other upheavals in world history, but that would be true only if a social revolution occurred. The work of John Franklin Jameson in the 1920s offered an early version of this interpretation.[8] If considered as a purely ideological shift toward liberal democracy, the focus on transformation would still emphasize an acute national difference. This was the influential approach adopted by Gordon Wood in *The Radicalism of the American*

Revolution (1992), wherein the revolution was treated as a change in political and social consciousness, rather than a societal cataclysm. Though Wood left open the possibility that the American Revolution might be compared with other democratic revolutions, in practice he reinforced the singularity of the American case.[9]

From the perspective of participants and contemporary observers, the Declaration of Independence was truly a break of an ideological kind. For the radical-liberal Thomas Paine, it constituted something new in world history. In a world in which monarchy and empire dominated, it is easy to imagine how the revolutionary action of 1775–76 appeared this way, and it is equally plausible to see how it released possibilities for egalitarian change in American society.[10] Because many of Paine's contemporaries saw the revolution as a split with the monarchical past, entailing a radical goal of equality, the emphasis was, in theory, on the future. This forward-looking ethos was an aspect of revolutionary ideology.[11]

The question of significance could not, however, be determined by participants or observers at that time. Paine himself framed the American Revolution in a transatlantic language of liberalism and Enlightenment doctrine. His famous pamphlet *Common Sense* (1776) made comparisons between monarchies and republics as different categories of countries, rather than treated the United States as an entirely singular case.[12] But, in *The Rights of Man* (1791), Paine made clear that the U.S. role was indeed exceptional: "As America was the only spot in the political world where the principle of universal reformation could begin, so also was it the best in the natural world."[13] In this view, the way events turned out made the revolutionary stance of 1776 special. As Paine's account suggests, the unity of the revolution and its meaning for the nation had to be fashioned over time. The revolution required consolidation, and so too did its ideological content. These ideas were woven together in the process of social change as war and revolution altered social circumstances. The military upheaval of 1776–81 removed key loyalists to the Crown, many of them Episcopalians, and caused great social tensions within American society. National homogeneity, either culturally or socially, did not result, however. Rather than "fostering a nascent nationalism," the revolutionary hostilities fractured society. They exposed, one historian has argued, "a growing antagonism between the states and especially an increasingly hostile relationship between citizens of the states and the new Continental Congress."[14] These tensions confirmed the new republic as not united, and far from egalitarian.[15] In this circumstance, national consolidation through national identity could not simply happen of its own accord. National identity did not emerge directly from the American Revolution but rather indirectly in its remembering over the course of the following decades.

National identity and exceptionalism are not necessarily connected, of course; one can conceive of a proud and secure national identity without thinking that it was unlike that of other nations and superior to them. The concept of the chosen nation, especially, implies such a sense of superiority, but the assumption of national singularity is also made by writers who have rejected the language of chosenness. Not an advocate for that religion-based idea, Lipset regarded American national identity as "derived from its revolutionary origins" and inculcated in individualist values; he treated those revolutionary values as the bedrock of the republic's enduring exceptionalism.[16]

Popular culture and recent political contention verify the importance of this revolutionary connection, not as history but as public memory. In the political and economic turmoil of 2008–10, Tea Party activists proclaimed the revolution's values as key to defining an exceptional nation, but they presented strange juxtapositions. In September 2009, I walked among the crowds on Capitol Hill at Tea Party rallies. At times, I felt like a time-traveling intruder watching demonstrators in coonskin caps and revolutionary-era costumes. Before me were slogans berating gun control, abortion, and "Obamacare" jostling alongside placards bearing minuteman catchphrases and antigovernment banners from the Gadsden flag of 1775. In the Gadsden slogan, "Don't Tread on Me," time was collapsed in popular memory—indeed, "time" as something that gives context to the events of the past was irrelevant to the protestors. They lived within the pre-historicist idea of exceptionalism: yesterday, today, and tomorrow, the United States was and will always be the same, always exceptional at its core.[17]

Long before, most academic historians had junked such "nostalgia for an imagined time" as Tea Party people recalled. The phrase was meant by historian Jill Lepore to refer to Tea Party enthusiasm for an exceptional America of the 1950s, but the nostalgia extended further back to popular memories of the American Revolution.[18] In remembering this revolution, nostalgia blurred the boundaries between the Declaration of Independence, the Revolutionary War (1776–81), the Confederation of 1781, the peace of 1783, the Federal Constitution of 1787, and the subsequent struggle over the Bill of Rights. The tensions and discontinuities between these events explored in academic study are not reproduced in the public discourse over the revolutionary legacy. As historian Richard Beeman noted in 2013, in one recent survey, 71 percent of Americans believed that the phrase "all men are created equal" appeared in the Constitution, not in the Declaration of Independence. "The Tea Party's passion about the 'destruction of the Constitution' by our government doesn't understand the history of what they were doing," Beeman observed. Proponents of the new federal constitution created a stronger national framework to avoid what Beeman argued were the mistakes of the decentralized government under the earlier Articles of Confederation.[19]

Despite some valiant efforts, academic attempts to demystify the American Revolution have failed to shape public opinion.[20] Popular confusion about the American Revolution and the U.S. Constitution has little to do with the emergence of highly partisan politics since the 1990s, to be sure. Anxiety over widespread public ignorance of revolutionary and early republican history went back at least to the early 1940s.[21] This deeper problem in historical consciousness reinforces the point that drawing attention to a "factual" or "empirical" history will most likely not alter public perspectives on the meaning of those events for American exceptionalism.

One alternative is to shift the debate from the actualities of the revolution to the memory of those events. It was not the circumstances of 1776, or the American War of Independence that followed, but the memories emerging during the period from the 1780s to the 1830s that have been crucial in shaping the meaning of the American Revolution for national identity. Those memories were constructed, and exceptionalism became intertwined in that process. Showing how historicizes the way Americans of the early republic recalled the revolution.

In this, the implementation or consolidation of the revolution was crucial. Lipset's approach allows us to reconsider how the United States developed its ideology of exceptionalism in a postcolonial situation, which was the driving point in his own present-centered analysis. While he made the simple observation that the American Revolution bequeathed a special national identity, Lipset's focus was not on those events but on their intellectual and value-centered inheritance. There was no revolutionary tradition to transmit without its being consolidated. He argued that the position of the early republic was analogous to new nations in the postcolonial world. Like modern African countries liberated from European imperialism, Americans had to work out a structure of authority—or fail. As a "new" society, the United States had no easy recourse to "tradition" but necessarily needed charismatic leaders to bolster national allegiance to what Lipset called the American Creed. More important, to create a settled government from the disunited colonies, leadership effecting a move from charisma to rational-legal authority was necessary.[22] Political instability might otherwise follow, Lipset believed, as happened in ex-colonial Africa of the 1960s or in various Latin American revolutions of the nineteenth century.[23]

Innovative as his application of modernization theory to the American Revolution promised to be, Lipset was unable to explain how national consolidation occurred. Instead of grounding it in social and political history, Lipset treated the shift from charismatic leadership to rational authority in idiosyncratic terms.[24] In his view, George Washington simply stayed around long enough as a charismatic independence leader to allow the rational-legal system as a framework for constitutional legitimacy to develop its norms. This explanation overestimates Washington's charisma and underestimates social discontent within the new states. In reality, the expectations of many Americans for more thorough and egalitarian reform had not been met in the fledgling republic.[25]

Like many other social scientists and historians, Lipset did not make the postcolonial condition anything other than an unfolding of a value system *within* an independent nation-state. In contrast, the transnational and global context allows us to extend Lipset's suggestion of the postcolonial moment as the ground on which the meaning of the revolution was cast. The United States was formally independent but still in some ways a colony of Great Britain and dependent on the British-imperial world system of mercantile trade. In this way, we can think of the American Revolution as a much longer "war" for independence in economic and cultural terms through to the Civil War. This view allows us to reperiodize the emergence and significance of exceptionalism and of the "Revolution"—making an intellectual, social, and economic declaration of independence in a slow-moving way until the 1840s (in some measures of achievement) or 1861–65 (in others).

This debate over the meaning of the republican and democratic polity intensified in the early to mid-nineteenth century and had effects on the understanding of exceptionalism. Instead of seeing the events of 1776–89 as part of a global system of change, and hence placing the United States inside history, it was possible for Americans after the Mexican War of 1846–48 to see the nation as both outside history, exempt from its laws, and yet free of a purely religious chosenness because it was more culturally independent, geopolitically secure, and resource rich as a result of continental expansion. At that time, the exceptionalism of the revolutionary generation, with its uncertainties, fears of failure, and circumspect attention to the power of greater nations and empires abroad, gave way to a progressive, future-oriented, and deterministic doctrine of inevitable rise and spatial realization. That process recast the meaning of 1776 as the progenitor of a great nation of "futurity." At every point, those who revised exceptionalism took the American Revolution as their benchmark for progress and for innovation on the original republican claims.

The Meaning of the American Revolution
for American Exceptionalism

In this narrative, a new nation destined to serve as a beacon of liberty to others was created, but the revolution as material circumstance consisted of a
highly contested and checkered set of events. It offered up no easy meaning.
Rather, its exceptional nature was retrospectively made in history books and
school texts, sermons, addresses, and other mediums of political and social
discourse. Its meanings for the nation's special character—and whether there
was one at all—changed over time and differed markedly according to political positions on the issues of the day.[26]

The Declaration of Independence was, Thomas Jefferson told his friend
Roger Weightman in 1826, "an instrument pregnant with our own, and the
fate of the world." It was the "signal of arousing men to burst the chains, under which monkish ignorance and superstition had persuaded them to bind
themselves, and to assume the blessings & security of self-government."[27] No
wonder Jefferson is invoked in public memory to prove the point of an im-
maculate creation for American exceptionalism in 1776. But the results of the
revolution were conditional, not preordained as exceptionalist. He concluded
in his autobiography of 1821 that the inception of the United States was a link in
a chain of "inscrutable" occurrences; one thing going wrong could change the
outcome. When the French Revolution began, it was that revolution, not the
American, that raised Jefferson's hopes for the global spread of freedom.[28]
The American Revolution became foundational to American exceptionalism
as a political idea, and as the spur to put the idea of liberty into practice,
but the events of 1776–83—the era of global war involving France, Spain, the
Dutch Republic, and Britain—were not sufficient as an example to the world.
It would require, Jefferson understood, the subsequent growth and power
of the nation, together with the course of human history abroad, to create
exceptionality. This meant that exceptionalism in Jeffersonian terms was a
qualified idea and an exercise in national caution.[29]

Jefferson's response to the fate of democratic revolutions was not unique.
The emergence of American national identity was entangled with international circumstances. In the first flush of revolutionary success, after defeating
the world's greatest military power at Yorktown, Virginia, in 1781, the Fourth
of July orations across the Northeast could announce with some confidence
the triumph of liberty and the nation's special position guided by providence.
Even so, the addresses that followed for a quarter of a century reflected practical exigencies rather than either ideology or a belief in divine intervention.
They responded to the progress of liberty across the globe and to the changing

prospects for democracy and national unity within the American republic. In 1787, Joel Barlow, the Jeffersonian diplomat and politician, stressed the work still to be done and did not judge the new republic as either created perfect or certain to succeed. As the nation considered the federal constitution for ratification, it faced what Barlow called "an alarming crisis; perhaps the most alarming that America ever saw. We have contended with the most powerful nation and subdued the bravest and best-appointed armies; but now we have to contend with ourselves, and encounter passions and prejudices more powerful than armies and more dangerous to our peace."[30]

Early republicans tempered enthusiasm for the global example they saw in the American Revolution with an acute awareness that the hold of liberty was tenuous at home and abroad. Like the Russian Bolsheviks who overthrew tsarist rule in 1917 only to find no other country able to join them in embracing communism, Americans looked anxiously abroad for endorsement of their revolutionary aspirations, and they had to contemplate that liberty "in one country," as it were, rather than a global democratic revolution, might result. That would imply a uniqueness not relevant to the future of other nations. But as democracy's prospects rose internationally after 1789 with the beginning of the French Revolution, hopes for a global validation of the American achievement soared, only to be either qualified or dashed in the mid-1790s. In the European case, the descent of the French Revolution into terror, then Napoleonic rule, made Americans think their own revolution sui generis, yet the chances for democracy revived again with the revolts in Spain's American colonies after 1810. Partly because of the uncertain future for republicanism and democracy, Fourth of July orations tended to be "sporadic" in incidence and replete with diverse meanings and indications. They interpreted history in the light of, and for, the present.[31]

The interpretation of the revolution forged in the course of the war and the years directly after reflected and even exacerbated social and political contention. Members of the political elite highlighted sources of nationalism in the historical record, but at the local level and among ordinary soldiers the idea of a grand historical narrative of the American republic was not central.[32] The memories of the rank-and-file soldiers are hard to uncover or generalize about, but they often focused their own Revolutionary War accounts on immediate circumstances; their membership of local militia counted for more than grand national strategies. They expressed "deeply personal experiences" and were sometimes scathing in their assessments of their leaders.[33]

The patchy development of a narrative for the American Revolution stemmed also from generational change. Occasionally the speakers who rose to defend the revolution through Fourth of July orations were veterans or military heroes. Their experience encompassed suffering and loss. They knew that unspeakable things had been done in the name of either freedom or its suppression. Such people were inclined to seek higher purpose in the blood-letting. Jonathan Loring Austin of Boston noted in 1786 the "solemn road of death we have often trod," as "the price at which" the "flourishing plant of AMERICAN LIBERTY" was purchased.[34] For Solomon Aiken of Newbury-port, Massachusetts, who had enlisted three times in the long revolutionary struggle, the bloody experience could not be in vain.[35] He found a meaning for sacrifice in the freedom of religious worship that the revolution encour-aged; in his view, this was an ample dividend implying exceptionality.[36]

More Fourth of July addresses in the early republic came, however, from the postrevolutionary generation. Most were uttered not by farmers, trades-men, and laborers but well-to-do, well-educated citizens including politi-cians, merchants, lawyers, doctors, and clergy.[37] From these ranks came those who gave Boston's official Fourth of July orations before the War of 1812. Aus-tin was unusual in being a former soldier, but he was only briefly a Revolu-tionary War officer and served mainly in diplomatic roles for the Continental Congress. In fact, some prominent revolutionary leaders, such as Benjamin Rush, a Philadelphia doctor, temperance advocate, and signatory to the Dec-laration of Independence, urged Americans to "forget the war"; it was the new "beginning" of the Constitution that was more important, he argued.[38]

Catherine Albanese has interpreted the glorification of the war and its he-roes in postrevolutionary America as a need to find common cause, to solid-ify the revolution in the light of real social, regional, and ideological divides. Whereas other nations possessed traditional creation stories derived from deep ethnic or religious attachments, the United States needed to replace the reverence toward ancestors accorded in New England to the Pilgrims. Cre-ating a common national origin would "function to unify and identify the citizen-heirs," revealing a "structure of consciousness which demanded one center for all the nations which formed the United States." While Albanese drew not upon Lipset but rather sociologist Robert Bellah's idea of a solidify-ing civil religion as the source of national identity, her interpretation of na-tion making remained top-down.[39]

In reality, the imposition of any "structure of consciousness" on the popu-lation was necessarily uneven and contested. It is far from clear how and to what extent nationalist yearnings for convincing myths meshed with local needs. It was not so much that the national discourse dispensed with the war as that orators sought to forget its details and glorify its higher purpose. The events were bloody, and they needed rationalization, whether that be through religious liberty or national unity. The glorification of the revolutionaries and their moment in history was part of a psychological adjustment for this post-revolutionary generation, which faced the problem of guilt over human loss. Similar responses to bloody wars sanctifying the coming of age of a newly independent nation through divisive conflict can be found elsewhere in modern history, such as World War I. The mythical origin story for Australia attained by the Gallipoli campaign of 1915 against the Ottoman Empire as the birth of nationhood—in practice rather than in legal status—is one such example. "They" died that "we" might be "free" is a customary refrain in the remembrance of war and nationhood.[40]

A key point for embracing the exceptionalism of the American Revolution was the patriotic effort to acknowledge the trials of the new nation's heroes. They had chosen "to sacrifice their present ease for honorable perils, and to bury themselves beneath the ruins of their country, rather than to survive the destruction of their freedom." So wrote Jonathan Maxcy, the president of Brown University in 1795.[41] Calls were made for the new generation to recognize the legacy. Suffice it to say that this glorification was a masculinist one, by and large.[42] But mostly it was the *political* heroes who came to be honored because they represented the side of the revolutionary cause more clearly identifiable with republican beliefs. As with war remembrance, the "heroes" were sanitized in the process of official or semiofficial memorialization.[43]

This assertion of sacrifice's dividend did not entail the actual achievement of exceptionality. Most orators continued to explain the revolution in terms that called into question the simple story of valor and reward. From 1789 to 1815, the nation's Fourth of July orators registered the geopolitical changes on the great anniversaries, such as that of 1796, with the second decade of independence completed. Most notable was the extent to which orators raised division and doubt, rather than confidence in an exceptional status.[44] Those writers who attempted to shape American national identity as a democratic experiment leaned toward Joel Barlow's view of the United States "as the universal type for future societies."[45] Here, the nation was considered as a model to be adopted everywhere in the fullness of time. This universalism was how Tom Paine had come by the time of his *Rights of Man* to treat the United States.[46] As the literary scholar Karen O'Brien has noted, a "Universal America" became "a distinctively radical vision in the Early Republic." For Barlow, the poet and diplomat, such an idea "prefiguring a secular millennium had potency," she points out. His long epic poem *The Vision of Columbus* (1787) had made "cultural progress a central aspect of this historical vision."[47]

This radical view of the American Revolution as example to the world was controversial. The French Revolution had raised, through its repercussions across Europe and the Americas, the specter of a global upheaval that was not

producing human progress. Speaking in 1796 in the wake of Jacobin extremism, Federalist congressman Samuel Thatcher admitted the "effect of former
oppression" in France. Underlying Thatcher's concern was an anticipated
cyclical decay of nations, giving rise to a fear that the United States would
not be an exception. Thatcher drew not from the ideas of the Enlightenment
or the Puritan tradition but from Court versus Country notions of a civic
(or classical) republicanism necessary to combat social decay and centralized power. For Thatcher, "Governments too frequently imbibe, at an early
period, the seeds of corruption, which incorporate with their constitutions,
grow with their age, and at length, effect their ruin. Luxury has destroyed the
most renowned empires of time. Faction, the fruitful mother of evil; faction,
the peculiar curse of republics, has already endangered our rising greatness."
Would this cyclical fate befall the United States? Thatcher understood what
a fluid situation it was for the American Revolution's place as an event of
world-historical importance. He still expressed hope that the "excesses" of
republican France would "totally subside" and that "her new constitution"
under the French Directorate taking power in 1795 would establish "liberty
upon law and reason." Thatcher continued to look upon America as the hope
of the world, but not as a singular power for liberty: France and the United
States would need to be twin Atlases holding up the world.[48]

A consolidation of national exceptionalism was not likely under such
turbulent conditions. Ideological contention over France was one issue, geopolitics another, and regional splintering a third. As historian Peter Messer
puts it, the early republic "saw the rise of a conservative ideology that emphasized the virtues of the status quo at the expense of the revolutionary sentiment of the period immediately following independence."[49] As part of this
shift, contemporary writers such as the historian David Ramsay flinched at
both the violence of European revolutions and the political discord within
the United States. A Federalist, Ramsay rooted American history in experience rather than God-given conditions, and he increasingly turned to a view
of American history at odds with the tradition of providentialism.[50] So too
the second president, John Adams, who went back on an exceptionalist outlook, announced in a private diary entry of 1765, over a decade before the
revolution began. Then he had held that "I always consider the settlement of
America with reverence and wonder," as "the opening of a grand scene and
design in Providence for the illumination of the ignorant and the emancipa-
tion of the slavish part of mankind all over the earth." But in 1814, he wrote,
"We may boast that *we* are the chosen people; we may even thank God that
we are not like other men; but, after all, it will be but flattery, and the delusion,

the self-deceit of the Pharisee."[51] It should not surprise one that Adams also rejected a view of the United States as egalitarian and thought that oligarchy would most probably develop in the republic. For this reason, political scientist Luke Mayville states that Adams was "perhaps the first critic of the idea of American exceptionalism."[52]

In reality, there were lesser-known orators and writers already thinking along similar lines of antiexceptionalism, and the criticisms were not limited to Federalists. Virginian Thomas Ritchie, the pro-Jeffersonian editor of the *Richmond Enquirer*, could fret in 1807 because "four memorable evils" threatened the supposed "unexampled freedom" of the republic: war, party spirit, disunion, and luxury. Here he invoked the fear latent in the civic republican critique of privileged elites usurping power and amassing wealth at the expense of the common good.[53]

At the root of this self-doubt over the future was the harsh fact of military conflict across the Atlantic as the Napoleonic Wars raged. That geopolitical contest of power drew the United States back into the affairs of Europe and the worldwide reach of the mercantilist empires. The War of 1812 marked a culmination of these fears.[54] The war's conduct and course threatened disunion, with New England resistance expressed in the Federalist Party's Hartford Convention of 1814–15. The proceedings of that convention professed dismay that the nation had so soon in its "infancy" exhibited the "embarrassments of old and rotten institutions" that were "not peculiar to any form of Government." Though the Federalists pragmatically stepped back from advocating disunion to register a more practical protest against "heavy taxes, wasteful expenditures, and unjust and ruinous wars," they prominently displayed, as Thatcher and Ritchie had already done, the antiexceptionalist idea of the United States as subject to the cyclical history of nations, obeying the same laws as others before them, "in all ages and countries."[55]

The War of 1812 also highlighted regional splits, though these sources of discord were not new and not confined to the Northeast. Local and state allegiances thrived in a still rural and far-flung nation. The Federalist opposition to the war had been regionally based, just as the earlier Virginia and Kentucky Resolves of 1798 and the Whiskey Rebellion of 1791–94 exposed the fissures of class and geography across the South and West. Even after 1815, the pattern of American life was still local rather than national.[56] North Carolina, Vermont, and Virginia, among others, had their own dates of celebration for local revolutionary events. In South Carolina, states' rights advocates cultivated a historical tradition of Palmetto Day to signify the separate resistance of that colony to the British that began on June 26, 1776. They employed a nascent and precocious South Carolinian nationalism to advance the cause of nullification against federal power, a struggle that came to a head from 1829 to 1833.[57] Given this growing sectional uncertainty, more than the fading memories of the revolution would be needed to solidify exceptionalism as a compelling ideology for nationalism. The revolution's significance required a new cultural nationalism based on the material foundations of a spatially expanding republic.

3

Cultural Nationalism and the Origins of American Exceptionalism

The post-1815 period did not foreclose the debate over the meaning of the American Revolution. Partly because the revolutionary generation was passing away, the struggle to define the federal state and make secure the revolutionary legacy intensified. That struggle was hampered by the decentralized political culture. The "Union" was a rather abstract concept, identified with limited federal power.[1] Even as orators in the 1820s professed loyalty to it, few of the cultural symbols of a civil religion that might generate or reinforce national cohesion around this Union yet existed. Celebrations of the Revolutionary War were markedly localized. The obelisk known as the Bunker Hill Monument, tucked away in Charlestown, Massachusetts, was begun in 1825, but work proceeded slowly. The inauguration in 1843 was marked by a Daniel Webster address notable not only for its verbosity but also for its emphasis on exceptionalism as an effort to "impose a national character," as historian Daniel Walker Howe puts it.[2] Though George Washington was already becoming idealized as "man" and "monument" through numerous books and public art, the project for a commanding physical memorial to him in the nation's capital remained unfulfilled owing to parsimonious financing and interstate squabbles.[3] The work was not commenced until 1848 and finished only in 1884. This tardiness in erecting truly national symbols in the setting of the federal capital reflected the republic's decentralized forces. As historian John Higham observed, "Cultural nationalism, in the sense of a deep popular consciousness of being a single people, hardly existed."[4] Though the nation was politically independent and able to expand westward with much diminished threat from European powers after 1815, cultural anxieties over the reality of American independence and its meaning persisted.

In a further constraint on exceptionalism, the nation's leaders were pain-fully aware that the United States lacked economic autonomy. Greeted as an impending "national calamity," the Panic of 1819, followed by the recession of 1820–21, showed the republic's reliance on European, particularly British, fi-nance and markets. The internationally connected recession produced much soul-searching over systemic economic weakness: "a capricious foreign mar-ket, the glut of foreign merchandize, and the balance of trade against us," as the New England clergyman Lyman Beecher put it in a widely circulated ad-dress.[5] The financial panic elicited calls to protect American industry from Eu-ropean competition.

The chorus of lament stimulated anti-British feeling over the source of the nation's economic woes, though not the means to channel it into functional independence. Some nationalists advocated high tariffs on manufacturing to strengthen the bonds of nation, even as the political and economic power of the South, dependent on free trade, meant that a consistently high tariff was not possible before the Civil War. In the 1820s, economic destiny remained in-tertwined with the vagaries of British capital flows and fluctuating interna-tional demand for agricultural products.[6] The growing geographic and political sectionalism, reflected in westward expansion, the lucrative cotton economy, and slavery in the South, further intensified anxieties over national identity. One Harvard College orator warned that, amid "warring sectaries" and the re-sultant "foundation of bitterness" between the states, the "dependence of our very national existence" rested on the "intelligence and morality of the people in general." That meant a "national literature" might be the only tie holding the country together.[7]

In cultural life, the United States was manifestly still derivative of Britain. For all its claims of cultural distinctiveness, historian Samuel Haynes has ar-gued, "the young republic exhibited a set of anxieties not uncommon among nation-states that have emerged from long periods of colonial rule."[8] Anglo-philia was almost as prevalent as a growing Anglophobic frustration. Ironi-cally, magazines and the infrastructure of literary society still mimicked Brit-ish cultural themes. American English, at least in the form of Noah Webster's now-famous *Dictionary*, struggled for recognition in the compiler's own life-time.[9] British publishers and cheap, often pirated editions of British titles in-fluenced the book market. It is hardly surprising that leading British poets of the era, such as William Wordsworth, were rated more highly than American ones, but the status of the American novel was not much different from that assessment. Thus, for example, Walter Scott had an "immense" popularity in the United States. Though a minority decried the celebration of a "luxurious and aristocratic" culture in Scott's Romanticist novels, few readers cared to join in endorsing that message by abstaining from the purchase of his books.[10] On the contrary, some writers, especially in the South, tried to emulate Scott and extracted from his work the very symbols of Romantic nationalism. In such ways, the nation's entanglement with British culture was insidious and commonplace.[11]

This reality of economic and cultural dependence was a mismatch for the political independence affirmed in the War of 1812's outcome; it was precisely this tension that generated sharper assertions of national cultural identity. The litany of demands for an independent literature backs the old claim of historian Russel Nye that the 1820s constituted a crucial period in the intellectual construction of the American nation.[12] In these years, the assertion of American exceptionalism began to depart from its diffident revolutionary-era precedents. Those had relied on the United States as part of an Enlightenment culture, in which the United States was a key example of European ideas in practice. As if it were an antidote for American subordination to Europe, orators now hailed a nascent national culture as the source of an "unexampled" promise for the future. Whereas the revolutionary generation by and large saw the United States as linked with other nations in a revolutionary enterprise, and remained tempered by awareness of the nation's precarious history, the post-1815 formulation sought to place the United States outside the international system of states as culturally separate as much as politically so. This distinctiveness built on the colonial era's intellectual apprehension of an American "nature."

A pugnacious American exceptionalism began to blossom in this context. To demonstrate cultural independence, intellectuals emphasized the things that gave the United States cultural advantage through the encounter with a wholly new environment. Instead of accepting the New World as a site of civilizational decay, they stressed the material and institutional grounds for self-improvement that American material life offered. The growth of cultural nationalism constructed an exceptionalist identity through individual efforts among intellectuals. They asserted a national literature rooted in American circumstances that they held to be backed by providential favor.

These conditions were, first, a growing internal market founded on a common language, rapidly rising population, and territorial expansion; second, the competition possible in such a market when access to culture was not limited, as it was said to be in Europe, by social class; and third, the flourishing, at an early stage of national existence, of colleges and universities competing with one another to spread higher standards of literature, learning, and republican mores. In this critique, Europe was identified with tradition in intellectual life, whereas the United States represented the new and innovative.

In cultural terms, this declaration of independence is commonly linked to Ralph Waldo Emerson's 1837 speech "The American Scholar."[13] Certainly, he grew to be more famous than other national literary luminaries of the time, but his contribution came relatively late. Emerson was indeed "American" in focus, but he did not completely abandon the Old World, as sometimes thought; he gave it his due. He was intellectually indebted to Thomas Carlyle's Romanticism, and, above all, conceded a common genuflection to European literature to be "the tax we pay for the splendid inheritance," as he wrote in 1834.[14] In *English Traits* (1856), he revealed a "conflictedness about England" and saw the United States as a future successor nation embodying and yet transcending the old mother country's contribution to world history and civilization.[15] Emerson's real achievement was not to repudiate the cultural inheritance but to build on it by diverting attention from artifice and convention, whether European or American, to self-reliance.[16] Still, what American writers wanted was international recognition (and sales) to validate their cultural achievements. It was in the 1840s and 1850s that American literature began to get such results in Britain.[17]

Everett and the Cultural Networks of Nationalism

Figures other than Emerson had already made an articulate case for a cultural declaration of independence. Among the earliest came in Edward Everett's 1824 address, *An Oration Pronounced at Cambridge, before the Society of Phi Beta Kappa.*[18] The speech was foundational to the new cultural nationalism, and it preceded the work of both Emerson and George Bancroft, a more famous ideologue of American exceptionalism. Everett had the good fortune to speak, with the Revolutionary War hero the Marquis de Lafayette present in the audience, during the marquis's valedictory tour of the Northeast in 1824. A "great triumph," Everett's address stirred listeners and launched his political career.[19] The *Oration* continued to be in demand for many years, being republished as "The Circumstances Favorable to Literary Improvement in America" (1833) and reprinted in 1840, 1850, and five more times by 1865. It was widely included in compendiums on "American Oratory" and similar titles.[20] The piece illustrated the relationship between exceptionalism and intellectual bravado. Everett is best remembered as the unfortunate politician who addressed the crowd in flowery language for two hours at Gettysburg to honor the Union dead in 1863, only to hear Abraham Lincoln follow him concisely with a two-minute speech that has become a canonical piece of American democratic nationalism, the Gettysburg Address. But Everett was better than this invidious comparison suggests—he had a distinguished life as a politician, governor, and senator; an educationist (as president of Harvard University); and an orator. Though long-winded like Webster, he was less florid and more original, analytical, and forward-looking in his conception of the nation's singularity. Like Bancroft, he obtained a doctorate studying in Germany.[21]

Everett was among a number of Americans who, as students in Europe, honed their ideas of a distinctive nation in response to their exposure to the rich cultural life of that continent after 1815. Influenced by the German philosopher Johann Gottfried Herder, a new generation of American republicans stressed the importance to a nation of a popular cultural identity. This identity would be achieved through education and the use of history to inculcate nationalist sentiments and principles. It was a German immigrant to the United States, Francis Lieber, who acquainted Americans with the very notion of "nationalism" as a concept in the English language.[22] Yet the substance of cultural nationalism was illustrated in Everett.[23]

Though Everett looked to the American Revolution as the source of national cohesion, that was not his novel contribution. Rather, the universal spirit of "national" identity was his interest, grounded in new material circumstances that enhanced cultural cohesion. Unlike Europe, American institutions "could not be limited to the privileged few," he proclaimed.[24] They sent out "a vital nerve to every member of the community, by which its talent and power, great or small," was "brought into living conjunction and strong sympathy with the kindred intellect of the nation."[25] In Everett's estimate, the American republic could be called an intellectual democracy. Freedom opened up a country's "universal mind," as Everett put it in imitation of Herder, whereas European culture was spoiled by "despotism." The "further you recede from such a despotism, in the establishment of a system of popular and constitutional liberty, the greater the assurance that the universal mind of the country will be powerfully and genially excited," Everett asserted.[26] Europe was theoretical in disposition as well as despotic, "America" was practical. To others, the epithet *practical* might be a pejorative in which, as Alexis de Tocqueville argued in 1835, culture was neglected in favor of getting and spending.[27] But Everett took as a compliment the argument that "Our country is called practical"; this was the best environment for "intellectual action" since all great literature derived, he argued, from the self-activity of the people.[28] Everett spoke of an American "character" as a national trait and argued that the foundation for these institutions and mores was "in dear nature." Thereby he extoled the virtues of the American material and intellectual environment against European criticism. According to Everett, these unique circumstances gave the American people a distinctive opportunity for creating great literature to back growing economic prosperity and provide an example of intellectual enlightenment to the world.[29]

The other distinctive infrastructural feature noted by Everett concerned the cultural consequences of geographic spread. A "continually expanding realm" was opening up to "American intellect, in the community of our language, throughout the wide spread settlements of this continent," he insisted.[30] Territorial expansion spawned "a state of society entirely new among men." It was "a vast empire" whose institutions were "wholly popular."[31] This association of freedom and cultural independence with a dynamic and spatial "empire" of white settlers would allow the United States to find the liberation from European domination that its intellectual champions wanted. In other words, knowledge production would respond to the inevitable growth in power that a larger population and resource-rich territory provided. Exposed to the stimulus of that material abundance, American intellectual achievement would swell too, and transcend European standards.

Providence did feature in Everett's views on exceptionalism, but not in a millenarian way. He noted what he saw as the extraordinary set of coincidences that put such a resourceful people as the English upon a continent as bountiful as North America, at the right time to exploit its resources before others got their hands on it. Americans were fortunate not to settle in the seventeenth century among the already "crowded population of savages" in Central America, but rather to encounter a New England only thinly peopled with Indian tribes.[32] Everett pronounced this and every other piece of good fortune down to a providential alignment rather than simple luck. Yet for Everett, providence remained the Enlightenment idea of a distant and impersonal force endowing social change in a progressive direction.[33] It was the individuals of the new nation who had to take charge of that force by asserting an exceptional national status.

Everett's approach shifted American professions of such a status away from the originating moments of either the Pilgrims or the Founding Fathers. Despite his concern to conserve history's traditions, Everett's focus actually moved from the past—the Puritan colony or the revolution—to the future, represented physically by the new western territory into which the nation's people poured in increasing numbers after 1815. For Everett, assertions of national identity possessing a uniquely auspicious future served to act out and affirm that special status. He thereby anticipated John L. O'Sullivan's more famous enunciation of "futurity" fifteen years later as the condition of American exceptionalism.[34]

However, Everett differed from O'Sullivan in being torn by the consequences of expansion for indigenous people. Everett's providential interpretation predicated the nation's exceptionality on the "scantiness of the native occupation" and thereby made endorsement of settler colonialism's legitimate occupancy an unacknowledged condition of cultural nationalism's rising trajectory. But there was a catch. This ex post facto endorsement of Indian removal in the Northeast raised the same issue in the West and South. When the Jacksonian Democrats enacted legislation for the forced removal of the Cherokee and other "civilized tribes" in 1830, Everett, at that time a National Republican congressman, opposed the move. These Indians in the Southeast were different, Everett argued. No longer were they a collection of "warriors" but a nation of Christian families with women, children, and old men. Not only were they no danger to white expansion; they had adopted the accoutrements of civilization. Christianization and assimilation, not coercion and exclusion, were Everett's preferences, as they were for the Whig Party that Everett joined in the 1830s. Though Everett fought removal, his argument meant that he did not oppose the cultural extirpation of Indian civilizations. The new cultural nationalism is almost inconceivable without this implicit endorsement that the new cultural networks of nationalism must replace tribal power and allegiance, because spatial expansion created the material sustenance for the new national confidence to flourish.[35]

The Infrastructure of Exceptionalism

As cultural nationalism took hold, its sentiments were regularly noted in college commencement addresses, Thanksgiving sermons, and Fourth of July orations, as well as congressional speeches. Helping to disseminate these texts was the transfer of knowledge through education, particularly the common (elementary) schools, which spread across the northern states from the 1830s on. The leading advocate for the common schools, Horace Mann, saw the nation as a "new experiment" in need of the shared values that only a public education system could generate. This view was compatible with Everett's ideas of a common literary infrastructure underpinning American exceptionalism. But what was the content of that national culture to be? For both Everett and Mann, exceptionalism was a value to be created by human effort to ensure the stability and progress of republican government.[36]

History textbooks for common schools and private colleges, such as Emma Willard's *History of the United States, or Republic of America* (1828), were similarly products and projections of the new cultural nationalism. The principal of Troy (New York) Female Academy, Willard had serious aims for women's education. She sought to supply "the deficiencies of our literature by filling up the chasms of truth" and argued that knowledge of history would "improve our national literature" and promote "the growth of wholesome national feel-ing." Willard included the study of the Declaration of Independence, Wash-ington's Farewell Address, and the U.S. Constitution as "political scriptures," and she hoped readers would recognize in her text "a superintending Provi-dence, whose time for exchanging, upon these shores, a savage for a civilized people, had now fully come."[37] The book was distinguished by maps illustrat-ing this settler colonial theme. Sales of more than a million copies of her text-books in her lifetime attested to her success.[38]

Imbued with Protestant intellectual assumptions, the common schools fos-tered democracy, nationalism, moral virtue, and economic progress. Hagio-graphic stories of the American Revolution underpinned these objectives.[39] Textbooks such as Samuel R. Hall and A. R. Baker's *School History of the United States* (1839) made the point plainly. Given the passing of almost all of the participants in the American Revolution, Hall and Baker told the younger generation, "To you, . . . the written page must supply the place of the ani-mated tale from the venerable men whose voice is silenced by the tomb."[40] Excerpts from politicians, clergy, and educators were disseminated through ubiquitous school readers, of which those published by William McGuffey became the most famous, selling some 120 million copies between 1838 and 1920. Compilations of this type furnished the intellectual and ideological con-tent of revolutionary-era remembrance to the common schools right through the nineteenth century.[41]

A theme in the McGuffey readers was American exceptionalism, especially regarding the 1776 revolution as a foundational achievement and in contrast-ing "republican" vigor and old-world decay.[42] An illustrative case is the 1795 Fourth of July oration delivered in the Baptist Meeting-House in Providence, Rhode Island, by President Jonathan Maxcy of Brown University. McGuffey's *Fourth Eclectic Reader* (1838) reproduced an excerpt from Maxcy's oration. It illustrated the millenarian promise of the United States as an example for the world's transformation and gave students stock questions and answers cover-ing the concepts present in the text. "What is our happiness, compared with that of other nations?" was one such question. The answer for schoolchildren was given in conjunction with Maxcy's excerpt: "No nation under heaven en-joys so much happiness as the Americans."[43]

The importance of the McGuffey readers should not be exaggerated. For one thing, their chief objective was the preservation of morals. They did not cover all varieties of exceptionalism since they concentrated on religious and moral conduct and tried to avoid partisan politics. Many entries were prosaic and often had nothing to do with the debates over the nation's singularity. It is also forgotten that McGuffey's work was only part of a larger landscape of

literary compilations used in schools, debating societies, lyceums, and colleges. There were, for example, Catholic competitor texts set in the parochial
school system that expanded in the mid- and late nineteenth century.[44] The
McGuffey readers are the best known because they survived the longest, but
their main markets in the antebellum period were the North and Midwest.[45]
Other compilations, such as *The United States Speaker*, edited by John Epy
Lovell and focusing on the Northeast, similarly reproduced the Maxcy ex-
tract found in the early McGuffey readers.[46] Maxcy's oration also appeared in
The Southern First Class Book. As the title page indicated, entries were "Selected principally from American authors, and designed for the use of schools
and academies in the Southern and Western states."[47] In this way, exceptionalist notions spread geographically and temporally, aided by communication
changes. Newspapers, cheap printing presses, and the railroads allowed the
distribution of such material in ways impossible in the 1780s.[48] This does not
mean that exceptionalist ideas were absorbed uniformly or without adaptation. The compilers of the *Southern First Class Book* railed, like other southern literary producers, against the radicalism of "Foreign and Northern books"
that "opposed our peculiar views and institutions."[49] The McGuffey compilations probably succeeded more over the longer term because they were the
blandest and strove to be inoffensive.

These compilations were not just books to read but ideas to act out. Elocution was considered an important component of education. As part of democratic citizenship training, it was recommended for students to speak the
printed words, and thereby the patriotic orations of the 1790s continued to be
practiced and presented by schoolchildren in the 1830s. Maxcy's speech and
others like it became part of the performance of exceptionalism as much as
the original oratory was, and the lessons of national singularity were articulated through the bodies as well as the minds of students by such performative
rituals—rituals reproduced in the temperance lodges and literary and self-
improvement societies such as the lyceums, which gave courses in elocution.[50]

Bancroft and Democratic Nationalism

Included in some though by no means all of the school texts were excerpts
from the work of George Bancroft. To historian Barry Joyce, Bancroft was "more
than a valued source" for textbooks. His writings identified republicanism and
democracy as key features of national identity and "authenticated the mythical timeless storyline that allowed American history to 'make sense' for future generations."[51] Dramatic excerpts such as Bancroft's account of the "Boston Massacre" of 1770 were included in school readers, but Bancroft is more

noteworthy for his intellectual contribution in shaping the writing and political projection of American history than for the educational impact of his
work in the common schools. Two Fourth of July speeches expressing the emerging values of American exceptionalism came from this man. The first, in 1826,
ignited Bancroft's career as a politician, orator, and intellectual. As a Democrat, Bancroft stood on the other side of the political fence from Everett.

Whereas Everett treated providence as an extension of the founders' own
sense of an inscrutable deity, Bancroft approached God's role very differently.
He added the idea that humans were not simply inheriting favorable circumstances but actually realizing God's plans by their everyday activity as citizens
of a democracy. He raised the endorsement of exceptionalism to a quasi-
spiritual level without succumbing to the Puritan idea of an elect telling the
community what to believe and do because Bancroft divined God's purpose
as intrinsically democratic, not hierarchical and theocratic. As the foremost
nation of the world from the 1820s to 1840s in the extension of a democratic
franchise to white males, the United States could become one with the purpose of all creation, Bancroft argued. The year in which he made his revelation public was 1826.

It was a year replete with providential overtones. The fiftieth anniversary
of the Declaration of Independence was an auspicious occasion to take stock
of the American Revolution. On that day in 1826, the day that Jefferson died
and John Adams too, the future historian and Democratic Party politician elec-
trified an audience in Northampton, Massachusetts. Bancroft had an impressive intellectual pedigree when he returned in 1822 to Boston from his European studies with a Göttingen doctorate.[52] His father, the Reverend Aaron
Bancroft, wrote a hagiographical *Life of Washington* (1807) and was a prominent liberal Congregational minister who opposed orthodox Calvinism. Despite his credentials, George Bancroft had few immediate prospects of advancement and languished in a minor and temporary post at Harvard, then
as principal of a Northampton school in 1823. But marriage to the well-to-do
Sarah Dwight in 1827 gave him the freedom to write, and he soon began his
ten-volume *History of the United States*, the first installment appearing in 1834.

The volumes charted the course of North American settlement as the in-
terconnected story of freedom planted in the first European colonies, growing to fruition and maturity in his own time. His story was not one of a special founding moment, such as the American Revolution, but a cumulative
buildup. The seeds of 1776 were not only in the Puritan settlements or Jamestown but also in the explorations of Spain's famed Genoan explorer, Christopher Columbus. All such human endeavor—and much before, in Europe's
Protestant Reformation and back to the time of ancient Greece—was swept

up in a universal history to which the United States was inheritor. Long before his death in 1891, Bancroft had become the preeminent historian of American nationalism and the bearer to a reading public of ideas that made the United States the exemplar of liberty to the world. Commanding a broad audience, selling many thousands of copies of his *History*, he gave readers a democratic (and Democratic) pedigree for that history.[53]

Just as Bancroft helped forge Americans exceptionalism as a doctrine, his advocacy facilitated his own political ascent along with the Democratic Party led by Andrew Jackson. In his writings of the 1820s and 1830s Bancroft illustrated the link between self-made achievement and the forging of exceptionalist doctrines. Through oratory and writing he advanced his own career and set out an exceptionalist platform for his intellectual engagement with the Second Party System that flowered in the Jacksonian period. His theory was elaborated in his monumental *History*. Appointed secretary of the navy in 1845, he later served as ambassador to Great Britain and Germany.[54] More important, Bancroft made charting the history of the United States his life's work. Bancroft's Northampton speech of July 4, 1826, was the inception of a lifetime's historical interpretation to establish and reinforce American exceptionalism.

Bancroft's purpose in the speech was to create a sense of nation as coterminous with democratic forms and the power of the people, not a social or religious hierarchy. Drawing on his German Romantic training, he saw as the defining quality of a nation "its origin in the will of the people" rather than a dynastic succession, as in Europe. Proclaiming that "our government is strictly national," he outlined its nationalizing and "levelling" role. The nation defined its object in the "happiness" of the "people," prohibiting "hereditary distinctions," diminishing "artificial ones," and promptly reforming governmental "abuses." In turn, the moral foundation of government was the rational judgment of free citizens.[55] This blend of egalitarianism, democracy, and nationalism was key to Bancroft's version of a universalist American creed. It was a break with the idea of history as the embodiment of merely local or state traditions.

This sense of a *nation* both democratic and egalitarian was nurtured in the ferment of cultural nationalism. A nation must have a collective identity and a collective history, Bancroft believed, and that was what he wished to create by embracing the common will as God's work. Though drawing on the same wellspring of cultural nationalism, Bancroft's work was distinct from that of the more materialist Everett. Bancroft's alternative was idealist in the philosophical sense and yet more political in a practical sense and collective in a social sense. Blending religion and material circumstances, Bancroft invested the latter with providential sanction. He took this stance not from the

Puritan inheritance of his Massachusetts origin, or from his upbringing, but from the German idealist philosophers, who advanced a teleological story of progress in which God's purpose was inherent.

In Bancroft's hands, this interpretation portrayed not a covenant with God, as under Puritanism, but a spiritual alignment through democracy and its connotations for freedom of conscience. In practice, it entailed sanctification of American democracy's forms that were beginning to emerge under the leadership of Jackson, the unsuccessful candidate for the presidency in 1824 and the future influential president who would be elected in 1828. This interpretation served tactical and strategic purposes. It enabled the Democrats to counter their political opponents' claims that the Jacksonians were corrupt, tyrannical, and immoral. To the contrary, Bancroft asked, were they not effecting God's plans, which were democratic? For this sanctification, Bancroft took Herder's idea of universal history and made the spirit of democracy that history. Bancroft therefore jettisoned the flirtation with the cyclical interpretation of history as evidenced in the writing of John Adams and in the fulminations of the Hartford Convention. In its place, he told a story of human ascent as if it were a relay race in which the United States took the baton, to sprint toward the finish line of human history.[56]

Although he singled out the special role of the United States as baton carrier, he grounded its exceptionalism within the universal story of liberty in which "all the nations of the earth have an interest." Of democracy, he wrote in 1826 that "humanity proclaims it sacred." Democracy and liberty had specific American manifestations that he celebrated, but the kernel of the idea was outside time itself as one of the principles "eternal, not only in their truth, but in their efficacy." The spark had been struck in the specific events of 1776, but his formulation was a pre-historicist endorsement. "The world" had "never been entirely without witnesses" to liberty's unfolding, he averred, and its ideas "have been safely transmitted through the succession of generations; they have survived the revolutions of individual states; and their final success has never been despaired of." Liberty had its foundation in "human nature."[57]

Bancroft agreed with Jefferson that the American Revolution had inspired the French Revolution and all other revolutionary movements to free Europe from autocracy. Certainly, those revolutions had gone to extremes, while the American stayed true to democratic principles. But he blamed European failures on aristocracy and monarchy: the "melancholy events" of the French Revolution's Jacobin phase he "distinguished from the original resistance to unlimited monarchy." In France, the "representatives of the people were true, while the nobles were false." Homing in on the eternal matter of principle, he warned that "evils, which resulted from anarchy in the royal councils," should not obscure the integrity and worth of the "popular effort," which "abolished the system of absolute rule and feudal subjection." The kernel of democracy was pure, even as its French *expression* had ceased to be so. With this French failure, the United States took the leadership in the struggle to embody the democratic purpose. Installed in the United States were "the equal rights of man, which reclaimed the sovereign power for the people, . . . established the responsibility of all public officers," and gave "a free course to the principles of liberty, to industry, and to truth." Liberty and democracy remained unsullied in this American expression.

The vantage point of 1826 allowed Bancroft to see the United States as more successful in spreading freedom than it had appeared to the revolutionary generation and its immediate offspring. While he believed Europe had blotted the copybook of liberty, the New World revived its prospect with the successful Latin American colonial wars against Spain. "Human culture has at length been transplanted to other climes, and already grown to a more beautiful maturity," Bancroft rejoiced. "Whatever destiny may hang over Europe, mankind is safe." In "our own hemisphere," a "family" of free states had come to flourish "on a soil, which till now had been drooping under colonial thraldom." Nothing could offer "a more admirable and cheering spectacle."[58] This point amounted to a New World exceptionalism, not purely an American one.

If Bancroft made the whole of the Americas the site of the rising democratic age, he also broke new ground by emphasizing how universal the promise of exceptionalism was on the question of race. He did not limit democracy to any one ethnic, racial, or national group. Viewing the aftermath of the Latin American revolutions as the colonists there consolidated their own independence, he argued that liberty belonged not only to whites but those of "mixt [racial] descent." The true Democrat worked for humankind, "not for a single race of men."[59] Bancroft did not, however, endorse opposition to slavery in 1826, and he stayed loyal to the Democratic Party until the sectional crisis of the 1850s.

American Exceptionalism and Pre-Historicism

So far as the theoretical and methodological underpinnings of American exceptionalism are concerned, Bancroft perpetuated pre-historicist tendencies in colonial American thought. It is not that the outcomes of American history were devoid of real-life contingencies; rather, the key was the idealist concept of God's immanence in human action. The events of that history expressed, in a Hegelian philosophical sense, the providential purpose. Liberty's course might be halted or slowed by individual quirks or missteps, but

not overturned. Its direction was upward, and the only question was whether
the United States or some other nation would be liberty's champion. In this
way, the historicist implications of the philosophical idealism that Bancroft
learned in Germany were absorbed into a preexisting "Christian and millennial frame."[60] This interpretation weighed heavily on early professional
historiography as it developed in the nineteenth century and worked its way
through universities, colleges, and school curricula. Echoes could still be seen
in the twentieth century, through the attempts of social analysts to treat the
American Revolution as embodying an unchanging liberal core, either as Hartz's
Liberal Tradition or as Lipset's American Creed.

Considered as part of a public and overtly political discourse, Bancroft's
approach was more hardheaded than it might seem. It legitimized the rising
Democratic Party and disentangled the memory of the American Revolution from the particular sway of any church, region, or ethnic group. Though
serving a spiritual purpose, Bancroft saw U.S. history as beyond sectarian identification since God's plan for "America" did not begin with the Puritans.[61]
Bancroft thus invoked the Christian religion without privileging one section of the country or one church. This befitted his Unitarian faith and rejec-
tion of church establishment in New England; it also suited the Democratic
Party's support base, which was cross-sectional, with strong backing in the
South and West, and with a promising allegiance from Irish Catholic immigrants. It therefore made political as well as theological sense for Bancroft to
reject a purely New England origin for American exceptionalism. At the same
time, Bancroft invested Americans with a stronger sense of a secular mission
to carry the message of democracy to all lands and thereby realize universal
freedom.

In its abandonment of the Puritan covenant, Bancroft's view lacked any
intercession of God in history by way of human conversion. "Religion" as
church or congregational action was also missing as a causative element. But,
a decade later, Bancroft's democratic and nationalist exceptionalism faced a
challenge from the resurgent forces of Protestant evangelicalism. On July 4,
1836, Bancroft spoke at Springfield, Massachusetts, and gave greater attention to religion as a social force than he had in 1826. He acknowledged a new
spirit of revivalism and its presence in politics. This later speech recognized
not only the Puritan contribution but also the role of contemporary religion
in safeguarding the morality of the republic. Notwithstanding, Bancroft still
assimilated the religious impulse to his democratic refrain, claiming that the
demonstrable growth of religious enthusiasm was due to democracy's flowering. "The enfranchising principle is a purifying principle . . . ; democracy,
following the counsels of religion, exults in 'the reality of spiritual light.'" See-

ing in "Each New England town a perfect democracy" promoting purity and morality, Bancroft put Puritanism in context as the local form of democratic government.[62]

Bancroft's intellectual gymnastics in the changes between the two speeches reveal the rising power of evangelical religion in American society, but it was a power deployed in a novel way. The old hierarchy in which the state supported the Puritan churches in New England was almost completely gone in 1826. Responding to this political environment, a new religious impulse supplied something lacking in Bancroft's version of exceptionalism—that is, the idea of joining democracy to a political state made moral and virtuous by a Christian people. A Christian social and intellectual movement sought to effect God's purpose of making the United States a republic in which religious conversion and an eschatology of spiritual millennialism, not democratic affiliation, would be key. That story, too, began in the 1820s, partly in reaction to the declining official sanction of religion that followed the revolution; it incorporated and transcended the themes of cultural nationalism sketched in this chapter.

For this reason, Bancroft's influence should not be overestimated. He influenced later historians, but within the broader community, his effect was diluted within the wider discourse of American exceptionalism. This point is revealed in the antebellum elocution texts and school readers. Surprising as it may seem, the excerpts from Bancroft in these sources do not stand out above the miscellany. McGuffey's readers were not called "eclectic" for nothing. They incorporated the work of Whigs such as Daniel Webster, writers from both sides of the Atlantic, and, most prominently, clergymen. The name Edward Everett was more often present than Bancroft, and the Reverend Lyman Beecher figured more than either of them. For this reason, it is to the work of Beecher and his family that we must next turn. They offered a different yet equally important interpretation of American exceptionalism and of the revolutionary inheritance, not as a democratic nation but as a Christian republic.

Both Everett and Bancroft had argued that the American republic created the conditions for individuals to prosper and become engaged with political institutions. Bancroft saw the Democratic Party as the chief agent of reform and key to the consequent attachment of citizens to the nation-state, while Everett championed individual improvement through education and other self-help measures. Both saw political and social institutions mediating between individuals and a republic whose history and promise both men considered exceptional. What neither writer did was to create a personal catalyst for binding the individual to the nation.

Beecher and the evangelical reform movement provided this deeper link, supplying an intermediary stage between the polity and the people—in the form of civil society. Voluntarist reform became powerful glue for the emerging cultural nationalism through personal conversion to moral causes. Voluntary societies promoting religion and morality, including temperance and education reform, served this purpose. Social improvement in prison systems, advocacy of women's rights and antislavery, and a host of lesser-known causes gave opportunities for individuals to take associational action to change their lives and the lives of those around them. Thereby, they expressed a new collective mission to reshape American society and the polity.[63]

Lyman Beecher, Personal Identity, and the Christian Republic

American Exceptionalism could not be imposed from the top down. This much was indicated in the careers of Edward Everett and George Bancroft, as discussed in chapter 3. Exceptionalism required the emotional investment of many people, who identified their own security, prosperity, or opportunity with that of the United States. Education could help, as could sermons and ubiquitous Fourth of July addresses. When students read homilies, histories, or other texts, when they playacted roles or took elocution lessons, and when adults gave speeches in lyceums and literary societies, they contributed to this wider participation. Ties to the nation could be strengthened through personal activity and alignment of many kinds. The most important influence came from voluntary associations, which had a key role in accentuating nationalism beyond the garden-variety type to an assertion of exceptionalism.[1]

In this age of rising voluntary organizations, one form was the political party, but its impacts were divisive of national unity and a stable conception of American exceptionalism. The mere act of joining a party likely played a role. The Jacksonian era saw a rapid rise of democratic participation measured by voting among adult (white) males. Voters became closely aligned with particular political programs in the 1830s, an alignment reinforced by the connection between parties and political appointments to local and state office, and by the internal improvements that oiled the system. Canal, river, harbor, and other public works were notably parochial, not national, legislation, and parties cultivated an allegiance that was transactional rather than transformative in identity terms.

Another form of association differed. Unlike political parties, moral reform societies, churches, and missionary activity mediated personal identity and national values via individual conversion. Personal identity and exceptionalism

became linked through Christian evangelicalism and the rise of morals societies. This connection changed American exceptionalism by emphasizing a
postmillennial triumph of a Christian republic. One striking moment in the
life of the most famous observer of American difference brought the personal
and the social into an illuminating alignment.

Soon after the French reformer, writer, politician, and aristocrat Alexis de
Tocqueville arrived in Boston on September 7, 1831, he attended an extraordinary meeting at Faneuil Hall. As recalled in his *Democracy in America*, a
crowd swept in from a procession, carrying banners and Polish flags to hear
an assortment of speakers denounce the Russian government.[2] The meeting
attendees expressed sympathy with the Poles seeking freedom from the tsar
in the uprising that began as part of the failed European revolutions of 1830. A
clergyman strode to the platform to call on Almighty God to extend his providential blessing to the Polish people in their struggle for independence. The
"priest," as Tocqueville put it, beseeched God to repeat the divine aid given
to the American colonists in their war of independence.[3] Tocqueville's trav-
eling companion Gustave de Beaumont dismissed the oration as a "pomp-
ous eulogy," but Tocqueville saw evidence of an extraordinary, if puzzling,
alignment between patriotic sentiment, religious institutions, and republican
liberty.[4] How strange to see a clergyman in the supposedly secular American
republic calling on God's spiritual battalions to free the Polish people. Tocqueville noted the respect given to this man and to his message. His name was Lyman Beecher, and he was a Congregational minister with a stern air in public
and a reputation, paradoxically, for his fine sense of humor.

Reverend Beecher had a towering presence in American religious and moral
reform circles. His was the time that the idea of the United States as a Christian republic first gained widespread credence. Protestant evangelical advocacy
of American exceptionalism was crucial to this process. Identifying with this
notion, Beecher merged his religious heritage, as the intellectual descendant
of the Puritans and the biological descendant of early English settlers, with a
teleological description of American history as fulfilling God's purpose under
the dynamic freedom of republican government. A Christian republic would,
it was hoped, facilitate innovation and allow organization over a vast area
without legal restriction, under the spur of religious competition for truth and
faith. The gains for the republic would be reciprocal. A religion strengthened
under these favored conditions would provide the moral content to structure
the new polity without infringing on religious liberties. In Beecher's eyes, the
republic was especially well endowed through prosperity and liberal institutions to take a leadership role from the Old World and its "Christian" nations.
The case shows how certain Americans sought actively to make their country

exceptional, rather than took it to be exceptional as if given from God or the Founding Fathers—and how personal trajectories of coming to know one's identity fused with the identification of the United States as exceptional.

This is not to say that Beecher deserves all the credit or discredit for the birth of a new exceptionalism, but that is no reason to forget him. As the most senior figure in the movement to establish a republic suffused with Protestant values, it is appropriate to explore his ideas in detail because they shaped and represented Christian republicanism and because they have been misunderstood. Beecher was not simply the father of three famous offspring in the Beecher clan, whose work also contributed to American exceptionalism. He was more, too, than a bitter anti-Catholic preoccupied with stopping Irish immigration to the American West.[5]

The context of his rise to fame was New England disestablishment, which directly affected his own Congregational church. From 1776 to the 1810s, one by one the states across the nation severed the ties between church and state, complementing the federal constitution's prohibition of an established church under the First Amendment. In Rhode Island and Pennsylvania, no state-supported church had existed, and to the south, the churches had been disestablished before 1800 amid the already strong presence of Enlightenment and revolutionary-era doctrines as well as the agitation of Methodists and Baptist dissenters. In New England, circumstances differed. There, the crisis of the Protestant elite came to a head in the 1810s, with the end of state support for an official church in Connecticut (in 1818) and the undermining of the established order in Massachusetts by judicial interpretation (in 1817).[6] In response, clergy and Christian moral reformers, especially those associated with the Congregational and Presbyterian churches, sought to replace their lost privileges with an evangelized, Christian citizenry. Thereby, it would not matter if religion lacked state aid; in fact, a Christianized republic would be a far better vehicle for the purposes of providence than state enforcement of church authority, because the new Christian order would be the moral and ecclesiastical equivalent of consent by the governed. From that time, all churches had to compete for adherents in a spiritual marketplace.

There was an extra dimension to this open market in religion. Changes in evangelicalism with the emergence of Methodism and Baptist sects as major forces gave primacy to the (democratic) individual as personally coming to crisis and conversion. Though compatible in reliance on the Gospels with old-school Calvinism, the newer doctrine emphasized the individual's exercise of free choice. In the open market of disestablishment, the measure of success was voluntary joining. For preachers, what now came to matter most was sentiment, technique, and persuasion. This evangelical imperative dovetailed nicely with the emphasis on a moral public as the foundation for American democracy. The doctrine was named "Arminian" after the venerated Dutch theologian Jacobus Arminius, who opposed predestination under a God-ordained "elect."

This merger of Christianity with republicanism through a mobilized Christian citizenry need not be exceptional. Ultimately, it would not be if, as American evangelicals hoped, other countries attained a truly Christianized citizenship aligning God's and human law. But only in a republic could this symmetry be fully obtained, the new Christian republicans argued, and only in the United States did the conditions yet exist for change. Though Christian reformers prayed and preached for the conversion of the world, they saw the republican United States as a prototype of this desired state. It is important to note that this exceptionalist program was postmillennialist in its assumption that conversion of the world under American leadership would precede the Second Coming of Christ. The United States should seize the providential opportunity, not passively await the Apocalypse. This positive program for a special evangelical influence in society necessarily focused on individual agency, a circumstance that advanced personal attachment to the nation-state as an exceptional republic.

Four years before he prayed for the Poles, Beecher had already confronted the post establishment options of the New England clergy. He collapsed the Puritan heritage into America's—and his own—in a landmark address before the Connecticut legislature in 1826, converted the following year into a sermon at the Third Congregational Church in Plymouth, Massachusetts, where the English colonists had arrived in 1620.[7] In this sermon, published as *The Memory of Our Fathers*, Reverend Beecher honored the collective Puritan identity but set out the terms in which accession to a republican form of government was central to the continued prosperity of the Christian enterprise. Beecher began with the proposition that no "state of society" had lasted forever; all had failed as a result of moral deficiencies. Much of world history consisted in "barbarism and despotism" while, for a favored few nations, a condition of happiness had been achieved only partially and temporarily. The United States could be an exception to this cyclical tale of misery, pain, and ultimate perdition. Republican America was in a position to change the course of history by providing a template for human redemption. "This nation has been raised up by Providence to exert an efficient instrumentality in this work of moral renovation," Beecher asserted.[8] His postmillennial eschatology worked on the idea of human action to hasten the millennium and Christ's return. It was to become key to making America Christian—and making the nation into the central instrument of God's plans.

For Beecher, the United States had a fortunate legacy. Like many nineteenth-century thinkers, secular and religious, he regarded American exceptionality as a product of favorable material conditions: the nation was prosperous because of its environment. Beecher drew attention to "the unexampled resources of this country," including "soil, climate, sea-coast, rivers, [and] lakes," that had "secured our prosperity."[9] In this observation, Beecher ventured an early version of the frontier thesis. The opportunity for ordinary people to acquire their own stake in the land made for American singularity compared with all previous societies, where the tillers of the soil were divorced from ownership and consigned to grinding poverty in vice-ridden cities. Herein were echoes of Jefferson's own views on the circumstances necessary for democracy.[10] But material conditions did not work without the "human mind" supplying the ingenuity to develop those assets; the opportunity to do so came through liberty to think and act to improve society. This liberty was nurtured "in connexion with the influence of republican and religious institutions" bequeathed, Beecher believed, by the Puritans.[11]

It was neither the material state of society nor its political institutions alone that made the United States exceptional but rather the moral chemistry of religious and political liberty under evangelical leadership. Morality underpinned political institutions, and that, in turn, built on the Puritan inheritance. The celebrated preacher's own ancestors had arrived in 1638, and he took particular pride in his family's achievements as examples of a stern Puritan faith.[12] For Beecher, the New England colonies were already different from Europe prior to the American Revolution because they had patiently crafted a stable, prosperous society in which religion and morality were central to the social order. That process must be continued by new means, Beecher concluded.[13] The Puritans had used their religious hegemony to prepare New England for self-governing liberty. Downplaying the evidence for Puritan persecution of those deemed nonbelievers or heretics, Beecher emphasized that "it was by training men for self-government" that his ancestors had "expected to make free men." This model, Beecher believed, was the essential basis for the national government in which power was not exercised by an autocrat. It was a point taken up by Tocqueville in the 1830s.[14]

The focus on creating a vibrant civil society through moral influence was doubly important, given the geographic extent of the American union, which already stretched well beyond the Puritan boundaries. Others had "doubted, whether a republic so extensive" could be "held together and efficiently governed." No matter. Provided there was an intellectual and moral influence, and the practice of civil and religious liberty among families, Beecher could not see "why a republic may not be extended indefinitely, and still be the strongest, and most effective government in the world."[15] His position was little different in its material aspects from Jefferson's own "Empire for Liberty," but it departed from the traditional local and regional identity of the New England colonies before the American Revolution.

For this happy state of affairs, Beecher thanked providential intervention. God had a plan for the United States, and this plan was evident in the successful colonizing movement of the Pilgrim fathers and the attainment of political independence against great odds. He saw the hand of God in the struggles against the "savage tribes," then the papist French in the Seven Years' War, and finally the British imperial rulers. It was "a history of perils and deliverances, and of strength ordained out of weakness."[16] So improbable did he find this series of triumphs that "some great design" must have been behind its unfolding, he concluded. The result was to draw a straight line between the New England colonial founding in 1620 and the emergence of the United States in 1776–89. From the start, the Pilgrims were "laying the foundations of a nation," and the question of nation became a key theme of Beecher's *Memory of Our Fathers*, not the history of the Puritans.[17] This was a religious redefinition of American cultural nationalism.

Such providential assistance came at a price. With material prosperity and the attainment of republican liberty, God clearly expected an American role in the coming millennium, Beecher proclaimed. In the "whole history of the world," God had "not been accustomed to grant signal interpositions, without ends of corresponding magnitude to be answered by them." Beecher could not conceive of the country's past as anything other than "the design of heaven to establish a powerful nation, . . . where all the energies of man might find scope and excitement, on purpose to show the world by experiment, of what man is capable."[18] Given God's aid, the United States must, in return, become a spiritual, moral, and political exemplar to the world.

For this reason, the national moral order underpinning republican liberty must be maintained. It was the duty of Christians to deliver for God. This line of thinking offered a new covenant. In return for being so favored a nation, Americans must serve God's purpose by spreading the gospel across the earth. Missions were therefore imperative. This alone did not make the United States exceptional since the unity of Christianity and especially Protestant Christianity in missions was acknowledged. The American missionary force was smaller than the British up to the end of the nineteenth century. But over time, the organization of strong missionary support groups, including for mission education, reinforced a growing reputation of the United States as the most innovative and energetic exporter of morals and religion.

In practice, the relation between nation and providence differed from its deterministic context under traditional Puritanism and also differed from the Enlightenment notion of a distant providential autonomy. Beecher worked to spread the new moral order as a self-generating influence, shifting the emphasis from a reaction to the work of providence and the threat of moral decline onto an active engagement to attain the status of a Christian republic. Beecher did not come to his conclusion while Congregational political and institutional power remained state-entrenched. But once the severing of the church from state support in Connecticut was completed in 1818 over his objections, Beecher turned from being a conservative defender of the social order to an enthusiastic exponent of religious liberty.

So far, it seemed to Beecher in 1826, the change of heart had worked, and God must have been pleased. Noting the greater number of religious denominations flourishing, Beecher now believed that God had rescued social stability through the emergence of the religious revivals sweeping the Protestant congregations of the Northeast. God "began to pour out his Spirit upon the churches; and voluntary associations of Christians were raised up to apply and extend that influence, which the law could no longer apply."[19] Beecher saw every reason to press ahead.

This idea of a covenant with God meant living on a knife-edge between success and failure. Lest Americans should become self-satisfied, Beecher argued they needed to inject themselves actively into the stream of history to fulfill God's purpose. The theology behind this stance differed from Beecher's Calvinist background. It reflected the rise of the Arminian doctrines of the individual believer's free agency as key to society's regeneration. Influenced by those Methodists and Baptists who abandoned Calvinist theology for a faith spread by religious revivals that raised the emotional pitch, Beecher became a leader in the practical application of so-called New School theology. The Calvinist focus on predestination was modified, and individual faith and conversion were stressed. The competition of the sects that proliferated in the era of church-state separation thus intensified the belief that religious liberty was part of God's bequeathing an "unexampled" capacity to the nation.[20]

Not only were the evangelical revivals viewed by Americans and many foreign commentators as exceptional; the material conditions behind them were too. America's astounding population increase was considered key. Surely God intended this human bounty to be the foundation of a global revival, making the new nation a bearer of supernatural will. This reasoning allowed Beecher to accept material progress, including the geographic expansion of a settler empire over Native American tribes, as essential. The United States must attain ever-greater demographic and economic power; it must "multiply its millions and its resources," in order to bring the whole world "under the influence of our civil and religious institutions," Beecher contended. Thereby, the evangelization of the globe could be completed on a platform of American prosperity, through "the energies" of a "concentrated benevolence" made possible by the nation's booming numbers.[21]

Spreading the Puritan Inheritance:
The Machinery of Exceptionalist Belief

It has become conventional to play down the role of the reformed Calvinists such as Beecher in American religious change and social reform, but this argument should not be overstressed. Granted, the newer sects and churches grew at a faster rate than those Beecher represented. The firepower came not from any one church but rather from the combined church and reform institutions that Protestants devised to extend the idea of a Christian republic. More than church-state divisions, it was the competitiveness between churches in the search for souls to save that led denominations to draw on one another's techniques for success. Denominationalism and theology became in this way less important than before 1800. More critical than differences over freedom of religion were splits within denominations between freewill beliefs and more rigidly Calvinist ones. Beecher's campaign was a product of these energies, not the cause. He was, however, at the forefront of the intellectual efforts to create the national institutions that would underpin a religiously driven exceptionalism and spread its influence.

The idea of the nation's providential role made manifest in the actions of Christian Americans became central to this cross-denominational fertilization. The influence of evangelicalism became cooperative and even cathartic in moral reform activities as Arminian techniques spread. Though Baptists and Methodists had disparate positions on church organization, their views of the nation's special status encompassed the creation of a Christian republic as part of the nation's exceptionalism.[22] After the memory of religious discrimination against dissenters began to fade, "latent areas of agreement among different groups" on public action to promote morality emerged. Interdenominational collaboration in voluntary institutions encouraged such a shift, duplicated across the nation. Even some old-school Calvinists began to adopt moral reform measures as their vehicle by the 1850s.[23]

During this time, the social power of evangelical religion surged. Out of 31 million people before the Civil War, avers historian Richard Carwardine, "about 40 percent of the total population, appear . . . to have been in close sympathy with evangelical Christianity." This was the nation's "largest, and most formidable, subculture."[24] "The important fact here is comparative," states historian Mark Noll. "No other organized promoter of values, no other generator of print, no other source of popular music or compelling public imagery, no other comforter (and agitator) of internal life—none came anywhere close to the organized strength of the evangelical churches in the three-quarters of a century after the dawn of the republic."[25] Within these stronger churches, it was Beecher and his cohort who summarized in many sermons "the faith that was frequently preached in much of America in the first half of the nineteenth century."[26] Though originally concerned with individual salvation, by the 1850s evangelicals had begun to move from moral influence to the altering of law, and they displayed a strong evangelical interest in politics.[27]

The political influence of evangelicalism notwithstanding, exceptionalist beliefs needed to be validated through individual human experience and identity. The years in which Beecher first became a figure of national importance saw the expansion of moral reform societies that encouraged individuals to take practical action by identifying with others in associations. The American Bible Society (founded 1816); the American Tract Society (reorganized as a national institution in 1824); the American Sunday School Union (1824); and the American Society for the Promotion of Temperance (1826) were among the many national organizations that made Protestant evangelicalism a force in politics and society.[28] These and kindred groups collectively became known as the *Benevolent Empire*, a term that rose to prominence between 1819 and 1822. In the two decades that followed, the colporteurs of the tract societies penetrated deep into the countryside; the steamboats and, a little later, early railroads allowed preachers to travel more swiftly than ever before; and the new steam printing presses facilitated cheap moral tracts, newspapers, and periodicals that challenged Americans to renounce sin and pursue moral reform. Historians call this period from the 1820s to 1840s the *Ferment (or Era) of Reform*. Voluntary associations preaching not only religious causes and temperance but also antislavery, prison reform, and prostitution reform spread the content of Christian republicanism far and wide through what evangelicals described as moral benevolence.[29]

In part, the significance of these associations was to demonstrate that God was actually turning the United States into a Christian republic. The success of the American Tract Society Beecher interpreted as such a sign. "Now we are blessed with societies to aid in the support of the Gospel at home, to extend it to the new settlements, and through the earth. We have Bible societies, and Tract societies, and associations of individuals, who make it their business to see that every family has a Bible, and every church a pastor, and every child a catechism," he declared.[30] Human action inspired by providential power made the United States seem ever more exceptional. Revivals of religion and moral reform in the New England states were, Beecher boasted, "without a parallel in the history of the world" because of their extent and their persistence. In his boastful estimate of world history, "these revivals [were] constituting an era of moral power entirely new."[31] Not born so, the United States was being made exceptional by revivals sweeping across the land.

This interpretation raised the possibility of chosenness, but the Bible and tract societies did not explicitly endorse it. In fact, they saw their task as a global agenda undertaken by all of Protestant Christianity. Within the United States, the new, voluntaristic societies had practical religious and moral objectives and stuck to them. Even the missionary societies working abroad generally abstained from invidious comparisons with other Christian nations. It was "Christian" versus "heathen" polities that constituted the reference point.[32] To accept national chosenness would depend on a sense of collective identity not firmly formed when Beecher first championed Christian republicanism. Political nationalism was a still fragile and self-conscious promotion. Cultural nationalism had begun to develop, but this protean force remained decentralized until evangelical reform grew in the 1820s.[33] The real strength of the reform movements was demonstrated at the local level and in their innovative tactics for individual conversion. National reform was envisaged as the cumulative effect of local renunciation of sinful conduct. Organizing at the local and state level made sense because most morals legislation came under local and state law through the so-called police powers.

Nevertheless, evangelical reformers were vital in the leap toward a national *imaginary*. They provided a structure and a moral trajectory for cultural nationalist sentiment to consolidate by aligning local and state action with the reaffirmation of the United States not as a chosen people of a certain place but as a Christian nation aspiring to future global leadership. Equally important, evangelical reformers created a material infrastructure to assist this change by building national institutions as a symbol of reform's expected trajectory.[34] These institutions encouraged members to think of a national transformation and to spread the administrative practices of reform. Moving the organizational, financial, and publishing headquarters of many benevolent reform societies to New York facilitated this shift by aligning national trade, communications, and philanthropy with the refurbished traditions of New England Protestantism. Thereby, moral activists worked to expand their relevance for the whole nation.[35] New School Calvinism was a key part of this coalition, and like-minded Presbyterians in New Jersey, New York, and Pennsylvania were prominent. The businessmen, lawyers, and politicians as well as clergy of the major northeastern cities were tapped for funding and administrative roles in the organization. Forceful Mid-Atlantic preachers such as Philadelphia's Presbyterian firebrand Albert Barnes merged liberty, moral causes, and revivalism, and they understood the importance of a national focus for moral reform.[36]

New England was, therefore, no longer enough in itself. Its culture must also colonize the western states and territories to survive as a moral force, and it must represent the entire East as essentially an augmented version of New England's agenda. Geopolitical realities made the frontier key because, west of the Appalachian Mountains, "a nation [was] being 'born in a day,'" Beecher stated. For the Protestant worldview to survive, northerners had to expand territorially, just as Southerners believed was necessary to do for slavery's survival. If the West came under the control of the South, northern evangelical reformers feared that laxer moral standards would apply more generally, owing to the effects of slavery.[37] Beecher wanted to avoid being seen as the bearer of purely New England ideas, but he wished for a northern dominance of moral reform incorporating the West and the South in his vision. If the United States was going to provide the catalyst for the coming millennium, New England needed to be, behind the scenes, the orchestrator of U.S. moral power, Beecher believed, because there the work of rearing moral institutions had "been most nearly accomplished."[38]

With the peopling of the West prompting Beecher's alarm, material circumstances shaped his geopolitical calculation of the millennial struggle. Jonathan Edwards had predicted in the mid-eighteenth century that the United States would have a role in the world's potential salvation, but Beecher claimed to have questioned that thought until he witnessed the economic success of the United States after the American Revolution.[39] Through the political possibilities of the United States as a civil society structured by voluntary organizations of moral citizens came the impetus to see the American "nation" as the site for his work. In this way, the post-1815 explosion in westward expansion and the creation of national institutions jointly shaped antebellum exceptionalism. Beecher noted that "all other nations have gone up slowly from semi-barbarism to a civilized manhood," but Americans experienced uneven spurts of development. What became the United States began in the 1600s with "the best materials of a nation" in New England and, at that time, was "the most favored nation in the world," yet further progress was delayed for two hundred years, "by policy, and power, and war, and taxation, and want of capital." Then, liberated from Britain, the United States suddenly surged forward in population and economic growth. "It is less than fifty years since our resources have begun to be developed in great power," Beecher rejoiced. The opening of the

West had driven this shift.[40] This emphasis on expansion, both geographic and demographic, was full of bravado not far in its inflection from the cultural nationalism that Everett and Bancroft announced.

Identity Formation and Moral Reform

Analyzing the role of evangelical reform and religious revivalism in creating a national identity in these years provides a link between personal experience and a national narrative. How was it that so many Americans could believe in national exceptionalism when the empirical evidence for that idea was uneven and sometimes, in political, economic, or cultural terms, quite weak? To the extent that the polity could be seen as a Christian republic in the making, individual conversion encouraged a broadening of allegiance from community and church to the nation-state as expressive of personal identity and guarantor of individual conversion.

The sense of identity as American and evangelical was not completely fused. As Bancroft's version of exceptionalism suggests, national consciousness had a wider historical origin in the period when nationalism in Europe as well as the Americas was spreading. But political and evangelical identity became allied in the conversion process. This nexus created a new personal life experience, one in which the nation's liberal democratic progress facilitated individual commitment to evangelicalism and elicited in turn an attachment to the American nation-state, which protected that freedom through the First Amendment. Converts invested the institutions of the nation with the spiritual purpose of millennial salvation. Such was the conclusion of mainstream Baptists who, unlike certain old-school Baptists, supported global missions. They cherished a memory of special origins in the struggle for religious autonomy even before the American Revolution. In their hard-won denominational identity, they considered themselves exceptional prior to embracing the nation in a merged sense of patriotic exceptionality, to which they claimed to have made a unique contribution.[41]

Identity formation within the churches stemmed not only from the revivals but also from the life changes induced by the moral reform societies in which the evangelicals participated. Of all the religious and moral institutions of the Benevolent Empire, the most numerically expansive and influential were the proliferating temperance societies that emerged from 1826 to 1836. In those years, national membership rose from less than a few hundred people to more than one million. In this early iteration, the temperance movement aligned closely with evangelicalism and the arguments of Beecher. Delivered in 1826, his *Six Sermons on the Nature, Occasions, Signs, Evils, and Remedy of Intem-*

perance was reprinted and distributed for decades as propaganda for the cause, alongside a barrage of advice and sermonizing literature from a wide variety of Protestant clergy and their allies among the medical profession, industrialists, merchants, politicians, and judges.[42] It was not so much from the Bible and tract societies that the new iteration of American exceptionalism spread as it was from temperance and other reform groups associated with the Protestant churches.

The temperance surge coincided with a decline in U.S. alcohol consumption from very high levels, but the movement's importance exceeded purely drink-related impacts. Its organizational success and novel methods of conversion caught the attention of Tocqueville. He used the movement's apparent might as evidence for the innovative potential of the American society that fascinated him.[43] The reform movement's associational model of democracy Tocqueville proposed as the essence of American distinctiveness. The phenomenon of individual, public profession of allegiance to temperance reform appeared, to the French observer, to distinguish the United States from Europe as the exemplar of civil society against state power.[44]

When the drinker not only abstained but also pledged sobriety as an example to one's community, a public demonstration of faith in the moral cause was asserted. This collective moral force Tocqueville believed was absent in Europe, where morality had to be imposed. His interest centered on the effects this demonstration of public opinion had on the nurturing of a society capable of adjusting conflict through law and popular participation. But the impact on the individual's, not the association's, identification with the republic was key for exceptionalism. The signer of the temperance pledge took on a new personal and civic identity as a moral citizen, whether he or she was a church member or not. In this way, the temperance movement indirectly championed American exceptionalism and extended its power beyond the evangelical ambit.

Not only did the temperance movement promise national reform via individual conversion, it also campaigned to cleanse the rituals and institutions of the republic. Reformers established a Congressional Temperance Society (CTS) to change behavior in government and demonstrate political leadership throughout the land. Fourth of July ceremonies were affected all over the country where temperance societies campaigned and where their orators championed the antispirits cause as liberating, not repressive. Senator Felix Grundy of Tennessee persuaded the CTS to resolve that "the practice of not using ardent spirits, at the celebration of the 4th of July, the great day of American liberty, is truly republican; and tends to prevent that corruption of public morals, which is the deadliest foe to the prosperity of our country."[45] Here temperance signified the virtue that classical republicanism required, and that Christian republicanism proposed to achieve.

The temperance movement identified its objective for many thousands of temperance members as a moral republic, advancing the cause of righteousness everywhere. The United States, once rendered sober, could be contrasted with (mostly European) countries that did not shun alcohol. According to former justice of the New York Supreme Court Jonas Platt, experiments in republicanism across Latin America and Europe conducted in the absence of a vigorous temperance movement could only be the action of a species of "mock-republic," not a true manifestation of exceptionality against monarchical tyranny.[46] In an authentic and "unexampled" republic, personal temperance would become a marker of national identity. Such action, even concerning the lobbying of members of Congress, did not involve a formal alliance with the state but rather moral suasion.[47]

While the movement did not initially make the state the enforcer of morality through law, temperance reformers soon saw the government licensing of hard liquor as promoting a bad example, whereas the state should be free of such moral taint. Temperance societies therefore began to advocate changing the laws to reflect what they regarded as the true character of society.[48] Reformers succeeded by limiting public-house hours and pushing for local option legislation in the 1840s, and even for state prohibition in thirteen northern states and territories in the 1850s. Of course, the latter were contentious laws, and most were overthrown or greatly modified between 1855 and 1865, but the larger, antialcohol social movement persisted and revived in the 1870s and beyond. Its successor crusade, alcohol prohibition, continued to influence state and national politics profoundly until the 1930s.

The link between individual identity and collective morality was manifest in temperance arguments. In the religiously motivated temperance societies under the banner of the American Society for the Promotion of Temperance, "each individual who names the name of Christ" was called upon, "by the providence of God, to act on this subject openly and decidedly for him" in order "to cause temperance and all its attendant benefits universally to prevail." It was the duty of the individual to abstain in the interests of the "animating prospects of this great and mighty republic," which would otherwise be "darkened" and "its precious institutions ruined."[49] Only thus could the nation's pioneering work be made global. Temperate behavior through conversion would underpin the "virtue" of "our American Republic," asserted temperance proponent David Daggett, Connecticut chief justice. Energized by Christian values, this moral nation would in turn enable international progress toward a sober and humane world following the U.S. example, he predicted.[50] The American

Society for the Promotion of Temperance and its huge affiliated membership aimed for an alcohol-free world through individual pledge taking.

The connection of conversion and personal identity with national identity was made even clearer in the new, ostensibly secular self-help temperance societies of the 1840s that featured conversion narratives from erstwhile drunkards. These new, "teetotal" groups abjuring fermented as well as distilled liquor were paradigmatic of a merged personal and national identity. They designated themselves the "Washingtonians" in honor of the first president, and they equated liberation from the thraldom of drink to the unshackling of the thirteen colonies from the yoke of Britain in 1776. More conventional abstainers saluted this embrace in Boston at a Faneuil Hall meeting devoted to the veritable "Temple of Liberty." Temperance fraternal orders that enrolled hundreds of thousands of members in the 1840s and 1850s, notably the numerous Sons of Temperance lodges, included in their rituals the self-conscious reference to the "Temple of Liberty" not as a physical place but a condition of sobriety.[51] The reference to "temple" in the Sons of Temperance transcended a specifically Christian focus. It reflected classical Roman notions of a "Temple of Honor," the name of another temperance fraternal order, and the seat of figurative worship became recast as a "Temple of Sobriety" to which followers were drawn by conversion. Its messages indicated that total abstinence was key to the stability and future prosperity of the republic.[52] Patriotism and the process of conversion coincided in this rhetoric and practice.

The Limits of Christian Republicanism

The vogue for temperance associations was close to the heart of antebellum manifestations of American exceptionalism; but this phenomenon did not function as a set of consensual institutions promoting legal and democratic norms.[53] Rather, the temperance movement was riven in the 1840s by conflict over how far to take moral suasion, and by ethnic and religious opposition within the larger society. The young Abraham Lincoln's 1842 speech in Springfield, Illinois, on the role of temperance groups showed both the strengths and the limits of the Christian republican program. Praising the temperance movement, Lincoln aligned himself with voluntary action promoting reform, not the use of law. He acknowledged how important temperance "advocates" were but specifically endorsed the anti-institutional dynamic of the Washingtonian movement with its reformed drunkards and teetotal policies of self-help in place of lawyers and preachers denouncing boozers and legislating against alcohol.[54]

The limits to Christian republicanism were centered to a considerable

extent on this question of how voluntary associations could appropriately effect social change. Though Lincoln praised the Washingtonians, the latter
group was not a source of comity within the republic. Temperance advocates
of the 1830s had a habit of becoming prohibitionists quite quickly in the 1840s.
That they became teetotalers was already a source of controversy among the
many Christians who took the biblical sanction of wine literally. The ubiquitous temperance networks were inherently unstable because they disrupted
the social and legal order through the strong evangelical influence on them;
the same happened with moderate antislavery giving way to radical abolitionism.[55] It was precisely the tendency to move toward enforcement of moral
reform through both personal intimidation and law that threatened disunity.

Because of divided opinion over reform tactics and objectives, Lincoln's
avoidance of coercion revealed an astute political sense of compromise. The
divisions went further than those over alcohol. The reformed Calvinist churches
of the Northeast were not able to speak even for all the nation's Protestants on
the hierarchies of donating and proselytizing. Methodists, Southern Baptists,
and a plethora of sects such as the Disciples of Christ and the Seventh-Day
Adventists thrived in the new republic. Along with Catholics, many of these
groups objected to the demands from tract and bible societies for centralized
programs of giving. They sometimes rejected the importance of missionary
work in other countries as well. These activities certain dissenters denounced
as the work of financial parasites.[56]

The recalcitrant groups did not add up anywhere near to a majority of
American Protestants, but their carping and grumbling did undermine a nationwide Christian consensus on the role of religion in politics. The so-called
Anti-Mission Baptists were old-school Calvinists on the western frontier of
the 1830s, as in the Wabash Valley of Indiana and in the South. They opposed
what they called "the craft of missions." The "missionary" would "not preach
to the heathen and many others, or help get these poor creatures out of hell,
without money," exclaimed one southern clergyman.[57] Later called Primitive
Baptists, Anti-Mission critics rejected anything without precedent in their own
literal interpretation of biblical teaching. In southern states such as North Carolina, the purveyors of temperance tracts were denounced because their total
abstinence extremism did not "agree with Scripture."[58] By opposing "the missionary establishment," these critics offered a different view of American exceptionalism, stressing individual rights, local self-government, and the need
to guard against those "usurping" liberties won by blood in the revolutionary
struggle. This meant limiting state power and supporting Jacksonian democracy in politics against interfering missionaries and reformers such as antislavery and temperance campaigners.[59]

In this and other ways, politics and sectional rivalry interfered with the spread of the Benevolent Empire agenda. The chief accusation was that New School Calvinists wanted to reinstate an established church by stealth. Dissenting Christian sects, Jews, and secularists responded to the perceived threat and "galvanized Jacksonian opposition to church-state collusion."[60] An early target was the Pennsylvanian Presbyterian clergyman Ezra Stiles Ely, whose tactless call in 1827 for "a truly Christian party in politics" inadvertently crystallized secularist and dissenter objections. Unitarians as well as Universalists protested.[61] William Morse, a pastor of the Universalist Church in Nantucket, Massachusetts, condemned the "Christian party" as "theological tyrants."[62] Others, like New York State assemblymen David Moulton and Mordecai Myers, argued that the synagogue, the mosque, and "all other churches and religions" were "placed on equal grounds" under the U.S. Constitution.[63]

Opposition to the opening of the U.S. Post Office on Sundays became a cause célèbre for evangelical campaigns, and in this practical attempt at a Sabbatarian measure the Christian republicans were defeated.[64] The advocates of church-state separation triumphed, demonstrating that other Christians and even people of non-Christian or no faith exercised considerable influence in the political and social spheres in the 1830s among Jacksonian Democrats, whose political fortunes were ascendant.[65] These groups relied on the constitution's First Amendment rights. The consequences for ideas of an exceptional nation were profound; they indicated how disparate the articulation of national exceptionalism might be. The Anti-Mission Baptists were exceptionalists, but they specified what the nation could not and should not be and left open the contest of beliefs between all religious denominations. They differed sharply from Beecher's idea of a positively Christianized people, a notion in later generations thought to be indicative of Christian nation beliefs.

The negative view of the state in regard to religion was designed to curb federal power, and it contrasted a properly limited government in the United States with despotic European monarchs. Though this formulation expressed the exceptionalist dichotomy of "Europe" versus "America" and the corresponding trope of "aristocracy" versus "democracy," it lacked the concept of the United States as an example to the world, or as a liberating, missionizing force. Anti-Mission Baptists were closer to the idea of the United States as a unique society—unrepeatable—but also conceded that the United States was not the only country guided by God since, "in his providence," God sent "rain on the just and unjust, giving life, health and blessing to all."[66]

A second roadblock threatening Beecher's goal of a homogeneous Christian republicanism came from "Rome." Roman Catholics of German and Irish origin became the fastest-growing religious group in the late 1840s and 1850s, owing to the first wave of mass European immigration, but even in 1835, Beecher foresaw these immigrant groups as a threat to his agenda. Rather than attempt to persuade Catholics to support his model, Beecher wished to discourage their move to the United States and to curb their political influence when they arrived. Within the Roman Catholic Church, Bishop John J. Hughes of New York opposed this attempted Protestant ascendancy and promoted parish schools where Catholic religious education could be freely taught.[67] Since Protestants considered the public schools to be foundational in promoting American singularity, education was inevitably a contested field. The severe religious and ethnocultural conflict that followed over temperance and public education necessarily checked the growth of a hegemonic Protestant discourse on exceptionalism.[68]

Given this divided moral geography, other faces of religiously motivated exceptionalism than Beecher's must be addressed. Ironically, Bishop Hughes did not deny U.S. exceptionalism but saw America's fortunate past and future identity another way. In the wake of the 1848 revolutions that threatened the papacy in Europe, he developed a conservative defense of the United States as the bastion of moderate change and republican continuity against radical European anticlericalism. Catholics he portrayed as positive contributors to stable American growth and nationhood.[69] In Hughes's opinion, Catholics, particularly Irish Catholics, were already fashioning their own exceptionalist beliefs in the promise of the nation as they made their way in American society. This intervention by Hughes presaged the idea that Catholicism could be compatible with liberal republican government, provided the government was not taken over by a Protestant ascendancy through the activities of the Benevolent Empire.

Tempering the anxieties over Catholics at midcentury was the contrast between a "provincial republican prosperity" in the United States and the radical republicanism sweeping across the European continent in 1848 and threatening property as much as religion. Those European revolutions were widely reported and discussed in the United States; Americans welcomed visits from leading revolutionaries of the liberal nationalist type such as Louis Kossuth and Giuseppe Garibaldi, but most Americans drew the line at joining actively in European political quarrels. In the wake of the "distant revolutions" of 1848, the interpretation of the American Revolution as the work of a more moderate political culture had strong attractions. It was one that "Americans of different faiths could commonly embrace," historian Timothy Roberts has argued.[70]

Stubborn Catholic and ethnic differences over exceptionalism flared again in the 1850s, but religious contention *within* the Protestant majority was more malleable. The pattern was revealed in the case of the so-called Christian Church, later known as the Disciples of Christ. It was not the mainstream churches alone which supported the idea of a Christianized republic serving providence. Sects claiming the mantle of a Bible-centered Christianity also found providence at work in secular American history. Prominent leaders included Elias Smith (1769–1846), a fractious Baptist preacher who became a Universalist and then a member of the Christian Church as he progressed through his spiritual journey. Smith's newspaper, the *Herald of Gospel Liberty*, founded in 1808, conveyed the importance of religious freedom under the U.S. Constitution in its title and content as the key to personal identity tied to exceptionalism.[71] Another foundational figure was Barton Stone (1772–1844), whose sect merged in the 1820s with one led by Thomas and Alexander Campbell. The merged group (the Christian Church) became known by more orthodox denominations as the "Campbellites" under its most influential preacher, Alexander Campbell (1788–1866), and numbered about one hundred thousand members in 1860.

Alexander Campbell's writings reveal a story of exceptionalism remarkably similar in practice, though not in theological doctrine, to that of the Benevolent Empire. Campbell argued for restoring a purely Bible-based and nondenominational religion focused on the original church forms and customs of the early Christian era, hence the movement was called Restorationist in theology. Regarding the freedom of religion, Restorationists eschewed a close identification with the public rituals of the American state. "We remember with gratitude the achievements of the patriots of the land," Campbell wrote of the Fourth of July observances in 1830, but "we ought to rejoice with joy unspeakable and full of glory in recollecting the Christian Chief, and his holy apostles, who has made us free indeed, and given us the rank and dignity, not of citizens of earthly states, but of heaven."[72] Campbell subordinated his patriotism to a higher loyalty—God. For this reason, Campbell would not give an address on the Fourth of July when the date fell on a Sunday. Yet Campbell was a very successful preacher and, as Restorationist churches consolidated and assimilated to the cultural norms of American society, Campbell's following grew and shed its rough frontier image that displeased some mainstream Protestants. As it did, Restorationist institutions developed the marks of older, more settled denominations. Campbell became wealthy and founded Bethany College in 1840 to promote an educated ministry. Restorationists also established what became Butler University in Indiana, for liberal and professional education.

National vanity or glory was not the objective of Campbell's teaching but, by 1847, he too placed the United States among the greatest countries in

education, climate, soils, population, natural beauty, and other material en-
dowments.[73] Compared with the Old World, the United States was already
ahead in the "elements" of national achievement, despite the nation's "infancy," Campbell asserted. "We excel all the world beside," he argued, because
the United States had a destiny powered "in part through the Protestant Reformation, carried to this continent by our stern, uncompromising Puritan
ancestors."[74] Providentialist history, millennial expectations, and hopes for
a pure Christianity bound Restorationists to the mainstream New England
clergy on the importance of exceptionalist tenets, even though they differed
from evangelicals over legislating morality, church hierarchies, and undi-
vided allegiance to the nation-state.[75]

✶

Writing from abroad in 1844 and 1851, the Presbyterian minister Robert Baird
could be expected to rejoice in all this effort by evangelists and moral reform
allies. With his wide experience working for the American Sunday School
Union and the American Bible Society at home and in Europe, Baird was in
some ways doing the work of Tocqueville by explaining American distinctiveness to a European audience. From headquarters in Paris, he interpreted
American religious movements to Europeans, and the story he told was one
of extensive and positive influence. Yet even Baird, the first serious if amateur
historian of nineteenth-century Protestant revivalism, conceded that Christian republicanism had limits. While the number of formally churched people
jumped markedly from 1800 to 1850, evangelicalism did not command a clear
majority among Americans.[76] Beecher and his allies had not succeeded in
converting all segments of opinion. Yet, the quest to spread Christian republican ideas of exceptionalism had a secret weapon whose significance Baird
did not register—Catharine Beecher.

Women and Exceptionalism: The Self-Made Woman and the Power of Catharine Beecher

Opposition to the exceptionalist agenda of Christian republicans revealed the need for other, indirect supports. The cultural elaboration of a separate sphere for women fitted the bill, allowing for a wider field in which women could find identity and attachment to exceptionalism via self-reform. This chapter continues the emphasis on exceptionalist personal identification by focusing on how women, who made up roughly half of society, acquired and asserted a reputation for the American home as the site of women's advancement and the stability of the social structure. Despite the limits revealed in its political muscle flexing, Christian republican ideas spread in noninstitutional ways through these changes in the position of women.

Even as exceptionalism was to become, in the twentieth century, associated with political economy (class, labor, capital, and the institutions of the state), its (American) underpinning in the nineteenth century could be found in patterns of family life critical to a civil society. Here the role of gender was particularly important. The realm of the state was a largely masculinist space, but, in republican society, females were assigned moral leadership in the home. From this foundation, far-reaching changes that took the role of women out of the home and into society quickly came. The implications for American democracy and the idea of exceptionalism were profound. Articulated by middle-class Protestant women, this agenda cut across class and denominational categories to produce explicit discussion of exceptionalism as a gender issue and a matter of religious chosenness. These social and cultural changes paralleled Jacksonian democracy and its mythic image of the self-made man, with the emergence of the self-made woman achieved through domestic self-reform. As with the spread of personal identification in the self-help temperance societies and the conversion of Baptists, Campbellites, and other dissenter sects, exceptionalism ceased to be imparted from above but became manifest in American families and the education of children.

Women's critical importance for the stability of society was one of the major observations made by European commentators and nineteenth-century visitors to the United States.[1] Alexis de Tocqueville noted the shift, in principle, away from the patriarchal authority expressed in social life in the European world. This contrast already placed women in the mainstream of speculation about the nation's singularity by 1835. The role of women as moral guardians through their piety and religion was a point pushed by the Protestant clergy, duly registered by the French traveler.[2]

That role in the early republic was two-edged. On the one hand, it suggested possibilities for women as well-informed and responsible individual citizens; on the other, it reflected Enlightenment thought that inscribed gendered roles and associated women with the highest stage of "civilization." In this schema, "savage" Indians or "barbaric" polities such as the Ottoman Empire degraded women. "Civilized" societies flourished by exalting women. But this was not an exceptionalist position marked merely by the blending of Christian republicanism with Enlightenment ideas. At first women developed their own sense of engagement with the new republican enterprise by establishing or participating in schools to improve literacy and general knowledge as well as social skills among young women. Improvements in women's education and the emergence of women writers as a distinctive cohort were noticeable trends in the United States as in Britain. American women and men necessarily responded to the ground-breaking discussions on the role of women that the American Revolution and later the French Revolution exposed, especially through the English-woman Mary Wollstonecraft's *A Vindication of the Rights of Woman* (1792).[3]

A conservative reaction to the French Revolution's implications in the work of Wollstonecraft took shape soon after. The evangelicals' initial response to her call for woman's autonomy and human rights stressed religious piety within the "traditional" idea of family, at whose head would be a male. Timothy Dwight's sermons and Federalist political practice were at the center of this counterrevolution against both secularism and a possible American protofeminism based on the Declaration of Independence.[4] This conservative agenda might seem at odds with an American exceptionalism in the treatment of women based on individual rights, but conflict over the impact of the French Revolution was an important spur to the eastern American evangelical revivals (1790s–1810s), from which a distinctive phase in the growth of women's activism was well under way in missionary, education, temperance, and anti-slavery societies by the 1820s. Lyman Beecher's Christian republicanism provided a political and social outlet for this highly gendered civil society work.

Certainly, women took up the challenge to make the most of a greater moral influence in the home that evangelical preachers insisted was necessary to the defeat of irreligion stemming from the French Revolution. This agency made the changing position of gender central to the inculcation of exceptionalist sentiments, since women were increasingly held responsible for child-rearing in a specifically republican social experiment. Women's domesticity and morality became the essential underpinning of the new liberty that Lyman Beecher promised.

The growth of a presumed moral power on the part of women was connected to the extension of church membership during the early nineteenth-century religious revivals. Big increases came with the rising numbers of women converting to an active Christian role after 1800. This shift in audience has become known as the "feminization" of American religion. It affected most obviously the evangelical denominations, though a version of ladylike domesticity also existed under Roman Catholicism later in the century, with its pantheon of revered images, such as of Mother Mary. The presence of women in the churches provided foot-soldiers in the evangelical wars for the nation's soul that the Benevolent Empire undertook.[5]

This story directly involved the Beecher family. Lyman Beecher's moral and social impact was hugely extended by his progeny, especially two of his daughters, Catharine Beecher and Harriet Beecher Stowe. Among sons, the Reverend Henry Ward Beecher was the best known because of his abolitionist sentiments, his impassioned preaching, and, after the Civil War, his scandalous affair with a parishioner, but Lyman's eldest child, Catharine, was the more important for exceptionalism's genealogy.[6] She became the chief dispenser of domestic advice to American women, and she combined this vocation with a strong dose of support for a Christian republic. Through Catharine, the program of Lyman Beecher was disseminated interdenominationally among middle-class American families.

Catharine embraced Lyman's republican exceptionalism and applied it to women, the greatest consumers of Christian evangelism in the nineteenth century. In her best-selling book *A Treatise on Domestic Economy* (1841), she wrote that democracy had already given American women a higher place in world history than any other national grouping of their gender.[7] Catharine was not drawing on her father directly in this exceptionalist statement but rather mixing his interpretation of U.S. history with the ideas of Tocqueville. In fact, four pages on the position of women is a set of block quotations from the French political thinker, who noticed the greater freedom before marriage that American women enjoyed.[8] But Catharine did draw on her father in attributing to religious freedom the favored state of democratic institutions, from which she extrapolated the exceptional potential of the American republic for woman's role. Democracy became inextricably linked in Catharine's mind with religion, national destiny, and gender. "The democratic institutions of this Country are in reality no other than the principles of Christianity carried into operation," she insisted. These institutions had placed woman "in her true position in society, as having equal rights with the other sex." Equal rights, Catharine Beecher style, meant not the equal rights championed by Frances Wright or Mary Wollstonecraft, in which women would be autonomous individuals, but highly gendered moral rights, in which the family was the basic unit of the republic and the source of its necessary virtues.[9]

Catharine Beecher's work was not the modern version of American exceptionalism. It created two categories of sociological analysis to the extent that it acknowledged a key distinction between "aristocratic" and "democratic" countries. Again, this dichotomy followed Tocqueville's model, which generalized these types and did not ascribe exceptionality to the United States on its own but instead considered democracy analytically and comparatively as a social system. Beecher also followed Tocqueville in criticizing certain negative aspects of gender relations on the North American continent. He commented on exhausted frontier women, and so did Beecher, building on Tocqueville's critique by discussing the social causes of women's apparent ill health. According to her, American women had it worse in a material sense than the women of aristocratic lands. Gender everywhere consigned women to a second-class status, Beecher acknowledged, but argued that "it would seem as if the primeval curse, which has written the doom of pain and sorrow on one period of a young mother's life, in this Country had been extended over all; so that the hour seldom arrives, when 'she forgetteth her sorrow for joy that a man is born into the world.'"[10]

These democratic discriminations of gender in the United States were not grounded in "nature" but economics and culture. In this analysis, the economic energy unleashed through individual property rights in early republican and Jacksonian America had produced economic change that disconnected women from extended family relations. Social change placed upon them increased housework, with families forced to move west, or husbands forced to labor outside the home or village, leaving mothers to care alone for children, especially on the western frontier.[11]

Because of rapid economic development, the argument went, women in the United States faced collateral mental and physical damage from excessive "excitement" thrust upon them by hard-pressed husbands and fathers, thus producing symptoms of anxiety in female carers.[12] Writing in the shadows of the 1837–43 depression, Beecher emphasized "the fluctuating state of society."

No one could question "that women were exposed to a far greater amount of intellectual and moral excitement, than those of any other land." In her judgment, American women were truly exceptional in their psychic state. In the "responsibilities of domestic life, the degree in which their minds and feelings are taxed, is altogether greater than it is in any other nation."[13] These draining physical and mental effects on American women were thought to be even more pronounced in the western states. Quoting again from Tocqueville, but also reflecting her own time in the Midwest, Beecher highlighted the debilitating impact of frontier life on young women forced to raise a family in primitive domestic conditions and a rugged climate.

Beecher was not the only prominent woman to decry the economic upheavals of antebellum America and to deal with American exceptionalism. The future abolitionist Lydia Child wrote *The Frugal Housewife* (1829), wherein she condemned the growing inequality in U.S. society and its materialistic culture, arguing that this social change presented a challenge to republican values. She feared the loss of "our virtue and our freedom," warning that the United States was not exempt from the laws of history. Because "decay has begun in all republics," she challenged her readers, "let them calmly ask themselves whether we are in no danger." Nations did "not plunge at once into ruin," since the causes built up insidiously over time and had their origins in "luxury."[14] Child's practical answer was for the American housewife to inculcate habits of frugality in her family, but her analysis was hostile to exceptionalism.

Child's book sold thousands of copies and went through many editions, perhaps demonstrating in the process a certain sympathy for her antiexceptionalist message among women. Nevertheless, she gained only a fraction of the long-term impact that Beecher's blockbuster of a decade later did. That may have been because Child became embroiled in antislavery agitation, and, partly as a consequence, sales of her works slumped. More likely, Child's classical republican theme was too gloomy; it differed from Beecher's Christian republic, which presented a more optimistic outcome, bolstering the moral framework of society, whereas Child could only bemoan the decay of American promise. Beecher offered a future-oriented morality by blending her father's millennialist and Christian republican agenda with the political analysis of Tocqueville.

Beecher turned Tocqueville's bleak condemnation of the frontier's rough and rude society into a triumph for American women. Supposing that "American women of the East" merited applause "for their skill and success as accomplished housekeepers, still more [was] due to the heroines of the West, who, with such unyielding fortitude and cheerful endurance, attempt similar duties, amid so many disadvantages and deprivations."[15] If this was exceptionalism,

it was still a negative type in its description of women's conditions as a direct
result of social and cultural practices in the early republic. What the suffering
mother endured was not so much the natural process of childbirth but the
grueling experience of "nourishing her child" alone, "week after week" when
sick or tired.[16] It was not the innate condition of women that physically subordinated them to men but the parlous economic circumstances that left them
without help in raising infants.

How was this mismanagement of "early life" produced? Catharine depicted
a gulf between overworked American women and Europeans able to meet the
physical demands on them much better. Unlike their European counterparts,
Beecher claimed, well-educated young American women did insufficient exercise. In the "aristocratic" lands of Europe, the population split between the
pampered women of leisure in the upper class, where servants provided for
every whim, and peasants who, she asserted, were used to hard physical tasks.
But even the middle-class woman of Britain got more exercise than did young
Americans of comparable socioeconomic status. The former, she argued, was
used to horse-riding and distance walking. Such paths to physical fitness were
said to be unknown to the educated young American woman. "In consequence
of a different physical training, English women, in those circles which enjoy
competency, present an appearance which always strikes American gentle-
men as a contrast to what they see at home."[17] This contrast revealed Beecher's
middle-class sensibilities regarding social and economic "competency" as well
as her superficial grasp of the English class structure.

Beecher went further than a litany of complaints about domestic chores
and the difficulties of dealing with distressed husbands pushed by the pace of
American life. She also condemned the stresses on daughters facing a grueling program of education in "ladies'" seminaries. These stresses arose from
the very education designed to create woman citizens better able to fulfill the
aspirations of republican motherhood. An insufficiently rigorous physical and
mental preparation in the school system failed to make American women
strong enough to fill the new roles assigned to them.

To those physical, mental, and psychological aspects Beecher added the
moral question. Mere equality of legal rights promised in the Declaration of
Independence could not explain the pressures on women nor provide solutions. In the moral perspective, American women faced challenges that presented exceptional pressures but also special opportunities. Christian womanhood in a republic put extra obligations on women, she averred. "No women
on earth have a higher sense of their moral and religious responsibilities, or
better understand, not only what is demanded of them, as housekeepers, but
all the claims that rest upon them as wives, mothers, and members of a social

community." The American woman as mistress of a family felt obligations toward the care of her husband but felt "a still greater responsibility in rearing
and educating her children." Those who did possess servants also faced the
pressures that "the moral interests of her domestics have on her watchful care."
Social life offered no escape, for the American woman recognized and fulfilled the claims on her "of hospitality, and the demands of friendly visiting."[18]

Beecher's *Treatise on Domestic Economy* is best understood as an attempt
to rise to the challenge of her father's Christian republican dream, criticize its
blind spots, and improve its likely outcome. In fact, her social analysis contained a covert critique of her father's program; she did not wish to jettison
the Christian republic but to draw attention to its very debilitating effects when
translated into the work of women within families. Moral reform societies
gave scope for women's influence, but "the regular worship of the Lord's day,
and all the various religious meetings and benevolent societies" placed "so
much dependence on female influence and example" that the average mother
felt "obligated" to sustain every demanding moral activity.[19] This pressure increased the workload of women and accounted for mental stress. For this
challenge Beecher sought an American womanhood able to realize the republic's potential, thus requiring social acceptance of a more forthright type
of mother, daughter, and sister. She wished to achieve this end by rendering
American women both physically and mentally fit for such arduous and conflicting challenges as, she believed, the women of no other country faced.

Beecher presented solutions to aid women in these peculiar conditions, not
to make the same choices on women's rights as Europeans. She did not flinch
from the importance of women's education. Rather, she wished to shape that
learning by including physical education that incorporated contemporary standards of professional advice. Organized, programmatic exercise, not the personal, idiosyncratic English walk or country horse-ride, was important to her
system. The program included calisthenics. Beecher did not say precisely where
she got the idea of physical education, but she developed her own version of
the regimen. Her plans were adapted to American practice and fused the personal experience of Americans with her ideological purpose. Her system combined "singing with a great variety of amusing and graceful evolutions, designed to promote both health and easy manners." Intellectual development
would not be neglected, either, with Beecher offering "an elevated and invigo-
rating course of mental discipline."[20]

It is key that Beecher's work was underpinned by a class perspective, reflecting middle-class anxieties and aspirations. But its genius was the capacity
of her practical advice to transcend class and make gender more important in
American exceptionalism than a simple contrast between "aristocracy" and

"democracy." This transclass dimension enabled Beecher's work to contribute to the Protestant moral hegemony that supported the social order. Thereby, the social and political upheavals of Jacksonian America could be managed by women's moral reform work in the community and domestic work in the revitalization of the family. The key to unlock this approach was the place of servants in relation to housewives. Beecher did not write for an elite, but she did aim for a middle class for whom there was already a servant "problem."

At the heart of her analysis was the unequal supply of servants on one side of the Atlantic in the 1840s, which she called "the deficiency of domestic service."[21] It was assumed that most American women, particularly in the West, would have little or no access to servants and that the skills of modern home management ought to be inculcated in all American women, not outsourced. Under Beecher's plan, the "true" woman of flowery romantic literature would surrender to the organized woman intended as an efficient domestic helper as well as moral preceptor, yet would spare enough energy for her own well-being. Such advice would help democratize society and level the condition of women by eliminating the class distinctions of a servant-based family economy, thus raising the social standard as a whole and producing a more egalitarian and exceptional republican outcome.

In Beecher's assessment, democratic housewives would be different from European ones in attitudes toward work. She opposed "the aristocratic feeling, that labor is degrading." Instead she wished to make common the assumption "that it is refined and ladylike to engage in domestic pursuits." Here she drew on Jeffersonian and European Enlightenment critiques of aristocratic corruption and supported the moral woman as a female equivalent of the yeoman farmer idea. "In past ages, and in aristocratic countries, leisure and indolence and frivolous pursuits have been deemed lady-like and refined, because those classes, which were most refined, countenanced such an opinion," Beecher explained.[22] Such pampered indolence could not produce the virtuous womanhood that Christian republicanism demanded.

To this end, she stressed practical domestic change. Better-designed residences would reduce the distance from the kitchen to the dining room to save labor in serving meals. Homes should be built square and functional for easier cleaning, and they should be devoid of outbuildings difficult to reach and heat. Technology should be brought to bear on the home as much as on industry. The traditional task of carrying water from a well should give way to reticulated water. All this and more she addressed toward an audience of women, and she served to create an autonomous sphere for their operation within the republican system of liberty.[23]

Just as the evangelical ideal of the true woman contained the seeds of its own destruction, Beecher's recipe for women's practical roles within the home had implications for undermining existing social relations. Her published works conveyed, as in physical education and home management, revolutionary ideas about the organization of that home and about women's health. These ideas encouraged women to think beyond the home by questioning how it was to be organized. There was no indication that women should accept a lesser standard of material life within the home, and women were in her view entitled to manage homes themselves, whether accompanied by a male or not.

The result was to provide a bridge from republican liberty supported by Christian evangelicalism to a more secular version of woman's role as the basis of the moral order. Within that order, the utility of women's work outside the home would be put on a firmer footing. By encouraging labor-saving organization within the home, Beecher promised the ostensibly housebound woman the means of fulfilling her deeply felt "responsibility" to aid the "institutions of benevolence and religion" in the wider society. By campaigning for training woman teachers, including in the women's educational institutions that she established, and by her own example as a single woman educator, she also provided her sex with a role model for women working for wages outside the home.

This work was conceived in the late 1830s, at a time of economic distress and before the Irish famine era's deluge of Hibernian labor. When Irish servants became more available after 1845, Beecher turned her campaign in an ethnic as much as a middle-class direction by asserting the authority of the Protestant mistress over immigrant servants, whom she dismissed as inadequate. A section of her revised opus with her sister Harriet, *The American Woman's Home* (1869), dwelled on the importance of supervising, as they saw it, the problematic raw material that Irish servants constituted.[24]

The Reception of Catharine Beecher

Although the appeal of the morality behind her arguments is impossible to measure precisely, the impact of Catharine Beecher's work was roughly registered in huge sales. Her books were extraordinarily successful. First published in 1841, the *Treatise on Domestic Economy* appeared through the prominent Harper and Brothers imprint in 1842, and "was reprinted nearly every year from 1841 to 1856." With a supplementary recipe book released in 1846, along with two other volumes, *Letters to Persons Who Are Engaged in Domestic Service*

(1842), and *Letters to the People on Health and Happiness* (1855), Beecher's books fueled a juggernaut of an industry devoted to household advice and female conduct. She "became a national authority" on the domestic well-being of women.[25] Her work attempted to compete with and surpass by its more democratic pitch the English advice and cookbook literature aimed mainly at wealthier people. Beecher's efforts were to be thoroughly republican in this way. In the process, she disseminated the ideas of both her father and Tocqueville on religion, gender, and American democracy much further through the American population than otherwise possible. Though class and racial lines remained within women's work and child-rearing, Beecher's ideological objective gained considerable sway and penetrated the "respectable" working-class as well as middle-class women.[26]

Not simply through Beecher but also through the women who read her, the collective experience of (white) wives and mothers, gender identity, and national identity became linked to U.S. exceptionalism. In Beecher's approach, American women were not created different from and superior to other women because of their constitutional rights, or by a providentially imposed plan as the existing protoexceptionalisms would have it, but through personal application and practical activity. Exceptionalism became strongly welded to personal striving for excellence within the home. For large sections of middle-class womanhood, personal identity and American identity became intertwined in the phenomenon of self-help and upward social mobility. Much as the ideal of the self-made man emerged in Jacksonian America as a key tenet of what fashioned the United States as a singular nation, a self-made woman became identified with an ideal womanhood to run parallel to the masculinist version. The activity of this self-made woman was to be selfless, not individualist. Thereby, women were to provide the community infrastructure for an otherwise individualistic democracy.

Against mostly male written or endorsed literature praising true womanhood, Beecher's influence also spread a more professionalized version of domesticity and woman's moral authority. Over time, her message gained more of an expert tenor because of its ties to women's education, its practical orientation as an advice manual, and its appeal to "science" as an authority for its many recommendations. Experts on English public health, physiology, and fitness were prominently cited.[27] Nor should her work's continued invocation of the Christian home obscure its functional analysis of the domestic space as a cog in building the secular American nation. The change can be seen in the collaboration with Harriet Beecher Stowe in *The American Woman's Home*.[28] By 1869, the harder edge of Christian republicanism had mellowed into veneration of the Victorian family as a companionate institution. This book carried further the accepted dichotomy between a Europe of hierarchical institutions, with its prevalence of servants, and a more democratic American ethos. By emphasizing even more than the 1841 volume the reskilling of housewives, it aimed to put the ideal of American women's exceptional status as the moral preceptor of the home into practice—to make it work.

Granted, this approach did not win accord from the (then) minority of women led by women's rights advocates such as Elizabeth Cady Stanton and Susan B. Anthony. Feminists used the Declaration of Independence to demand full citizenship for women as independent beings. This call became enshrined in the hagiography of the women's rights movement through the Seneca Falls Convention of 1848, which asserted in the language of the Declaration that all women as well as men were created equal. Ironically, it was the 1848 revolutions in Europe highlighting demands for equality against monarchy and aristocracy that prodded American women finally to hold the long-planned conference at Seneca Falls, New York. In the pre-Civil War years, a transatlantic ferment of ideas on women's rights influenced American women. Harriet Taylor Mill's "On the Enfranchisement of Women," a British tract, became popular stateside. The prominent Quaker women's rights advocate Lucretia Mott tapped these transnational reform circuits for ideas and inspiration, and she was aware of the European revolutionary impact in enhancing demands for "a larger liberty" among the oppressed, which, in her eyes, included women.[29]

Both sides of this discussion used exceptionalist arguments. The advocates of women's influence within the home stressed the unique moral foundations of American republicanism, while advocates of women's rights drew on the revolutionary inheritance of equal rights. Yet the latter approach drew women across national boundaries together and posed problems for a simple belief in American exceptionalism as the sign of an incomparable nation, since the message was the Jeffersonian assumption of universal natural rights, its global dissemination by example, and the importation of European sources of feminist inspiration running back as far as Mary Wollstonecraft.[30]

In the equal rights tradition, American women were exceptional only insofar as they were able to assert themselves in the vanguard of this global change. This they ultimately succeeded in doing to some degree, not by their legislative and constitutional achievements but by their advocacy. In *The American Commonwealth* (1888), the influential British observer James Bryce praised American women. He noted that, in work and in education, "the eagerness to make full provision for women has been keener" in the United States than in Britain. No country owed more to its women, and in no country except perhaps Russia did women have a "greater measure of freedom."[31]

The cluster of women's suffrage organizations eventually made American feminism a model in more than a few other nations, but not until around 1900, and, even then, the achievements of American women in voting rights lagged behind the precocious Antipodean woman suffrage victories of New Zealand (1893) and Australia (1894 to 1902). As in Europe, the U.S. suffrage struggle was a protracted one; the early signs favored Beecher's more conservative approach. She accepted the language of her father's Christian republicanism and bypassed the republican tradition of equal rights by making the Christian family, not individualism, its bedrock. In the context of antebellum America, this position had greater appeal for most women, at least those able to make their opinions known to a wider public audience.[32]

Before the Civil War, the balance was very much in favor of Beecher's womanhood ideal. Reforms favoring divorce, citizenship, woman suffrage, and equal wages gained only marginal acceptance in this period, despite a succession of women's rights conventions to 1860 that demanded true equality. Tellingly, the American women's rights movement split over how far to take the principle. One of the most widely known of American woman writers in the 1850s, Amelia Bloomer, advocated women's voting rights but favored campaigning on social reforms such as alcohol prohibition to prepare the way for women's improved position in society.[33] Because of the idea that women supposedly possessed innate female qualities, the roles of women, like slaves, were still bound by society's informal and legal discriminations in 1860.

Harriet Beecher Stowe, the third daughter and sixth child of Lyman Beecher, drew on the domesticity theme that Catharine Beecher publicized. Through *Uncle Tom's Cabin*, Harriet became Lyman's most famous offspring. This book is remembered for its impact on slavery, but it did even more intellectual and cultural work than that. Its underlying themes concerned the importance of domestic tranquility to the Christian family structure, women's presumed innate difference from men, and the role of women's Christian sensibilities in moral uplift. Stowe used the idea of domesticity to generate empathy with slaves; the slave and the (white) woman are assigned in *Uncle Tom's Cabin* an emotional connection because they were both said to be full of "feeling" rather than "reason."[34] Stowe wrote that the one thing people could do to challenge slavery was this: "they can see to it that they feel right." Here Stowe relied on culture to overcome economic interests. Sympathy could work, but only by changing the culture within the family to turn men into receptacles for sympathy. Women and children could effect this change, Stowe believed.[35] Framing the issue in terms of the new evangelical Romanticism that flourished in the 1840s and 1850s, Stowe understood that families, not just women, must be emotionally converted to the antislavery cause.[36] She saw in women's

(Romantic) sensibilities the route to national regeneration by the exertion of feeling within the family and beyond the family through the influence of women in literature.

Stowe's argument for the importance of individual moral conscience, sympathy with slaves, and an emotional identification with the cause of freedom fitted well with antebellum society. Stowe's version of the American family and her attempts to show slavery's impacts on family life—through slave sales, deaths, and other family separations—could be recast as parallel with the emotional travail of the white family in midcentury America, which experienced the impact of rapid industrialization in the Northeast and westward movement of people. Women whose own extended families were so gravely disrupted by demographic change and by the medical uncertainties of childbirth and child-rearing could, under assumptions of Christian sentimentality, have greater empathy with slave women.[37] Not only was *Uncle Tom's Cabin* the best-selling fiction work of the century; Stowe had indirect influence over attitudes toward womanhood among a vast number of young people through her support for the publication and dissemination of the McGuffey readers, which, as detailed in chapter 3, became staple textbooks for the teaching of morality and patriotism in American schools.[38]

Yet it is doubtful whether Stowe was an advocate of American exceptionalism without qualification. She was acutely aware that her work spoke to wider, even global audiences. *Uncle Tom's Cabin* was a best seller across the British Empire for the rest of the century, and the mobilization of international opinion was a key to slavery's abolition. She traveled to Britain in aid of the anti-slavery cause, and she corresponded internationally with literary and political figures and used their endorsements of her position in the book. She saw human oppression as a global issue, not an American peculiarity. But within this international view, she reserved a special place for one transnational cultural group, the Anglo-Saxon peoples. In *Sunny Memories of Foreign Lands* (1854), Stowe declared the American experiment in equality and democracy to be part of a common racial enterprise: she swept American uniqueness into a larger pattern, stressing close ties to the mother country.[39] In a much-quoted piece, she enthused:

> Say what we will, an American, particularly a New Englander, can never approach the old country without a kind of thrill and pulsation of kindred. Its history for two centuries was our history. Its literature, laws, and language are our literature, laws, and language. Spenser, Shakspeare [sic], Bacon, Milton, were a glorious inheritance, which we share in common. Our very life-blood is English life-blood. It is Anglo-Saxon vigor that is spreading our country from Atlantic to Pacific, and leading on a new era in the world's development.

America is a tall, slightly young shoot, that has grown from the old royal oak
of England.[40]

Of that little offspring, she added that the "sap in it" was still "the same."[41]
Nevertheless, extending the imagery, it is significant that she wrote of the
"new, rich soil" and "genial, brilliant skies" stimulating "a new type of growth
and foliage" in the figurative oak of the New World.[42] This further imagery
was compatible with the idea that, though a British offshoot, American civilization developed as an expansionist settler society in a land especially condu-
cive to the spread of Protestant morality and the idealization of domesticity.

In this way, the concept of Anglo-Saxonism added to the heady brew of
exceptionalist sentiment. This racialist doctrine became common by the mid-
nineteenth century. It is unlikely that, if Stowe had written her remarks before
1840, she would have emphasized this heritage of race. A major change had
just begun in the language and meaning of exceptionalism, one that would
ultimately make ethnonationalist sentiment important among republicanism's
Christian devotees, and perhaps more important even than Christian republicanism itself. This Anglo-Saxonism boosted the idea of exceptionalism, yet
also rendered the notion more complex by putting the United States into a
partnership with Great Britain and, potentially, its white setter colonies emerging in Canada and Australasia. Subsuming the history of American women
within a racial phalanx did not render the sway of the Beecher clan any less,
however. They embraced the sentiment.

Race, Anglo-Saxonism, and Manifest Destiny

This chapter reveals exceptionalism's growing imbrication with race and westward expansion, a social formation that would inform later versions of American imperialism. Through its emphasis on space rather than time, the exceptionalism of the 1840s amplified the inherited sense of material abundance, making American exceptionalism less obviously religious and shifting chosenness to spatial realization. Material power and abundance were always latent in American exceptionalism, but the connection received a boost in the 1840s. Two circumstances underpinned the change: a new intellectual explanation of the nation's singular importance from the rise of Anglo-Saxonism as an ideology; and the emergence of Manifest Destiny as a program for future American greatness, based on the right, duty, and God-ordained process of continental expansion. While Manifest Destiny rose to be a key subsidiary myth of exceptionalism, neither it nor Anglo-Saxonism lacked ambiguity. Neither sprang forth fully made in the American DNA. Neither washed over American history explaining all within it. Each faced opposition, and both ideas were shaped and limited by their time.[1]

The crystalizing event was the Mexican War of 1846–48. Despite dissension within the United States over the justice, morality, and possible political consequences of the war, success enhanced the conditions for exceptionalism. Military victory over Mexico was itself cathartic, but much more came from the huge accretion of territory that followed in the Treaty of Guadalupe Hidalgo (1848). Comprising over half a million square miles, this "Mexican Cession" bequeathed to the nation two world-class harbors and, with the quick discovery of gold that started the California boom times, delivered de facto continental hegemony. In turn, the material fruits of victory further stimulated ideas that the nation's path must have been providential. Manifest

Destiny constituted a new and self-confident phase of exceptionalism, thoroughly based on material prospects for future greatness, while a belief in the cultural and economic superiority of the Anglo-Saxon race arose almost simultaneously. Anglo-Saxonism was not causal in the geographic expansion, but acceptance of the idea became a consequence of demographic and economic success. That confidence stemmed from the very act of peopling the American continent, through high birth rates thought to be remarkable in world history and the fact that many of the immigrants entering from the 1820s to 1840s came from the British Isles.

Nevertheless, Anglo-Saxonism had a problematic relationship with exceptionalism. Prior to the Mexican War, the term *Anglo-Saxon* was rarely used and little known. Its specifically racial content was far from clear, and *Anglo-American* was the more prevalent epithet. Protestant churches saw the United States as part of a global partnership to bring about the Christianizing of the world in preparation for the Second Coming of Christ. Even as Anglo-Saxonism began to give racial content to this preexisting idea of an Anglo-American sharing of cultural power, it did not mean the United States had cut loose from European constraints. Anglo-Saxonism still operated within assumptions of an Anglo-American comity in the spread of cultural values and economic progress. Christian republicans were prominent in shaping these ideas, tempering the racial and exceptionalist implications of Anglo-Saxonism in this context.

Foreshadowed in the 1830s, Anglo-Saxonist justifications for exceptionalism and U.S. "expansion" surged abruptly in American publications of the 1840s.[2] One stimulus was the lobbying for such expansion in regard to the annexation of Texas, while another was a rising concern about race, as Enlightenment ideas on the unity of humankind faded. Not yet the era of Darwinian theory, the mid-nineteenth-century period was foundational to new racialized stereotypes layered over the older categories of "barbaric" and "savage" peoples—using physical characteristics as a central organizing principle of a systematic racism.[3] These were transnational ideas that took deep root in the United States.

Yet race understood as biology did not uniformly dominate the 1840s version of Anglo-Saxonist exceptionalism. It was more a "cultural" discourse (of "civilization" against "barbarism") that characterized representations at that time among Christian republicans in the Benevolent Empire reform organizations. Anglo-Saxonism was commonly associated with the party that took the Whig name in the 1830s and 1840s and battled against Andrew Jackson's Democrats, but the latter also adopted the term. Protestant Americans associated with New School Calvinism tended to align with the Whigs.[4] Their

version was set out in American Home Missionary Society publications such
as *Our Country: Its Capabilities, Its Perils, and Its Hope* (1842). This manifesto
for missions to the American West and South stressed economic progress, the
English language, and a mutual heritage of self-government and legal institutions. The American people shared a tongue that contained "so much of the
science and literature of the world" and had used these cultural resources to
develop economically. But "Anglo-Saxon" was not employed. Rather, it was
"Anglo-American" commerce that "spreads her sail on every sea, and drops
her anchor on every strand," the Home Missionary Society argued.[5] Immense
resources and growing demographic strength were also pertinent, when combined with British naval power and a common language. Thereby, Anglo-
Americans would achieve leadership of the world, the manifesto proclaimed.
This was almost sixty years before the formal empire of the United States
abroad made its major surge (1898), and forty-three before the Reverend Josiah Strong wrote a more famous discourse that simply updated with the aid
of a racialized social Darwinism the thesis of Congregationalists and Baptists
of the 1840s under the same name—"Our Country."[6]

Not merely an assertion of superior culture or political institutions, a religious influence was vital in this Anglo-Saxon mix. Christian republicans
held that the nation's economic infrastructure built by people of Anglo-Saxon
heritage both facilitated and reflected Christianity's geographic and demographic expansion. More important, they saw the English language as the chief
instrument for spreading God's word globally, in effect arguing that an Anglo-
Saxon heritage lay behind the success of Protestantism. These ideas thrived
well beyond the New School Calvinist ambit. Granted, Home Missionary Society clergy despised, for example, the Restorationist theology of Alexander
Campbell as vulgar and opportunistic. That was said to be a form of salvation
by nothing more than dunking a person in water.[7] Yet, just as many Presbyterians, Methodists, and Congregationalists did, Campbellites argued that "the
destiny of the Anglo-Saxon tongue," as a regnant cultural force in the world,
was derived from "the Anglo-Saxon missionary spirit." Campbell himself put
it this way in 1849.[8]

American Christianity was, the Home Missionary Society declared, blessed
because it was "comparatively fresh from the [biblical] fountain." "Unmixed"
with and "unfettered" by the "traditions" of Europe, Anglo-American Protestantism was considered more likely to yield conversions than Roman Catholicism could, given the deadweight of Catholicism's European monarchical, aristocratic, and corrupt institutions as a burden. Protestant exceptionalism gained
a confidence boost from the florescence of Anglo-Saxonism as a culturally
powerful force. With Americans having an Anglo-Saxon type of Christianity

in their instincts and heritage, "such a people" would be "responsible for a large share of the instrumentality of converting the world," the society predicted.[9]

At the same time, the new cultural comity meant acknowledging that the United States and Great Britain retained complementary and cooperative roles in God's providential purpose because both were Protestant dominated and influenced by Anglo-Saxonism. A purely *American* exceptionalism was thereby qualified at the same time that it was emboldened. Because of this Anglo-American connection, the United States could still not be treated as a true singularity. American leadership had not been obtained in all fields, supporters of Anglo-Saxonism conceded.[10] At a time when Britain loomed large in the trade and investment of the United States and influenced antebellum culture, this was not an unreasonable or fringe position, despite much posturing of anti-British, antimonarchical sentiments from the ranks of Jacksonian Democrats. This is why John L. O'Sullivan, who coined the term *Manifest Destiny*, issued yet another call for a cultural declaration of independence. It came in his article of 1839 on "The Great Nation of Futurity" in the *United States Magazine and Democratic Review*.[11] By 1845, O'Sullivan concurred that the United States was the prime site of the further development of Anglo-Saxonism in a new country, untrammeled by "old" Europe. This synergy was opening up geographic opportunities to fulfill the generic Anglo-Saxon promise as a spatially oriented ideology.

The embrace of Anglo-Saxonism reinforced a progressive interpretation of the United States and its role in world history. By 1850, this inheritance was commonly thought to account for the dynamic quality of American life as westward expansion occurred. Migration west would bring the cultural accoutrements of Anglo-Saxonism, as O'Sullivan put it in 1845, through settlers "armed with the plough and the rifle, and marking its trail with schools and colleges, courts and representative halls, mills and meeting-houses."[12] The elements of Anglo-Saxonism as a source of liberty, the rule of law, and freedom of thought that would lead to innovation meant the idea could serve as both a justification for territorial expansion and an explanation of it.

American interest in Anglo-Saxonism was not a spontaneous or endemic creation. Advances in scholarship in Europe brought, from the disciplines of philology and history, greater knowledge of Anglo-Saxon language and institutions.[13] American editions of British works on Anglo-Saxon culture, language, and literature appeared in the 1830s and 1840s, and Christian publications were at the forefront in spreading publicity for these works by reviewing them and recycling their ideas. Important was the contribution of the British conservative writer Sir Archibald Alison. An heir of the Scottish Enlightenment, he sold one hundred thousand copies of his histories in cheap U.S. editions in the early 1840s.[14] Alison's *History of Europe* mainly told the tales of battles and revolutions across the Atlantic, but its moral content and its subscription to the providential role of the Anglo-Saxon peoples appealed to educated Protestant audiences in the United States, especially when Alison turned his attention to the British Empire's colonists in North America. Therein, Alison explored the future course of settlement and the capacity of the new American nation to build on British achievements and densely populate the Mississippi Valley. His study treated the United States as the beneficiary of the nation's God-endowed material abundance and transmitted this idea along with the substance of Manifest Destiny, though without the term. The Home Missionary Society saw this new western territory as a geopolitical opportunity, and it found Alison's ruminations a stimulus to embrace the United States as the launching pad for the worldwide enterprise of civilization.[15]

The Anglo-Saxon idea crossed sectarian as well as political boundaries. The Baptist editor of *Christian Review*, Samuel F. Smith is better known as the author of the song "America" ("My Country 'Tis of Thee"), the nation's early (unofficial) national anthem. But, waxing lyrical on the works of Alison, Smith co-opted the idea of a providential Anglo-Saxonism. For Smith, Anglo-Saxon language, history, and traditions supplied "the connecting link" from "barbarism" to "the highest civilization." As "the parent-stock" of the Anglo-Saxon heritage, Smith announced in 1843, the British peoples must be acknowledged "as our fathers. They are neither strangers nor enemies, but they belong to ourselves."[16] This was roughly the stance taken by the Restorationist preacher Alexander Campbell: "the Anglo-Saxon race, language, politics and religion" provided "the key to human progress."[17] Even naval strategy and commercial technology favored the Anglo-Saxons, Campbell believed, with Britain and the United States seeming more and more united in a de facto global partnership. "No event in the future, next to the anticipated millennial triumph, appears more natural, more probable, more practicable or more morally certain and desirable, than this Anglo-Saxon triumph in the great work of human civilization and redemption," Campbell wrote.[18]

Even a famous African American advocate for equal rights in the 1850s was touched by the Anglo-Saxon idea. Frederick Douglass, who escaped from enslavement and became an eloquent orator and abolitionist, acknowledged the economic, literary, and cultural progress of Anglo-Saxon countries as a shared legacy for all Americans. But Douglass insisted that Anglo-Saxonism should not be considered evidence of racial superiority or an excuse for racial exclusion from the polity. The Anglo-Saxon ascent to civilization was said to be quite recent in terms of humanity's history and actually the product of racial intermixture, not separation of races.[19] That he felt compelled to argue the antislavery case this way testified to the hegemonic, albeit contestable, status that the notion of Anglo-Saxonism had achieved by the 1850s. Douglass wanted inclusion in the linear and exceptionalist progress of the United States that had reputedly been achieved under Anglo-Saxon leadership. In this respect, he differed from those African Americans who would renounce the American promise. Among the latter, some even sought a new promised land in Africa, as abolitionists Robert Campbell and Martin Delany did in the 1850s.[20]

Anglo-Saxonism and the Coming of Manifest Destiny

This cross-denominational Anglo-Saxonism stressed cultural superiority and resourcefulness stemming from a Protestant inheritance of individual initiative. When linked to Christian republicanism, Anglo-Saxonism supplied the intellectual materials for a theory of American geographic expansion as an attribute of exceptionalism. Anglo-Saxon Protestantism now preached the inevitability of Americans filling up not just the Mississippi Valley but the entire North American continent because they were such a culturally vigorous and demographically fertile people, yet still in partnership with Britain. In Manifest Destiny, Protestantism and Anglo-Saxonism hypercharged exceptionalism. First articulated in that specific form in 1845 at the time of the annexation of Texas and the moves toward war with Mexico, Manifest Destiny opened the possibility of reconciling, through spatial expansion, the evangelical religious outreach of the Benevolent Empire with the Jacksonian resistance to its religious and cultural leadership.[21]

This synthesis was possible because of the evangelicals' groundwork in the 1830s to "civilize" the American frontier and publicize the achievement as Christian and republican. Fearful of the fact that American settlement west into Ohio, Illinois, Indiana, Tennessee, and Kentucky after the War of 1812 had outstripped the provision of churches, Protestant evangelicals organized to fill the gap. When Lyman Beecher went to Cincinnati to head the Lane Theological Seminary, to train teachers and missionaries in the theology and morals of Christian republicanism, in support of his mission he published *A Plea for the West* (1835). Therein he called on easterners to send money and ministers to save the region from irreligion and Catholicism.[22]

Though northern evangelicals accepted the westward march of civilization, they did so with qualms. They tended to oppose removal of the Cherokee and other "civilized tribes," as did Edward Everett and Catharine Beecher. Jeremiah Evarts, the lawyer and official of the American Board of Commissioners for Foreign Missions was a key Christian republican and ally of Lyman Beecher. Urging opposition to Cherokee removal, Evarts wrote, "The character of our government, and of our country, may be deeply involved. Most certainly an indelible stigma will be fixed upon us, if, in the plenitude of our power, and in the pride of our superiority, we shall be guilty of manifest injustice to our weak and defenceless neighbours."[23] This was not a demonstration of American exceptionalism but a jeremiad urging the nation to abandon its vanity and pride. Otherwise, it would face mockery among the Christian nations of the world. The "character which a nation sustains, in its intercourse with the great community of nations," was, Evarts stated, "of more value than any other of its public possessions."[24] Petitioners to Congress chimed in with support. Developing antiexceptionalist arguments, they deplored removal of the southern tribes as actions hostile to democratic and republican rights.[25]

Neither Evarts's eloquence nor grassroots petitions in the North overcame the splenetic will of President Andrew Jackson (1829–37). After Evarts's untimely death in 1831, the premier missionary institutions of the Benevolent Empire caved in to government pressure, much to the discomfort of some white missionaries on the ground in Cherokee country. Also contributing to the abandonment of a strong moral position on Indian rights was the growing racialist "conviction that the United States was indeed a 'White Man's country.'"[26] Nascent Anglo-Saxonism supplied the intellectual rationale for the argument that Indian tribes were weak and unworthy of continued occupation of the land. Their removal was now regarded as an inevitable consequence of white settlers' racial strength. Visceral prejudice assisted the argument. The 1825–26 dispute over intermarriage of white women to Cherokee students in the Foreign (Missionary) School at Cornwall, Connecticut, had already foreshadowed racial and sexual rather than humanitarian concerns among the rank and file in the evangelical congregations of the eastern states ostensibly backing the Indian missions. Support for equal rights and the Enlightenment promise of Indian assimilation into American society was fading at the very time that Christian republican agitation became most vocal.[27]

Awkward choices had to be made by Christian republicans in decisions affecting indigenous dispossession, but the imperatives of westward movement prevailed. While Beecher was one of many evangelicals who believed frontier expansion had been too rapid, he worried equally that social stability would inevitably unravel without Christian republicans coming to the rescue. Christian republicans had to transform the spatial expansion of the republic into a Protestant enterprise rather than simply oppose it on the grounds that it might adversely affect missionary work among Native Americans. The controversial Congregationalist clergyman Horace Bushnell of Connecticut

agreed. Though sometimes regarded as "the father of American religious liberalism" for his protomodernist inclinations, in 1847 Bushnell as much as
Beecher feared intellectual and social decay in western states as European
and eastern American immigrants poured in, but Bushnell believed that a
Protestant-dominated westward expansion would be a positive force for Christianity.[28] Despite other disagreements over theology, Beecher and Bushnell
concurred that the West would be the crucible of change. Here was to be the
defining struggle for the soul of America, because the Mississippi Valley had
such resources that these alone would provide a Christian nation with the
power to project across the entire globe and take Christianity to its farthest
corners. As Beecher put it, the "West is destined to be the great central power
of the nation, and under heaven, must affect powerfully the cause of free institutions and the liberty of the world."[29]

Apart from these global and millennialist ambitions, the most notable feature of *A Plea for the West* was its focus on a perceived Catholic menace, not
Indian removal. With immigration from Ireland on the rise, Beecher and his
allies feared Irish Catholics would swarm across the frontier states and territories as a "terrific inundation."[30] For him, the immigrant problem was not
ethnicity. Rather, the aversion was political, and it concerned the centraliza-
tion of church political power that, evangelicals reasoned, had arisen so often
in Europe's history to subvert liberal freedoms. It was the "union of church
and state" in Europe that Beecher feared as a feudal vestige incompatible with
his American exceptionalism.[31] Compared with this politically based anti-
Catholicism, the absence of references to Indian removal or the problem of
slavery as it affected the peopling and geopolitics of westward expansion is
palpable in *A Plea for the West*. Beecher's implicit endorsement of settler colonial expansionism was a given, and his attempt to identify westward motion
with Christian republicanism laid the basis for mainstream Protestantism's
intellectual and political acquiescence in Manifest Destiny as a God-ordained
process.[32]

Notwithstanding this de facto endorsement of Manifest Destiny in 1835, a
decade before the term was used, the Mexican War failed to win the enthusiastic approval of Christian republicans. Many Protestant northerners were either lukewarm toward the war or opposed to it. Neither did President James K.
Polk's policy impress antislavery and Whig politicians as far afield as Abraham Lincoln in Illinois. The war actually rekindled sectional conflict over
slavery, provoking radical abolitionism to partisan political action. Opposing
the Mexican War did not mean Christian republicans dropped the idea of
geographic expansion connected to a providential destiny; rather, they simultaneously criticized the war for enforcing republicanism by bayonet and

praised the U.S. push to the Pacific. They even took the quixotic opportunity presented by the American invasion of Mexico to introduce Christian missions there, in order to turn Catholics into evangelicals.[33] The conquest of northern Mexico heightened the Christian republicans' sense of power and opportunity to become not only a national missionary force but also a global one backed by the material resources of the enlarged West. They trusted that American settlers in the Pacific Northwest would outcompete and outreproduce the southerners who might pour into the Southwest with their slaves. The acquisition of a potentially Protestant-dominated and abolitionist Oregon Territory in 1846 served in part to mollify northern opinion over slavery's expansion. It demonstrated that, for all their hand-wringing over the removal of the Cherokee, Benevolent Empire reformers stood for the manifest nature of Manifest Destiny and supported the American settlers' dominion of the continent over indigenous people.[34]

Christian republicans not only rejoiced in what they saw as the spiritual spread of Anglo-Saxon Protestantism. They also lent legitimacy to the economic progress that resulted. They argued that material infrastructure together with Christian education would civilize the American West. "The sooner we have railroads and telegraphs spinning into the wilderness, and setting the remotest hamlets in connexion and close proximity with the east, the more certain it is that light, good manners and Christian refinement, will become universally diffused," Bushnell asserted.[35] This argument in *Barbarism the First Danger* (1847) anticipated by twenty-five years the widely disseminated *American Progress* lithograph of 1872 by John Gast, in which liberty and technological growth were displayed mutually sustaining the coming national greatness.[36] Bushnell's sermon was one that prepared the groundwork for that stunning and representative image of American exceptionalism and Manifest Destiny. Bushnell not only acquiesced in westward movement; he also justified it and shifted the balance of evangelical concern from the politicoreligious sphere under Beecher to material advances in capitalism. This maneuver helped normalize Christian republican exceptionalism as an expression of an ostensibly secular nation. The idea of the United States having a special role in human history could thereby gain support from both the northeastern Protestant Whig Party sympathizers like Bushnell and more secular protagonists of expansion among the Jacksonian Democrats.

The accommodation between Christian republicanism and Manifest Destiny could not be imposed by a few church leaders, to be sure. The idea of an expansive Christian republic was grounded in individual experience as white settlers and their clergy moved west. One of Beecher's students illustrates the melding process. The Reverend John J. Miter of Milwaukee, Wisconsin, was born in Lansingburgh, New York, in 1809; underwent a conversion experience in the upstate New York revivals of 1827; and attended Lane Theological Seminary in 1833–34. He took part in the split of 1834 within the seminary over the slavery question, against Beecher's tepid support on that issue, and embraced the abolitionist cause.[37] He then studied at what became Union Theological Seminary as a protégé of the prominent temperance reformer, educator, and Congregational minister Nathan Beman. An agent of the American Home Missionary Society, Miter served in Illinois and then Wisconsin from 1837 to 1856. As a pioneer in Milwaukee and later in Dodge County, eighty miles to the west, he "speedily and heartily identified himself, not only with the spiritual, but with the material development and growth of the city and country."[38] His congregation boomed in numbers in the 1840s, allowing him to depict the pioneering experience of Christian revivals as a part of peopling and civilizing the West.

The result was a personal identification between moral cause and physical space. "With the West I have united my destiny," he wrote in 1846. "From love to Christ, I trust, and the institutions of my country, hallowed by ten thousand sacred associations, I have consecrated myself to the moral cultivation of that natural Eden." This work of possessing the land (and dispossessing indigenous people) would go all the way to Oregon, as the proponents of Manifest Destiny proclaimed. He told colleagues:

> In consequence of the wise, liberal and highly successful efforts . . . to take *possession* of Wisconsin in its infancy, I expect to see that rich territory become the New England of the West. And with the same prompt and judicious outlay upon the opening field west of us, we may see a continuation of the magnificent, *moral scenery* of New England, extending from the Penobscot to the Columbia River. To accomplish a work of such imperishable grandeur, constitutes the God-like aim of the American Home Missionary Society. For this I love it.[39]

The consecrated seizure of a continental domain characterized by "moral scenery" embodied providence in human action, imposed on wild nature and "savages" in the aid of white American settlers. Christian republicanism became incarnate in this cultural landscape and achieved a personal identification with it as an expression of Manifest Destiny.

Just as Frederick Jackson Turner concluded decades later, Christian republicans understood that the West was a space for turning the mélange of frontier cultures into a national culture. This was an argument Bushnell made in 1847. He emphasized that this mixture would be a cooperative venture, a growing collaboration of Protestant sects, and he urged close liaison with

Methodist preachers who, he believed, had obtained more success than his own Congregationalists on the frontier. But there were limits to this proto-melting pot. Bushnell was not sanctioning ethnocultural intermixture when discussing westward movement. "Romanism" was definitely not part of this synthesis, and Bushnell feared that without provision of adequate education through Protestant churches, colleges, Sunday schools, and missions, the region would, in its "ignorance," be susceptible to Catholic encroachment. One could posit the United States, if it were truly to become a Protestant nation, as destined to possess and transform the West into the core of a distinctively American "civilization."[40]

The Christian republicans' version of a destiny made manifest in the United States entailed, therefore, anti-Catholicism. This stance paralleled the way that the larger political and military struggle against Mexico raised shades of a religious war against Rome's imagined influence in the Western Hemisphere, but religion should not be abstracted from the wider geopolitical frame. American evangelicals depicted Romanism as anti-individualist; in contrast, Anglo-Saxon Protestantism favored individualism, democracy, and economic development. The American fear of Catholicism in Mexico's north was closely tied to concerns about Rome's likely effects on liberal freedoms, ideas that reflected exceptionalist anxieties over the absence of church-state separation in Europe. In short, anti-Catholicism did not stand on its own. Rather, it became a touchstone for interpreting westward expansion and for defending the Christian republican version of American exceptionalism.[41] Anti-Catholicism was neither the beginning nor the end of Manifest Destiny, as the career of the man who popularized the latter term indicated.

Manifest Destiny and American Exceptionalism

It might seem ironic that the explicit Manifest Destiny ideology of 1845 was named by a man with a Catholic heritage from his wayward and adventuresome father. But journalist and editor John L. O'Sullivan was not a practicing Catholic until years later and had been raised as an Episcopalian by his widowed mother. Rather than a reconciliation directly of Catholic and Protestant views, Manifest Destiny ideology secularized the Christian republican outlook on expansion in a way that made it more acceptable to Democrats and Catholics.[42]

Considered geopolitically, O'Sullivan's was not simply a boundless view of exceptionalism. He recognized historical contingency while paradoxically preaching inevitable agency under providential authority. The context that he identified viewed exceptionalism marked off against the machinations of

European powers that could still control American aspirations. The future remained uncertain unless destiny was acted out by citizens who seized the providential offer. O'Sullivan condemned the subordination of American economics and culture to Britain, just as cultural nationalists had. Not yet exceptional, the United States continued to be seen as a quasi colony of the British Empire twenty years after the emergence of cultural nationalism. For O'Sullivan, the key to the colonial status lay not in the material world but in the mind and spirit of the people, who too easily gravitated toward British fashions. Westward expansion was a way to declare cultural independence in practice, to make the nation exceptional through collective human action.[43]

As a secular concept in the hands of an autonomous nation, Manifest Destiny was foreshadowed in O'Sullivan's astounding essay on space and time, "The Great Nation of Futurity," though O'Sullivan did not mention "Anglo-Saxonism" there. Instead, O'Sullivan drew on a wellspring of secular republican notions more than Protestant ones. He gave no recognition of a religious inheritance: "Our national birth was the beginning of a new history, the formation and progress of an untried political system, which separates us from the past and connects us with the future only." It was in *natural rights* that the United States was destined to be superior, not through a Calvinist or any other Christian heritage: "So far as regards the entire development of the natural rights of man, in moral, political, and national life, we may confidently assume that our country is destined to be the great nation of futurity." Here providence remained an abstract idea, as it was for the Founding Fathers in the era of the American Revolution. To be sure, O'Sullivan argued that "Providence is with us," and "no earthly power" could limit the republic.[44] However, the hand of God did not involve an intimate exchange with the deity, a covenant, or a conversion experience. Unlike Beecher's ideas, past traditions of the Pilgrims and Puritans played no part in this thesis. The future was all that counted.

O'Sullivan's words are reminiscent of religious language drawn from Christian revivalism—but in a completely secular application concerning the spread of democracy. "For this *blessed mission* to the nations of the world, which are shut out from the life-giving light of truth, has America been *chosen*; and her high example shall *smite* unto death the tyranny of kings, hierarchs, and oligarchs, and carry the *glad tidings* of peace and good will where myriads now endure an existence scarcely more enviable than that of beasts of the field," O'Sullivan declared.[45] This millenarian statement tracked the rhetoric and morality of the Bible's Hebraic symbols and metaphors—and their influence in antebellum political culture. Manifest Destiny's "mission" was not to convert souls or create a Christian state. Rather, the task was to spread democratic institutions and the power and prosperity of white Americans. In O'Sullivan's work, providence is presented in a quasi-Hegelian sense of immanence—as "spirit," akin to the Democratic Party ideology popularized by Bancroft a decade earlier.[46] With Manifest Destiny, Americans were depicted as working their sacred principles out through demographic and economic advance, which O'Sullivan asserted was irresistible. The American people did not need to convert to or express a Christian faith. They simply had to carry on their daily lives as restless expansionists, thereby realizing in material form the immanent presence of God's purpose.

It is likely O'Sullivan took his complicated mix of contingency and immanent force from family experience and personal mobility. It came through the career of his father, John Thomas O'Sullivan, a knockabout Anglo-Irish ship captain and sometime U.S. consul to the Barbary Coast, whose life illustrated the vicissitudes of young men making their way in the new and insecure republic within the Atlantic world. The family faced financial ruin after the U.S. government seized the father's vessel in 1823 for alleged "piracy." To make matters worse, the elder O'Sullivan died at sea on a mission to recover the ship's cargo and reclaim his fortune. The family experience of the American republic as a site of dangerous and speculative quests for survival and social mobility was not uncommon.[47] Capitalism's market forces and the political turbulence of the transatlantic republican revolutions of the late eighteenth and early nineteenth centuries underpinned a sense of personal deracination, movement, and travail as central to securing the future of individuals and republican institutions.

The son inherited the father's derring-do but, as a landlubber, applied this quality to intellectual and political pursuits in aid of westward annexations. Filibusters and westward-bound farmers as much as maritime adventurers embodied a personal destiny woven together with American destiny through attempted territorial expansion in the Caribbean and the western United States. For O'Sullivan, years of battling for compensation ended in 1836 when his mother secured a federal payout for the wrongful government expropriation of her husband's ship and cargo.[48] This recompense probably convinced the family that an attachment to flag and nation was worthwhile after all. More certainly, it gave the younger O'Sullivan the wherewithal to enter his journalistic career as editor and proprietor of the *United States Democratic Review*, where his seminal writings appeared.

The most impressive feature of O'Sullivan's literary and political career was not actually the Manifest Destiny slogan, which synthesized the thinking of Democrats and Whigs alike, but its spatial assertions of an ahistorical entity, the United States, outside of history and its "laws." The "Great Nation of Futurity" collapsed time into space. No other nation could be conceived in such a purely spatial and ahistorical way, O'Sullivan believed. This was not an evangelical influence. Spatial expansion, not a religious teleology, character-ized his thinking. Nor did it seem compatible with the Whig Party emphasis on the consolidation of historical institutions and revolutionary traditions. It was, however, congenial to Beecher's plans, which saw the American West as the space on which to inscribe the moral geography of a Christian republic.[49] The realization of Manifest Destiny in a continental dimension would signal a secular and spatial version of millennialism's impending triumph.

That O'Sullivan shared with Christian republicanism a moral sense of space is clear. He preferred westward migration to be peaceful, just as Protes-tant Whigs and reformers did. War was not needed in 1845–46, since Ameri-can success he considered inevitable. Besides, war's spiteful consequences could sour the spread of American notions of liberty to Latin America. It is significant that in his "Annexation" essay on Texas in 1845, which revealed Manifest Destiny unadorned by circumlocution, O'Sullivan introduced the terminology of an "irresistible army of *Anglo-Saxon* emigration" bound to conquer the continent through demographical change.[50] He echoed the Prot-estant speculation about a global takeover on the platform of a numerically ascendant American nation of continental dimensions.[51] Christian republi-cans had made such concepts familiar ground for expansionism's justifica-tion. By framing the question in this way, O'Sullivan reached out to proclaim Manifest Destiny a broader creed for the nation as a whole—Catholic, Prot-estant, and secularist.

In reality, a shared commitment to such a creed proved tenuous because of Manifest Destiny's fractious impact on political stability.[52] In a torturous commentary on the Texas annexation, O'Sullivan had suggested that acquir-ing Texas would help drain the African American slave population toward the Southwest and into Mexico. Leaving aside the sophistry of this demographic argument and its metaphor of drainage, O'Sullivan opened Manifest Destiny to charges of partisanship since it justified Democratic obfuscation on the slavery question. Still fueled by a subterranean Anglophobia and desirous of liberating the American people from British industrial and trade domination, O'Sullivan became an apologist for further territorial aggrandizement. Com-pared with the Christian republicans, he spoke in more starkly racist terms of Mexicans, with their "mixed and confused blood" considered inherently in-ferior, and depicted Central America as a site for miscegenation with African American slaves, as if it were a racial sewer.[53] Such overtly racist sentiments were common among Democrats but more controversial among northern evangelicals, who tended to see "the radical inferiority of the [African American] race" as a product of subordination under slavery.[54] After the Mexican War, O'Sullivan contemplated the possible purchase of Cuba under the Manifest Destiny slogan to aid the racial drainage. By such action, the Democrats would prove themselves "the true American party, the party entrusted by God & Nature with the mission of the American policy and destiny."[55] Here American exceptionalism became explicitly tied to the Democrats.

Previously muted within the Home Missionary Society, Christian republican tension over southern expansionism and hostility to slavery grew in the early 1850s. The more radical among the evangelical reformers, including the *New England Freewill Baptist Quarterly's* editors and contributors, condemned slavery as inconsistent with Christianity and liberty.[56] The Home Missionary Society saw the assimilation of new Catholic citizens in the southwestern territory gained in 1848 as a fearful challenge, but one that might be met with intensified educational campaigns and missions to convert Catholics. In contrast, slavery was, by definition, law, and practice, a coercive force that blocked individual autonomy to accept the evangelical message. Moreover, slavery undermined the nation's reputation as a liberal democratic exemplar abroad. The continued agitation of southerners and their northern Democratic Party allies to extend slavery made it clear that the problem of slavery would not go away on its own.[57] That is what made abolitionism and the idea of a "Slave Power" conspiring to control national politics through the Democratic Party a potent catchcry in the 1850s.

In national politics, ethnic and religious conflict fueled these sectional strains between North and South. The early 1850s witnessed the political apotheosis of antebellum anxieties over Catholicism with the emergence of the Know-Nothings. Officially the American Party, this political movement favored restricting immigration and ending easy naturalization of foreign arrivals, principally Catholics. Peaking in 1854, Irish immigration agitated Protestant clergy, who saw the newcomers as a foreign and papist threat outweighing the opportunities that the Mexican Cession provided for Protestant domination of the North American continent. Moreover, (mostly Protestant) advocates of alcohol prohibition believed the achievement of a sober nation through liquor reform would be undermined by Irish and German Catholic drinking cultures. Duplication throughout the North of the Maine Law (1851) for statewide alcohol prohibition might fail because of the immigrant challenge.[58]

The fracturing of the political culture demonstrated in anti-Catholic and prohibitionist agitation prompted a self-conscious question: how could Americans find, or agree on, a slogan to repair the damage and identify the coherence of national values? Under the banner of the "American Idea," the Universalist preacher Edwin H. Chapin of New York's Church of the Divine

Paternity gave a Fourth of July address in 1854. Ever eloquent, Chapin spoke of citizenship, democracy, unity, acceptance of immigration, and global mission.[59] His American Idea expressed shared beliefs that approximated those of the modern American Creed.[60] Yet Chapin's work was reprinted in an anti-immigration collection edited by William Ryder and dedicated to "Our Country First." Chapin's gesture of tolerance was intended by the editor to show the reader that the charges of bigotry leveled at the "American Movement" were unfair, but it was swamped in the collection by those opposed to foreign and especially Catholic influences deviating from the American Idea.[61] One contributor, A. D. Challoner, articulated the common refrain of nativists that "we are engaged in rallying to the defence of the rights of American born."[62] In its interpretation, the American Idea proved to be an empty vessel. It was capable of being filled with many different ideas that could be either inclusive or exclusive regarding groups with different ethnic, religious or cultural traditions.

The practical and ethical challenge over slavery's extension that resurfaced in the same year of 1854 through the Kansas-Nebraska Act overrode the generalities of the American Idea until after the Civil War. The nativist Know-Nothings were politically disruptive and destroyed the Whigs as a national force but failed to supplant it as an established party. Instead, the Republican Party emerged from the ashes of the highly competitive Second Party System to defend American freedom defined as free labor, free soil, and free men, rather than racial equality. Indeed, the Republican Party incorporated elements of ethnoexceptionalism by offering a vision of the West as a space preserved for white settlers.[63] By 1856 it was clear that, although anti-Catholicism had damaged the Christian republican crusade for a new moral order, slavery threatened the nation's exceptionalism more. With the fear of further settler-based spreading of slavery using the rhetoric of Manifest Destiny on the rise, the intellectual synthesis of Christian republicanism unraveled.

In the Hands of an Angry God:
The Antislavery Jeremiad and the Origins
of the Christian Nation

For northern evangelicals, the sectional conflict of the 1850s increasingly focused on defending the republic against slavery's extension in the West. But this conflict and the war that followed also introduced the issue of the Christian nation, as antislavery activists pressed home the idea of the judgment of God against an entire nation for its shortcomings. Exceptionalism came under attack, even as the actual term was still almost unknown. Because the contest became by 1863 a matter of either slavery or freedom, Americans were fighting over the kind of republic the United States should be. In this sense, the Civil War was a moral conflict grounded in a dispute over the nature of American exceptionalism. While the outcome was a victory for a particular Northern vision of exceptionalism, the alternative, Southern exceptionalism, was not defeated. The South solidified around race and a regionally shared history rather than join in conferring equal rights and citizenship of African American people, as radical Reconstruction in the North proposed to do. By the end of Reconstruction in 1877, the rest of the country had acquiesced in this outcome.[1]

It was in the Civil War that "exceptionalism" was first named, albeit fleetingly. In 1861, the *Times* of London correspondent William Howard Russell noted how Americans thought themselves exceptional, and he implicitly apologized for using the "ism" as if he were coining the term. The awkward word would not easily roll off anyone's lips, and Russell did not start a trend. Still, his usage was apt. Observing the chaos of the First Battle of Bull Run (July 21, 1861), he concluded that the United States was exceptional in the second-rate character of its military preparation and the ill discipline of its troops, such that neither side could easily win. The nation would have to adapt to modern ways of thinking about political and military authority if a long, drawn-out war were to be averted. In fact, Russell was implying that a civil war would bring an end to American exceptionalism, or what others saw as the "American experiment." A state apparatus of size and substance must develop, Russell inferred, and a culture to counter fractious democratic tendencies. The United States must modernize its thinking and its action, and pull together. This did not happen easily. Russell was right that many Americans thought themselves exceptional but wrong that exceptionalism would end. This was not to be the last time in which a pundit erred in so predicting.[2]

As Russell intimated, the Civil War expressed the contested trajectory of American exceptionalism. Through the energy and advocacy of its supporters, exceptionalism was widely embedded in the consciousness of Americans, but the idea's substance was the source of ever-greater contention. Exceptionalism was both enhanced and compromised by the cleavage of opinion over Manifest Destiny's political implications for slavery. So too did an Anglo-Saxonism that spurned Catholics as inferior spell fraught division, but more ominous still was the conflict generated by Christian republicanism. The critical and potentially fractious language of the Puritan jeremiad was intrinsic to Christian republicanism's campaigning. Evangelical Protestantism's relative success in welding personal conversion to national identity intensified allegiance to an American "nation" as a vehicle of providence, but the moral logic of the jeremiad produced waves of criticism when political issues became articles of faith for individual citizens. This conflict threatened the very survival of the nation, and its singularity.

The critical fault line concerned abolitionism's rise. A crisis generated by the conceptual frame of exceptionalism arose because the attack on slavery took the jeremiad's form to a considerable extent. Abolitionists appropriated its tradition of goading a whole people for collective sin, but they used the jeremiad's condemnatory language to cast such grave doubts on the nation's exceptionality that some critics repudiated the protean tradition altogether, and others tested exceptionalism's limits as a coherent belief system. The questioning of the nation's practice and values became so ferocious that it turned, through the radical abolitionists, into a critique of the Christian republic idea. Exceptionalism could no longer be identified with the existing American state because its institutions lacked the qualities that God ordained. Yet the result was two-edged. On the one hand, belief in American exceptionalism was challenged and antiexceptionalism flourished. On the other, the ruin of the republic might still be overcome by recolonizing the nation as a Christian province. During the Civil War this latter approach would prompt calls to make the United States not merely Christian republican in sentiment but also in legal terms, with Christian values recognized in the Constitution and legal practice. In turn, this attempt to impose on the United States a post-Civil War "Christian Nation" framework further divided the advocates of exceptionalism.

Chief among the prosecutors were, ironically, disciples of the Benevolent Empire who cherished republican political liberty but found the republic wanting as a moral order. Opposition to slavery grew as evangelical conversions in the North tied sin to moral and political deficiencies. Antislavery advocates based their condemnation of human bondage, American style, largely on its violation of the right to individual liberty, and therefore as a sin in their estimate. The holding of slaves appeared to block the path of individual conversion to God and the ability to lead a moral life without the brutalizing effects of the "peculiar institution."

Within that unequivocal understanding of sinfulness, personal identity became both entangled with religious identity and highly disruptive of patriotic identity. The sternest opponents of slavery such as William Lloyd Garrison attacked American institutions as compromised by evil and incompatible with following God's word and spirit. Garrison condemned the U.S. Constitution on this ground. Some abolitionists, like the anti-institutionalists from whom Garrison received support, preached Christian perfectionism and separation from institutional religion as a way to achieve the millennium through individual repentance reproduced on mass scale. But the resistance of slaveholders invited other blistering denunciations.[3]

Slavery's persistence in the face of attempts to persuade southern Christian converts of its evil nature inevitably led antislavery reformers to criticize not only Christianity but also the republican liberty associated with it by moral reformers. Frederick Douglass's abolitionist Fifth of July speech (1852), delivered at the invitation of the "Ladies" of the Rochester Anti-Slavery Sewing Society, highlighted how the promise of liberty under the Declaration of Independence had exactly the opposite result for African Americans. But Douglass still hoped to redeem the American nation. He separated the potential for human fulfillment of the Declaration from the arguments of politicians and southern churchmen defending their interpretation of the Constitution as proslavery.[4] After his final break in 1851 with the Garrisonian abolitionists, Douglass sought a political place within the liberal democratic polity for African Americans liberated from slavery. This effort paralleled the position of antislavery advocates within the newly formed Republican Party in 1854. Rather than renounce the United States, Douglass offered a jeremiad as a warning, drawn from the parallel casting out of Israel by a God angry over collective sin.[5]

Less well known is the highly negative assessment of exceptionalism coming from some white abolitionists. Hailing from upstate New York, William Goodell first came to prominence as editor of the *Genius of Temperance* (1829–33).[6] Therein he preached the need for universal and benevolent reform to spread liberty across the globe. His audience was "humanity" as a whole, and his vehicle was the range of moral reforms first championed on the national stage under Benevolent Empire leadership. But the failure of the United States to abolish slavery led Goodell to a radical course. In the eyes of the world, he reasoned, the United States had not embraced the high moral example that the Benevolent Empire professed. By tolerating slavery, the American people and American institutions were shown to be uncivilized in a world where key European nations had eliminated the evil.[7] Ironically, the one way that the nation seemed truly exceptional to Goodell was its embarrassingly sinful status as a slaveholding *republic*. It was "an anomalous republic," in his words, not an exception in a positive sense but in a derelict way. The anomaly was not simply the failure to follow religious teaching but the "incongruity" between "universal human rights" inspired by the French and American revolutions and republican practice. Abject support of "human chattelhood" had actually undermined the spread of republicanism globally, Goodell argued. The United States "armed the world's despots with their most plausible pleas against republican institutions" and thus vitiated Lyman Beecher's religious plans.[8]

With the American republic considered a garden-variety nation that condoned oppression, it would be necessary to bring about a global revolution of the masses to end this circumstance. Writing after the failed European revolutions of 1848, Goodell was sensitized to the fact that slavery was a form of labor and therefore part of a larger pattern of class oppression that included the peasants of Ireland and the serfs of Russia. He did not, however, overtly connect his argument to the *Communist Manifesto* written by Karl Marx in that same, turbulent year in European history. Instead, Goodell deployed the classic jeremiad that went back to the Puritans. He treated the dialectic of slavery and freedom as moral as much as economic. As a "political abolitionist," Goodell did not single out the government for condemnation but included the people, who either elected corrupt representatives or failed to right the wrongs of the existing constitution by active protest.[9] As an heir to the jeremiad, Goodell attempted to hold the United States to its nominally high standards. He joined James Birney's Liberty Party to effect change and was the party's presidential candidate in 1852.

Goodell went further than a nationally specific ideal of liberty to attack the entire organization of society and argued for a universal revolution of freedom that drew on hope for a Christian millennium. Goodell represented modified Calvinist views akin to those of the Benevolent Empire. He argued that slavery represented "absolute authority." "True" Calvinism, with its "knowledge of divine sovereignty and human depravity" could recognize that in such a system, "the slaveholder was playing God"—thus interfering with the spiritual life of the slave. Far from being an anti-institutionalist like Garrison, Goodell presented radicalism as the "application of the governmental view of God" to the question of slavery. Goodell later argued that violence, in the form of John Brown's raid on Harpers Ferry in 1859, was "the providential remedy" for slavery when warnings went unheeded and when government did not act.[10]

Similar antiexceptionalist beliefs could be found among more conservative Christian republicans such as George Barrell Cheever. He won notoriety as the author of *Deacon Giles' Distillery*, a tract that condemned a Salem, Massachusetts, church elder and distiller for his compromise with the evils of the demon drink. Cheever was jailed in 1835 for libel over this issue. He also crossed swords with the Democrat-journalist John L. O'Sullivan, debating in the affirmative the merits of capital punishment with him. Cheever then scandalized Protestant clergy with his frank condemnation of slavery. Later, Cheever wrote for Goodell's *Principia* magazine, but he accepted Beecher's position on the advantages of complete separation of church and state.[11]

Even as his application of Beecher was fairly orthodox Christian republicanism, Cheever angrily denounced Christian preachers who did not condemn slavery. They used the "Christian name to palliate if not to justify and sanctify the wrong." Like Goodell, Cheever deployed the jeremiad to excoriate the republic's vaunted claims of special status in the eyes of God. He made the Bible his standard for both human conduct and the Constitution. The sin of slavery "could never be, if we, as a people, had kept the word of God in view, and had not forgotten or denied its principles." National catastrophe was nigh, he warned in 1857. Even politicians "must take [a] stand on God's word, and square our policy, our platform, according to it, or we shall surely perish as a nation." The Civil War gave even theologically conservative Protestants an opening to condemn the American state using their own version of the moral order. For Cheever, the United States would be damned to a truly exceptional fate if slavery were not abolished; the nation would face "such a destruction as the world never beheld."[12]

Questioning American exceptionalism in the light of slavery was not a prerogative of evangelicals alone. Unitarians such as the prominent historian John Lothrop Motley were scathing about national vanity. Motley denied the nation's "singular" status in the rise of democracy. American history was not "born of the cloud-embraces of a false Divinity," he declared.[13] A rationalist

and secularist with a Unitarian background, Richard Hildreth matched Motley's and Goodell's critiques, writing pioneering antislavery novels in the 1840s.
He conceded the exceptionalist point that the United States was a "social experiment," but he argued that the nation was also an exhibition of "despotism"
through the coercive nature of the slave system. Moreover, the American experience was not "universal" in significance. Universal laws would inevitably
produce their "necessary effects," not any "single experiment" located in a
particular country, no matter how convinced its citizens were of their own
self-importance.[14] Embodying these ideas, Hildreth's multivolume *History of
the United States* (1851–52) was an antiexceptionalist riposte to George Bancroft. Hildreth professed facts over patriotic guff and was especially critical
of pseudohistorical literature centered on Fourth of July and similar political
orations.[15]

In *An Appeal in Favor of That Class of Americans Called Africans*, yet another reformer of Unitarian background, Lydia Child, added her criticism of
exceptionalism and slavery. She compared slavery across the ages and analyzed it as a historical creation of social forces, not something outside time.
Though condemning both Great Britain and the United States for displaying
the worst examples of slavery, the cookbook author and novelist proclaimed
that "my countrymen are fond of preeminence, and I am afraid they deserve
it here."[16] Widespread and boastful proclamations of exceptionalism invited
this critique of American vanity. As has often been the case in condemnations
of the United States, the criticism retained residual tinges of exceptionalism
in its negativity, but the substance of her work was analytical and empirical.

While American exceptionalism came under fire from antislavery evangelicals and from Unitarian and secular abolitionists, their proslavery opponents embraced the exceptionalist idea—for themselves. Edgefield County,
South Carolina, planter Arthur Simkins noted in a widely circulated address
of 1855 that "the Southern people of the American Union are the chosen race
of modern times." Observing that God's original chosen country was an agrarian society like the South, and that Old Testament stories sanctioned slavery,
Simkins claimed that only the South, not the industrializing and urbanizing
North, could possibly be the successor state of ancient Israel uniquely favored
by God.[17] Southern opinion was divided over the merits of secession, but its
accomplishment solidified the idea of the South as a chosen nation in its own
right. Though originally opposed to a breakup of the Union, Alexander Stephen, vice president of the newly created Confederacy, spoke for the fledging
Southern nation when he attacked the "pestilent heresy" of the Declaration
of Independence that "all men, of all races, were equal." He vowed that an
independent South, with white supremacy its "corner-stone," would be the

genuine "model nation of history," founded on a superior social order and the primacy of cotton in the world economy.[18]

As the "chosen race" idea and its Old Testament justifications hinted, Southern exceptionalism made religion as much as race central to its singularity. The Confederate Constitution invoked in its preamble "the favor and guidance of Almighty God," whereas the U.S. Constitution had no such mention. Some proslavery writers speculated that it was the Calvinist belief in a God-ordained country that rendered the South superior. Northerners responded that their own section was the model republic but, to many abolitionists, the presence of slavery's indirect constitutional sanction and the repeated threats of disunion in the 1850s indicated otherwise.[19]

The antislavery jeremiad insisted that the failed promise of the republic could register, through the South's secession from the Union, a greater damnation than any other nation had ever faced. As one preacher complained, "Our failure to stand up before the nations of the earth as a model nation, to exhibit to them the beauty and glory of free institutions—of a self-governed people—a great moral fountain whose fertilizing streams should go out to bless a desert world; these and a long list of our national sins, have provoked our Lord and King to subject us to his chastening hand."[20] So railed Hollis Read, a best-selling author and former missionary to India.[21]

If, for Southerners, war victory could confirm their own existing exceptionalism asserted in secession, for Northerners, only a bloody triumph could enable redemption of the nation's lost promise. This was the conclusion of John Brown in his preexecution speech after the failed raid on Harpers Ferry of October 1859, when he referenced the nation as a "guilty land."[22] But people far less radical thought much the same. The Civil War gave Northern Protestant exceptionalists a chance to consolidate their position and to equate their version of the doctrine with the forward march of history. Freeing the slaves and redeeming the republic became inseparable. In *The Coming Crisis of the World*, Hollis Read saw the Civil War as the linchpin in the final liberation of humankind.[23] Like Harriet Beecher Stowe and William Goodell, he viewed the conflict as a world-historical event. The issue in the United States was chattel slavery, which Read saw as a particular case of the global need to overthrow tyranny. As sin was everywhere, the United States was not exceptional. It could only hope to make itself exceptional by winning the war and ushering in the global Protestant millennium.[24]

This position was most famously extended through American popular culture in Julia Ward Howe's "Battle Hymn of the Republic" (1862). An alternative military marching piece, "The Battle Cry of Freedom" was popular at the time, and more practical to perform, but had an innocuous theological content.[25] In contrast, Howe's words expressed a providential tale in which the blood of Christ was equated with the blood of soldiers lost in patriotic battle. In the rivalry of the Civil War songs, evangelical religion proved more productive of nationalism than secular causes, however important the freeing of the slaves and the progress of liberty became as the war rolled on. That Howe was a Unitarian, yet could make so much of providential power, suggests how far the Christian republic idea had penetrated, as she was no Calvinist, either "Old" or "New" School. One could argue that the question of slavery blurred doctrinal differences even further than the Benevolent Empire did, to create a moral, interdenominational discourse that both displayed the achievements of evangelicalism, and underscored its moral fragilities on exceptionalism.[26]

A Christian Nation in the Civil War and Reconstruction

In part, the fratricidal conflict could be used to verify the existence of a "Redeemer Nation" through an "ennobling war" to transcend slavery's stain.[27] In historian Ernest Tuveson's words, "a new rationale of national mission was constructed."[28] But the national mission was sectional in origins. The victory of the North offered the prospect of imposing the Northern version of exceptionalism on the whole nation. This agenda involved eliminating the chattel slavery on which Southern exceptionalism rested and asserting African American human rights through the Fourteenth Amendment. This radical Reconstruction program sowed the seeds of modern liberal exceptionalism in race relations by creating national citizenship and equal protection under the laws. In the aftermath of a bloody war, however, it also meant an attempted imposition of Northern values of competitive individualism and Protestant-based moral reforms on the South.[29]

The irony lay in how the war and its aftermath of Union Army occupation actually strengthened the South's own sense of a special identity. Reinforced in the military defeat, Southern exceptionalism thrived on the memory and mourning of collective loss. Based formerly on the incongruous idea of plantation slavery as the foundation of a modern economy, Southern exceptionalism now forged purely racial distinctions in which—"free" or not—black people were considered inferior to white ones. Racial caste replaced class as the basis of Southern society. The North's attempt to reconstruct the South ended in 1877, as a racially based social Darwinist sentiment spread nationally and internationally in the Anglo-American world, but true sectional rapprochement could not be achieved until the Spanish-American War of 1898 allowed patriotic sentiment to be projected outward, against a common and external enemy, in the name of liberating Cuba from Spanish "oppression."

In the North, the Civil War did not solve the old question of exception-alism's religious foundations. Doubts about that religious form of national identity continued precisely because of the wartime cataclysm and the com-parison with the rebel states. That the Confederacy could do a better job of including God in its constitution was galling for Northern Christians. Cen-tral to the questioning was a group of orthodox Calvinists who emerged as a political and intellectual force aware that the United States was not yet a Christian nation.[30] That idea fed not on exceptionalist opinion but on anxiety over the perilous status of the nation that the war revealed. While numerous Northern evangelical clergy preached the coalescence of their faith with the progress of the Union Army, the National Reform Association (NRA) met in 1863, calling for an amendment to recognize God in the U.S. Constitution. The drive originated in the more orthodox or "Ultra-Calvinist" (Presbyterian and Reformed) churches opposing Arminian theology and the "new measures" of the revivals. They adhered to the old idea of a pact with God as a Christian covenant. Called *covenanters*, they offered a sterner rebuke to a sinful nation than Beecher had. To these more severe Calvinists, not only was the war a divine punishment wrought against a people who had broken a precious bar-gain with God; the error lay also in a kind of original sin, in which the repub-lic was born neither perfect nor Christian. This meant Christianity must—for the first time—be constitutionally enshrined by amendment, a position at odds with antebellum Christian republican strategy. This initiative departed from Lyman Beecher's emphasis on a steadily more Christian tenor in civil society through voluntary work. Indeed, the covenanters condemned as inadequate the work of reform associations and even urged abstention from voting on the grounds that the state was not yet God's institution.[31]

Nevertheless, the wartime prognosis for the Calvinists was promising. In February 1864, NRA representatives met President Lincoln, who seemed sym-pathetic at first, and some senators, notably Charles Sumner of Massachusetts, gave tentative support for an amendment. Soon, however, politicians admit-ted the obvious: the move threatened the constitutional basis of church-state separation, and political backing faltered. Nevertheless, the movement con-tinued, claiming ten thousand readers of its journal, the *Christian Statesman*, and up to fifty thousand signers for its petitions in the mid-1870s. In contrast, the failed civil rights bill of 1874 received four thousand signatures. This was "less than half" the number campaigning for "the God Amendment."[32]

With slavery officially abolished, the doctrinal issue that led covenanters to abstain from voting before 1865 abated. Though starting from an orthodox Calvinist base in 1863–65, organized support for the NRA grew more vocal yet diffuse during Reconstruction. The movement retained its emphasis on a future Christian status for the nation while trying to clarify that concept not as a church-state union but as a religion-state alliance in which even Catholics should be able to find common purpose, but Catholic officials did not attend NRA conventions.[33] In fact, the 1874 convention saw the movement's secretary attacking Catholicism as a "counterfeit" faith in which "the whole Roman Catholic Church" undermined the Christian Sunday.[34]

Exceptionalist influences were clear in the idea of an example to the world. A Christian nation would spread the hemispheric and worldwide moral influence of a Christianized republic, some supporters stated. The vice president of the NRA, John Alexander put it thus in 1873: "The commanding influence of our American republicanism is causing republics to be born in a day"; yet the global credentials of the United States remained out of kilter with the nation's practice.[35] The NRA desired "to preserve and perpetuate for ourselves, our children, and for the *example of all the world*, the glorious inheritance which we have received from our Christian patriotic ancestors." Yet a warning was attached to this boast: "We know from other history of the past, as well as from Holy Writ, that the nation that will not serve Him shall perish."[36] The jeremiad continued.

Rhetoric aside, the campaign for a constitutional amendment was not as closely aligned with exceptionalism as advocates of a Christian nation post-1970 have been. Other countries had God in their constitutions, said the Reverend David Kerr at the 1874 NRA convention, and the United States should too.[37] General Secretary David McAllister of the Reformed Presbyterian Church felt sure that Islamic people of the Middle East would have included the name of God in a constitution, if they had possessed one.[38] Neither of these points illustrated national hubris; rather, soul-searching and an unfavorable international comparison prevailed. The NRA charged that the American republic had, in law, moved away from God, even as the culture and the practice of politics and common law remained Christian. Though the United States might be deemed "Christian" in this way, unlike Christian nation reformers of later times, the earlier advocates conceded the technically secular nature of the U.S. Constitution. For these Christians, the Civil War's result could not sanctify or legitimate the ideal of an exceptional nation. Only legal reform to empower a Christian state apparatus could do so.

Some in the NRA did assert a Christian-based practice that would strengthen the nation's esteemed place in the world; so opined President Solomon Pool of the University of North Carolina in 1874. It was, in a spiritual sense, transcending any law, Pool argued, that "we were born a Christian nation. God gave us our freedom, and upon the great principles of Christian liberty our institutions are founded, and our laws administered." As a nation, he asserted, the United States was "as essentially and distinctively Christian, as is Turkey Mohammedan, or China Pagan." A direct result of these distinctive conditions was "our rapid progress and exalted place among the people of the earth. The loftiest destiny which patriots and statesmen claim for us is based upon Christian revelation," he concluded.[39] The inconsistency between choosing to be like Islamic states in their institutionalized obedience to God and the exceptionalist idea of a Christian example to the world was palpable in the rhetoric of the NRA. The contradiction disclosed an underlying weakness. The NRA lacked a clear position on its purpose, which was hypercritical of the United States yet rejoiced in the nation's essential goodness and could not get widespread support to push beyond Beecher's Christian republicanism into law-based religious exceptionalism.

There was another unusual feature to the campaign. Rather than single out the United States as a chosen nation in a pre-historicist sense, the new campaigners exposed organicist themes foreign to the notions of either Christian republicans or the American Revolution. The NRA of the 1870s went well beyond revolutionary and antebellum ideas to champion an organic state. The latter was not an aggregation of soon-to-be-converted individuals, as Beecher had seen it. Now, "nations" were treated as "growths, not mere *voluntary associations*." Alexis de Tocqueville's version of exceptionalism as organized moral influence was therefore discounted.[40] The argument not only drew on the practical and legal change resulting from the Civil War, which made the nation-state supreme and the Union indissoluble; it also proposed a historicist concept of the state similar to contemporary European thinking. Displaying a Hegelian influence, the NRA championed the abstract concept of such a "state" embodying the "spirit" of the age. Those ideas made "nation" superior to individual "rights" and therefore supplied the need for an explicit sanction of Christianity in the constitution. At the 1873 meeting, the Reverend Dr. Elijah Craven, a Presbyterian minister in Newark, New Jersey, and secretary of the board of trustees of Princeton University, spoke of colonial-era settlements in evolutionary terms; they were the "germ of a nation" in need of moral discipline to be forged into an "organic" creation constituting a "special form of life."[41] Judge John Hagans, a Republican congressman from West Virginia, championed before the 1872 NRA convention "the State as a sovereign, conscious, moral personality." It was "not a historical accident," Hagans claimed, but "an external circumstance of its being."[42] The phrase invoked a historical "essence," a Hegelian formulation of the state and law at odds with individualism and pre-historicist understandings of the nation's origins. For the NRA, American Christianity must be reflected in an organically developed constitution, expressing the substance of a Christian state, drawing on the assertion that the nation had already developed such an "un-written Constitution" of Christian assumptions needing only to be set into constitutional law.[43]

These aspirations were translated into concrete issues. Christian teaching in the public schools and restoring the Christian Sabbath quickly dominated the NRA agenda. According to Hagans, the "dictate of true patriotism and statesmanship" was clear: "The Bible must not be cast out of our schools; our Christian laws of marriage, and of the Sabbath, must not be abrogated; the oath of God must not be banished from our courts of justice."[44] The Reverend Dr. A. M. Milligan of Pittsburgh blamed the "infidel theory" of the French Enlightenment and its influence on the Founding Fathers for the canker he identified at the heart of the American polity.[45] The Fathers' Enlightenment interpretation of the American place in world history was treated as indica-tive of the mechanistic way they had used "providence" and offended the new organicism of the Christian nation variety.

Organizationally speaking, the climax of Christian nation activities came in the 1870s and 1880s. The NRA allied with moral reform groups such as the Woman's Christian Temperance Union (WCTU) to promote the Christian Sabbath, oppose gambling, and push antiobscenity initiatives.[46] The WCTU and Christian Endeavor, a prominent Christian coeducational youth group, campaigned for "Christian Citizenship" toward this end, and both were closely allied with the NRA. Both enrolled a mass membership, numbering in the millions for Christian Endeavor, and both petitioned the U.S. Congress for their causes on a vast scale.[47] This Christian nation program continued to influence American politics and law during the Progressive Era (1890s–1920s) through National Citizenship Conferences.

Though the NRA lost a good many of its concrete political contests, a legal high-water mark for the Christian nation agitation came in Supreme Court Justice David J. Brewer's obiter dictum in the *Church of the Holy Trinity v. United States* decision (1892).[48] Born in the Ottoman Empire as the son of a Congregational missionary and himself a lifelong Christian evangelical, Brewer did not push the NRA's earlier constitutional amendment proposal but aligned with the NRA ethos of an "organic" Christian connection under-pinning the Constitution.[49] He told his Congregational Church parishioners in a rare lawyer's address from the pulpit in 1890 that "the law and the Gospel ought always to go together."[50] The *Holy Trinity* judgment referred to the nu-merous "organic utterances" in politics and law "that this is a Christian na-tion." Brewer's opinion represented the nineteenth-century legal apotheosis of the NRA's demands for an alliance with the federal state. He declared that the United States was indeed a "Christian people" in a Christian country, but not that it was uniquely privileged among the nations in this way.[51] Nor could it be, because of the widespread use of "Christian nation" to describe other countries.

As with so much of the NRA agitation, exceptionalism remained ambiguous in the *Holy Trinity* case. The decision was the unanimous verdict of all Supreme Court judges, and it rested not on the grounds of the oft-cited Christian nation formula but rather the faulty application of statute law in the case. The case involved the barring of a (white) English clergyman from entering the United States under a labor contract.[52] The legal dispute stemmed from an 1885 immigration law against migration of "aliens" or "foreigners, to perform labor or service." This law was clearly intended to exclude low-wage Chinese manual laborers contracted for railroad construction and other tasks across the American West. The court ruled that the clergyman's vocation among the "brain toilers" of the world could not be equated with ordinary understandings of "cheap, unskilled labor."[53] Consequently, Brewer's Christian nation statement stood only as an additional assertion—through the obiter dictum—of evangelical aspirations.

Not until a lecture in 1905 did Brewer go further. By that time, he could assert that the republic was not only "classified among the Christian nations of the world" but also spoken of internationally as "the leading Christian nation."[54] The "Christian character of this republic shines out with richest promise," he claimed then, for the redemption of the world. Perhaps the difference reflected the gap between a court judgment requiring consensus in 1892 and Brewer's own views in lecture form. Yet the intervening years had also seen, in the victorious Spanish-American War of 1898, changes underwriting the estimate of national capacity, which Brewer claimed now shone with the "richest promise" due to the country's new global position.[55]

Brewer's belief that the United States was uniquely charged by God to be the bearer of world peace was not a new one, but was rearticulated when the nation's growing material power made such a reassessment of its world role almost inevitable. In 1910, the NRA began to promote "World Citizenship" as a condition of a forthcoming Pax Americana, to be modeled globally on the American ethnic and national blend of peoples. Brewer believed that such a mixture forged through immigration in the United States could redeem the biblical "dispersal" of Babel by fusing the races to usher in the peace of the world.[56]

Except for Brewer's efforts, the Christian nation idea did not reach wider constitutional standing. This failure lay in the growing complexity of American culture after 1880 as immigrants poured in, bringing greater ethnic and cultural diversity. Too many Americans now sided with either the more practical compromise of a Christian republic grounded in moral voluntarism or those who rallied to make the nation even more secular than before. Because the Christian nation project to turn religious concepts into law actually spurred other Americans to mobilize opposition to it in state and national politics, the NRA campaign proved to be self-defeating.[57] It stimulated secularists, Christian sects such as the Seventh-Day Adventists, and adherents of non-Christian faiths to sharpen their own understanding of the U.S. Constitution based on freedom of belief—and of the nation as exceptional for this reason. For the Jewish Reform Rabbi Max Lilienthal in 1870, strict separation of church and state meant that "our beloved country will not only prosper and succeed as heretofore, but will always lead the van of human liberty and civilization."[58]

In retrospect, the weakness of the Christian nation movement was not revealed in the Civil War, where, after all, the "sin" of slavery was ultimately overcome; the victory of 1865 undermined, if only temporarily for some, the argument of national sinfulness requiring national repentance. More important was the rise of secular threats to the status of Christian practice in the common law, and state court rulings that the U.S. Constitution never had been specifically Christian. Repeated attempts to preserve the holy Sabbath met with opposition in the cities of the East and Midwest where German immigrants violated the Sunday observance derived from the Puritan heritage.[59] In this context, the attempt to create a Christian Nation in name and law revealed its own defensive and anxious character.

The Brewer judgment came at a time when the forces of evangelically driven exceptionalism were being sharply challenged on several fronts. A widening gap between rich and poor, together with labor violence, raised the prospect of lost promise for the nation. The egalitarian hope of a harmonious and socially homogeneous America was at risk. Simultaneously the new immigration of Catholics, Eastern Orthodox, and nonwhite people—signaled as a legal issue in *Trinity*—spurred Christian patriots to seek other ways than the Christian nation concept to bolster American credentials for exceptional status.

Fin de Siècle Challenges: The Frontier, Labor, and American Imperialism

October 28, 1886, was a rainy and foggy day in New York Harbor. A crowd of 2,500 people gathered on Bedloe's Island to hear President Grover Cleveland accept the Statue of Liberty, a gift from France, with the words, "We will not forget that Liberty has here made her home; nor shall her chosen altar be neglected."[1] Spectators aboard the numerous pleasure craft that plied the harbor had come out to witness the auspicious event, but they could hardly see the statue for the fog, and the fireworks display was postponed until November 1. This natural event could be seen as a metaphor for growing criticism of American exceptionalism shaped increasingly by foreign complications. Immigration, the global rise of industrial and financial capitalism, and the European contests for empire were all circumstances that called into question the newly solidified liberal exceptionalism of the Reconstruction settlement, with its focus on individual freedom. The attempts to deal with these challenges saw Americans adapting, modifying, or even abandoning the compass of exceptionalist values.

The Fog of Liberty

Being mired in fog was a slightly deflated beginning to an illustrious career as a monument, but the Statue of Liberty still connoted for visitors the promise of America. The statue became an early example of "monumental" exceptionalism: the resort to the built environment to materialize exceptionalist notions. Through sheer size or beauty, Lady Liberty would impress nations and American citizens with the idea of the United States as an exemplar of freedom. Few nation-inspired monuments had been completed prior to this time. Standing just over three hundred feet or twenty stories high, the statue towered over the harbor and was the tallest structure in the nation's largest city. Immigrants to the United States could not miss it as they arrived in New York by ship, thereby making the statue and its principles better known to millions of future citizens. But the circumstances of the 1880s and 1890s were indeed to put a fog of uncertainty around the face of liberty.

The erection of this statue symbolized the arrival of the United States as a unified nation at the end of Reconstruction. With national consolidation achieved and the formal end to the problem of slavery that stood in the way of individual liberty for so long, for the first time one could think exclusively of an exceptionalism centered on an American nation-state. The celebration of the first one hundred years of the nation in 1876 symbolized this achievement. Speaking in Arkansas on July 4, Isaac Parker (later famous as "Hanging Judge Parker") could declare that the country had experienced great tribulation since 1861 but had pulled through. He referenced the "thankful" passing of slavery so that liberty would include all. There "treads not a slave on the soil of free America," he proclaimed.[2] This was something Southerners and Northerners could agree on, Parker affirmed.

The story of the Statue of Liberty goes back to these events of the era in which the United States was emerging from the Civil War as a nation indivisible. It was also a time of upheaval in France, where the statue had its origins. The subsequent history was quite ironic, as the original name was "Liberty Enlightening the World," and its designers did not have a singular national story in mind. The purpose of the statue was not to set the United States apart but to draw it and France together. The project's origin was not, as some commentators have thought, an homage to the American republic for an exclusive achievement but instead an attempt to build on cordial relations with France at a time when the French sorely needed them. The French had just experienced military defeat in the Franco-Prussian War (1870–71). Meanwhile, they had witnessed the humiliation of Paris becoming the site of a bloody socialist uprising, the Paris Commune. Noting German-American rejoicing over the Prussian victory and the subsequent unification of Germany, a small group of Frenchmen decided that France needed friends abroad to compensate for the new menace to the east; they wished to develop cultural diplomacy on a popular level to capitalize on the good feeling toward France in the United States that could be traced back to the Marquis de Lafayette's intervention in the American Revolution. The offer of the Statue of Liberty as a gift from the French people was conceived in this transatlantic milieu.[3] But the American government and people lagged behind the French in interest, and financing of the proposal remained unresolved for nearly ten years. When the inauguration occurred in 1886, the political landscape had changed. The

United States once more seemed faced with turmoil that challenged American exceptionalism.

In the very year that the statue project was proceeding on New York Harbor, another set of events was occurring eight hundred miles away that called into question the achievements of liberty. A group of anarchists had been declared guilty of a May 1886 bombing in the Haymarket district of Chicago and awaited execution as their lawyers filed appeals. The conviction of these foreign-born "incendiaries" was greeted with shock by the international labor movement, since the legal processes were dubious, and critics disputed the capital punishment meted out. Despite divisions over whether violence was the correct course of action for dissenters to take, many trade unionists and other labor representatives in Europe and the United States regarded "America" no longer as the land of liberty but the site of grinding poverty and strife between labor and capital. The spring of 1886 saw huge strikes across western states against cuts to wages in the railroad industry, and it was this strife that the anarchists attempted to exploit with their agitation in May that produced the Haymarket riot. Just when the Statue of Liberty was being touted as a tribute to the global significance of that idea, the United States seemed to be moving toward political repression and social instability. As one of the condemned Haymarketers, Albert Parsons, proclaimed, "The American flag protects as much economic despotism as any other flag on the face of the earth to-day to the ratio of population." Of what then, he went on, "does the boasted freedom of the American workingman consist?" This critique plainly revealed antiexceptionalism.[4]

These were pressing issues for American exceptionalism. Slavery had been defeated, but wage "slavery" had not, radicals argued. Workers across the United States were periodically restive and rebellious as wages dropped and unemployment rose in the depression and labor violence of 1873–77, again in the mid-1880s, and yet again in 1893. Labor presented a challenge to an exceptionalist ideology made more fragile as frontier expansion slowed because the best public land available to settle appeared to have been taken up already and because farmers protested against the growing power of railroads that moved goods to market at high prices relative to demand for agricultural products.

There was more to anxiety over and criticism of American prospects than that. "Expansionism," hitherto largely protected from general opprobrium under the values of republicanism as "continental," now focused on overseas trade, investment, and the quest for an isthmian canal in Nicaragua or Columbia. Agitation for colonies was held in check in the 1870s and 1880s but caused great controversy after 1898, when the United States acquired an overseas colonial empire—the Philippine Islands, Guam, and Puerto Rico—as a result of the Spanish-American War.[5] American Samoa, the Panama Canal Zone, and Hawaii also joined the empire column quickly.

These circumstances disturbed many Americans. Labor conflict, the termination of the frontier, and the threat posed by U.S. imperialist ambitions abroad to a republican form of government collectively raised concern over a possible end to exceptionalism. These comprised the trinity of issues that challenged the old democratic and patriotic traditions newly reinforced by the Civil War's outcome. From these circumstances arose the first true crisis in exceptionalism, running from the mid-1880s to World War I. It was "true" in the sense that the political ideals at the root of American identity were challenged across such a range of issues as to suggest a systemic crisis. Previous conflicts had centered on the perceived failure to implement liberal democratic values of individual freedom, but the distinctiveness and worth of the ideals that made the United States seem qualitatively different from other nations were now disputed.

Frontier's End

These three issues simmered through the 1870s and 1880s but came in full force in the 1890s. Two were based on the material prosperity underpinning the society and polity. While both religious exceptionalism and nineteenth-century liberal ideals emphasized the ideational structures making the United States a special country, material circumstances had always been an important underlying condition fostering these ideas. The most obvious aspect of material change was the frontier's end, as announced by the U.S. Census Office in 1890. Throughout the nineteenth century, the small-scale "yeoman" farmer ideal was essential to American political stability by appearing to give the ordinary person an opportunity to take a stake in society through the ownership of (landed) property. Through property, not only would individual families be fed, clothed, and housed, but the moral virtue and independence considered essential to civic republicanism could also be sustained. That is, only the property owner could be free from the corruption of the powerful. Given the decline in available fertile land, a substitute was now needed.

Widespread anxiety over the "end" of the frontier ensued, with the debate dragging on episodically until the 1930s.[6] The most important intellectual contributor was the academic historian Frederick Jackson Turner. In "The Significance of the Frontier in American History" (1893), Turner presented civic republicanism as a secularized process grounded in the environmental origins of American institutions. Turner supplied several exceptionalist tropes, making his essay famous as a statement of the general doctrine. He presented

European-American differences in the dichotomous form associated with American exceptionalism: "Since the days when the fleet of Columbus sailed into the waters of the New World, America has been another name for opportunity, and the people of the United States have taken their tone from the incessant expansion which has not only been open but has even been forced upon them."[7] The contrast with the "Old World" was clear enough. The new environment had unleashed the dynamism that shaped a new nation.

What Turner stated about the availability of land for small-scale farmers and its significance for democracy and equality of opportunity was hardly news. Turner simply developed the point about the importance of free land in an academic direction. His frontier thesis made him a forerunner of social science exceptionalism with its emphasis on the empirical studies of material conditions that made the nation radically distinctive. Seymour Martin Lipset took his contribution that way. But Turner was not a systematic and consistent thinker, and he left many aspects unclear. Indeed, he continued to modify his own thesis for the rest of his life. His address of 1893 was more poetic in form than analytical.[8]

Turner did not use the term *exceptionalism*, though he did believe that the United States had developed a cluster of unique characteristics; a rambunctious democracy and individual mobility had, he believed, served the nation well from its roots on the frontier. It had created across the West a rough egalitarianism, whose impacts eventually fed back to the East to shape a more democratic country. While he acknowledged the sharp sectional differences in the United States revealed in the Civil War and played down the idea of a melting pot, he also argued that a national character or "new type" had emerged over the interplay of forces on the frontier.[9]

All these ideas were open to empirical testing, and that was one serious caveat on Turner's work. Much of the needed evidence was not yet collected. In another qualification, he did not profess the full range of exceptionalist views we now associate with the idea. One huge absence is rarely noted: he presented no notion of a chosen people. Evolution, rather than God's word, shaped his worldview. Religion was not a theme, except in the social context of churches as frontier institutions promoting community. Certainly, he assumed that the United States differed sharply from Europe in the shaping of national character—based on individualism, nationalism, and democracy; and he viewed the nation as a land of opportunity and progress. But in none of these things was he advocating exceptionalism understood as outside the normal course of history. That idea had to be inferred from his work.

The closest he came to providing an explanation pertinent to exceptionalism was through the so-called safety valve. He argued that as Americans moved west, the labor vacuum created relief for urban discontent back east, thus mitigating the possibility of class conflict that might bring American exceptionalism to an end. This argument has long ago been questioned empirically.[10] But, whatever its validity, the concept was only hinted at in the original essay of 1893 as "a gate of escape." The "stubborn" American environment was there "with its imperious summons to accept its conditions; . . . and yet, in spite of environment, and in spite of custom, each frontier did indeed furnish a new field of opportunity, a gate of escape from the bondage of the past; and freshness, and confidence, and scorn of older society, impatience of its restraints and its ideas, and indifference to its lessons, have accompanied the frontier."[11] Only in 1910 did Turner explicitly declare a safety valve; even then, he put forth this argument and immediately stated that it was no longer functioning: "A new national development is before us *without the former safety valve* of abundant resources open to him who would take."[12]

Turner's students and critics have erected an American exceptionalism out of his unsystematic comments. More realistically, he was providing evidence for the crisis facing American exceptionalism, rather than providing a coherent doctrine supporting it. He viewed the discontent of the farmers, manifest in the Populist political movement of the 1890s, as evidence for the obstacles to American improvement previously achieved along classic Victorian lines of material and moral progress. The People's Party of that decade proposed new, "European-style" methods to retrieve American democracy from the plutocrats, who appeared to control it during the Gilded Age, but the Populists never lost faith in key exceptionalist ideas, whose promise they wished to restore. They blamed distant capitalists and even international Jewish bankers for undermining American opportunity. They urged such policies as government-owned railroads and telegraph services, as well as liberal monetary reform, to restore the welfare of farmers and others hurt by international competition and the banking system. The platform was promising, but the outcome was disappointing. Fractured by internal squabbles and confounded by the race issue that undermined their professions of equality, the Populists failed to achieve their goals in the 1890s.[13] The Progressivism that emerged from these disappointments offered an alternative. Along with electoral and welfare reform measures, incremental regulatory reform would deal with social and economic problems. After 1900, Turner allied with this emerging Progressive movement.[14]

Turner did not predict a solution to the social problems of the farmer in 1893, nor did he present clear alternatives. He simply suggested that the problem of blocked opportunity must be faced. Over the course of the next twenty-five years, he argued that the United States would need either to find new frontiers abroad or to reform the economy at home through industrial and social efficiency. The choice was the American people's, but either choice spelled the possible end of American exceptionalism, since greater regulation of the economy and a growing size of government limiting individualism would follow the actions he anticipated.

This antiexceptionalist aspect to his critique placed him in the ranks of the Progressive Republicans seeking to use the American state to rectify inequalities of power, if not completely remove the wealth disparities threatening the promise of America. President Theodore Roosevelt spearheaded this agenda at the federal level. Especially through efforts to conserve resources, Roosevelt tried to deal with the growing social problems of industrialization to replace traditional American exceptionalism with a modern polity resting upon science, technology, and innovation. Turner's writings between 1900 and 1914 favored this agenda.[15]

A related context for Turner's thesis on the end of the frontier was his argument that the American West had served as a site for ethnic mixture—a way of preventing the development of immigrant ghettos and promoting American nationality. But Turner feared this trend was ending in the 1890s too. "Pioneer Ideals" would have be to transformed into something else if the nation's potential were to be fulfilled. In reality, migration westward, especially by European immigrants, introduced ethnic enclaves rather than produced a homogeneous national culture. Turner had no easy answer to this racial and ethnic heterogeneity, precisely because he believed the frontier process no longer worked as it had. This is why he turned to Progressive Republicanism and its attempts to address the social questions of labor and class through better, more efficient government and technical management of social and economic conflict. The challenge to exceptionalism became focused on the end of that promise of cultural assimilation and the impact of ethnic and cultural diversity on American values.[16]

Despite his sympathies, Turner had no part to play in the political process of Progressivism; he was an observer and commentator rather than a partisan actor. As a result, the Turner thesis entered the wider public discourse based almost entirely on his academic work and its interpretation by later historians, journalists, and political figures. In the short term, the assimilation of his thesis merely reinforced the (old-time) American exceptionalism present in the wider culture. By the 1920s, it had become standard fare in American textbooks to see the frontier as a source of American uniqueness and a material foundation of American democracy, and to forget the many qualifications Turner put on exceptionalism between 1897 and 1917, when the United States entered World War I. The most formidable critiques of Turner did not emerge full-blown until the 1930s, as the nation faced new global crises, but in the post–World War II period, empirical studies, notably that undertaken by Merle Curti, countered and found some historical truth in the idea of greater equality on the frontier than in settled districts.[17]

The biggest lacuna in the frontier "school" interpretation was Turner's presentation of "free" land as if Native Americans comprised a side issue. Turner's continuing relevance reflected the fact that he did not disturb the comfortable neglect of settler colonialism's impact. Rather, he worked within nineteenth-century popular traditions about the role of the American West in sustaining American democracy and opportunity. This intellectual influence lingered for decades. The 1960s saw new work in history and in cultural and American studies exploring frontier violence and Indian expropriation, but not until the New Western Historians undertook their revisionism in the 1980s by applying social history with its triad of race, class, and gender to the western subject matter was Turner truly eclipsed. Even then, while critical of Turner, this new work conceded the importance of the frontier in shaping American life, but it spoke ambiguously on the question of exceptionalism, since frontier violence and expropriation of land were widely shared across many European empires in collision with indigenous peoples.[18]

Of course, Turner understood that land was not literally free and that its value changed according to the demands of particular politicoeconomic systems. He was well aware that colonists had to cultivate the land, that Indian tribes had fought to retain it in violent conflicts from which they suffered most, and that they adapted to European penetration. He could hardly have failed to acknowledge the prior occupation of the indigenous peoples because his earliest work was a study of the Indian fur trade as a process of evolutionary adaptation. Yet Turner treated the fur trade as part of an inevitable movement in which the evolution of civilization eroded the value of Native Americans as labor (that is, as hunters of furs). Thus, the expropriation of their land was both possible and, from the settler perspective, necessary. It was not settlers who destroyed Indian tribes, in his view, but the impersonal processes of survival of the fittest under a technically superior stage of evolution. Turner also believed that this was a global and not a purely American process.[19]

Despite his association with exceptionalist ideas, Turner was much aware of comparative frontier development, the existence of democracy in other lands, and the imperial history of North America from which the United States sprang.[20] Historians have played down this side to Turner's work. For him, the expansion of the United States was the latest wave in the rise of world civilization. During the late nineteenth and early twentieth centuries, he still saw U.S. history as part of a larger story in which frontier experience connected European empires with North America. Only later did he depict the United States as a model for the world. The shift came after the nation had joined the Allied cause in World War I, when he saw American federalism as a possible prototype for European political development. A democracy based on compromise and a federal-state allocation of powers was what Turner put forward as a solution to postwar chaos and the collapse of European empires. His argument after 1918 became allied to exceptionalist precepts that sharply divided the political experience of Europe (associated with social turmoil) and "America" (where pragmatic and moderate change occurred). Though the Civil War gave the lie to the idea that calamitous conflict could not occur in the United States—Turner understood this point—by 1919 the American achievement in democracy seemed far more secure than it did when he was born in 1861. It is not surprising, therefore, that he would now present the United States as an exception in light of wartime European catastrophes. America's role under Woodrow Wilson in turning the war into a crusade for freedom and democracy reinforced the exceptionalist view, but Turner never worked out a coherent theory behind the doctrine.[21]

National Parks and Exceptionalism

The development of Turner's frontier thesis was a subset within the larger question of the American relationship to nature. His departure point was the challenge to the myths about frontier abundance and the exceptionalist theories of history on which those myths depended.[22] While Americans had long thought of their natural world as different and superior, American nature was not defined purely as national space before the last third of the nineteenth century. Visual representations of nature in American art often associated the richness of the American West with Manifest Destiny, but they did not clearly distinguish between U.S. nature and the natural world of the Americas. Traditionally the idea of natural abundance had been applied prior to the nineteenth century by European explorers to the Americas as a whole, not the British colonies alone, the assets of which had been seen as somewhat deficient in comparison with the gold, silver, and other precious items found elsewhere in the Western Hemisphere. At a microcosmic level, the chief American philosopher of nature in the nineteenth century treated the physical world as transcendent and God given. Nature was rooted in particular places as well as nations, and all showed, as in Henry David Thoreau's *Walden*, that the immanence of God's creation could be found everywhere in nature.[23]

Nor was nature preservation a key part of the American state as late as the 1870s. The hitching of American nature to an explicitly national exceptionalism came with the beginnings of federal regulation through the creation of national parks. The first of these dated from 1872 when Congress acted to preserve Yellowstone under federal control. But it was around the century's turning that a cluster of national parks such as Yosemite was established or consolidated. This was the time that a wide reformation of American nationalism began, stimulated by the Spanish-American War. The "nationalization," as it were, of the spaces of nature accelerated with the 1906 National Monuments legislation (American Antiquities Act) under Theodore Roosevelt, and in 1916 the National Park Service was created as a unified system to administer national parks.

Though other nations began to set aside national parks at about the same time, Americans thought their own to be exceptional.[24] As the public visitations soared in the 1920s and beyond, the parks became yet another way in which the perceived abundance of the American environment contributed to the twentieth-century understanding of national exceptionalism. Like the more capacious nineteenth-century sense of transcendental nature, the parks became spaces blending the abundance of American nature with the sacred element of providential design. Even more than the Statue of Liberty, these parks developed into key examples of monumental exceptionalism, emphasizing its material reality, albeit still created, many Americans thought, by God. The national park system won recognition as "America's Best Idea," though the phrase was not American in origin any more than conservation of natural resources or ecological consciousness was exclusively American.[25] These complexities were lost as American state power and the nation's importance in the world increased. The changes were closely associated with the rise of the United States to the status of a global power and a formal empire, even as empire itself conflicted with inherited attributes of the nation's exceptionalism.

There was another side to this discovery of the nation as a "nature-state."[26] As Americans discovered the power of "America" in nature, they also discovered the fragility of that power. The emergence of the United States as a nation with global aspirations coincided with the increased emphasis on the damage being done to American nature. If the nation's superiority resided in natural resources, their destruction raised troubling questions about how to maintain and advance the nation's supposedly special status in the face of massive environmental change. The old conviction of an especially bountiful nature was challenged by settler society's depredations not only in marginalizing American Indian tribes but also in threatening the life-support systems of water, forests, and fauna. These anxieties both coincided with and contributed to the rise of national Progressivism. The strengthening of the nation required a national resource policy, through a stronger state apparatus promoting national control over nature to conserve it for the better and long-term use that American abundance would require as an underpinning for exceptionalism.

It is significant that this challenge to American wastefulness was framed, as it was in other settler offshoots of the European empires around the same time, through a jeremiad of decline. The Progressive Era policies of conservation promoted by Theodore Roosevelt as President (1901–9) were couched in those terms, not only of nature's impending destruction nationally but globally as well. This new worldview reflected heightened interest in overseas possessions. In this way, the crisis of the frontier blended into the creation of an American empire abroad. From the Louisiana Purchase (1803) to the frontier's "closing" (1890), a settler colonial state had developed. But it was, by 1900, in the process of transfiguration into a modern nation-state with far-flung overseas colonies and bases. In the view of Progressives, these new circumstances demanded a rationalized and efficient government at home and conservation-minded objectives abroad to maximize American influence and leadership in the world. The new imperial polity that Theodore Roosevelt envisaged during his presidency would transcend the long settler phase of American development even as the settler process remained as a powerful undercurrent and memory of the nation's founding in the takeover of a rich land.[27]

Roosevelt did not emphasize national providentialism but national self-realization. In contributing to a nearly "world-wide movement" of "civilized nations" developing democracy, he argued that the nation's high status depended on the condition of the fittest, demonstrated through practical action on the part of an entire people under strenuous, moral leadership. Not ordained to be so by God or the impersonal forces of nature, the nation's people had to decide themselves to be exceptional. Still, chosenness remained an element in the rationalization of imperial expansion through the racial hierarchies underpinning Anglo-Saxon expansionism. The link came from Protestant missionaries and their growing prestige in American society.[28]

Chosenness and World Power

Whereas the use of terms such as *chosen nation, chosen country,* and *chosen people* was most common in the first half of the nineteenth century, the Protestant churches did not completely discard them as the nation embarked upon a course of imperial influence. The 1890s to 1914 saw the most dramatic expansion of Anglo-American Protestant missions as a collective enterprise, powered by the Student Volunteer Movement for Foreign Missions founded in 1886. As the United States gained in power and ambition after the Civil War, evangelicals felt more confident about the decisive American role within this cooperative international work of spreading Christian evangelism across the globe. That gave the idea of chosenness a new lease on life. The Congregational minister and Andover Seminary president Austin Phelps stated in 1881, "Ours is the elect nation for the age to come. We are the chosen people."[29] The purpose was not to reflect on American grandeur or political domination, however, but to spur American donors and would-be missionaries to act abroad in support of the "heathen." There was a strongly hierarchical air to these claims. In his best-selling *Our Country* (1885), the Reverend Josiah Strong asserted that "our plea is not America for America's sake; but America for the world's sake." Strong predicted that "America" would "become God's right arm in his battle with the world's ignorance and oppression and sin." This was not a statement of achievement but of hope grounded in postmillennial Social Gospel thought. In this way, it stirred among Protestant evangelicals the idea of a national religious singularity marking the future importance of the United States.[30]

It was from these sources that politicians drew at the time of the Spanish-American War. Albert Beveridge famously stated the starkest case for the United States becoming a colonial and global power. The Indiana senator's speech on the Philippines in January 1900 used the language of chosenness with unparalleled vigor: "We will not renounce our part in the mission of our race, trustee, under God, of the civilization of the world. And we will move forward to our work, . . . with gratitude for a task worthy of our strength and thanksgiving to Almighty God that He has marked us as His chosen people, henceforth to lead in the regeneration of the world."[31] Three times in his "March of the Flag" speech of September 1898 Beveridge had already asserted American chosenness to urge annexation of the Philippines. Yet his powerful rhetoric was that of racial and moral connection to the "civilization of the world," not a national pattern outside of history.[32]

Just as Beveridge did, the far less florid Alfred Thayer Mahan used chosenness to justify the exertion of American power on the global stage. Mahan's observations are highly significant because he was a major geopolitical theorist and confidante of cabinet members and Theodore Roosevelt. His opinions, moreover, carried almost theological weight. He served on the Board of Missions of the Protestant Episcopal Church and wrote in 1909 *The Harvest Within*, based on work commissioned for the World Missionary Conference of 1910 by the American delegation to that meeting.[33] Therein, Mahan noted, "The parallelism, in order of consequences, between the occupation of Canaan by the Israelites and the occupation of America by the English race, is so close" that "an American of to-day, . . . may reverently trace the comparison, and see in both the finger of God."[34] He listed the "successive events in history" from the early days of settlement, which were to Christians the "overruling of human action by Divine Providence" and which led to the growth of English power and liberty in America, and from there to world power.[35]

This chosen status was not, however, so much vested in a nation as in a race. In *The Harvest Within*, chosenness was hypercharged with social Darwinism and invoked a racial formation rather than one of either religion or democracy as a route to ultimate conversion of the world. This was not an American singularity. Mahan assumed an imminent Anglo-American moral and material domination, with the English-speaking people "launched upon the world." Britain and the United States had developed, he argued, a "peculiar tradition of liberty and law differing in forms but identical in spirit, to become in the end a common heritage of mankind."[36] That tradition had first been bred in English insularity, then in the isolation of the North American colonies, he insisted. Not only was the American status as chosen tempered by being racial and transimperial rather than national or republican. Mahan repeated the caveat that, in making merely a tentative judgment of the nation's standing in the eyes of God, he was "guarding himself from ignoring his [own] country's shortcomings."[37] Reflecting Mahan's ambivalence, the shift in world power changed the valence of the chosen nation idea in global context. It became harder to see the United States as purely elect, set aside from other nations, because it functioned in a world of imperialism. American exceptionalism had to be reassessed in the context of a growing international and cosmopolitan sentiment, and in terms of transnational connections made speedier and denser by the advent of steamships, railroads, and telegraph cables linking countries around the world.[38]

Imperialism

This sudden acquisition of overseas territories was one of the challenges to exceptionalism that had perturbed Turner. In response, Turner elaborated on his 1893 thesis in insightful essays around the turn of the century that make more sense if seen within the changing frame of the nation's new imperial role. The aftermath of the Spanish-American War prompted vigorous though minority opposition nationwide and also spurred a self-conscious anti-imperialist movement after the annexation of the Philippine Islands, Guam, and Puerto Rico. The American Anti-Imperialist League functioned from June 1898 until dissolved in 1920, but its most important years were those immediately after the war of 1898.

Generally, the anti-imperialists understood their cause as exposing American policy as an abandonment of exceptionalism. They argued that the nation's republican values precluded the holding of foreign people as subjects, not citizens, as was the case in the "island empire." In the eyes of critics, this abrogation of republicanism reduced the United States to just another colonial power, like those in Europe, and opponents argued that the negative effects on civil liberties and the American reputation abroad as a liberal democratic state would be irrevocable. (The critics did not, for the most part, extend this condemnation to the settlement process across the western frontier). The anti-imperialists of 1898 argued that, provided the new colonies were quickly freed, the nation's exalted honor could be regained, just as many abolitionists had before 1860 seen the freeing of slaves as essential to the proper gestation of American exceptionalism in the first place.[39]

Enthusiasm for formal empire had limits quickly reached. After a period in which the Roosevelt administration and its backers championed the idea of a "Greater America" with colonies, protectorates, and other acquisitions as far-flung as Manila, Guam, Pago Pago, Panama, Havana, and San Juan, the denial of empire's significance or even existence began to gel. By 1916, a U.S. policy of "Filipinization" of the Philippine Islands civil service was well under way, and changes to the status of other colonies and protectorates distanced the United States from criticism of its imperialist conduct. This action did not completely stop opposition, since colonial nationalists in the Philippines, Puerto Rico, and elsewhere, as well as Marxists and Progressives within the United States, continued to agitate and demand independence for colonial peoples. These antiexceptionalists exposed the United States as both a formal and—through its protectorates, bases, and trade policies—an informal empire in Latin America and the Pacific.[40]

Wilsonian Internationalism

The changing status and reputation of the American empire was also deeply affected by World War I and the role of Woodrow Wilson in that war. On the one hand, Wilson built on the new assertiveness of American power and the desire expressed already by Roosevelt that the world must be transformed in line with American interests in international engagement. Wilsonianism differed, however, in its effort to transcend unilateral internationalism of the type Roosevelt had frequently exercised.

Wilsonianism has become a touchstone for the United States as a liberal exceptionalist nation and defender of democracy. In this context, the chosen nation idea made its last appearance in presidential rhetoric until the modern resurgence of the idea in the 1980s. Wilson is the most often quoted president on a Christian crusader status for the United States in the twentieth century.[41] Yet even he, despite his Christian moralism and his well-known Presbyterian missionary background from his father, stopped short of depicting the United States in explicitly chosen nation terms. The historian Malcolm Magee has argued that Wilson "believed the United States was divinely chosen to do God's will on earth," but he did not quote the words directly from Wilson.[42] The closest presidential statement was Wilson's 1912 electioneering assertion that "liberty" was "planted" by God in the American people. The then-presidential candidate expressed "the *hope* that we are chosen, and *prominently* chosen, to show the way to the nations of the world how they shall walk in the paths of liberty."[43] This was a conventional nineteenth-century exceptionalist endorsement of U.S. political and economic institutions as a model for the world, but it did not sanction intervention in it. Wilson did not say the United States was already "blessed among the nations," but he did say that he hoped it would be so viewed in the future, if the nation continued to pursue a policy of peace and prosperity amid the European war begun in 1914.[44] In any event, embroilment in war after 1917 tarnished this roseate image.

Despite his own missionary inflection, Wilson followed a shrewdly realist approach in which zeal for the export of American ideals did not exceed the geopolitical and economic considerations that he regarded as national interests. These he defended through an exertion of American political, financial, military, and diplomatic power in a fashion that would do justice to many an advocate of realpolitik in foreign relations. His prewar ruthlessness in the measured application of military and economic force against a turbulent and revolutionary Mexico pointed in this direction; so too his intervention in World War I. His campaign for a new postimperial economic system with the League of Nations at its centerpiece was designed to secure American global interests in a world in which the European balance of power had, by war and the Russian Revolution, been terminally overturned.[45] But, with Wilsonian diplomacy over the Treaty of Versailles negotiations and ratification failing in 1919–20, and in the light of his own vacillations regarding the declaration of religious freedom he wished nations to adopt under that treaty, the idea of the United States as a chosen nation destined for world leadership was damaged at home and abroad.[46]

By the 1920s it was possible for the public to regard the nation's flirtation with empire as finished. The colonies and protectorates were, with the exception of the Philippine Islands, relatively small places at a time when American power derived increasingly from its industrial base. This much was demonstrated in the impressive World War I mobilization of material resources and troops to help defeat Germany. Even more so after the establishment of an internally self-governing Commonwealth of the Philippines in 1935, the issue of the island possessions receded in public memory. The remnant colonies could be more easily concealed from public view. That led the eminent diplomatic historian Samuel Flagg Bemis in 1936 to describe American empire as the "great aberration of 1898"—a hasty transgression at odds with the nation's core liberal tradition, yet one quickly rectified.[47] Thereafter the idea of the United States as an anticolonial nation was reasserted as an exceptionalist trait, and anticolonialism was soon applied by the Franklin D. Roosevelt administration in judgment of European colonial empires during and after World War II. The holding by the United States of overseas territory became less important except as strategic platforms for naval and air power. That almost "hidden" residue of empire remained, however, and in fact grew surreptitiously into an "empire" of overseas bases after 1945.[48]

For all the intensity of American colonialism as an exceptionalist crisis, within the mainland United States it was an embarrassment more easily swept under the rug than the other late nineteenth-century challenges to the republic's special status, owing to the strength of liberal exceptionalist beliefs that did not probe much beyond the surface of American conduct abroad, ignored the acquisition and retention of other American outposts in the Pacific and Atlantic oceans, and failed to understand the full significance of settler colonial expansion across the American West.[49] It was the focus on specifically "overseas" colonies in the liberal theory of empire that allowed the United States to dismiss its settler colonial history. Not until the early part of the twenty-first century have historians and social theorists begun to consider the analytical apparatus of settler colonialism as the basis of a continental empire back to 1776.

Two Isms: Americanism and Socialism

The challenge of immigration and the growth of ethnic enclaves proved to be a more enduring problem for American exceptionalism than land, labor, or a formal empire abroad. Exceptionalism as a patriotic doctrine often rested on openness toward immigration, but in the late nineteenth century, intolerance toward immigrants challenged this image. Exceptionalism did not disappear; instead, open and restrictive interpretations of American ideals clashed, and exceptionalist elements were incorporated into both. The received interpretation in public memory reflected words emblazoned on a plaque at the base of the Statue of Liberty in 1903. There, poet Emma Lazarus's sonnet encapsulated the welcoming attitude toward immigrants, including the poor, the tired, and the huddled masses. Written in 1883, the poem had become a perverse reflection of social reality by the time the plaque was placed, since more and more Americans wished to abandon the generous immigration policy associated with liberal exceptionalist values.

Ethnonationalism and Racial Exclusion

Long before then, immigration spurred reactionary ideas of defending American values through a self-styled "Americanism." That concept is a slippery one that changed over time, however, and it comprised both inclusive and exclusionary impulses. The latter was first associated with the American (or Know-Nothing) Party in the 1850s. As seen in chapter 6, antebellum nativists championed an exceptionalism in which American values were identified with native-born whites and their descendants, but the crosshairs of religion complicated this simple split.[1] To nativists, Americanism meant an exclusionist policy directly more specifically toward Catholic immigrants.

Ironically, in the late nineteenth century an international controversy within the Roman Catholic Church occurred over what Pope Leo XIII called the heresy of "Americanism," where the meaning differed from the nativist version. Catholics who assimilated to American life were obliquely accused by the pope of undermining universal Catholic rituals and faith. The pope's *Testem Benevolentiae Nostrae* (1899) criticizing Catholics' apparent adaptation to American religious pluralism was a wild card in nativist politics. On the one hand, the pope's longing for a stronger and more uniform bond with the American church confirmed nativist fantasies about a dark ambition on the part of Rome to interfere in American politics. On the other hand, American Catholics were themselves divided in multiple ways over how much adaptation should occur (for example, regarding specific "national" or ethnic parishes among Catholic immigrants).[2] The intra-Catholic controversy demonstrated how malleable a concept Americanism could be, since the nativist demand was a weapon directed against the very people whom the pope condemned as being too American because they wanted to Americanize the nation's Catholicism. (In a second irony, the pope's futile attempt to curb American Catholic exceptionalism presaged the later efforts of Joseph Stalin to oppose any American exception to the prospects for global socialist revolution.)

The pope's usage of *Americanism* was confusing because it strayed into a debate in which the term's meaning had already been preempted for a xenophobic, anti-Catholic movement. The American Party as a mercurial political entity did not survive the rivalry between South and North culminating in the Civil War. But ethnoexceptionalism resurfaced in American politics, with a shifting basis. Even though the American Protective Association was formed in 1887 and prospered for several years by harping on the old anti-Catholic theme, it was riven with internal rivalries and poor leadership. It failed to influence national politics and did not address squarely what was novel in the so-called new immigration of the 1880s and 1890s, a phenomenon that made mere anti-Catholicism an ineffectual response. More successful were groups targeting the race or ethnicity of immigrants rather than the Catholic beliefs of what was by then a large and increasingly respectable segment of the voting population. The sheer volume and heterogeneity of the post-Civil War immigration required new solutions, even as Protestant hostility toward Catholics persisted. At the level of the social elite, these fresh approaches highlighted institutional reform, the use of expertise, and appeals to "science" to a degree far more than the older social protest against Catholics could encompass.[3] The new nativists sought to prohibit the entry of many immigrant groups, Catholic or not. The poor, anarchists, mental "defectives," and all racially inferior "stock" were barred. The targets of this venom included

Chinese, Japanese, Slavic, and Mediterranean people, as well as a religious miscellany of Eastern Orthodox Christians and Jews arriving from the 1880s to 1914. The erosion of the nation's Protestant foundations and the desire to preserve the position of old-stock Americans turned nativism into a racialized ethnonationalism.

Organized in 1894, the Immigration Restriction League (IRL) provides a window into the ideas of the new exclusionism, but not its electoral power. The IRL supplied intellectual leadership but found it harder to achieve legislative exclusion of Europeans than Asians. The 1882 Chinese Exclusion Act revealed the existence of a broad consensus on the unsuitability of "servile" nonwhite immigrants, which extended after 1908 to Japanese and later to Filipino newcomers, but not a consensus on European arrivals. Many Americans still believed the Europeans could be assimilated, even as they came increasingly from other parts of Europe than earlier arrivals. For this reason, the IRL needed to depict cultural and religious differences as immovable racial characteristics not amenable to "Americanization." A racialist nationalism grew from the 1890s to the 1920s and proposed restricted immigrant entry, with physical appearance and biology rather than nation or religion as the decisive points of difference. The IRL could not do this work alone. Wider congressional support for immigration restriction came through the influential Dillingham Commission of the U.S. Congress (1907–10), which, after extensive investigation, reported that the newcomers presented the nation with a serious social, economic, and political "immigration problem."[4]

The nativists of the IRL did not initially claim to represent an explicit ideology of Americanism. Drawing on the older American Idea of the mid-nineteenth century as a shared sentiment, they spoke of "American Ideals," a code for tradition and a presumed history of racial and cultural homogeneity. In contrast, "Americanism" would logically need to include all people born in or assimilated into the country, including the sons and daughters of immigrants and, at least notionally, African Americans and American Indians. This was too racially inclusive a position for the elitist, Protestant, and upper-class social stratum supporting the IRL.

National greatness was not born of the whole population, the IRL argued; rather, it reflected a "common racial origin" promoting "homogeneous institutions" and "the amalgamation of the people into a fairly definite national type." Acceptable immigrants should be Northern Europeans. They would restore the characteristics of early America, from which "energy, initiative, and self-reliance" were derived. Such "Baltic" or "Nordic" types—both these questionable categories were used—appeared to exhibit many of the values associated with American exceptionalism. As explained by one of the IRL leaders, Prescott Farnsworth Hall, these Northern European types were "impatient of much government, relying upon self-help rather than the paternalism of the State" and "firm" in allegiance to "certain pretty definite religious and social standards."[5] Without that common cultural origin at its heart, the IRL considered Americanism valueless. The group looked to the past as the source of a racial exceptionalism to preserve: it erected a historical interpretation of the nation's founding in which an exceptional status was explicit. It portrayed the founders of the U.S. Constitution as biologically homogeneous, in order to create the desired racialized tradition. "Even in the days of sparse settlement Washington, Adams, Jefferson and many others were strong in their demand for immigration restriction," Hall claimed.[6]

It was Madison Grant who pushed these ideas to the extreme. The lawyer, conservationist, lobbyist, and IRL member burst into national attention over eugenics in 1916 with *The Passing of the Great Race* and summed up the implications for the United States in 1933 in his *Conquest of a Continent*. In the latter work, Grant brandished a sweeping reinterpretation of U.S. history based on racial features that determined the republic's moral character. He found exceptionalism in the Puritans, not because of their religion or their "chosenness" but because they were physically "Nordic," and therefore mentally and morally superior for developing a new continent.[7] "Nordic blood was kept pure in the colonies," he suggested in his 1916 book. Though some intermixture occurred with Africans and Indians, he labeled those groups "inferior" stock that could be controlled by the white majority, as he believed they were by whites in the postbellum South and border states.[8] Hailing the "Nordic" origins of American institutions, he and his supporters depicted the Founding Fathers as cementing the "moral tendency" which made a special nation. Henry Fairfield Osborn, a distinguished paleontologist, museum director, and president of the New York Zoological Society, endorsed these opinions in his preface to *The Passing of the Great Race*. For Osborn, Nordic characteristics had created the superior democratic institutions commonly considered exceptional.[9]

To anti-immigrationists, the growing racial complexity of American society threatened to undermine that superiority. Immigration that was not of a common racial origin could destroy republicanism because of the characteristics that "inferior" immigrants brought with them. The immigrant threatened, nativists charged, to Europeanize and Asianize America and to blur the dichotomy between Old World and New. Osborn lamented "the gradual dying out among our people of those hereditary traits through which the principles of our religious, political and social foundations were laid down."[10] This prejudice extended even to influential advocates of workers' rights. According to economist John Commons of the University of Wisconsin in 1907, the American state had already "begun to despotize our institutions in order to deal with large masses of [immigrant] citizens not capable of intelligently supporting representative government."[11] In the nativists' view, the wrong kind of immigrants would produce a new and authoritarian polity in which native-born people were deprived of their rights. The consideration of certain European newcomers as bearers of a despotic political culture, associated with the Old World and its "monarchies," portended a merging of race and political exceptionalism through the criterion of literacy. The IRL official Prescott Hall charged that "the monarchical, semi-feudalistic, economically backward nations," from whose ranks unsuitable immigrants were coming, had "public education systems inadequate either in plan or administration"; their populations showed "a high percentage of illiteracy."[12] Such illiterates could be easily manipulated by priests and political bosses, using irrational appeals to religion or ethnicity. They would become a potential drain on democratic institutions. Change to a more restrictive policy was needed "not merely for our own sake, but that the United States may continue strong to uphold the cause of democracy and liberty throughout the world," Hall contended.[13] The IRL demand for a literacy test to exclude racially and mentally incompetent people was intended not only to protect domestic society but also to preserve the tenets of exceptionalism as an international example.

Immigration restriction did not easily prevail, and it actually took the charged atmosphere of World War I to achieve the political momentum for rigorous exclusion. First proposed in the 1880s, the legislation for a literacy test was vetoed by three U.S. presidents before being implemented over the protest of President Woodrow Wilson in 1917. Mass organizations such as the American Legion and the Ku Klux Klan that emerged between 1915 and 1920 with an antiforeign, antiradical agenda propelled the restrictive immigration agenda into law.[14] However, these groups mirrored or drew on the ideas of the IRL.

The nativists behind this legislative campaign were highly nationalistic and professedly patriotic, but singling out race as a characteristic did not mean a nation was truly exceptional. As was so often the case with other forms of exceptionalism, nativists were not sure how exceptional the United States actually was. In fact, almost by definition the United States was not. The late nineteenth-century era of high international migration had meant that correlations between race and place had become weakened, creating much racialist anxiety.[15] The IRL counted the United States as *among* the "modern industrial" nations.[16] This formulation allowed the IRL to endorse Northwestern Europe as the compatible "Nordic" site from which to draw new residents. The league drew from European racial thought and the mass psychology of French social theorist Gustave Le Bon to justify this de facto departure from exceptionalism. Influential senator Henry Cabot Lodge invoked Le Bon on racially specific "moral characteristics" in human evolution to justify exclusion of immigrants.[17] For Le Bon, "too large a preponderance of foreigners (meaning those foreign in ideas and customs)" destroyed "that most vital possession of a nation—its own soul." Paraphrasing Le Bon, the IRL through Hall attributed the "downfall of nearly every great civilization" in large part to "the peaceful invasion of large numbers of persons having different aims and customs."[18] Le Bon opined on the threat in Europe of mobs, riots, and revolutions, and he proclaimed the irrational nature of each, but the IRL thought his work applicable to shore up the absence of a mobbish revolution in America.

Invoking Le Bon put ethnonationalists on dangerous ground for American exceptionalism. It meant that their plight in defending national distinctiveness and uniqueness was shared with kindred "races" because whites everywhere were said to be smothered by a succession of nonwhite peoples as part of a worldwide challenge to white supremacy. This shared basis of ethnoexceptionalism in *The Passing of the Great Race* signified a global, not a national, "problem." The mechanism chosen to restore an imagined racial purity was a borrowed product too. Anti-immigrationists believed that U.S. entry restrictions were extraordinarily light by international standards and ought to be changed, using international examples. "It may be noted that the exclusion of Orientals from Australia, New Zealand and Canada is much more rigid than from the United States," observed Hall.[19] One could almost say that "We're all in this together" was the message being preached by the IRL to whites around the world. In reality, American ethnoexceptionalism was an expression of the transnational transfer of white nationalist sentiment.[20]

For the IRL, Americanization of immigrants was not a credible alternative because it suggested that assimilation could work. Grant denounced "the folly of the 'Melting Pot.'"[21] That exceptionalist metaphor could never be made into a viable program, immigration restrictionists argued, partly because of the immigrants' social and ethnic composition, and partly because of the sheer numbers to be assimilated. By 1921, the same IRL spokespeople who lobbied for the literacy test became advocates of overt racial prohibitions through immigration quotas: "Exclude the black, the brown and the yellow altogether; as to the white, favor the immigration of Nordic and Nordicized stocks."[22]

The culmination of this racially virulent pseudoscience was the 1924 Immigration Act. It embodied quotas for European immigrants by nation while almost totally excluding nonwhites from outside the Western Hemisphere. This act reflected the long-term work of the IRL and the short-term pressure of mass European immigration to the United States as a result of the world war. The "true spirit of Americanism," as Osborn put it, rested not on the melting pot, or wartime Americanization, but on the preservation of the dominant culture through conscious selection of a superior race. The act's demographic effects would shape a more racially "white" America for four decades thereafter.[23]

By concentrating on the notion of a superior race located in a nation-state, ethnonationalists drew on exceptionalism. The 1924 act linked race to the political ideology of national exceptionalism and made the latter a question of erecting hard borders between peoples. As Senator Ellison DuRant Smith of South Carolina put it, "Thank God we have in America perhaps the largest percentage of any country in the world of the pure, unadulterated Anglo-Saxon stock; certainly, the greatest of any nation in the Nordic breed. It is for the preservation of that splendid stock that has characterized us that I would make this not an asylum for the oppressed of all countries, but a country to assimilate and perfect that splendid type of manhood that has made America the foremost Nation in her progress and in her power, and yet the youngest of all the nations."[24] The United States would become a global example, but that included being a "model" against which other nations could test their racial policies. The German Nazi Party leader Adolf Hitler found the Madison Grant version in *The Passing of the Great Race* inspiring.[25]

The Civic Alternative

There was an alternative to this fierce ethnoexceptionalism—a more inclusive Americanism that we may consider civic nationalism. Ironically, in view of the earlier intolerance in the Know-Nothing movement and the American Protective Association, *Americanism* as a term had actually been deployed in the 1890s to combat ethnonationalism. This more inclusive Americanism was associated with the work of Theodore Roosevelt. In "What 'Americanism' Means" (1894), the future president attempted to distinguish the term from the rantings of anti-immigrationists. Roosevelt challenged racial conservatism with his "truest" and "most sincere and intense" form of "Americanism."[26] He called the American Protective Association "un-American" for wishing to "proscribe Catholics both politically and socially."[27] Roosevelt's version of Americanism was, historian Gary Gerstle points out, aiming to be as inclusive as possible while insisting on the value of nationalist sentiments tying a people together.[28] Despite his reputation as an imperialist and advocate of Anglo-Saxon superiority, Roosevelt was quite close in his Americanism to modern ideas of a liberal or cosmopolitan exceptionalism. "Our nation is that one among all the nations of the earth which holds in its hands the fate of the coming years. We enjoy exceptional advantages, and are menaced by exceptional dangers; and all signs indicate that we shall either fail greatly or succeed greatly. I firmly believe that we shall succeed; but we must not foolishly blink the dangers by which we are threatened, for that is the way to fail," he wrote. He believed the Anglo-Saxons must lead the world but understood Anglo-Saxonism as a mixture of peoples, not a distinct "race." He favored the melting-pot metaphor and borrowed ideas of social reform from overseas, including Europe and the colonies of the British Empire.[29]

Not everybody agreed, of course. Liberal pluralists of the time tried to divorce Americanism from its Anglo-Saxon roots. Harvard academic Horace Kallen and the antiwar critic Randolph Bourne were prominent in this intellectual work.[30] They hoped in various ways to assimilate both immigrants and native-born people into a new cultural identity that transcended the parochial stance and ethnic particularism of hierarchical Anglo-Saxon values. Yet, until the 1930s, theirs were the ideas of a minority with little influence in national politics.[31] Moreover, attacking Americanism, whether from these points of view or not, was tricky because the target was always a moving one.

Roosevelt likewise understood that Americanism was a capacious notion, with many nuances, pitfalls, and changes over time. Victorian era morality and sensibilities rather than race motived him, but his more temperate form of Americanism did not survive the coming of World War I.[32] Before the war there were still hopes of immigrants freely mixing cultures through "the Melting Pot." The metaphor was publicized by the Anglo-Jewish writer Israel Zangwill, in his play of that name in 1908; it endorsed assimilation and was very popular. The hero proclaims, "America is God's Crucible, the great Melting-Pot where all the races of Europe are melting and reforming . . . Germans and Frenchmen, Irishmen and Englishmen, Jews and Russians—into the Crucible with you all! God is making the American."[33] This was exceptionalist doctrine par excellence, though the metaphor did not include equal opportunity for nonwhites. It denied not only cross-racial comity but also the transnational loyalties and cultural pluralism that Bourne and Kallen, respectively, analyzed, and it gave God an interventionist role in the creation of the United States as a special nation.

World War I intensified the search for a strong sense of nationalism based on cultural conformity and revealed how marginalized cultural pluralists were. In 1917–18, the sentiment of Americanism became institutionalized in "The

American's Creed." It was reminiscent of the American Idea of the 1850s as a projected national consensus, but with a more elaborate content and ritual. The reference to *creed* suggested a religious basis, and so marked a stage in the explicit articulation of a civil religion. This wartime initiative gave Americans a standard political faith to recite, and one that exuded ideas associated with exceptionalism. The author of "The American's Creed," William Tyler Page, the clerk of the U.S. House of Representatives, strung together a brief statement of American liberal, republican, and democratic tenets taken from the Declaration of Independence, the Gettysburg Address, and other prized political texts. Cited by community groups and recited in schools, the House endorsed it in 1918, and the Daughters of the American Revolution (DAR) embraced it as part of its public rituals of nationalism.[34] From this time on, both critics and supporters of American exceptionalism have referenced various versions of an American Creed to measure the conformity to or deviation of the nation from its exceptional ideological origins, based not on ethnic but politico-ideological values. They have often equated the elements of this creed with Americanism.[35]

Though the wartime institutionalization of an American Creed served as a political bulwark for the American state, World War I's disruptive impact simultaneously called the exceptionalism of that creed into question. In the process, Roosevelt's compromise of "true Americanism" as a liberal or "civic" nationalism gave way. The war's circumstances brought the United States into conflict with foreign powers, breached American political isolation from Europe, and arguably crammed several decades of cultural change into just a few hectic years. Advocacy of Americanism continued but turned toward heightened patriotism and an exclusionist stance demanding ideological conformity. With "German-American" fealty in doubt, the question of divided loyalties among those identified as "hyphenated" became key. Roosevelt himself took this stance against "hyphenated Americans" in the lead up to American entry into the war.[36] In this context, the "true" version hardened into "100 percent Americanism." The latter doctrine was appropriated by the American Legion, formed in 1919 among military veterans to instill a patriotic and coercive nationalism in the increasingly polyglot nation.[37]

In the wake of the war, public anxiety over immigrants had added to it fears of political heresy against the American tradition now embodied in a formal creed. Foreigners were suspected of importing anarchism or communism. Now, Americanism gathered new connotations; it came to emphasize the social question of class conflict. To be an American was to favor free enterprise and to oppose communism, socialism, syndicalism, and Bolshevism in vituperative and Manichean fashion.[38] This reactive identity formation was not entirely new; elements could be traced back at least to the 1880s and the Haymarket trial, but the elision of "foreign" and "communist" or "anarchist" as the enemy of national identity was revealed as the new core of Americanism after 1918. The Sacco and Vanzetti affair of 1920, with its anarchist bombers in Massachusetts, crystallized the issue.[39] In the 1920s, the American Legion, the DAR, and other right-wing groups joined a chorus pestering school boards and state legislatures to eliminate "subversive" material from the nation's civics and history texts.[40]

Americanism and the Threat of Socialism

The hyperbolic wartime crusade against socialists and communists culminated in the Red Scare that peaked in 1919–20. Radicals were imprisoned and some even deported or, in the case of the Italian anarchists Nicola Sacco and Bartolomeo Vanzetti, executed, all in the name of Americanism and anticommunism. In this context, *Americanism* became a source of ideological polarization, with foreign nationals and international commentators also using the term, chiefly to denounce American capitalism. For foreign radicals, to be *against* Americanism became a rallying point. To do so, it was necessary to acknowledge its "reality" as the regnant expression of American distinctiveness. True anti-Americanism depended on the explicit image of Americanism as a coherent ideological foil for radicals to contest. But, in doing so, foreign observers helped make the new political xenophobia of postwar America seem not only nationally distinctive and coherent but also exceptional. Socialists and others labeled antiradicalism the natural tendency of Americanism, and they condemned the latter as the enemy of global social democracy. In singling out the United States, international critics endorsed a (negative) notion of exceptionalism. This was a change from the mid-nineteenth century, when, more often than not, American values seemed to stand, among radicals abroad, for the positive extension of democracy and the enhanced rights of common people. Through the outcome of the Civil War, this democratic image had been renewed, and it was registered in the Statue of Liberty's meaning as a welcoming symbol of liberal opportunity. The international reception of the image of the United States was never uniform, to be sure, and positive and negative images continued to be held by foreign observers during the late nineteenth and early twentieth centuries.[41] Nevertheless, European radicals, socialists, and even some liberals became more critical of American institutions, as inequality and the growth of both corporate and state power became evident.[42]

While labor strife before World War I confirmed the increasingly negative image of the United States among labor parties and trade unions abroad, the result of the war intensified radical critiques. This criticism occurred because of the nation's enhanced international power, demonstrated in wartime participation, and Woodrow Wilson's prominence at the Versailles Peace Conference. American suppression of radicalism at home and military aid abroad for the anticommunist White Russian resistance after the Bolshevik Revolution seemed to verify a growing ideological polarization globally. Writing in the shadow of World War I, radicals used "Americanism" as a synonym for an evil ideology of a rising world empire encroaching on Europe. For many European socialists, to be anti-American was not to be against the people of the United States but rather the export of its ideological system. The Anglo-American communist William T. Colyer conjured up the image in *Americanism: A World Menace*. A British national and alien resident of Boston, Colyer and his wife Amy faced deportation in the early 1920s for their antiwar activism and role in nascent American communist politics.[43] The prominent left-wing British trade unionist Tom Mann endorsed their position.[44] Though the analysis was sharpened by Colyer's specific personal experience of state intrusiveness and repression, what is significant about his work was the way he portrayed Americanism as a cultural and social formation. Therein, social issues such as religion, racial bigotry, and gender discrimination figured as well as class, while the immense economic productivity of the United States was recognized as key to Americanism's potential impact abroad.

Colyer was common among left-wingers in depicting Americanism as a distinctively American manifestation of capitalism threatening the world, but anti-Americanism in Europe was by no means restricted to radicals. Conservatives feared the incursion of cheap American consumer goods and the "vulgar" cultural attitudes associated with that consumerism. The potential economic impact in Europe of Americanization helped disperse quite widely the concept of Americanism as a global danger.[45] On the other hand, at least one singularly important Marxist abroad saw more hope than fear in Americanism. Written in the late 1920s, the Italian Marxist Antonio Gramsci's essay "Americanism and Fordism" posited American culture and its impact on Europe not as exceptional but as a new phase in capitalist production from which a powerful mass culture was derived. Gramsci believed that "Americanism" as a concept needed to be broken down to strip it of its exceptionalist characteristics. Its core was not the ubiquitous cultural influence but a specific economic formation of mass production and consumption on which the culture was based. This dynamic driver of change, which Gramsci labeled

"Fordism," could be helpful, he thought, to the world's working classes as a way of removing feudalistic elements from European social structures. His argument's subtleties have been noted and debated, but one simple point usually missed is the way Gramsci's use of the concept disclosed the common transatlantic discourse that posited Henry Ford's assembly-line methods, and modern American movies and advertising, as parts of a nascent U.S. cultural hegemony in the new world order of the 1920s.[46] Gramsci's antiexceptionalist work on Americanism was, however, composed furtively and fragmentedly in an Italian prison, and it was little known in the Anglophone world until translated into English decades later. Other European thinkers on socialism made a more immediate and cruder impact on the idea of American exceptionalism.

Most socialists abroad, like those within the United States, approached the phenomenon of Americanism through a more conventional and purely economic analysis of capitalism's inner logic than Gramsci's. In this line of thought, the United States needed to be assimilated to Marxist orthodoxy, thus denying exceptionalism entirely. Perversely, socialist analysis also became, through the clashes within international socialism, the source for the emergence of American exceptionalism as an explicit concept and theory of history. Discussion of the United States in terms of its capitalist production was already well established in the mid- to late nineteenth century, but the Marxist understanding of American distinctiveness did not emerge from relative obscurity until the Progressive Era.[47]

Socialism and American Exceptionalism

The period from the 1890s to 1919 witnessed recurrent crises in the relations of American capital and labor, with the blue-collar workforce reaching its zenith and industrial strikes becoming endemic. The exceptionalist question was necessarily connected to this conflict, but American labor and socialist responses were divided. Some radicals sided with Daniel De Leon and the small Socialist Labor Party, with which he was briefly affiliated. They advocated class struggle well before the Bolshevik Revolution of 1917. Taking a syndicalist approach stressing the organization of workers into industrial unions, with strike action the main theme of class resistance, De Leon depicted the United States as the modern vanguard of revolutionary politics. In 1906, he told the Socialist International, "If my reading of history is correct, . . . the prophecy of Marx will be fulfilled and America will ring the downfall of capitalism the world over."[48] In contrast, the larger Socialist Party of America, founded in 1901, was gradualist and reformist. In some cities, most prominently Milwaukee, socialists campaigned for practical urban reform to alleviate the condition of working-class people, while not abandoning the ideal of an eventual socialist outcome.[49] Yet even moderate socialists did not tend to see the United States as a true exception to development of the capitalist mode of production, although they did identify elements of American singularity in class formation. The German political economist Werner Sombart made the most extensive statement in this "vulgar materialist" vein.[50] For decades thereafter, Sombart continued to influence American socialists and liberals as a result of his study of socialism's "absence" in the United States.

Now considered a major statement of U.S. exceptionalism, Sombart's American observations are better understood as part of the transnational discourse over labor's place in the Progressive Era's social order.[51] The challenge to exceptionalism posed by strikes and the growth of labor unions sent American social reformers and academics abroad to find models for changing the social structure and implementing egalitarian reform. Europeans returned the compliment by visiting North America. Sombart was among them. He was in close contact with his "middle-class American friends" and American "experts," and he vetted his work with them.[52] In addition, Sombart acquired some personal knowledge of the great republic. He joined his fellow German academic Max Weber at the Congress of Arts and Science at the Universal Exposition in St. Louis in 1904. At that time, Sombart was a self-proclaimed socialist, but not a revolutionary. Working from an academic position rather than an activist one, he became disillusioned with socialism by 1913 and later emerged as a supporter of National Socialism—better known as Nazism.[53] Yet his unsavory intellectual destination should not obscure his importance in posing critical social questions for American democracy during the Progressive Era. In 1906, Sombart put the explicit question succinctly: Why is there no socialism in the United States? It became the classic way to frame American exceptionalism, considered in opposition to a supposedly socialist inclined Europe.

Despite the intellectual weight given to Sombart as a witness to exceptionalism, the irony is that Sombart did not actually embrace the notion. As historian Walter McDougall has explained, "nowhere did Sombart employ any word that could be fairly translated as exceptionalism."[54] More important than his terminology, Sombart rejected the very idea of an American "character" outside the laws of history. He poured scorn on the notion of an "idiosyncratic 'American spirit' that dropped out of the blue on to this chosen people for no particular reason and contrary to principles of social causation."[55] Rather, the United States exhibited the social conditions in which the general laws of capital could operate without restraint. That put the United

States within history's evolution, not separate from it; nor did he typecast it as a chosen nation. Sounding much like Frederick Jackson Turner in describing key social conditions, Sombart made abundant American resources and the frontier experience crucial to explaining class revolution's lack of appeal. Material conditions in such a "land of promise," with its ample supplies of raw materials, such as "precious metals" and "fertile soils," favored capitalism's full development.[56] The "mere knowledge" that he could become a "free farmer," Sombart concluded, "could not but make the American worker feel secure and content," compared with a "European counterpart."[57] This was akin to Turner's "safety-valve" argument.

Sombart's materialist analysis left open the possibility of an eventual conformity of the United States to the socialist revolution and the end of Americans' alleged disdain for socialism. He made exactly this point—that the factors preventing the development of socialism were "about to disappear" or be "converted into their opposite." Predicting that U.S. socialism would "very probably experience the greatest expansion of its appeal" over "the next few years," Sombart felt that the transition to class conflict needed more "thorough analysis," which he did not have time to undertake in 1906.[58] Perhaps Sombart's prediction was a gesture of socialist hope over the realities of academic despair, but it was a common stance among socialists before 1917 in the United States. In any case, academic and personal factors intervened. Sombart's career took a different direction, his support for German social democracy eroded, and the further theoretical work he promised was never done, leaving his position on American singularity an ambiguous one. He died a lonely figure during Hitler's war in 1941, but Sombart's earlier appraisal of socialist absence was not his alone. It was the product of his interaction with American colleagues and reflected the milieu of American socialism as well as Progressivism and European social theory.

Contrary to Sombart, it was not the natural evolution of capitalism that brought change. Instead, the contingencies of World War I disrupted moderate socialism and raised once more the question of the American nation's possible revolutionary future. The collapse of the German and Austro-Hungarian Empires appeared to portend major social changes and the rise in several European nations of a working class no longer willing to die in imperialist wars. A more radical socialism was emboldened by these events. The success of the Bolsheviks under V. I. Lenin in overthrowing the Russian tsar and establishing a communist state (1917–1922) was without precedent, and it split the socialist movement in Western countries, including the American Socialist Party. From this split came the forerunner of the Communist Party of the United States of America (CPUSA), which adhered to a Leninist position. This stance ordained that the revolution in Russia, not in an advanced capitalist country like the United States, would be the spark precipitating a world revolution. In Russia, Leon Trotsky pushed this idea until he fell out with the communist leadership and was eventually exiled, only to be targeted for assassination in Mexico in 1940. Though Trotsky's followers continued to believe in world revolution, they embraced the idea of combined and uneven development to explain why a communist revolution had occurred first in the least developed of the major European powers, Russia, which had "jumped the queue," as it were, of socialist parties waiting for the revolutionary millennium.[59]

It was in this world-historical situation of communism's arrival as a revolutionary force that the actual term *American exceptionalism* entered debate. Marxists were already much given to the conceptualization of "isms." They ideologized everything in political thought and sought systematic answers to tactical questions of political action. Lenin himself made the first known socialist references to "exceptionalism" in the mid-1890s, but, ironically, he was not at that time thinking about the United States. It was Russian exceptionalism that Lenin detected, because Russia's peculiar mix of rural backwardness and rapid proletarianization in industrializing towns posed obstacles for the interpretation of a Marxist revolutionary transformation. Lenin rejected the idea that the rural radicalism of the populist Narodniks made Russia exceptional. In 1897, he denounced "Narodism" for its "belief in Russia's exceptionalism, idealization of the peasantry, [and] the village community" because such an ideology obstructed the true development of a forward-looking proletariat.[60]

The Lovestoneite "Deviation"

Bizarrely, the Russian exceptionalism that Lenin in the 1890s professed to loathe appeared to be confirmed by the appearance of revolution in economically "backward" Russia after 1917. Yet the body tasked with exporting revolution abroad, the Comintern, still strove to create a picture of seething global masses about to follow the Russian example and create revolutionary situations in more "advanced" capitalist countries. Only from 1926 to 1928 did the Union of Soviet Socialist Republics change official tack to pursue Socialism in One Country, a policy which Lenin's successor as leader, Joseph Stalin, concluded was necessary because the revolutionary potential in Western industrial countries had been exaggerated. It was in this context—of bewildering changes in factional and strategic postures within international communism over the correct course of action for world revolution—that *American exceptionalism* arose as a term and a pejorative.

In the United States, the "Workers" (Communist) Party and its titular successor, the CPUSA, faced pressure from Comintern policy to conform. Granted, all communist parties outside Russia theoretically took orders from the Comintern, with that international communist organization firmly under Moscow's control. Western communist ideology and practice tended therefore to parrot the Soviet line, which in the American case meant accepting that the United States was building inexorably toward a class-based revolution despite evidence to the contrary. The growth of the U.S. economy in the 1920s and the failure of labor to make decisive inroads in what was a strike-prone decade brought some American communists to question Comintern tactics.[61]

As leader of the party from 1927 to 1929, the Lithuanian-American Jay Lovestone clashed with the Moscow-aligned faction associated with William Z. Foster. Lovestone and his allies, including John Pepper (Józef Pogány), a Hungarian Communist and self-proclaimed Comintern operative working in the United States, argued, as Sombart had done, that the conditions for revolution were not yet favorable.[62] Pepper and another colleague, the Swedish-American J. Louis Engdahl, asserted that capitalism was "still on its upward trend in America." In their view, the United States was the "single big industrial country in which there does not exist a mass political party of the proletariat."[63] The U.S. working class had a "privileged position" and mostly adhered to bourgeois parties. This meant that any communist organization was "small" and unlikely to challenge the capitalists and imperialists in the short term.[64] Lovestone and his allies did not abandon Marxist revolution as the ultimate goal, but they were expelled in 1929 on Comintern orders for the error of "exceptionalism."[65] Thereafter, Lovestone led a splinter group, the Communist Party (Opposition).[66]

Curiously enough, Stalin's critique of Lovestone made no reference to the term *American exceptionalism*. That is because the Soviet leader was preoccupied at the time with the endemic factionalism in the American party, not its ideological deviations. He attempted to knock the heads of the factions together to get the party to do what he saw as the hard work of building contacts and support within American trade unions. With the Americans having failed to achieve this unity, Stalin condemned the U.S. party for its inclination "to regard American capitalism as something apart from and above world capitalism."[67] This was exceptionalism in all but name. However, the ejection of the Lovestoneites that followed needed a snappy title to work as invective. It was Stalin's operatives in the Comintern and Lovestone's American opponents who pronounced the error "American exceptionalism."[68]

Far from being terminally embarrassed or intimidated, the Lovestoneites soon embraced the epithet enthusiastically. As the dissident communist writer

Bertram Wolfe put it in 1933, "In the queer jargon that takes the place of intel-
ligible English in upper party circles, the American Communist Opposition
is denounced as 'American exceptionalists.'" The Great Depression had not
produced a workers' revolt, though it did reveal capitalism's instability, Lovestoneites proclaimed. Wolfe stated, "If we understand what the party leaders
are driving at, we plead guilty to the charge. Yes, we consider that conditions
in America are different from conditions in Germany or Spain or the Soviet
Union."[69]

This frank acceptance of the "American exceptionalism" label was to become extremely important because it enabled a more realistic and sociologi-
cally based understanding of different national class trajectories. It was not
the United States that was exceptional, insisted the Lovestoneites. "We are
more than 'American exceptionalists,'" Wolfe exclaimed. "We are 'exceptionalists' for every country of the world!"[70] The idea of "many" exceptionalisms
eventually became an important weapon in scholarly analysis, including in
undermining the idea of U.S. exceptionalism as incomparable. The later scholarly discourse derived from this intra-Marxist debate over the meaning of the
American republic for world communism, not just for American history.[71]
Though originally a pejorative, *exceptionalism* became an analytic and com-
parativist tool.

When allied in the Communist Opposition to Trotskyite ideas, "exceptionalism" informed a cogent dissection of various national pathways to socialism. Wolfe and Lovestone both believed themselves true Marxists still
aligned with the interests of Soviet communism, even though they dissented
from Comintern instructions.[72] They turned to the doctrines of exceptionalism to expose the ideological rigidities of its policy. Only much later did
Wolfe and Lovestone abandon communism as an ideal and a guiding theory;
the Soviet government's execution of the Bolshevik revolutionary Nikolai
Bukharin in 1938 and the signing of the Nazi-Soviet Pact in 1939 were critical in changing their minds. The former convinced Wolfe of Stalin's incorri-
gible and dictatorial stance against dissent within Soviet communism, while
the latter event drove many communists out of the party ranks from 1939 to
1941 and prompted the ideological opponents of the CPUSA to harden their
analysis and see something fundamentally wrong with Marxist politics.[73] For
Lovestone and Wolfe, the partition of Poland, which the Nazi-Soviet Pact facilitated, confirmed suspicions of Stalin's imperialist ambitions.[74]

From these Lovestoneite and Trotskyite sources, post–World War II academic American exceptionalism grew. Mostly this growth was a general intellectual awakening, as in the case of the political scientist Louis Hartz, who admitted in *The Liberal Tradition in America* the "peculiar utility of Marxism,"

despite its sectarianism, and who echoed Leon Trotsky's concept of combined and uneven development that enabled countries to leapfrog others on the stages of economic and political growth.[75] Though spawning a "contested legacy," Hartz's book continued to influence political science and intellectual history for decades thereafter by emphasizing the idea of the United States as a uniquely liberal society.[76] Max Lerner, who taught American Studies at Brandeis University, came from a left-wing background to endorse American exceptionalism through his sprawling opus, *America as a Civilization* (1957), which was set for undergraduate reading in college courses. Notwithstanding his wide appeal as an unorthodox left-liberal critic, Lerner did not distinguish between "exceptional" and "unique." Rather, he treated American Exceptionalism as the sum total of American characteristics. More important, he failed to create a research program in which a central hypothesis and subsidiary propositions on exceptionalism could be tested by future scholars.[77] In contrast, this was exactly what Seymour Martin Lipset achieved. In his case, there was a direct, if brief, Trotskyite affiliation at City College of New York. In other instances, as with Daniel Bell, the link came more through independent democratic socialism, which in turn absorbed some of these exceptionalist analytical tools. Through such people, the failure of the United States to follow a revolutionary trajectory was translated into sociological and political discourse.[78]

Marxist influences should not, however, be considered in terms of direct impact alone. The indirect effect of Marxist politics included the emergence of an *anti*-Marxian sociology in the United States. These ideas were tied to and shaped by Weberian modernization theory. This connection came especially through Talcott Parsons, the preeminent Harvard sociologist, who self-consciously tried to formulate a sociology in which values provided the controlling element in society rather than material production, as in classical Marxism.[79] Parson's theories influenced Lipset's answer to Sombart's famous question on socialism's absence. Instead of class polarization, Lipset postulated a liberal creed as a value system shaping and constraining the nation's class development and enabling American exceptionalism.

A publishing juggernaut, Lipset completed thirteen single-authored books, twelve coauthored works, and thirty-three edited tomes. Including articles, Lipset tallied 587 publications between 1947 and 2003. Quantity does not guarantee quality, yet Lipset became the most widely known political sociologist in post–World War II America and won international acclaim in his field. The only person to serve as president of both the American Political Science Association and the American Sociological Association, his academic career encompassed stints at Harvard, Columbia, Berkeley, Stanford, and George

Mason universities. Lipset did more than anyone else to make the use of the term *American exceptionalism* respectable in academic scholarship. He did not invent the concept, but he applied it to empirical research. A large number of the most important sociologists and political scientists emerging from the 1950s to 1970s either worked under Lipset as students or with him on research projects. Though his modernization theory and structural functionalism fell from favor by the 1970s, exceptionalist analysis of American political development and political economy continues as a theme in academic discourse.[80] Contemporary public discourse on American exceptionalism also reveals similar assumptions to Lipset's about comparative empirical research and the essence of a political culture derived from quantitative national differences in attitudes and values. Public polling and surveying methods to establish "outliers" in behavior and values among "comparable" countries are still routinely employed in mass media and think tanks to draw exceptionalist conclusions about the United States.[81]

If the challenge of socialism produced a self-conscious American exceptionalism, it did so not only in negative terms of being antisocialist or anti-Marxist. Its supporters also advanced a positive picture of American democracy by resurrecting Tocqueville's work. Though the latter had never been forgotten entirely, a Tocqueville revival did occur in the 1940s through the dissemination of cheap editions of *Democracy in America*.[82] The writings of the Founding Fathers also appeared in accessible reprints. Cold War antitotalitarianism and the need to find a values-based defense of the "free world" were behind this ideological offensive by publishers and intellectuals to reinforce the canon of Jefferson, Washington, Madison, and Lincoln over Marx. But there was something else that made this defense possible, and that ingredient was not conservatism. It was liberalism emboldened under the impact of the Great Depression and World War II.

In the longer term, American exceptionalism would align with anticommunist doctrine, but liberal exceptionalist belief rested in the 1940s on the positive performance of progressive reform that had survived the challenge of war and fascism. The cornucopia of the American post–World War II economy verified the value of the New Deal turn toward government intervention and a modified welfare state. Exceptionalism after 1945 was not merely against socialism but *for* liberal democracy revamped by the New Deal version of democracy. This change from a repressive ideology of Americanism to a positive exceptionalism of an expanded and pluralistic liberal democracy requires examining the crisis of the Great Depression and World War II from an angle other than the antitotalitarian and free market ideology associated with the American Enterprise Institute and free market economic thinkers such as

Milton Friedman and Friedrich von Hayek.[83] The triumph of a New Deal version of exceptionalism was a distinctive and forward-looking legacy for postwar America. This perspective directs attention once more to the material foundations of exceptionalism in abundance, not simply its religious or political pillars.

The Dream and the Century: The Liberal Exceptionalism of the New Deal State, 1930s–1960s

Crises have had a habit of shaking up American exceptionalism. We have documented that pattern for slavery, the Civil War, the upheavals of the 1890s, and World War I. Hardly had the nation recovered from the First World War than it faced another series of challenges, beginning with the Great Depression and continuing on through the Second World War and the Cold War.[1] The effect of each predicament of the 1930s to 1950s was distinctive, but the cumulative impact reinforced exceptionalism. While the American Cold War culture is commonly associated with religiosity and a strengthening public discourse on civil religion, material abundance underpinned exceptionalism as much as, if not more than, ever before because of the changing global position of the United States.

This reinforcement was mediated through twin concepts. Coupled with exceptionalism in the post–World War II period was the idea of the American Dream. First becoming prominent in 1931, the development of the American Dream as a concept can be considered part of exceptionalism's *domestic* intellectual infrastructure bequeathed by the New Deal experience.[2] Its twin in foreign policy, the American Century (1941), which will be outlined further on in this chapter, justified the changing American global position by articulating national greatness, international purpose, and potential world empire status.[3] These two were among the notions that I have labeled *subsidiary myths*. Neither the American Dream nor the American Century could be considered a substitute for American exceptionalism because they were transient in character and bounded by historical time. They drew on the deeper wellspring of exceptionalist beliefs to support them but were limited and concrete manifestations at particular points in time. Both notions supported a new version of exceptionalism reemphasizing its liberal character but embodied more than ever before in an activist state with universalist ambitions for citizens—and for the world.

The Great Depression, the New Deal, and American Exceptionalism

The spread of the Marxist-derived concept of exceptionalism to American academic life discussed in chapter 9 came at a less than optimal moment. Its genesis from the late 1920s to 1941 did not coincide with either national self-congratulation or singular achievement. Considered objectively, the 1930s actually witnessed a current of antiexceptionalism, concerning the apparently diminishing differences between the United States and the wider world in economic success, government intervention in economies, and the growth of welfare states. In addition, many ordinary Americans were feeling far from exceptional. More than a quarter of the population was out of work in 1933, and collectivism rather than individualism through industrial unions gained for the first time a measure of legal protection for bargaining through the Wagner Act (1935). Farmers driven off the land in the Dust Bowl of the American West did not feel exceptional either; their hopes for America were chastened, and the legacy remains so in American memory. The interviewees in the Ken Burns documentary *The Dust Bowl* (2012) projected a narrative of survival, not triumph.[4] Individualism was certainly the slogan of Republicans Herbert Hoover and Alfred Landon, who decisively lost the 1932 and 1936 presidential elections, respectively, but champions of free enterprise were in a (noisy) minority in the 1930s.

In the longer term, the New Deal itself could be seen as an exception to exceptionalism. As historian Jefferson Cowie puts it, "the political era between the 1930s and the 1970s marks . . . a sustained deviation, an extended detour—from some of the main contours of American political practice, economic structure, and cultural outlook." Exceptionalism was subdued rather than defeated in the 1930s, while principles of social democracy reached high tide.[5] As would fit Cowie's argument in *The Great Exception* (2016), presidents did not dwell on the chosen status of the republic. But, ironically, it was New Deal liberalism that set up the nation's economically most "successful" era, the post–World War II years to 1970, and galvanized an iteration of American exceptionalism in which chosenness could flourish again. Because Cowie treated New Deal liberalism as a matter of internal changes, he did not regard the impact of the Cold War as anything more than helping to consolidate the "ideological and political strength of the New Deal order."[6] The outward projection of American power and its exceptionalist objectives were not considered.

A somewhat different story emerges if we examine the U.S. relationship with the rest of the world. On the one hand, many elements in the New Deal were far from distinctive in global context as nations grappled with the worldwide economic crisis. Some countries were more successful than the United States in dealing with that crisis, others less so.[7] On the other hand, the New Deal mobilization of the state enabled a different kind of economic, military, and ideological projection abroad. In this context, the New Deal legacy seems far more a story of positive exceptionalism than antiexceptionalism. The New Deal became a model for those who wanted to export American values, and American success, but this point was not clear until the war years, when the United States came to the aid of a Europe at the mercy of fascism and took the lead in the war against Japan in the Pacific. Ideas of a patriotic Americanism with a nation pulling together in wartime flourished.[8] The victory over Germany in 1945, widely though wrongly attributed solely to American action, brought the United States to the apex of leadership in the Western world and, for a time, conferred a power unrivaled by any nation, including the Soviet Union. New Deal exceptionalism, modified by wartime experiences and opportunities, meant that the nation became once more an example for others to copy.

The result was an American exceptionalism focused on world leadership, material abundance as the basis of American power, and the promotion of economic development abroad. The religious aspect of exceptionalism was nested within this material and geopolitical context. *Freedom* of religion became more closely linked with the nation's role in the world, as anticommunism and the contest for global power with the Soviet Union replaced the issues of World War II. Especially in the 1950s, the United States projected on the world stage its role as an enemy of "godless" communism. World leadership was tied to this assertion, but it did not entail a special destiny, and politics deployed religion rather than the other way around. Only later in the century did the chosen nation undergo national political resurgence as a concept. Only then did religion return to its key place within the ideology of exceptionalism. Even then, it was not the stern religion of the Puritans that prevailed, nor the evangelicalism of the nineteenth-century Christian republicans; rather, it was a therapeutic form of politicoreligious exceptionalism championed by President Ronald Reagan that prevailed. The other major change was the emergence of an explicit concept of American exceptionalism as a quasi-state ideology. Increasingly, the promotion of exceptionalism relied on the expanding American state. The New Deal did not start this process but accelerated it and turned it in new directions.[9] A patriotic civil religion that went beyond any specific Christian content and which identified with the institutions of the nation-state bloomed in this context.

Examining the thinkers who canvassed exceptionalism in this period confirms that it was not the New Deal itself that made the nation appear more exceptional but rather its changing geopolitical position in that turmoil and in the events of World War II and its aftermath. The new connection between world power and American exceptionalism could be described as the latter's New Deal manifestation because it rested on the New Deal settlement in which (mainly white) labor was incorporated into a fledgling welfare state. That state was characterized by a post–World War II economic prosperity thought to be unparalleled and by global economic and military supremacy. The whole period from 1933 to the 1960s could be called the "Long New Deal," as the effects of the liberal state's consolidation became clear in American global power and international prosperity.[10] In this context, New Deal liberalism proved to be more exceptionalist in outlook than not; an exceptionalist program emerged as policy makers repudiated political isolationism and turned outward to seek worldwide change in light of the American example, and they also presumed a political preeminence. Exceptionalism did not determine foreign policy, it must be emphasized. Rather, geopolitics, economics, and other considerations of power shaped the direction that debates over exceptionalism took.[11] To project power abroad, the nation needed to be more united internally than it was in the 1920s for the global challenges of leadership that the inheritors of the New Deal would face. It is therefore necessary to consider how the New Deal transcended the divisiveness of the 1920s that had been centered on a defensive Americanism.

The Nation of Immigrants and Cultural Pluralism

The internal achievements of the New Deal are frequently studied, but its ideological significance for nation-building through exceptionalism requires emphasis. The New Deal stressed national incorporation of immigrants under cultural pluralism. Franklin D. Roosevelt inspired the new program; he sought to broaden the concept of Americanism, to reclaim its more inclusive tone, and to end the intolerance and cultural division of the 1920s. Part of the reasoning came from the strategy to build a New Deal coalition of urban voters and labor unions to join the older sources of Democratic sentiment in the South and among urban reformers and Roman Catholics. Defense of immigrants had political significance in incorporating into the body politic the predominantly city-based immigrant voters who had arrived from the 1880s to

1924. There were also international roots to the Democratic strategy. The cultural initiative occurred at the time of fascist stirrings at home and the external threat posed by Adolf Hitler's Germany. To project unity abroad, the project to disseminate ideas of cultural pluralism and the immigrant contribution as the foundation of the American democratic alternative to fascism began.

This solidification of American exceptionalism as a culture of pluralism had its negative consequences for Native Americans. In 1938, the U.S. Office of Education launched a New Deal program in the Department of the Interior for the broadcast of twenty-six thirty-minute radio programs "about the contributions of immigrants to American society." The series aired on more than one hundred Columbia Broadcasting System (CBS)-affiliated radio stations and was said to be "enormously popular." The federal government was "literally deluged with congratulatory mail from listeners."[12] This was part of a New Deal initiative to portray American democracy and the national struggle to extend it to all citizens. The CBS series was called *Americans All: Immigrants All*, and the Department of Interior booklet describing the series portrayed western pioneers shaping a great nation.[13] It outlined their hardships and triumph over the adversities of nature; the contributions of immigrants from Europe and enslaved people from Africa were also included. Yet Native Americans were absent from the broadcast subjects, which dealt with patterns of "settlement" and progress. The colonists' "thanks" to the Indians was given only insofar as the indigenous "lore" of cultivation aided white survival in the earliest days. In this telling, wherever the Indian "transmitted his lore," peaceful relations ensued, until "white men of hostile nations" provoked Indian wars and undermined the sharing of the land. Functionally, Indians supplemented for white settlement the natural advantages of American abundance wherever their "lore" was adopted in pioneering cultivation, but, as stated in the final episode, "the Red Man himself was supposed to be an immigrant of long before," who implicitly must give way to a higher (i.e., white Anglo-American) civilization.[14]

The slight of American Indian culture was made clear in that final interpretative twist. By turning Native Americans into *actual* immigrants, *Americans All* and its New Deal supporters sidelined indigenous identity. Praising the radio series, the booklet version noted, "There is no such person as a native American, nor was there ever such a person if we are to be strictly accurate. We are told that even the American Indian is an immigrant who came from far off Asia by way of the Bering Straits and Alaska." Whether "our ancestors" came "on the Mayflower or in the steerage," the broadcasters averred, Americans "ARE ALL IMMIGRANTS."[15] Addressing the Daughters of the American Revolution (DAR) in 1938, Franklin Roosevelt concurred: "Remember,

remember always that all of us, and you and I especially, are descended from immigrants and revolutionists."[16]

The CBS radio series presaged a wartime and post–World War II shift to a more positive appreciation of the nation's ethnic history. Increasingly, the narrative of "A Nation of Immigrants" as central to American identity took hold. In 1951, Harvard historian Oscar Handlin could state of his Pulitzer Prize-winning book, *The Uprooted*, "Once I thought to write a history of the immigrant in America. Then I discovered that the immigrants were American history."[17] The *Americans All* project was foundational to that movement to reexamine history and understand national identity as a product of diverse ethnic contributions within a pluralistic exceptionalist framework.[18]

The already well-known Nation of Immigrants idea registered the political imperatives of civil rights and the Cold War to show the nation striving against prejudice. John F. Kennedy published *A Nation of Immigrants* in 1958; the book stemmed from a lecture delivered before the Jewish Anti-Defamation League and was intended to further Kennedy's legislative ambitions for immigration law reform to remove discriminatory provisions, but it also signaled the possibility of his nomination as a presidential candidate of Irish Catholic derivation and the great-grandson of immigrants. Yet the book's influence was further propelled by the outpouring of grief at his untimely death. In 1964, a second, expanded edition appeared. From that time, at least until the early years of the twenty-first century, the "nation of immigrants" idea reigned as a key to exceptionalist doctrine, especially for the Democratic Party and its supporters derived originally from the New Deal coalition of voters.[19]

The unintended damage of the Nation of Immigrants idea was to remove any sense of responsibility for Indian subjugation in an American population derived increasingly from ethnic stock that arrived post-1890, when the frontier was presumed closed. In this context, the indigenous population lost significance as First Peoples. Kennedy repeated the conventional wisdom: "Some anthropologists" believed that even the Indians "were immigrants from another continent who displaced the original Americans—the aborigines."[20] The Native American rights activist and historian Vine Deloria Jr. has noted that, for many citizens, it was now possible to think Indians "were latecomers who had barely unpacked before Columbus came knocking on the door."[21] These "myths" undermined the message of the Native American population's ancient occupation of and prior claims to the land.[22]

Settler colonialism as an alternative discourse of U.S. history to replace exceptionalism as the guiding theme of national identity was thereby precluded. But it was not only the Nation of Immigrants idea that provided new support for exceptionalism. Underpinning the expansion of the New Deal state in the 1930s and American leadership of the Western world post-1945 was the restoration of economic prosperity. The precondition for this achievement was material abundance, mediated by mass consumerism, which in turn became linked to the concept of the American Dream.

The American Dream

The economic upheaval of the Great Depression greatly disturbed exceptionalism's assumptions of prosperity and progress. Americans had already begun to debate the meaning of the American Dream before James Truslow Adams told them, in *The Epic of America* (1931), that "a dream of motor cars and high wages" was not enough to be nationally or personally fulfilling.[23] Reflecting on the 1920s as a decade of mass production and consumption, and manipulative advertising to sell products, Adams reminded the American people that the embrace of material goods should not be the essence of American dreaming. It was, rather, the opportunity for all, irrespective of station in life. He preferred "a dream of social order in which each man and each woman shall be able to attain to the fullest stature of which they are innately capable."[24] Though Adams was no fan of the New Deal, his very general statement anticipated certain intellectual aspirations of the American people for community and fraternity during the New Deal. The content of the American Dream was challenged as workers and farmers sought economic security and protection, through state power, from vast economic interests. Together with the values of social democracy, fraternal and communal impulses gained ground over individualism for a time.[25] But, if we include the wartime economic progress, the achievements of the New Deal subtly altered the debate in a way more favorable to a materialist dream.

Through the reform of capitalism under the New Deal and the military-economic expansion of the Cold War era, the dream was transformed. It became one in which the distribution of resources would rest on an enlarged economic "pie" available to consumers from an ever more productive capitalist market system. Under the influence of mass advertising, the American Dream of the 1950s expressed a mostly suburban ideal of family homes with mowed lawns and white picket fences. In this context, consumer capitalism turned out to be the dream's new foundation and the chief way in which exceptionalism and the success of the U.S. economy aligned.[26]

The renowned American historian David Potter had lived through the Great Depression as a young man, but twenty years later he could sum up the American past as a story of how abundance shaped a distinctive national character. In an acclaimed set of essays, *People of Plenty* (1954), he traced how the "frontier" of consumer capitalism had replaced the frontier of the American West and extended the capacity of the nation to deliver on its material promise. Like a number of other historians and social scientists in the 1950s, Potter was uneasy about the achievements of consumer capitalism for their superficiality, conformism, materialism, and maladroit policies in engagement with a much poorer world. He criticized naive ideas of exporting American-style democracy's example to countries that lacked the requisite resources and technology. Yet his analysis remained indebted to the idea of American exceptionalism as material abundance and technological improvement.[27]

The American Dream was not open to all Americans, as the post–World War II civil rights struggles showed, but many people excluded from its promise wanted inclusion rather than something entirely different. While black separatists renounced the American way of life and even left the country as expatriates, more influential was Martin Luther King's famous "I Have a Dream" speech in August 1963, which asked how African Americans could be part of the dream. With its biblical references, citation of the Declaration of Independence, and invocation of the American Creed of equality, King drew on themes that have sustained modern American exceptionalism.[28]

Even as his appeal was confessedly "rooted in the American Dream," King made no attempt to assert national superiority, moral or otherwise, nor a chosen nation status. America was not even a "*great* nation," he announced, in view of its racial discrimination, though he believed it was capable of becoming one.[29] Like the American Dream itself, King's version was patriotic but not necessarily exceptionalist. He did not compare the United States with other countries in the dream speech, and his goal was "the brotherhood of man," an aspiration beyond nation.[30] Opposing the Vietnam War and denouncing the American war machine as an instrument of imperialism, King actually moved toward an antiexceptionalist analysis of the United States in the last few years before his assassination in 1968.[31]

Exporting Exceptionalism in the American Century

By the time King died, the American Dream was dimming in its appeal, a theme even more apparent in the grimmer decade of the 1970s. So too the idea of the American Century, which now seemed to deliver only pain to the American people, not to mention pain for the Vietnamese people. This section considers the ideas of American exceptionalism held by thinkers of the 1940s who shaped and confronted the concept of the American Century. These writers were not just reflective observers but, in most cases, political participants.

They pondered the significance of the New Deal state and its global projection. Each exerted some political or intellectual influence in this period of the Long New Deal. Their predictions on the future of the United States from the perspective of the nation's arrival as a hegemonic world power differed but were interwoven with commitments to exceptionalism: Henry Luce, Wendell Willkie, Henry A. Wallace, and, as a critic of these projections, the theologian Reinhold Niebuhr. During wartime, all these thinkers were impressed with the likely special position of the United States after World War II. Scholars have noted their public interventions and their disagreements; that was the way the debates were perceived at the time, but what stands out is how American power was reshaping exceptionalism.[32] While the New Deal began with inward-looking economic reforms, part of its long-term significance was as a strong platform to project American ideas for organizing the international political and economic order.

When one thinks of American exceptionalism and the nation's enhanced world power, it is *Time* and *Life* magazine founder Henry Luce who provides Exhibit A. Luce condemned the collectivism that he saw as a threat in the 1930s, and his alternative was liberal individualism. This would not be the partly planned economy of the New Deal but a political culture consistent with the more traditional antistate message of exceptionalism through "passionate devotion to great American ideals."[33] In the changing circumstances of 1941, however, he offered an olive branch—in effect, a pact with FDR to advance American interests and values. He proclaimed the onset of the first "American Century" and a program of involvement in world affairs focused on a positive U.S. example. In contrast to what Luce saw as the isolationism of FDR's first two terms, the United States in the American Century should, he argued, engage with the world, grounded in support for freedom against totalitarian aggression.[34]

Luce's American Century has been used as a catchcry for American postwar power. It was, the historian Michael Hunt stated of East Asian policy, "arguably the dominant American . . . approach."[35] Imbued with the language of American singularity, forged by a son of American missionaries to China, Luce's observations were nevertheless contingent, linked with the perilous wartime situation; they did not in 1941 apply far into the future in the way subsequently used. Tentative and vague about the nature of American military intervention in the wider world, Luce's ideas did not provide a blueprint for the day-to-day conduct of foreign policy either.[36]

Rather, it is the wartime ideological framework that shall be considered here. Despite its title, the American Century article was a plea to enlist the nation in the economic and political struggle to prevent an Axis takeover of

Europe, though Luce did not openly advocate entry into the war. Instead, he advanced an alternative American hegemony to the old colonial empires. Scornful of communism, Luce wanted the United States to lead the world in promoting free markets and individual freedom. It was a Republican platform that he offered, but founded on internationalism, not the isolationism that distinguished Republican foreign policy in the 1930s. Acknowledging the reality in 1941 of "one world, fundamentally indivisible," he argued that the United States had to be actively engaged in that world.[37]

That conceded, he considered the United States unique within global geopolitics. Its economic strength (ironically secured by the New Deal that he disliked) meant that Americans could choose their own destiny. In theory, Americans could live with a Hitler-dominated Europe but, already affected by the European war, the nation would be irrevocably connected to the world through the need to preserve American "ideals," which stressed "free economic enterprise" and the "freedom of the seas" to travel and trade with whomsoever Americans pleased. But this liberal concern for global capitalism was couched within a broader assertion of American internationalism.[38]

In Luce's formulation, interventionism should come not only by aiding the Allies but also by providing humanitarian assistance across the globe. In this he reflected the belief in an American mission that went way beyond geopolitical alliances and was long part of exceptionalist thinking. "We must undertake now to be the Good Samaritan of the entire world," he proclaimed. It was "the manifest duty" of the United States "to feed all the people of the world who as a result of this worldwide collapse of civilization are hungry and destitute."[39] According to Luce, the American Century did not sanction unlimited foreign military intervention. "Emphatically our only alternative to isolationism is not to undertake to police the whole world nor to impose democratic institutions on all mankind."[40] Later, he would be a cheerleader for U.S. military involvement in both Korea and Vietnam but, in 1941, his vision relied on soft power and the setting of ground rules for a global order, not interfering in individual countries, thus resulting in a U.S. hegemony, not an empire as conventionally conceived in terms of political control. This vision drew on an anti-imperialist tradition with a long inheritance in exceptionalist thought.

Luce's forward-looking and positive exceptionalism was tempered only by his commitment to preserving Western civilization because Americans were "the inheritors of all the great principles" of that civilization. The lineage recalls the metaphor of the relay baton, with the United States destined to anchor the great relay race of humanity, thus realizing the "one world" dream held together by American values of "Justice, the love of Truth, [and] the ideal of Charity."[41] This fealty to Western civilization could be seen as a conservative program, consonant with former president Herbert Hoover's statement that the nation was "fast becoming the sanctuary for the ideals of civilization."[42] But Luce saw the U.S. role as more than such a defensive posture implied; it would be the source for the future intellectual recolonization of the world under American liberalism.

Luce wove nation-state patriotism into the doctrines of American singularity. Drawing his vision together was "an allegiance to the most exciting flag of all the world and of all history," and one dedicated to "the triumphal purpose of freedom." Whereas the Four Freedoms of the Roosevelt administration stressed global commonalties, Luce asserted that "we have some things in this country which are infinitely precious and especially American—a love of freedom, a feeling for the equality of opportunity, a tradition of self-reliance and independence and also of co-operation."[43] This liberalism struck the balance between American superiority and peculiarity, on the one hand, and, on the other, a leadership role that required other countries to accept American dominance, in order for liberal democracy to be secured and extended globally.

If Luce did not want to escape the doctrines of exceptionalism, Wendell Willkie, the defeated 1940 Republican presidential candidate, was unable to do so. Returning from his forty-nine-day air trip around the world for the Roosevelt administration as a special envoy in 1942, the former Republican opponent of FDR wrote *One World*; the work exuded internationalism and, evoking the need for Americans to help "unify the peoples of the earth in the human quest for freedom and justice," gave more ground to international partnership and human commonalities than Luce did.[44] A publishing blockbuster, translated into many languages, the book was an important turning point registering American acceptance of greater global interconnectedness.[45] That said, Willkie mixed internationalism and cosmopolitanism with exceptionalism, as Luce did. Willkie's globally "connective impulse" rested, historian Samuel Zipp has argued, on "a sense that foreigners were no different from Americans and that other nations were like the US in its pioneer youth." In this way, American values functioned "as both a connective tissue" with the world "and the standard by which intimate international relations were established." Not only did the wartime enthusiasm for *One World* suggest the potentially hierarchical nature of a global relationship in which the United States set the standard of excellence; the antiexceptionalist strain in Willkie could not be realized because he died suddenly in 1944.[46] It must be conceded that he had already given too much ground to Roosevelt and the New Deal to make him a viable candidate as the Republican Party's 1944 standard-bearer for president.

Even as serendipitous circumstances reduced Willkie's impact, he was not the only thinker to challenge a highly nationalistic exceptionalism, yet still demonstrate the latter's pull. In theory, Vice President Henry Wallace's position was diametrically opposed to Luce's. The years ahead would not be the American Century, Wallace stated, but the "Century of the Common Man."[47] This view made him the true inheritor of the New Deal's most progressive impulses. In some ways, Wallace followed the antiexceptionalist line coming from the economic experience of the New Deal at home. His "Common Man" statement of 1942 was a direct reply to Luce. Therein Wallace renounced exceptionalism: "There can be no privileged peoples. We ourselves in the United States are no more a master race than the Nazis." He put the American Revolution in the context of global revolutions advancing human freedom: "Each spoke for the common man in terms of blood on the battlefield," even as "some went to excess." The significant point was that in other countries too, "the people groped their way to the light."[48] Wallace envisaged the entire world embarked on a collectivist journey, in contradiction to Luce's concern to preserve liberal individualism. Through revolutions, "More of them [the world's peoples] learned to think and work together."[49]

Given its appearance of antiexceptionalism, it is notable that Wallace raised notions of a chosen people. A practicing Presbyterian, Wallace believed the United States was part of God's plans, and Wallace saw the U.S. system of government as an expression of Social Gospel traditions. Though sensed by the prophets of the Old Testament, the idea of social justice was not, in Wallace's opinion, given "complete and powerful political expression until our nation, here in the United States, was formed as a Federal Union a century and a half ago." The statement could have come from that preeminent historian of the nineteenth century, George Bancroft. Since "democracy" was the "only true political expression of Christianity," the United States was the modern bearer of God's democratic design for the world.[50] Wallace's advocacy of an American interventionist role across the world also exposed a millenarian cast: "The people, in their millennial and revolutionary march toward manifesting here on earth the dignity that is in every human soul, hold as their credo the Four Freedoms enunciated by President Roosevelt." This movement would extend exceptionalism's values to all peoples by common agreement, not imposition. Like Luce, Wallace positioned the United States as empire's nemesis since he endorsed "neither military nor economic imperialism."[51]

Notwithstanding Wallace's social-democratic aspirations for government in producing a better life, his appeal sounded quite like Luce's idea of an exceptional American example to the world.[52] Neither Luce nor Wallace thought this example could be simply admired from afar; U.S. engagement must involve a vigorous agenda to change the world. Yet there was a difference. Luce saw the United States as separate, setting its own rules and exporting ideas and material assistance abroad. For Wallace, the United States must act within the stream of history, not outside it. While foreign methods differed from Americans' own, Wallace affirmed that all were part of the democratic strivings of the world's peoples. This idea of a collective humanity beyond individual national solidarity distinguished his interpretation from a simplistic exceptionalism.

Wallace was an important figure on the progressive wing of the Democratic Party, but he became widely vilified as a fellow traveler of communists, and his career was cut short. Conservatives and hardheaded pragmatists lobbied against his continuing as vice president, and he lost the Democratic nomination to Harry S. Truman in 1944. Post-1947, this de facto palace coup looked very much like preparation for the Cold War. But it must be remembered that the New Deal agenda of exporting the ideals of American democracy, through peaceful cooperation with other countries, was not lost.

After 1945, New Dealers transformed the Tennessee Valley Authority and other domestic initiatives of the 1930s into a modernization program for third world countries during the Cold War struggle. International institutions such as the Food and Agriculture Organization (FAO) of the United Nations (UN) relied to some degree on American expertise in agrarian reform. Experts in tropical forestry conservation, with their experience in Puerto Rico and the Philippine Islands, provided examples of postwar global impacts of the New Deal through the FAO. The Peace Corps of the 1960s, as envisaged by President Kennedy, could be seen as a successor to this New Deal liberal exceptionalism, crystalizing a sense of national identity as "essentially positive," Elizabeth Cobbs Hoffman has argued. This was a time of "widespread belief that American norms represented the pinnacle of progress and were self-evidently good."[53]

The New Deal's idealistic liberalism went further and underwrote the U.S. contribution to the UN Declaration of Human Rights. The document incorporated the spirit of the Declaration of Independence and the New Deal's emphasis on human welfare. A statement of principles, it soon fell victim to Cold War rivalries in geopolitics, but it still established standards of international law that have retained global significance. Eleanor Roosevelt, the widow of Franklin D., chaired the Universal Declaration of Human Rights drafting committee. Though others, especially John Peters Humphrey of

Canada, director of the UN's Human Rights Division, prepared the "Declaration's blueprint," the former first lady was "recognized as the driving force for the Declaration's adoption."[54] This collaborative and internationalist work bore the traces of the progressive New Deal update on exceptionalism.

Even so, with a fervent anticommunism providing convincing backup for his agenda, Luce's prediction that the twentieth century would be an American Century won out as the national narrative on international engagement.[55] Within the United States it rested on a hierarchical assumption that the majority of the world's inhabitants shared his enthusiasm for U.S. leadership.[56] In Luce's terms, the American Century projected the idea of a single nation dedicated to becoming "the powerhouse from which . . . [liberal democratic] ideals spread throughout the world."[57] Luce's asymmetrical vision concerning global power in 1941 was confirmed by the political, military, and economic realities of postwar American hegemony.

That hegemony was based on the command of material resources that made the nation seem exceptional in comparative perspective. In 1945, the United States accounted for nearly half the world's use of fossil fuels, mostly from domestic production.[58] It was the abundance of cheap energy through coal and oil that underpinned American manufacturing and the war effort. Despite consumer demand for tropical products such as coffee and bananas, the continental United States could still furnish most of the nation's essential needs in 1945. Even among tropical products, natural rubber had been partly bypassed through the development of synthetic rubber before the end of World War II. The food supply was also ample in wheat, corn, hogs, and cattle, as the West recovered from the Great Depression and the Dust Bowl crisis. The extension of chemical treatments to improve agricultural productivity allowed the nation to continue exporting vast quantities of food.

Nevertheless, strategic circumstances made American leaders anxious about abundance. Multilateral alliances drew government and corporations into global webs of resource depletion and dependence at the same time that exceptional consumer abundance was being celebrated. Despite the nation's legacy of cornucopia, the materials needed for strategic purposes became more problematic as technological developments in aerospace for defense made it necessary to take a greater interest in global mineral exploitation. This theme first emerged full-blown in President Truman's Materials Policy Commission (1951) and the subsequent work of the Resources for the Future think tank (from 1952). The commission drew attention to "the widening gap within the United States between requirements and our domestic means of satisfying them."[59] It urged the nation to "reject self-sufficiency" and seek "the lowest cost acquisition of materials" wherever possible. This economic internationalism was not an exceptionalist reading of modern American history but rather an antiexceptionalism embracing cooperation with "all freedom-loving peoples of the earth."[60]

What Truman's successor as president said about Southeast Asia indicated the drift of strategic thinking. The U.S. supply of $400 million in aid to the beleaguered French forces in Vietnam in 1953 was undertaken, President Dwight D. Eisenhower explained, because "if Indochina goes, several things happen right away. The Malayan peninsula would be scarcely defensible—and tin and tungsten we so greatly value from that area would cease coming." Such an outcome would be "very ominous" for the United States because "if we lost all that, how would the free world hold the rich empire of Indonesia?"[61] The United States became acutely concerned over the reservation of such sources of raw materials, which were needed for the nation's worldwide military commitments gained as a result of the Cold War. In this way, the paradoxes of an anxious hegemony haunted the Cold War arrival of the United States at the pinnacle of its material power.

The Cold War

Perhaps because of this anxiety on the question of limits, quantitative power did not create a consensus about a qualitatively different national destiny. The unofficial architect of containment policy, George Kennan, mentioned "providence" in his anonymous outline of the proposed American strategy to deal with Soviet communism in the late 1940s, but he made it clear that the United States must act like other great powers. The challenge of the Soviet Union was a test for American maturity in his view. "Surely, there was never a fairer test of national quality than this," the Department of State official wrote. "In the light of these circumstances, the thoughtful observer of Russian-American relations will find no cause for complaint in the Kremlin's challenge to American society. He will rather experience a certain gratitude to a Providence which, by providing the American people with this implacable challenge, has made their entire security as a nation dependent on their pulling themselves together and accepting the responsibilities of moral and political leadership that history plainly intended them to bear." U.S. "leadership" was a matter of geopolitical and material circumstances, not ideology, and should be conducted through statecraft.[62]

This realist approach does not mean that American governments applied containment policy in a subtle way. Religious profession blended with realism. On the ideological front, the rhetoric of anticommunism continually intruded, with practical consequences. Implacable opposition to the communist

bloc led the way, albeit incrementally, to direct American involvement in the
Vietnam War.[63] Nor did the realist component in containment strategy mean
that religious idealism was abandoned in government pronouncements. Secretary of State John Foster Dulles exemplified the use of Christian moralism
as a political and ideological weapon to reinforce the transatlantic alliance.
This Christian influence in politics entailed the application of religion to a
global political cause.[64] There were elements of a self-referential destiny in
this position. Dulles found an "indispensable" role for Americans in the preservation of "freedom" because they were among the "small minority" of the
world's people who held in their hands the capacity to preserve that freedom.
He called on citizens to defend the "great American experiment" because it
had produced rich "spiritual, intellectual and material" fruits inspiring people
globally. Defending this tradition of "liberty" would promote "political freedom" and "a large improvement in economic and social welfare."[65]

   This exceptionalist campaign sounded more like a patriotic civil religion
in its emphases than an assertion of chosenness. Official and semiofficial professions of faith abounded, especially through making "In God We Trust" the
national motto (1956), after adding "under God" to the Pledge of Allegiance
in 1954.[66] President Eisenhower made sure that he held White House prayer
breakfasts and included the Reverend Billy Graham as an adviser, yet he had
no record as a church member in the decades before his presidential candidacy. Sincere Eisenhower may have been, but his sincerity coincided with
political expediency and religious fashion. Injected into foreign policy, opposition to "godless" communism inspired spiritual renewal at home, manifest
in Graham's revivalist crusades. Though based on grassroots anxieties, government rhetoric assisted the new anticommunist push in religion, and the
postwar elaboration of a generalized civil religion became prominent as justification for state policy and promotion of patriotism.

   As part of this attempt to find a national religious consensus, the language
of a Judeo-Christian tradition consolidated from its prewar beginnings. Yet
it was not a central rallying cry for conservatives in the way it became in the
culture wars of the 1980s and beyond, and its relationship with exceptionalism was unclear. Proponents of the Judeo-Christian theme tried to argue,
in effect, for a Judeo-Christian exceptionalism leading Western civilization
against communism, but this formulation logically transcended *American*
exceptionalism. It also excluded or offended many Americans who were nonbelievers, those who stood for the strict separation of church and state, Mus-
lims, and the advocates of nontheistic faiths. Some Catholic leaders did not
like the Judeo-Christian terminology either. Ever the pragmatist, Eisenhower
himself avoided it after 1954, preferring instead the even more generalized and

vacuous "spirituality."[67] Tellingly, the U.S. government's "national goals" announced in 1960 omitted "religion" entirely, though this initiative included a passing reference to "spirituality," while focusing on more tangible and practical matters.[68]

Despite religious intimations, postwar American policy makers mostly refrained from the overbearing rhetoric of a chosen nation. "Under God" appeared commonly enough in presidential pronouncements, but the volume of references to "providence" was minuscule. The explicit doctrine of chosenness did not figure at all. As Truman once bluntly stated in another context, "I never thought God picked any favorites."[69] Even as freedom of religion in a pluralistic society was a key value in the campaign against communism, American exceptionalism now emphasized political freedoms, and economic and military strength projected abroad. If the possession of the atom bomb initially fueled a sense of omnipotence and even an air of "imperial hubris," Russian possession of the same nuclear weaponry within a few years meant that economics and the measurement of economic growth moved to the center of public discourse.[70] This was a circumstance forgotten in the wake of the Reagan revolution of the 1980s, when patriotic chosenness became more central in exceptionalist thinking.[71]

While the economy's capacity to meet the nation's strategic needs still worried policy analysts, it was consumer abundance that seemed most exceptional and promising. As much as the threat of nuclear weapons, American consumption loomed large in the competition with the USSR in the 1950s. This emphasis was revealed in the widely publicized "kitchen debate" in the American National Exhibition at Sokol'niki Park, Moscow, in the summer of 1959. The exhibit featured a modern home display. Visiting Vice President Nixon highlighted the exhibit to demonstrate to Soviet Premier Nikita Khrushchev the opportunities for American citizens to consume and to rejoice in the prosperity of U.S. capitalism that underpinned this largesse.[72] The debate was broadcast back home.

In the feisty exchange, Nixon's presentation blended American abundance with representations of American women as modern and exceptional. Just as Catharine Beecher's hardy and self-made housewife was integral to the gestation of American exceptionalism and its dissemination across classes in the nineteenth century, now consumerism was central, along with the image of American women as more emancipated than other women because of consumer capitalism's abundance. In this sense, spreading American culture abroad became a "heroic enterprise" for improving the lives of foreign women.[73] Khrushchev and Nixon put their "respective countries' claims to progress and goodness through representations about women's lives."[74] Nixon collapsed "freedom" into consumer calculation and depicted the home in each country as "the exemplar of standards of living."[75] Though in a different way from the nineteenth-century version, women remained markers of civilization, in which "'free' women, empowered by consumer choice and discretionary leisure time, signified advancement."[76] In all, the Moscow display revealed "a consistent trope of American exceptionalism" exemplified in the supposedly superior advantages possessed by American women.[77]

The freedom to choose consumer goods and possess a modern kitchen did not reach the lofty level of less overtly materialist iterations of an exceptionalist ideology. At the time, the practical limitations were also apparent. Liberal intellectuals, such as John Kenneth Galbraith in *The Affluent Society*, showed in the 1960s how shallow the substance of consumer culture was, but in doing so, they illustrated its pervasive influence.[78] In *The New Industrial State*, Galbraith proclaimed that "the individual serves the industrial system not by supplying it with savings and the resulting capital; he serves it far more by consuming its products. On no other activity, religious, political or moral, is he so elaborately, skillfully and expensively instructed."[79] Therein, impulses for equality in America were channeled into a Keynesian enlargement of the economic "pie." Only in the 1970s would the environmental consequences of this strategy based on material abundance become clear, when intensified resource extraction under global capitalism threatened American exceptionalism.

Ironically, idealistic critics of U.S. foreign policy often ground their arguments in similar notions of exceptional abundance. A case in point came from foreign aid. Arguing that U.S. prosperity required greater equality of distribution internationally, eighty-eight American religious leaders "endorsed a policy statement on American Abundance and World Need" published by the National Catholic Rural Life Conference.[80] The year was 1955, deep into the Cold War. The impetus originated from a transnational campaign of the Roman Catholic Church, but the American manifestation was based on assumed international power and responsibility. The representatives were adamant that, in a "moral universe, the continued prosperity of one nation can only be justified by its faithful and courageous efforts to make comparable abundance available to all nations." This was exceptionalism as example, but it meant intervention in other countries via foreign aid, a potent political and ideological weapon. Despite the tensions and imperatives of Cold War geopolitical alignments, these religious leaders averred that "nationalistic or imperialistic motivation on the part of the United States" must be avoided. Foreign aid should be dispensed "in a genuine spirit of international friendship and goodwill."[81] They opposed "making our participation contingent upon political conformity or subservience on the part of other nations," and they campaigned to "reduce international tension and to promote world peace" through private aid and "maximum utilization of the United Nations."[82]

The project summoned up the complexity and diversity of Cold War responses to American power and of liberal exceptionalism. The group appealed to the distinctive characteristics of American democracy, the idea of the fundamental goodness of the nation's democratic institutions, and international cooperation: "In the last analysis, American policies and programs are determined by the will of the people. This is the glory of our free and democratic society." They called on "all Americans of moral idealism and righteous conviction to join us and their neighbors in an all-out crusade to employ the God-given abundance of America in an expanded program of world development, human progress, and international peace."[83] Genuine as such initiatives were, in reality this "program for shared abundance" meant utilizing the existing Food for Peace initiative. Combining strategic and political objectives with improving the lot of American farmers, that approach also meant reinforcing American moral and material exceptionalism.[84]

In these postwar years, when the American Century idea spread well beyond its original articulation, the National Catholic Rural Life Conference was not alone among religious groups questioning the priorities of American foreign policy. Some Christian realists "witnessed to the non-military uses that 'chosen' American power could be consecrated."[85] But few got closer to the heart of the problem than Reinhold Niebuhr. He not only grappled with the ethical and practical responsibilities entailed in distributing the fruits of economic largesse; he also tackled the very idea of God's providential sanction for American policy. In *The Politics of Hope* (1963), Harvard historian Arthur Schlesinger Jr. praised Niebuhr's "searching realism" for giving American liberalism "renewed sources of strength."[86] From World War II through the Kennedy years, Niebuhr might almost be considered the country's "official establishment theologian" (as *New Yorker* journalist Richard Rovere put it).[87] Featured in the *Saturday Evening Post* and *Reader's Digest*, Niebuhr was, antiwar critic Noam Chomsky has argued, "a figure familiar to the general public, the state managers and the intellectual community, which regarded him with great respect if not awe."[88] He influenced not only Schlesinger, who served in the Kennedy administration, but also eminent academic historians such as C. Vann Woodward and Richard Hofstadter. Partly as a result, American historians of the 1950s and 1960s adopted a more cautious and critical approach to American exceptionalism than the American Century idea connoted. Niebuhr critiqued American "innocency" and assertions of a special national status. Regarding Cold War leadership, he urged a realist approach in which outlandish aims were tempered by pragmatism. He rebuffed suggestions of national chosenness and declared all human society affected by the taint of evil. He noted that "man as an historical creature never has as pure and disinterested a mind and his 'values' and 'socially approved goals' are never as universally valid as the prospective managers and manipulators of historical destiny assume theirs to be." What was true of zealous Soviet ideologues was "also true of an American nation, or any other nation with Messianic illusions," Niebuhr asserted.[89] This statement was antiexceptionalist in its inflection.

Yet the irony of Niebuhr's *The Irony of American History* (1952) was its indebtedness to the underlying historical assumptions of American exceptionalism as material force. Niebuhr tacitly conceded that the conventional (exceptionalist) narrative was broadly true of the past. His work was theologically sound but indifferent history. It questioned contemporary American illusions, not the historical myths on which these illusions were based.[90] Niebuhr glided lightly over previous U.S. involvement with imperialism. He did not (as he had done in a 1932 essay) mention the treatment of the Philippine Islands annexed by the United States, and he followed the common narrative that Americans were an anticolonial people at heart, albeit not as innocent of imperialist urges as they assumed themselves to be.[91] He accepted also the frontier thesis of abundance and prosperity deriving from it, and he drew a good deal of that commentary from Alexis de Tocqueville and (selectively) from Frederick Jackson Turner.[92] Disregarding the impact on indigenous Americans, Niebuhr simply treated this frontier and its egalitarian cast as an aspect of an exceptionalism which shaped national character.[93] He wrote of the nation as a consensual unit of the "we" in terms of its Americanism. All this was fairly conventional thinking. He also held David Potter's idea that technology had provided in the twentieth century the capacity to replace the frontier as a source of opportunity, while conceding that a reckoning in terms of social and economic inequality would occur sooner or later.[94] He underestimated the extent of such inequality in American history and the degree of Machiavellian activity that had nearly always applied in both foreign policy and domestic politics.

In the wake of the Iraq War of 2003, Niebuhr became a praised and influential thinker once more. Both conservatives and liberal antiwar critics found his call for understanding the limits of American power salutary. As a liberal Democrat calculating the measure of state power to be applied in any circumstance, Barack Obama confessed that Niebuhr was "one of my favorite philosophers."[95] But, before this latter-day revival, Niebuhr's influence had fallen for decades. Historian Jackson Lears has noted that, "during the years after the Vietnam War, when liberal realism revealed itself as little more than a portentous version of Cold War orthodoxy, Niebuhr's reputation lost some lustre."[96] From the opposite direction, his religious liberalism and criticism of chosenness made his work increasingly out of touch with resurgent American evangelicalism. Niebuhr's influence suffered because the chosen nation idea was, by 1980, on the way to an importance within exceptionalism unmatched since the antebellum period. Paradoxically, however, renewed assertions of American chosenness came in almost direct correlation with an apparent decline of the nation's material superiority. The roots of this revival lay in the early Cold War struggles, though it was the political and economic challenges of the 1970s that forged the new exceptionalism expressed through the presidential candidacy of Ronald Reagan.

The Newly Chosen Nation:
Exceptionalism from Reagan to Trump

Shifts in the mental worlds of a people may be precipitated by sudden change, but they usually have deep roots. The revival of a religiously based sense of American exceptionalism in the 1980s came from two long-evolving circumstances. The first was changes in attitudes toward church-state relations. After World War II, Christian fundamentalists sought to resist the perceived problems of an aggressive communism abroad and materialism at home by calling on the government to engage in a holy war. Spearheading this reinvigoration of evangelicalism as a political force was the Congregational preacher Harold Ockenga, who, starting in the late 1930s, gained a reputation for his conservative theology of anticommunism and opposition to big government. With the threat of totalitarianism from both the Soviets and the Nazis looming in 1939, Ockenga proclaimed American exceptionalism linked to biblical interpretation. The dangers facing the world from totalitarianism were "a fulfillment of Scripture prophecy in the 38th and 39th chapters of Ezekiel," he insisted. Due to the "distinctly Biblical basis" of the U.S. Constitution, the nation had a providential leadership role to play, he argued: "Our country is the fruit of the great Protestant reformation. Our continent was preserved to incarnate the development of the best of civilization. Humanly speaking, it is almost as though God pinned His last hope on America."[1] Ockenga's political and religious exceptionalism flowed into the new evangelicalism after World War II. The evangelical magazine *Christianity Today* (founded in 1956) and the Billy Graham crusades, both of which Ockenga supported and inspired, sought to turn fundamentalism away from internal introspection to address the issues of the contemporary world from a biblical perspective. The new evangelicals wanted to enhance the religiosity of the American state, whether by a conservative moral agenda, an emphasis on free enterprise as the American Way, or the foreign policy struggle with the Soviet Union.[2]

The second circumstance was a new language in which to encapsulate the idea of chosenness.[3] Harvard University became an unwitting incubator for the intellectual development of the latter through the work of Perry Miller, which took shape almost simultaneously with Reinhold Niebuhr's in the 1940s and 1950s. It fueled an academic debate and helped construct a new problematic for scholarly interest in American culture. Among those making innovative contributions in response to Miller was Sacvan Bercovitch, whose *The American Jeremiad* (1978) made Protestant self-searching foundational to American culture and exceptionalism. The debt to Miller was evident, despite the modification of his ideas.[4]

Perry Miller and the Winthrop Revival

A commanding figure in intellectual history from the 1930s to the 1960s, Miller was not a present-centered scholar. He understood from the corpus of his research that a simple line could not be drawn between the past and the contemporary world. In his view, the Puritans were not democrats, nor liberals, but "deliberately, vigorously, and consistently intolerant."[5] They were not Cold War warriors either, but the Cold War created for Miller anxieties and opportunities, especially since Harvard colleagues, such as Arthur Schlesinger Jr., were responding to the world-historical change in American power. Miller turned from a seemingly otherworldly concern with understanding the Puritans on their own terms to seeking the relevance of his work on the Puritan experience for the post–World War II geopolitical context, wherein American economic, military, and strategic ascendancy was impossible to miss.[6] In his now-famous 1953 article "Errand into the Wilderness," Miller treated the Puritan concept of a spiritual errand as foundational to John Winthrop's Massachusetts Bay Colony and metaphorically comparable to the dilemmas of World War II and Cold War America. In his rhetorical exposition, Miller made a jarringly ahistorical reference to mass prison camps to locate the contemporary significance of his story and complained of how "early" in the history of the nation there "commenced that chronic weakness in the foreign policy of Americans, an inability to recognize who in truth constitute their best friends abroad."[7]

Not a cheerleader for American nationalism, Miller nevertheless committed the very scholarly sin he abhorred by drawing a line between the distant past of the New England colonists and postwar America. In discussing the Puritan jeremiad, Miller treated the Puritan settlement and its mission, defined in Winthrop's "City upon a Hill," as the intellectual ground zero of American identity. Upon the failure by 1660 of Oliver Cromwell's revolution in England, New England Puritans could no longer see their mission as part of a transnational project to save European Christendom. They had, according to Miller, "no other place to search but within themselves" for the meaning of their seventeenth-century enterprise. Winthrop's "city" metaphor changed its import in this context, as Miller tells it: "Having failed to rivet the eyes of the world upon their city on the hill, they were left alone with America."[8] From that time to his death in 1963, Miller in his work turned to understanding and documenting this American self-interrogation over the meaning of U.S. history and nationality as the nation asserted its role as leader of the free world.[9] This question of meaning was a focus, too, of the relatively new academic field of American studies, and of the national character studies of the 1950s and 1960s. Miller's work is often taken in American studies as the essence of this shift in scholarly sensibilities.[10]

Miller's enormous contribution to American history and American studies should not be reduced to this single intervention, but it was from this work that the prominence of the "City upon a Hill" idea took hold. It is unlikely that Miller's work directly influenced John F. Kennedy's understanding of the "City" metaphor.[11] More likely it came from the background knowledge of his speechwriters. Kennedy had some professions to being a historian, and he had on his staff a historian tutored and mentored by Miller, Arthur Schlesinger Jr.[12] Possibly with background from Schlesinger, Kennedy showed familiarity with the work of American historians, including Miller. In a 1958 address to the Mississippi Valley Historical Association in Minneapolis, Kennedy regaled the assembled historians with his knowledgeable summations of their work, though it is doubtful whether he had personally read any of the content he mentioned. But Theodore Sorensen, who actually wrote the speech from which the modern use of the "City upon a Hill" phrase derives, may have simply seen the text on the tercentenary monument to the 1630 settlement, on Boston Common, opposite the Massachusetts State House, where Kennedy spoke those now-famous words.[13]

Whatever the origins and inspiration, Kennedy used the "City upon a Hill" idea when addressing the Massachusetts General Court on January 9, 1961, just weeks before being sworn in as president:

> I have been guided by the standard John Winthrop set before his shipmates on the flagship *Arbella* three hundred and thirty-one years ago, as they, too, faced the task of building a new government on a perilous frontier. "We must

always consider," [Winthrop] said, "that we shall be as a city upon a hill—the eyes of all people are upon us." Today the eyes of all people are truly upon us—and our governments, in every branch, at every level, national, state and local, must be as a city upon a hill—constructed and inhabited by men aware of their great trust and their great responsibilities. For we are setting out upon a voyage in 1961 no less hazardous than that undertaken by the *Arbella* in 1630. We are committing ourselves to tasks of statecraft no less awesome than that of governing the Massachusetts Bay Colony, beset as it was then by terror without and disorder within.[14]

While Kennedy's reference was a parting shot at the state politics of Massachusetts, after Kennedy's death the idea of the American nation as a sacred project initiated by Winthrop and rekindled by Kennedy was copied by Lyndon Johnson in 1964 and then reworked by Ronald Reagan.[15] Using the concept repeatedly from the 1970s onward, Reagan added the adjective *shining* to the image: "I have quoted John Winthrop's words more than once on the campaign trail this year—for I believe that Americans in 1980 are every bit as committed to that vision of a shining 'city on a hill,' as were those long-ago settlers."[16]

The metaphor had limited impact on academia. It made none at all on that emissary of American exceptionalism, Seymour Martin Lipset. He did not cite Miller, and he continued to study the social roots of American religious pluralism, not religion's role as a state ideology, legitimating force, or source of national identity.[17] For this reason, the serious study of the social science and chosen nation ideas of American exceptionalism persisted along parallel but clearly separate paths. Simultaneously, the mainstream of American historiography took a temporary turn away from interest in religion, except as social history, an emphasis broadly compatible with Lipset's social science approach.[18]

It was the sociologist Robert Bellah who realized the importance of religion for the entire polity as a system of belief. Bellah's *The Broken Covenant* (1975) made the Puritans' pact with God key. Influenced by Miller, Bellah cited Miller's posthumously published *The Life of the Mind in America* (1965) and quoted at length from Winthrop's "A Modell of Christian Charity." But Bellah used Miller's work to stress American civil religion and conceded that civil religion was neither denominationally Christian nor unique to the United States.[19]

The Answer to Almost Everything Lay in the 1970s

The opportunity for the chosen nation idea to flourish within exceptionalism came not so much from academic controversies as from a perceived "malaise" of the 1970s and a new religious environment to interpret it.[20] Quick to identify flaws in American culture, morals, and politics were the newly vocal evangelical preachers of conservative and, especially, so-called dispensational theology. This premillennial theology toughened fundamentalist resolution with a stark worldview of the end-time and the nation's key role within it. First introduced into the United States in the mid-nineteenth century but gaining mainstream attention after the cultural and political conflicts of the 1960s, dispensationalism stressed the physical reappearance of Christ to inaugurate his thousand-year rule that would precede the Day of Judgment.[21]

Televangelists moved these premillennialist debates to center stage from their obscure fundamentalist origins. Reverend Jerry Falwell's best-selling *Listen, America!* (1980) was predicated on the analysis that American society was "crumbling" under the weight of immorality and unbelief, with the nation in decline because of threats from big government, communism, and a weakened national defense.[22] The evangelist Hal Lindsey had earlier summoned premillennialist opinions to produce *The Late Great Planet Earth* (1970), a best-selling book, which presented a dystopian view of the United States. In a sequel, Lindsey predicted the imminent Second Coming of Christ, achieved with the assistance of a repentant nation. The television program associated with the book was watched by seventeen million followers. A seemingly endless torrent of such works followed, in which American Christians were exhorted to fulfill prophecy and realize the U.S. role in the End of History. Lindsey and other prominent televangelists envisioned "a special dispensation of the United States" that would "revive America's station as an exceptional nation."[23]

The loss of confidence during the 1970s was not troubling to Christian clerics alone. In a widely discussed *New York Times* piece in 1972, sociologist Herbert Gans announced "The American Malaise."[24] Academics and journalists located the beginning of the modern crisis in American exceptionalism in the late 1960s and early 1970s.[25] The failures of Vietnam and the scandal of Watergate eroded American self-confidence. In 1975, sociologist Daniel Bell announced "The End of American Exceptionalism," concluding that the "American Century" had "foundered on the shoals of Vietnam"; the experience made Americans realize that "we are a nation like all other nations."[26] In the revised Norton edition of *The First New Nation* (1979), even Lipset was preoccupied with defending against the apparent demise of the American Dream. He conceded that "pollsters registered a steady decline in the public's confidence in the country's institutions and in the people running them."[27]

Notwithstanding the importance of the Vietnam and Watergate experiences, a key predicament of the 1970s was the economic stagnation of capitalism in that decade, along with the closely related environmental awareness of growing resource depletion on a global scale. The simultaneous appearance of inflation and rising unemployment led to the widespread use of a new word, *stagflation*, to describe the sorry state of the global capitalist order developed under American tutelage since the 1944 Bretton Woods Agreement. The year 1970 witnessed the first Earth Day, and transnational environmental organizations such as Greenpeace began to preach the end of resource abundance. The first oil crisis came when the Organization of Petroleum Exporting Countries cut production in 1973 in retaliation against Israel's supporters during the Arab-Israeli (Yom Kippur) War. Reliance on foreign oil predicted in the 1950s was suddenly manifest. President Richard Nixon countered by imposing gasoline rationing and conservation measures. In 1978–79, the Iranian Revolution shattered U.S. relations with Iran and disrupted the oil supply once more; output dropped, prices soared, and the second great oil shock of the 1970s resulted. Rather than simply blame the Iranians, however, President Jimmy Carter pointed to the material limits that the nation appeared to face. For him it was the end of abundance, which had underwritten so much of American exceptionalism. He saw a "crisis of confidence" rooted in energy scarcity and its attendant problems. His nationally televised speech of July 15, 1979, seemed to confirm "the American malaise," and thereafter it was known as the "Malaise Speech."[28]

Carter did not abandon exceptionalism entirely. He believed the nation could regain its special position as the exemplary world leader if Americans harnessed their inner resourcefulness as a people. As political commentators have noted, he also "attempted to conduct a foreign policy consistent with the belief in American exceptionalism, particularly through his human rights policy."[29] In any case, the response of liberal intellectuals to the imminent "end of American exceptionalism" was less alarmist than Carter's. In 1978, before Carter's speech, an interesting symposium, "From Abundance to Scarcity: Implications for the American Tradition," brought together contributions from economist Kenneth Boulding, historian Michael Kammen, and political sociologist Lipset. The tenor of the discussion was cautiously optimistic and did not endorse exceptionalism's disappearance. Kammen and Lipset, especially, affirmed reliance on the resourcefulness of the American people and on technology to rescue the United States from its then-current "malaise."[30]

The wider context of Carter's speech often has been forgotten. The evangelical Baptist Carter was the heir to the long tradition of Christian-inspired exceptionalism, and thereby the president made a crucial error in misreading his audience. In keeping with the religiously inflected exceptionalism of antebellum America, his appeal to the American people rested on a jeremiad.

It was their wrongdoing, one might almost still say sin, that lay at the heart of the nation's problems. This analytical frame was compatible with the Puritan jeremiad.[31] Translated into the practical issues facing the nation, from domestic energy problems and a flagging economy, Carter accused the American people of wrongdoing. Individual Americans he held responsible for overproduction through their wasteful ways, and for the more general morass into which the nation had reputedly sunk. "Too many of us now tend to worship self-indulgence and consumption," Carter complained. "Human identity is no longer defined by what one does, but by what one owns." Carter decried the "growing disrespect for government" and the "fragmentation and self-interest" that prevented Americans from tackling the energy crisis but added that the problem was the result of their own dependence on materialism.[32] This was a traditional jeremiad in which exceptionalist discourse provided the implicit standard of judgment.

So startling was this accusation that many observers failed to notice Carter spreading the blame around. While chastising the nation's people, he also faulted government for the nation's failings, asserting that in looking "for a way out of this crisis, our people have turned to the Federal Government and found it isolated from the mainstream of our nation's life."[33] Confusingly, this part of his indictment recalled the Court versus Country tradition, not the excoriation of the people's sin through a jeremiad.[34] Carter was caught in the middle of these two concepts because the polling evidence fed to him indicated that there was indeed growing dissatisfaction with government, as the Court versus Country dichotomy required.[35]

The incumbent Carter's nemesis in the 1980 presidential campaign, Ronald Reagan, differed in that he focused single-mindedly on the ills of government.[36] Aligned with growing antigovernment feeling, Reagan took advantage of the mood and, in practice, adopted a Court versus Country position.[37] Reversing the point of the jeremiad, Reagan made "the people" the source of virtue and the cleansing of government the solution. This was a highly successful strategy. In this context of wanting to maintain American abundance and self-certainty in an era of global insecurity, the more charismatic Reagan provided an easygoing wish fulfillment for American exceptionalist ideas over Carter's emphasis on the nation's "inner faults."[38] But, in doing so, Reagan departed from the Puritan jeremiad and dumbed down the idea of chosenness into a patriotic exercise. He invented an optimistic or "modern" jeremiad, some scholars argue, yet the target was not the collective community as the true jeremiad required.[39]

Prominent evangelicals persisted with a jeremiad, but they distorted its meaning and worked with Reagan in the promotion of a new American conservatism. Thus, the pro-Reagan Moral Majority founder Falwell moved away from the traditional lament. Even as he bemoaned neglect of time-honored "family values," Falwell condemned liberal elites and abstractions such as "humanism" and "communism" for such national failings, rather than focused on the collective sin of a people. As an antidote, he championed the "free enterprise system" as "clearly outlined in the Book of Proverbs in the Bible." Business success was key to God's plan for the American people, Falwell asserted. His authorities were more often secular ones like the free market economist Milton Friedman than theologians.[40] Other televangelist preachers, including Jim Bakker and Jimmy Swaggart (until disgrace over fraud and sexual scandal) also stressed material prosperity.[41] Swaggart and Falwell put their organizational, financial, and media support behind Reagan's successful presidential campaigns of 1980 and 1984.

The Power of the Positive

Under these cultural influences, a far from self-critical American exceptionalism took hold as the Reagan administration repudiated the 1970s "malaise." Identifying the decade with Carter's impotent presidency, Reagan's "shining" alternative exuded a warmer and fuzzier civil religion. Confessing that he had "always believed this blessed land was set apart in a special way," Reagan gave the idea of a chosen status an entirely new gloss.[42] Although Reagan's stern sense of a Manichean battle between good and evil—represented in the form of the United States versus the Soviet Union—was prominent in his rhetoric, an alignment with positive thinking was overarching. His optimistic outlook resembled the mood of the Reverend Norman Vincent Peale's message and Peale's best-selling book, *The Power of Positive Thinking* (1952). Reagan was able to transform American exceptionalism into a signifier of positivity based on the Shining City, an idea shed of negativity or conflict.[43] This connection is hinted at in Reagan's bestowing of the Presidential Medal of Freedom on Peale for his contribution to "theology." Reinhold Niebuhr (who died in 1967) would probably not have been impressed.[44]

By vigorously reasserting American singularity, Reagan stimulated national confidence from the beginning of his presidency. Political scientist David Forsythe observed that "it was Reagan's victory in 1980 that more than any other event restored a moralistic American exceptionalism to dominance."[45] But moralism was not the only result. Proclaiming "morning in America" in his 1984 campaign, and therefore just the beginning of American power and influence, Reagan raised morale as well as moralism, and he scored enormously successful political points among ordinary American voters. His achievement was reinforced with the subsequent collapse of state communism in Eastern Europe (1989–91), which further enhanced the prestige of American exceptionalism in an era glibly proclaimed "The End of History."[46] It is one of history's ironies that *exceptionalism* was a term taken from Soviet-era Russia, since Russians after the Cold War's end wanted nothing more than to abandon the idea that their own history had messianic implications worth copying. At precisely this moment, the United States was embracing its own sense of messianic, utopian exceptionalism, borrowed in terminology from Soviet communism, as a blueprint for the future of the world based on a free market, liberal globality.[47]

The post–Cold War environment changed U.S. global relationships in ways favorable to the legacy of Reagan's exceptionalism. From the 1950s to 1980s, the United States had been widely acknowledged in the West, though perhaps not among unaligned nations, as the leader of the "free world." Yet, until 1989, a restraining influence operated on American hubris. Limiting extravagant statements was the Soviet Union's presence as a hydrogen bomb-possessing superpower from 1953. To some academic observers of Soviet development, the Soviets actually represented another form of exceptionalism, and, as long as that perception survived, it kept the lid on American exceptionalist doctrine as an unbounded claim. In the Cold War, the United States had necessarily to depend on its allies, especially its treaty partners, not all of whom liked the idea of a nation set apart from history, and who found the idea out of kilter with the American postwar abandonment of political and diplomatic isolationism. Though different in many ways, both the United States and the Soviet Union had a history of abundant natural resources; both had a "frontier" experience, and the Soviets were even held to possess potential for "modernization." This was the origin of the convergence theories of political development reflected, in diverse ways, in the works of Marshall Goldman, Marion J. Levy, and other social scientists.[48] The success of the space satellite Sputnik in 1957 had raised the image of the USSR as a modernizing, scientific and technological, albeit malevolent, system.[49] This is why the assertions of American exceptionalism in the era of postwar economic expansion were not wedded to an assigned religious status.[50]

Only the Cold War's end allowed an exceptionalism endowed by "History" itself to flourish uninhibited. It was in the first post–Cold War decade that the Clinton administration, through Secretary of State Madeleine Albright, spoke of the United States as the "indispensable" nation, though that still presumed allies and multilateralism, not isolationism or unilateralism.[51] "If we have to use force," Albright declared in regard to American pressure on Iraq, "it is because we are America; we are the indispensable nation." Albright failed to use the word *exceptionalism*, but her focus on the American republic transcended time, in the way exceptionalism requires. Only "America" could see time unfolding and survey capital *H* History from above, Albright claimed: "We stand tall and we see further than other countries into the future, and we see the danger here to all of us." The "indispensable nation" was a declaration of exceptionalism as the supreme rationale for U.S. foreign policy, and it remained an assumption until the time of Donald Trump.[52]

Endgame

The underlying ideas of exceptionalism had not died during the upheavals of the 1970s; they flourished in its aftermath. Moreover, those ideas had assumed new and more potent forms understood not as heuristic possibilities for social science investigation but as established truth. That was not enough, however. The sentiment still lacked a way to consolidate the disparate elements of American singularity. Seymour Martin Lipset's tireless work could be harnessed to that need. The new expression for articulating the nation's radical difference was to become capitalized "American Exceptionalism." After a lifetime of thinking about the issue, Lipset returned to write three books exploring the idea, in 1990, 1996, and 2000 (this third one coauthored with Gary Marks).[53] Soon after, the terrorist attacks of September 11, 2001, opened the way for Lipset's term to synthesize and express the underlying concept manifest in numerous permutations over the course of American history.

The use of an explicit and "exclusive" sense of American Exceptionalism as a state ideology arose in this context of the war on terror.[54] In 2007, former New York mayor Rudy Giuliani spoke as an aspiring presidential candidate at the National Lawyers Convention sponsored by the Federalist Society. Giuliani tried to rally the conservative lawyers and judges assembled by trademarking his candidacy with explicit reference to the term.[55] In this intervention, the influence of Lipset was not far from the surface. The prominent neoconservative and editor of *Commentary* Norman Podhoretz was Giuliani's foreign policy "adviser," friend, and ally in the failed presidential campaign. Podhoretz attributed his own fervent belief in American Exceptionalism to the Lipset book of that title published in 1996, and Lipset was a respected contributor to *Commentary*. It is plausible to suggest that Podhoretz influenced the ex-mayor, but the speech also reflected a wider context.[56]

The source was an upwelling of ideas during George W. Bush's presidency. Bush began to talk more openly about chosenness and liberty as distinguishing national features. He also used the old settler rhetoric of the frontier and the subjugation of American Indians legitimated through Manifest Destiny

as a parallel with the task to eliminate transnational Islamic terrorism, especially in Afghanistan.[57] Discussion of exceptionalism in the national press
rose, and progressive critics of the Bush administration drew on ideas of a
(nobler) exceptionalism of good example and high moral standards. Senator
Barack Obama of Illinois tried to present his own position affirming a positive
reclamation of the American Dream in *The Audacity of Hope* (2006).[58] But
some progressives and conservatives attacked exceptionalism as necessarily
a source of American hubris. The invasion of Iraq in 2003 and the American
military conduct there ensured a mixed reception for exceptionalist claims.
To many Americans and others around the world, the United States looked
more like an empire than a shining example of liberal universalism.

In defense of exceptionalism, neoconservatives gave shrill emphasis to
how the United States would bring democracy to the Arab world. Middle
East policy was, in reality, largely a matter of geopolitical calculation, but the
Bush administration nevertheless mobilized an ideology of American singularity to preserve and extend democracy. Alongside thinly veiled assertions
of the chosen nation, the arguments pointedly included not only a patriotic
alignment with God but also the universalist implications of the American
Creed applied to the Islamic world. In this context, gender became an ideological centerpiece. The analysis of women's (symbolic) role in American
society—from Alexis de Tocqueville and Catharine Beecher in Jacksonian
times, to James Bryce's *American Commonwealth* in 1888, and Richard Nixon
against the Soviet Union in 1959—now reached its apotheosis. Noticeable in
George W. Bush's articulation of his agenda was the attention not to economic
equality of opportunity but to the poor treatment of women under Islamic
fundamentalism. Bush assumed the equal status of women in the United States,
a dubious point, and made the liberation of all women an important justification for the invasion of Afghanistan in 2001. To a lesser extent, he raised
similar arguments for the Iraq War in 2003. In reaction, progressive critics
distinguished between rhetoric and reality, since the impact of the Middle
East wars on the position of women internationally—and, indeed, on democracy itself—was far from positive.[59] That opinion was shared by some conservatives. The former military officer, prolific historian, and self-professed conservative Andrew Bacevich denounced the Iraq War and saw in it evidence of
exceptionalism's baleful effects.[60]

Other conservatives doubled down on criticism as antipatriotic and seemed
barely shaken in their enthusiasm for exceptionalism. The Federalist Society
convention at which Giuliani spoke was revealing of conservative tendencies
as the political and economic circumstances deteriorated at the end of the
Bush presidency. The convention made (capitalized) American Exceptional-

ism its overarching theme, and keynote sessions announced its importance. Could the United States continue to maintain the global hegemony that many conservatives regarded as central to the survival of the world as they knew it in November 2007? That was the context for the new interest in an up-front exceptionalist doctrine.[61]

One of the keynote speakers was historian Gordon Wood of Brown University, who dismissed the ideas of "antiexceptionalist" historians. Wood asserted that American Exceptionalism was born in the American Revolution, an event that made the nation different from all other countries because of the way it changed the "national" mind-set. Americans were, stated Wood, "leaders . . . of the free world as early as 1776." Wood told how, in the minds of Americans, that revolution was responsible for the French upheaval of 1789, colonial rebellions in Latin America, and other salutary developments in the progress of freedom across the globe.[62] No mention was made of the slave rebellion led by Toussaint L'Ouverture in Saint-Domingue (later Haiti) and the American government's mostly negative response to those events. Wood elided the distinction between what the American Revolution actually was and what it was believed to be. The assumptions that the United States was different in both "fact" and values to other nations merged.[63]

Despite Giuliani's intervention, this new assertion of U.S. singularity did not come to dominate national political discourse until after the 2008 election. As the presidency of George W. Bush imploded amid the global financial crisis, its economic impacts stole the political show at first. It was the confluence of global economic instability and the election of an African American as president that provided the tipping point, spurring a conservative Republican revolt to defend a national creed. When President Obama gave his now-famous press conference in Strasbourg in April 2009, he explained the sense in which he supported the exceptionalist doctrine, and only then did the high-level political reaction begin.[64] The outcome was the Republican Party's remaking of American Exceptionalism into the central intellectual rationale of its 2012 platform against Obama's reelection.

Labeling Obama as against exceptionalism enabled his enemies to make the concept stand for two things: white power and antisocialism. Obama's blackness offended old ethnonationalist assumptions that power should never be shared with nonwhites. But critics, including Donald Trump, also began to undermine Obama by falsely claiming that Obama was not born in the United States. Foreignness blended into blackness as stigma, even as Obama was, biologically, "half" white. But racial and xenophobic bigotry was not enough. For the right-wing Fox News and *Washington Times*, Monica Crowley applied the political implications of the president's stance on exceptionalism to domestic policy and used the idea as a way of galvanizing opposition to "big government." She focused especially on the Affordable Care Act, referred to derisively as "Obamacare," as an example of creeping socialism, claiming that "the American people have been shackled by a new set of chains. The United States of America—once great, grand and free—is on the path to becoming just another country," like those in "socialist" Europe. In Crowley's view, Obama was "accomplishing this by expanding government in unprecedented ways. It's unprecedented for us, although it's certainly not unprecedented in the kinds of countries into which he's trying to turn us. By expanding government into every nook and cranny of your life . . . he will exponentially grow the base of people dependent on the federal government." The "Europe" versus "America" trope served her well. Obama's health care "reform" was about remaking "America into a two-bit, second-rate, debt-laden European socialist backwater"—such as those revealed in the financial crisis of 2007–10. In response to the challenge, Crowley issued a "note" to the president and his congressional allies: "We are exceptional Americans, and you are wholly unexceptional thieves of freedom. We want our liberty and exceptionalism back. We're throwing off the chains."[65]

Declinism and Contemporary Exceptionalism

We can only speculate what Seymour Martin Lipset might have made of such rhetoric. In 2001, he suffered a severe stroke. As a result of this considerable incapacity, he was unable to write in the wake of the 9/11 Al-Qaeda attacks, and collaborators completed his final publications. He died December 31, 2006. Likely his response would have conformed to his own version of exceptionalism based on an interest in empirical facts of American difference from other countries, not the rhetoric of chosenness. What he would have thought of President Donald Trump is also a matter for speculation, though he might well have slotted the businessman-showman-president into the cases he and Earl Raab had analyzed on right-wing and populist movements as a "strain" on the social system—yet an irritation incapable of overturning the key values of the American (liberal and democratic) Creed.[66]

That stated, since 2006 the history of American exceptionalism has become quite perverse in ways that Lipset would have struggled to comprehend. He would probably have observed the many economic and political challenges to American hegemony on a global scale since 2001. Concern over the "decline" of the United States reached a shrill pitch in this period. Writer Morris Berman produced the luridly titled *Dark Ages America: The Final Phase of Empire* in 2006.[67] In 2017, the prominent University of Wisconsin historian Alfred W. McCoy published *In the Shadows of the American Century: The Rise and Decline of US Global Power*.[68] It is tempting to consider these titles as bookends for an anguished era, but the prediction of, if not lamentation over, imperial decline has continued. Trump's rise led to what might be termed hyperspeculation on the end of exceptionalism. This was compounded by the 2020 coronavirus pandemic, in which the United States became emblematic of failed global leadership after vying with Brazil for the title of worst-handled virus outbreak worldwide.[69] Yet exceptionalism cannot be so easily displaced.

The discourse of American decline has grown at the same time that the affirmation of exceptionalism has intensified and become a matter of political and ideological conformity. This is a departure from the past, when the gap between the material condition of the United States and belief in the doctrine was not so pronounced; and when episodes of declinist anxiety tended to alternate with more positive outlooks on exceptionalism. The debate over whether or not Obama was an exceptionalist, as discussed in the introduction of this book, became part of this struggle to control the central concepts of American identity. In turn, this alignment of national and personal identity helps explain why the contemporary battle over the slogan of a capitalized American Exceptionalism has been so fiercely fought.

Critics of declinism offered reasonable empirical propositions for the continuing preeminence of the United States. After about 2011 the nation began to emerge from the Great Recession and by 2018 was deemed in better shape in gross domestic product growth than many other countries. A self-confessed declinist, Clyde Prestowitz, the president of the Washington-based Economic Strategy Institute, swiftly changed tack to argue that the resource base of the American economy made the nation exceptionally strong in global perspective. The coming of the fracking revolution in the petroleum and gas industry led to cheaper energy and, with the touted extension of 3D printing, created possibilities for the repatriation of manufacturing to the United States, thus providing hope for the future.

The other problem for antideclinists is the short-term vision of most predictive observations. Rome was not built in a day, so the saying goes, nor was the decline of the Roman Empire a hasty affair. It was protracted, as was the demise of the British Empire. Current supporters of American Exceptionalism forget time because their mental map is one of a country outside of time. In the actually existing world, if the United States were to decline, that would take a considerable period to be complete and, most probably, would reflect a *relative* slump as the American nation-state became less and less a self-contained vessel in a world of globalization and transnational cultural connections. Since the 1970s, the United States has recovered from prophecies of economic decay common in that decade and moved to a more pervasive global preeminence in military and some technological capacities, but the arc of economic growth has been less and less able at each peak to match that of the 1950s and 1960s, the period in which Lipset analyzed the American Creed. Inequality has increased and social mobility has fallen.[70]

This longer-term tendency toward chastened material outcomes would not necessarily shake exceptionalism. Some commentators have used the evidence of decline to focus on the negative aspects of the doctrine, such as the indices of anything from mass incarceration to COVID-19 failures. In this telling, the United States remains exceptional, albeit in undesirable ways. Positive judgments on the nation's prospects continue to be made too, partly because the evidence on economic and social performance since 2009 is very mixed, but also because many assertions of exceptionalism depart from concern with empirical testing. That is because the belief in exceptionalism is closely tied to political and personal identity. In the era of "fake news," facts of relative decline versus other countries did not matter to the ideologues of contemporary American Exceptionalism.[71]

The capacity of individuals to ignore the changing geopolitical "reality" of the American position in the world means that belief in exceptionalism is likely to persist. If so, it will become an ever-greater social "strain," to recall Lipset's term. The travails of Trump might eventually come to seem like a sideshow or, more likely, a portent. If the Trump presidency signifies anything for the future, it shows how difficult it has been to implement his agenda of "America First" as a way to greatness because the transnational connections between the United States and "the world" are so deep and wide—this, thanks in no small part to the role of the United States as the chief agent of globalization since 1945. That legacy, in immigration policy, trade, and security, proved harder to unwind than Trump anticipated.

Trump may not have believed in American Exceptionalism, if his words are to be taken at face value, but context leads one to question that judgment. Even as America First's ethnonationalism is not an exceptionalist program per se, in the past ethnonationalism cohabited with, and sometimes absorbed or shaped, exceptionalism by treating "America" as a racially special nation. Moreover, in the present circumstances many of Trump's backers within the Republican Party, such as Newt Gingrich, and conservative media and think tanks certainly do endorse American Exceptionalism.[72] Among these allies is the Heartland Institute, which supported Trump in the 2020 presidential election and which continues to ply climate change denial.

In 2016, the Heartland Institute joined the #OurAmerica coalition—"a nationwide movement to bring our country together to emphasize what makes America fundamentally good and what distinguishes it from other nations—in short American Exceptionalism."[73] The partners in #OurAmerica included organizations devoted to such themes as geopolitical supremacy, support for Israel, confrontation with Iran, immigration restriction, hostility to affirmative action in education and employment, and opposition to liberal progressivism on campuses.[74] This conservative Republican program is very close to the actual policy objectives of the Trump administration. But largely lost in this contemporary conservative agenda is Lipset's judgment on exceptionalism as having both positive and negative consequences. In the ideology of #OurAmerica, the Lipsetian approach of establishing exceptionalism by empirical comparison with other countries is also lost. Superiority is taken for granted, and the narrative of the egalitarian American Creed is muted in favor of patriotic rhetoric about the nation's "special role in the world and in human history."[75]

Among Trump's opponents, the reaction to his presidency has also been strongly infused with exceptionalism—namely, the liberal iteration of the New Deal and post–World War II period. Trump's conduct as both an individual and a representative of the nation has offended the idea of an American global leadership based on trust and rules rather than purely transactional politics, and it has played havoc with the nation's conception of itself as a positive example to humanity. Trump's immigration policies, in particular, transgressed the Nation of Immigrants idea that has informed modern liberal exceptionalism, especially since the 1940s. Given this bipartisan resort to exceptionalist hopes and fears, debates over exceptionalism's content will probably remain influential for decades to come.

What can we conclude about the substance of American exceptionalism as a description of the United States and its history? The simple answer is this: exceptionalism cannot be proven either by logical reasoning or by empirical evidence, and its existence as a "thing" can be understood only as a cumulative set of beliefs. The history of American exceptionalism is the sum total of the efforts to explain or interpret American experience as exceptional. The circulatory implications of this statement are as inevitable as they are obvious: The United States is exceptional because a large majority of Americans have believed it to be so. They have been taught to think it so, or have in their own experience come to identify with the nation's ideals and commitments. This task of outlining the shifting discourse expressing this allegiance has been undertaken in this book.

That is not to say that U.S. history and institutions lack empirically distinctive characteristics. For contemporary comparisons, this would include mass incarceration, the electoral college, and the very high incidence of private gun ownership. There are other distinctive, even exceptional, aspects, many far more positive, but a bunch of such cases either negative or positive does not amount to a system of exceptionality. The only observable "exceptional" phenomena transcending individual national differences are the constructed systems of beliefs or collective mentalities that Americans hold, but those beliefs are not truly exceptional either, as many other countries have claimed to be exceptional or religiously "chosen," as discussed in chapter 1. The rejoinder that those other places are not important in contemporary geopolitics or hegemonic in global status misunderstands the necessarily qualitative and transhistorical nature of exceptionalist claims.

Many characteristics often proffered as evidence for American exceptionalism are more correctly quantitative difference. The modern notion of U.S. exceptionalism has been bolstered by preponderant wealth and power, especially since 1945. That makes the nation seem exceptional, at least in its influence and perception if not in its essence. But "exceptional" is unconsciously confused in these cases with "greatest," where the latter is part of a numerical scale, not something outside the scale. Whether consciously or not, wealth and power have also projected through the modern mass media an image of American specialness associated with modernity. Already extensive across Western Europe and the British Empire's settler dominions in the 1920s because of Hollywood films and the export of mass-produced consumer goods, this cultural influence has become global since 1945 and particularly since the fall of communism in Europe as an ideological alternative to liberal capitalism.[1]

The importance of the United States also reflects, in the contemporary world, its continuing status as an imperial project. Many researchers prefer to call the geopolitical preponderance of the post-1945 United States "hegemonic" because it has not focused on large overseas land acquisitions or rule over subject peoples. Like other imperial powers, the United States faced pressures in the global wave of postcolonial movements of the post-1945 period to give self-government, independence, or citizenship rights to overseas territories, but the United States actually retained sovereignty or de facto control over its widely spread island territories, except for the Philippines.[2] More important, if empire involves the exertion of force to change sovereign regimes or their policies, then the United States may legitimately be considered an empire, even today. To interfere with the sovereignty of another country (whether through unilateral economic coercion, especially as applied in extraterritorial contexts, threatened military action, the use of drones as extrajudicial killing of foreign nationals, or actual invasion and regime change), and to combine that attempt to control others with the occupation of (some eight hundred) overseas bases around the global is quintessentially imperial, precisely because it relies on force, not a mutually acknowledged and agreed hegemony.[3] The nation's earlier "expansion" as a settler democracy involving or incorporating indigenous peoples is still part of this modern story, though settler colonialism is obscured in traditional narratives as a frontier or "pioneer" myth and has been swept, in the twentieth century, into the larger bureaucratic and political mechanisms of the American state.[4] Since the nineteenth century, this American empire has been distinctive in its specific configurations, but so too have other empires. Never has empire been based on a single template as the exceptionalist, anti-imperialist critique of empire studied in chapter 8 assumed. U.S. anti-imperialism's importance has chiefly been in structuring self-perceptions of American exceptionalism, in which it follows that only other places can have "real" empires.[5]

The critical features that have appeared to set the United States aside are not the quantitative differences in contemporary times but certain novel applications of political ideals and institutions. The most important distinction of this type was posed by Europeans as much as Americans regarding the American Revolution. That revolution served, many historians have assumed, as progenitor and model for the transition from empire to nation-state that characterized modern world history from the late eighteenth century to the twentieth. Europeans and Americans alike described republican government as the "American experiment" in the nineteenth century. By the 1820s, republics spread across Latin America and the Caribbean, but the influence came principally from the French Revolution of 1789.[6] The Swiss constitution of 1848 was a republican confederation influenced to some extent by American precedents, and later, the U.S. Constitution became a partial model in some other countries, such as Australia in several features of its federal constitution, though that country retained the Westminster parliamentary system (1901). The U.S. Constitution has been considered one of the most globally distinctive in its "brevity" and "omission of positive rights," though these characteristics do not apply to the state constitutions that form an important part of the American state structure.[7] The federal constitution is widely touted as the longest lasting and most stable worldwide, yet, as historian Eric Foner has argued, the Civil War and Reconstruction (1861–77) marked a sharp break and a de facto "second founding" moment.[8]

Seymour Martin Lipset made much of the American Revolution's novelty as a pioneering republic in *The First New Nation*: "The United States was the first major colony successfully to revolt against colonial rule." But Lipset knew an anticolonial revolt was not enough to make his case for American exceptionalism. The Dutch Republic of the seventeenth century was not only an earlier example of republicanism but also a major imperial and trading power, as discussed in chapter 2. Lipset could escape from this criticism because he elided republicanism and democracy, stating that "America's key values—equality and achievement—stem from our revolutionary origins." American political leaders "in the first half-century of our existence were instinctively 'democrats' believing that the United States had a special mission to perform in introducing a new form of political order to the world."[9] As Lipset tacitly conceded, it was less the revolution than the advent of democracy, with (supposedly) manhood suffrage progressively extended from 1800 to the 1840s, that made the United States worthy of the title it bore for foreigners as a great experiment. That accolade rang true whether foreigners applauded democracy or not. A harbinger of democracy was how Alexis de Tocqueville viewed North America in 1831, but he did not like all that he saw, nor did he characterize the United States as a system of exceptionalism to copy.[10]

How did that democratic exceptionalist image square with "reality"? Lipset found exceptionalism in the commitment to democracy through "the introduction of universal suffrage in America long before it came in other nations."[11] In this way he summoned a common perception of American specialness. But the historian Alex Keyssar has shown this quotidian assertion to be patently exaggerated. His magisterial opus on voting rights shows that by the 1850s, American suffrage was notionally extended to adult males in almost all states. However, the detail was mind-bogglingly complex. Voting rights were limited, except in six northeastern states, to white men. In five New England states alone, free, so-called colored American men could vote in the 1850s and, in New York, property-owning qualifications removed all but a fraction of potential black voters.[12] In addition, pauper or taxation status, criminal conviction, and length of residence were used in a considerable number of states to cut further the voting of the poor or transient. Objectively viewed, voting restrictions constituted, even before the Jim Crow segregation era excluded almost all Southern "free" black people from civil rights until the 1950s and 1960s, a massive impediment to seeing the United States as quintessentially democratic.

As Keyssar has stated, the right to vote was developed exceptionally well in the United States only if we ignore these qualifications and the specific social context. The elements of singularity were not the outcome of "a distinctive American commitment to democracy," Keyssar puts it, but "an unusual configuration of historical circumstances." Generous voting rights for whites were mostly achieved in the absence of a large (free) laboring class. If there had been more of one in the early nineteenth century, the right to vote would likely have been bitterly opposed by elites, as it was in Rhode Island in the 1840s, where there was already such a laboring class and where voting rights had not been extended earlier.[13]

Racism, especially, impeded the progress of American democracy. Tocqueville himself saw race relations as an exception to the generally positive prospects for equality in the United States and predicted that a race war would likely occur.[14] That would have nipped American exceptionalism in the bud. The sectional war that came in 1861 was different from what Tocqueville feared because it set North against South, not white against black. Both sides claimed to be "model" nations, as discussed in chapter 7, but the South invoked ideas of limited government and state rights to defend property in a racially based

slave system. The victory of the North meant an advance of sorts for democracy, as human slavery was declared off limits, yet democracy still meant individualism in a racially structured society, a condition that has persisted, sometimes being undermined but at other times becoming more entrenched. As a
result, the United States faced, and still does face, the flares and embers of an
inner civil war. The Black Lives Matter protests that have erupted periodically
since 2015 provide cumulative evidence for this characteristic of persistent and
systemic racism as a feature of modern American life.[15]

Nevertheless, the United States stood up fairly well, democratically, against
most European countries throughout the nineteenth century. Monarchy or autocracy still held the key political powers before World War I, especially in the
German, Austro-Hungarian, and Russian empires. The extension of suffrage to
the (male) middle class in Britain occurred under the Reform Acts of 1832 and
1867, and to many working-class males in 1884, but substantial numbers of male
adults could still not vote before 1918, while women's voting rights were only
extended in 1918 and not complete until 1928. French men first received the vote
in 1792 and again in 1848 and then permanently in 1870. In much of continental
Europe, as illustrated in France, male suffrage was either limited in extent or periodically rescinded by war or monarchical and aristocratic restoration, hence
the attribution to the United States of exceptionality. As in so many matters, perceptions of, and comparisons with, Europe shaped American exceptionalism.[16]

However, U.S. singularity in democracy is challenged if we consider, as we
should, settler colonial societies outside Europe, and particularly if we extend
the idea of democracy to social conditions. The extension of "universal"—
that is, manhood—suffrage came to the "self-governing" Australian colonies
of New South Wales, Victoria, and South Australia from 1855 to 1857. New
Zealand achieved manhood suffrage in 1879. The influences in Australasia
came not from the United States but from British liberal reformers and
working-class agitators who migrated to those British colonies, mostly after
the end of convict transportation to eastern Australia in 1840. Despite European Australia's early convict origins, the influence of Chartist sentiment
among immigrants from the British Isles helped make most Australian colonies and New Zealand more inclusive as democracies than the United States
by the 1870s because a far higher proportion of the adult male population
could vote.[17] To be sure, indigenous people were still shamefully excluded
from voting in Australia, as in the United States. Many Native Americans,
particularly those on reservations, lacked citizenship until 1924, and in some
cases lacked voting rights until the 1960s, just as Aboriginal Australians did.

The arrival in 1902 of womanhood suffrage for the newly constituted Australian federation, the Commonwealth of Australia, with similar but earlier

success in New Zealand (1893), made those new British self-governing dominions into polities more socially democratic than the American version.[18]
Australian parliaments extended the democratic legacy by introducing structural measures to increase inclusiveness and eliminate corruption and bias
in polling arrangements. These admittedly imperfect changes included the
nineteenth-century secret ballot, which was then exported to Europe and the
United States. Other innovations were federal electoral procedures and ma-
chinery (1902), and "compulsory" voting (1924). Though the idea of compulsory voting has been anathema in the United States, casting a valid vote was
not strictly compulsory in Australia, only being marked off the electoral roll
at a polling place.[19]

Progressive social and labor legislation that Americans reformers envied
followed greater representativeness. Socialists, social scientists, and labor reformers, both Americans and Europeans, traveled to Australia and New Zealand to see the Antipodean "socialisme sans doctrines," as the French scholar
Albert Métin phrased it—a pragmatic social democracy that gave Australia
the first national Labor Party government in the world in 1904 and a majority Labor government in 1910.[20] Theodore Roosevelt was impressed. He sent
one astute government economist to study the innovations in labor relations,
especially arbitration systems, and another federal official to examine land
tenure.[21] By then, Australasia was much more at the forefront of social democracy than the United States, where the practice of even political equality
fell far short of the rhetoric. As one Australian senator boasted, "We are in
politics the pacemakers of the world."[22] Hot air aside, on grounds of democracy, late nineteenth- and early twentieth-century Australia and New Zealand
had at least as strong a case to be considered exceptional, an argument rarely
heard by modern-day Americans because the almost exclusive measurement
of American exceptionalism against purely Western European standards has
blinkered perceptions. American exceptionalists could not escape the compelling antiexceptionalist argument of Australasian examples without re-
sorting to questions of size and latter-day importance as nations rather than
qualitative differences.[23]

It has not been the point of this book to substitute one form of national
exceptionalism (whether Australia, New Zealand, or any other country's) for
another. That would be both unnecessary and inaccurate.[24] There was exaggeration in Australian boasting, just as there was American bombast in
the "spread-eagle oratory" at Fourth of July celebrations that irritated British observers in the nineteenth century. Moreover, the novelty of the Australian form of social democracy has long since faded. Yet, such awkward
comparisons allow us to see that the U.S. record on democracy has been a

mixed—not exceptional—one; at first it was an "experiment" piquing great interest abroad, but later the United States was superseded as a radical example. American exceptionalism became focused more squarely on the nation's economic achievements in the growth of capitalism, but rising inequality caused labor unions and socialists in the United States and Europe to question whether the promise of American republican citizenship could be kept for all (as discussed in chapters 8 and 9). In this brief set of comparisons, one can see that exceptionalism does not arise from empirical reality in comparative perspective. Rather, it reflects the reproduction of belief.

The penultimate observation to make on democracy is that Americans have been riven by division over whether the United States could be simply an example to the world or whether a mission to spread American values around the world was intrinsic to the national experience. But that distinction is beside the point. Neither boasting of a specialness rooted in an example to the world nor a proclivity to export that example in a missionary or messianic enthusiasm was limited to the United States. Such pressures of ideological expansionism were part of the agenda of global modernity in the nineteenth century and after. Most notably, French republican armies tried to export the French Revolution in Europe after 1793, and, after 1917, the Bolshevik revolutionaries in Russia cheered on their own agenda as a socialist model for the world over seven decades.[25]

As noted in the introduction, an exemplar status versus activist or missionary expansion presents a false dichotomy. American values have often been admired from afar, specifically the ideals of democracy and freedom rather than the practice. The Declaration of Independence traveled metaphorically around the world and inspired many reformers and revolutionaries. In such enthusiasm, foreigners broke down the gap between a singular American experience and a globally relevant example because they chose to use (and adapt) democratic ideas of the inalienable rights of a people for their own purposes. In 1945, Ho Chi Minh could deploy the U.S. Declaration of Independence in a Vietnamese Marxist revolution. So too did South Asian and Irish nationalists, among others, draw on the declaration to varying degrees.[26] Democracy is a shared value even as it is interpreted differently by conservatives, liberals, and radicals across the globe. But, as Soviet messianism suggests, the tendency to seek exportation of a national ideological system was not limited to the United States.

The final point is that material superiority offers a different and even trickier case for exceptionality than democracy or mission. The abundance of American resources in the eighteenth and nineteenth centuries, and of the American economy, particularly the consumer-based economy since the

1920s, has attracted great attention abroad, partly in envy and hostility but also in desires for emulation. The large internal market economy, accompanied by the idea of the "American Dream" to express that material abundance, has had great appeal for many peoples, but the sources of this appeal are mundane and nonexceptional. They concern questions of quantity, not for all time but historically conditioned. The example of immigration is pertinent to this question.

It is often argued that the attraction of immigrants to the United States reflects a belief in the American "promise" or "dream."[27] I have discussed the rise of this concept and its increasingly tarnished image of the American material performance since the 1960s (in chapters 10 and 11). Certainly, the United States has long been a refuge for persecuted people, but so too have some other nations. Regarding exceptionality in immigration, the U.S. profile is not notably distinctive in qualitative standards. Historically speaking, immigration to the United States has been quantitatively larger than any other competitor destination, and ethnically and regionally more diverse. But the *proportion* of the population from immigrant sources, even at its peak in the 1850s, was far less than comparable Anglo settler societies such as Canada, New Zealand, and Australia have registered since 1945. Literally speaking, Australia is now more a nation of immigrants than the United States has ever been in percentage terms.[28]

In evaluating the immigrant question, the Nation of Immigrants idea has been important in reinforcing American exceptionalism through rituals of public repetition. The concept reflected a social process of constructing exceptionalism in self-conscious ways, especially from the 1930s to the 1960s. To a considerable extent, the image abroad of the United States as a Nation of Immigrants continues to appeal, but within the historical record and even in contemporary events, the reasons for migrating to the United States may best be explained less in terms of an exceptional attraction than happenstance or commonplace opportunity, such as the fluctuating conditions for work in the business cycles of the Atlantic economy. Otherwise, it is hard to account for the often forgotten but huge out-migration or "repatriation" to Europe in the late nineteenth and early twentieth centuries. Equally important, immigrant reception in the United States has been mixed, at best, rather than generally welcoming (as discussed in chapters 8 and 9). Movement to the United States was part of Atlantic and even world migration patterns, in which people journeyed to and fro under the influences of industrialization, urbanization, war, and political upheaval. For Europeans, the main nineteenth-century source of (free) migration to the Western Hemisphere, it was far easier and cheaper to reach the United States before 1914 than either Latin America or Australasia, the other two obvious competitor destinations. Australasia especially had a huge disadvantage in distance.[29]

Even today, the United States is a mecca for migrants and a subject of fraught political division over them, but the attractions are not qualitatively exceptional. The majority of illegal migrants now come from close by the United States, but they often follow familiar national patterns largely regional in nature, and to that extent, they parallel the early twenty-first-century African and Middle Eastern refugee migration to Europe.[30] Nevertheless, it is true that the American Dream is still a factor in migration to the United States for the ambitious from many countries, and for terrorized people from the Global South with little or nothing to lose and with nowhere better to head without access to expensive airline tickets.[31] The latter groups, many of them Central Americans and Mexicans, seek work and wish for security, both items not assured in the United States but better covered than in their homelands.

Like most Americans, many foreigners are still caught in the image of the United States as exceptional. Despite widespread international dismay over Trump's presidential performance, a majority of non-Americans retain a positive view of the United States, according to Pew Research. This is probably because there is no viable alternative for global leadership, but it is the desire of most non-Americans who think about these issues to seek international cooperation rather than a single geopolitical hegemon. To a considerable degree, the repudiation of Trump by the national electorate on November 3, 2020, might give the United States a second chance to reconsider its place in the international order, and even to move beyond the framework of American exceptionalism.[32]

✳

These words were written before Trump supporters marched to the Capitol on January 6, 2021, egged on by the soon-to-be-ex-president, and stormed the U.S. Congress. The much-vaunted capacity of the U.S. political system to effect a smooth transfer of power and to recognize the results of a presidential election was compromised in a way that raised uncomfortable antiexceptionalist comparisons with coup attempts in other nations. The ensuing violence did not make the United States seem exceptional on a global scale, either. On the other hand, the presidential election raised the prospect of a more circumspect and reflective reworking of exceptionalism. Joseph R. Biden Jr.'s victory creates opportunities to reconsider the hubris, vanity, and belief in inevitable triumph that has come to be considered a distinguishing part of exceptionalist doctrine since the 1990s. Whatever may be his flaws, Biden began his term fortunately placed for this task because, in his own life, he has experienced well-documented and indelible personal tragedy and loss. The capacity to understand, absorb, and deal with disappointment and failure is not usually considered an asset in the United States, as the historian C. Vann Woodward pointed out in 1953, but defeat and collective loss are circumstances that all humans, including Americans, must confront at some time. The current political, economic, and cultural conjuncture of a deeply flawed response to the coronavirus pandemic has raised the question of national disappointment and failure. Biden's experience might give him empathy, modesty, and sober judgment to deal with this contemporary circumstance.[33]

An even modest change in national consciousness regarding exceptionalism and identity is far from assured, of course. Faith in the redemption of the United States through electoral politics may be the triumph of wishful thinking over the pessimism of sober reality because the challenges are deeper than can be met by the removal of what many observers (non-Americans and Americans alike) have regarded, at a minimum, as an idiosyncratic and temperamentally unqualified president. The history of American exceptionalism is pertinent here because it may be considered as a set of sedimentary deposits on American memory, which have informed personal and community beliefs on the role of the United States in world history. Such a deep and entrenched "sediment" means that change is likely to be incremental and uneven, though earthquakes may occur. For all that, the United States in a post-Trump world remains an important object of global hope.

Acknowledgments

Sometimes I feel I have been writing this book all of my life. In fact, I began to think about this topic seriously in the mid-1980s. I am forever thankful to Dorothy Ross, James Gilbert, and the late John Higham for giving me the opportunity to present my earliest thoughts to the Organization of American Historians Annual Meeting in St. Louis, Missouri, in 1989; from which followed my "American Exceptionalism in an Age of International History," *American Historical Review* (1991). Work on this project proceeded intermittently thereafter. Some preliminary but possibly too crude conclusions were presented in a lecture at Brasenose College, Oxford University, in 2011; and in "The Myth(s) That Will Not Die: American National Exceptionalism," in *National Myths: Constructed Pasts, Contested Presents*, edited by Gérard Bouchard (New York: Routledge, 2013). Subsequently I have benefited from an Australian Research Council Discovery Grant (2015-18), without which it would have been impossible to finish the research and the manuscript. I have been aided by a number of able research assistants at various times under that grant: Marie McKenzie, Michael Thompson, Stuart Rollo, and James Keating. Among colleagues in Australia, David Goodman was unstintingly generous (and perceptive) in his reading of the entire text, and Mike McDonnell, as Australia's leading expert on the American Revolution and early republican era, helped greatly with the early chapters.

In an important sense, all of my friends and colleagues among historians in the United States have contributed, and without them my work would be nothing. But I must single out for special thanks discussions (over many years) with and comments by Dorothy Ross, Thomas Bender, David Thelen, and the late Roy Rosenzweig, Doug Mitchell, and Joyce Appleby. Jay Sexton and Gareth Davies have been important intellectual companions and friends since my time at Oxford University as Harmsworth Professor in 2010–11, as has Shane White (University of Sydney), for longer than either of us would care to remember. All these people have in various ways encouraged, challenged, and inspired my views on this topic. Two anonymous readers for the University of Chicago Press helped me persist and improve this work, through their interesting and supportive comments, and I thank them for everything, even when I did not totally agree with particular judgments. John Corrigan (Florida State University) supplied erudition on American religion, and I thank him for his generous donation of time. My editor, Tim Mennel, has provided astute advice. This has been a difficult project for me, and I am indebted to him for his support throughout the final year of work.

The background to this book is the stimulating intellectual environment of the University of New South Wales School of History, from the day I arrived in 1975. I thank my UNSW colleagues over the decades and also the members of the Australian and New Zealand American Studies Association. The latter provided a forum for me to talk in Auckland in 2019 on Seymour Martin Lipset and social science exceptionalism, and in Sydney in 2017 on Donald Trump. In addition, the Australian Historical Association Annual Conference provided a helpful forum for my presentation on "Australian and American Exceptionalism: The Question of Chosenness" in 2019.

As has been the case for forty-two years, my partner Diane Collins has been an inspiration. My daughters Jessica and Ellen provide me with hope for the coming generations; we are all going to need that.

Notes

Introduction

1. Gerhard Peters and John T. Woolley, "2012 Republican Party Platform," *American Presidency Project*, August 27, 2012, https://www.presidency.ucsb.edu/node/302338. The term "American exceptionalism" appeared in U.S. publications 457 times from 1980 to 2000, and 2,558 times from 2001 to 2009, leaping to 4,172 times in 2010–12. Robert R. Tomes, "American Exceptionalism in the Twenty-First Century," *Survival* 56, no. 1 (2014): 27–50, at 27.

2. Charles W. Dunn, ed., *American Exceptionalism: The Origins, History, and Future of the Nation's Greatest Strength* (Lanham, MD: Rowman and Littlefield, 2013), 3.

3. Ian Tyrrell, "The Myth(s) That Will Not Die: American National Exceptionalism," in *National Myths: Constructed Pasts, Contested Presents*, ed. Gérard Bouchard (New York: Routledge, 2013), 46–64.

4. Barack Obama, "The President's News Conference in Strasbourg," April 4, 2009, American Presidency Project, https://www.presidency.ucsb.edu/node/286249; Robert G. Patman and Laura Southgate, "Globalization, the Obama Administration and the Refashioning of US Exceptionalism," *International Politics* 53, no. 2 (March 2016): 220–38.

5. See, e.g., Sarah Palin's remarks in Gerhard Peters and John T. Woolley, "Vice-Presidential Debate at Washington University in St. Louis," October 2, 2008, American Presidency Project, https://www.presidency.ucsb.edu/node/285560.

6. David Frum, "The Sunset of American Exceptionalism," *Atlantic*, July 3, 2017, https://www.theatlantic.com/politics/archive/2017/07/the-sunset-of-american-exceptionalism/532548/.

7. Greg Sargent, "Donald Trump's Revealing Quote about 'American Exceptionalism,'" *Plum Line* (blog), *Washington Post*, June 7, 2016, https://www.washingtonpost.com/blogs/plum-line/wp/2016/06/07/donald-trumps-revealing-quote-about-american-exceptionalism/.

8. George Bennett, "Trump Defends Putin in Super Bowl Interview: 'You Think Our Country's So Innocent?'" *Atlanta Journal-Constitution*, February 5, 2017, https://www.ajc.com/news/national/trump-defends-putin-super-bowl-interview-you-think-our-country-innocent/4HJG8UTMQVjRsWso1bhMbJ/.

9. Reinhold Niebuhr, *The Irony of American History* (New York: Charles Scribner's Sons, 1952), 4.

10. Sarah Churchwell, *Behold, America: A History of America First and the American Dream* (New York: Basic Books, 2018).

11. See, e.g., Ronald Reagan, "Election Eve Address 'A Vision for America,'" November 3, 1980, American Presidency Project, https://www.presidency.ucsb.edu/node/285591; in which Reagan says, "That's when we're the shining light on the hill. Not when we respond on the basis of fear." See also Barack Obama, "Remarks at the Dignity for Children Foundation in Kuala Lumpur, Malaysia," November 21, 2015, American Presidency Project, https://www.presidency.ucsb .edu/node/311502; Barack Obama, "Remarks at the University of Nebraska Omaha in Omaha, Nebraska," January 13, 2016, American Presidency Project, https://www.presidency.ucsb.edu/node /313386.

12. Churchwell, *Behold, America*.

13. One earlier use of the term has been unearthed, but no replication has been found. [William Howard Russell], "The Civil War in America," *Times* (London), August 20, 1861, 7.

14. Hilde Eliassen Restad, *American Exceptionalism: An Idea that Made a Nation and Remade the World* (New York: Routledge, 2014), 70.

15. For some examples, see A. C. McClure, "Our Unexampled Republic," *McCook (NE) Tribune*, June 29, 1906, 7; John W. Bain, *The Golden Pot* (Philadelphia: J. M. White, 1898), 230; "Whig Meeting at Bayou Chicot," *St. Landry (LA) Whig*, September 19, 1844, 2; "Mr. Douglas' Essay on the 'Dividing Line between Federal and State Authority,'" *Nevada National*, October 8, 1859, 2; Frederick Saunders, ed., *National Centennial Jubilee* (New York: E. B. Treat, 1877), 249; L. B. Woolfolk, "Memorial Address at the Baptist Centennial of Kentucky, at Louisville, May 25th," *New North-west* (Deer Lodge, MT), June 23, 1876, 4.

16. For pre-historicism as a way of thinking about historical time before, and in tension with, the emergence of historicism as an analytical tool of historians, see Dorothy Ross, "Historical Consciousness in Nineteenth-Century America," *American Historical Review* 89 (October 1984): 909–28; Ross, *Origins of American Social Science* (New York: Cambridge University Press, 1991); Patrick Smith, *Time No Longer: Americans after the American Century* (New Haven, CT: Yale University Press, 2013), 61, 70, 88.

17. Clifford Geertz, *Agricultural Involution: The Processes of Ecological Change in Indonesia* (Berkeley, CA: University of California Press, 1970), 79–82; Seymour Martin Lipset, *Continental Divide: The Values and Institutions of the United States and Canada* (New York: Routledge, 1990), 212; Seymour Martin Lipset, "Pacific Divide: American Exceptionalism–Japanese Uniqueness," *International Journal of Public Opinion Research*, 5 (June 1993): 121–66, at 159–60. Lipset also used the alternative concept of the "loaded dice," in 1963 and in 1996; see Seymour Martin Lipset, *American Exceptionalism: A Double-Edged Sword* (New York: W. W. Norton, 1996), 23–24; Seymour Martin Lipset, *The First New Nation: The United States in Historical and Comparative Perspective* (1963; repr., Garden City, NY: Anchor Books, 1967), 8.

18. Terrence McCoy, "How Joseph Stalin Invented 'American Exceptionalism,'" *Atlantic*, March 15, 2012, https://www.theatlantic.com/politics/archive/2012/03/how-joseph-stalin-invented -american-exceptionalism/254534/.

19. Daniel T. Rodgers, "Exceptionalism," in *Imagined Histories: American Historians Interpret the Past*, ed. Anthony Molho and Gordon S. Wood (Princeton, NJ: Princeton University Press, 1998), 21–40; Daniel T. Rodgers, "American Exceptionalism Revisited," *Raritan* 24, no. 2 (2004): 21–47.

20. Ulrich Gehmann, "Modern Myths," *Culture and Organization* 9 (June 2003): 105–19.

21. See Robert N. Bellah, "Civil Religion in America," *Daedalus* 96 (Winter 1967): 13; Robert N. Bellah, *The Broken Covenant: American Civil Religion in Time of Trial* (New York: Seabury, 1975), 3; Robert N. Bellah and Phillip E. Hammond, *Varieties of Civil Religion* (New York: Harper

and Row, 1980); Anthony D. Smith, *Chosen Peoples: Sacred Sources of National Identity* (Oxford: Oxford University Press, 2003), 236–37, 238–53. A notable case is France, where a civil religion was grounded in that nation's own revolutionary experience. See Charlotte Linde, *Working the Past: Narrative and Institutional Memory* (Oxford: Oxford University Press, 2006), 59; Pierre Nora, ed., *Rethinking France: Les Lieux de Mémoire*, vol. 4, *Histories and Memories* (Chicago: University of Chicago Press, 2010).

22. Alexis de Tocqueville, *Democracy in America*, trans. Henry Reeve, 2 vols. (1835–40; repr., New York: Schocken Books, 1961).

23. See, e.g., Seymour Martin Lipset, *Revolution and Counterrevolution: Change and Persistence in Social Structures* (New York: Basic Books, 1968), ch. 10.

24. See, e.g., Pandita Ramabai, *Pandita Ramabai's American Encounter: The Peoples of the United States (1889)*; ed. and trans. Meera Kosambi (Bloomington: Indiana University Press, 2003).

25. Stephen Mennell, "An Exceptional Civilizing Process?" *Journal of Classical Sociology* 9, no. 1 (2009): 97–115, at 111.

26. J. Hector St. John de Crèvecoeur, *Letters from an American Farmer and Other Essays*, edited and with an introduction by Dennis D. Moore (Cambridge, MA: Belknap Press of Harvard University Press, 2013), 32; Percy G. Adams, ed., *Crèvecoeur's Eighteenth-Century Travels in Pennsylvania and New York* (Lexington: University of Kentucky Press, 1961), xv.

27. Alan Taylor, "The American Beginning: The Dark Side of Crèvecoeur's 'Letters from an American Farmer,'" *New Republic*, July 18, 2013, https://newrepublic.com/article/113571/crevecoeurs -letters-american-farmer-dark-side.

28. Ludwig Lewisohn, introduction to *Letters from an American Farmer: Reprinted from the Original Edition*, ed. Ludwig Lewisohn (New York: Fox, Duffield, 1904), ix–xxv; J. Hector St. John de Crèvecoeur, *Sketches of Eighteenth-Century America*, ed. Henry L. Bourdin, Ralph H. Gabriel, and Stanley Williams (New Haven, CT: Yale University Press, 1925); Norman A. Plotkin, "Saint-John de Crèvecoeur Rediscovered: Critic or Paneygyrist?" *French Historical Studies* 3 (Spring 1964): 390–404, at 390–91; Rodgers, "Exceptionalism," 26.

29. "Spread-Eagle Oratory," *North Otago* (New Zealand) *Times*, November 3, 1876, 2; G. R. Coyne, *Woodrow Wilson: British Perspectives, 1912–21* (New York: St. Martin's, 1992), 4.

30. Richard Pells, "From Modernism to the Movies: The Globalization of American Culture in the Twentieth Century," *European Journal of American Culture* 23 (September 2004): 144; Richard Pells, *Not Like Us: How Europeans Have Loved, Hated, and Transformed American Culture since World War II* (New York: Basic Books, 1997).

31. Aristide R. Zolberg, "How Many Exceptionalisms?" in *Working-Class Formation: Nineteenth-Century Patterns in Western Europe and the United States*, ed. Ira Katznelson and Aristide R. Zolberg (Princeton, NJ: Princeton University Press, 1986), 397–455. One case of proliferating exceptionalisms is Scandinavian or "Nordic" exceptionalism, which sometimes becomes "Norwegian exceptionalism," and so on. See, e.g., Sofie Louise Kastrup Marcussen, "Is Scandinavian Exceptionalism Similar to American Exceptionalism?" *Slate*, January 29, 2015, https://slate .com/human-interest/2015/01/scandinavian-exceptionalism-is-it-like-american-exceptional ism.html.

32. Sacvan Bercovitch, *The American Jeremiad* (Madison: University of Wisconsin Press, 1978), 176.

33. For a selection of antiexceptionalist writings, mostly before 1860, see Timothy Roberts and Lindsay DiCuirci, ed., *American Exceptionalism*, vol. 4, *Anti-Exceptionalism* (London: Chatto and Windus, 2013).

34. John Murrin, "The Great Inversion, or, Court versus Country: A Comparison of the Revolution Settlements in England (1688–1721) and America (1776–1816)," in *Three British Revolutions: 1641, 1688, 1776*, ed. J. G. A. Pocock (Princeton, NJ: Princeton University Press, 1980), 368–453; John Murrin, "Escaping Perfidious Albion: Federalism, Fear of Aristocracy, and the Democratization of Corruption in Postrevolutionary America," in *Virtue, Corruption, and Self-Interest: Political Values in the Eighteenth Century*, ed. Richard K. Matthews (Bethlehem, PA: Lehigh University Press, 1994), 103–47.

35. See, e.g., Major L. Wilson, "The 'Country' versus the 'Court': A Republican Consensus and Party Debate in the Bank War," *Journal of the Early Republic* 15 (Winter 1995): 619–47; Murrin, "Escaping Perfidious Albion," 137–39.

36. Wendy L. Wall, *Inventing the "American Way": The Politics of Consensus from the New Deal to the Civil Rights Movement* (New York: Oxford University Press, 2008), 15–17; Lawrence R. Samuel, *The American Way of Life: A Cultural History* (Lanham, MD: Rowman and Littlefield, 2017).

37. Churchwell, *Behold, America*, 25–26, 105, 169–74; James Truslow Adams, *The Epic of America* (Boston, MA: Little, Brown, 1931), 404; Allan Nevins, *James Truslow Adams: Historian of the American Dream* (Urbana: University of Illinois Press, 1968), 68; Jim Cullen, *The American Dream: A Short History of an Idea that Shaped a Nation* (New York: Oxford University Press, 2003), 4–5.

38. Cyril Ghosh, *The Politics of the American Dream: Democratic Inclusion in Contemporary American Political Culture* (New York: Palgrave Macmillan, 2013), 35–37; Tyrrell, "Myth(s) That Will Not Die," 60n5; Jennifer L. Hochschild, *Facing Up to the American Dream: Race, Class, and the Soul of the Nation* (Princeton, NJ: Princeton University Press, 1995).

39. Gunnar Myrdal, *An American Dilemma: The Negro Problem and Modern Democracy* (New York: Harper and Brothers, 1944); Lipset, *First New Nation*, 366; Lipset, *American Exceptionalism: Double-Edged Sword*, 20. Stray references to an "American Creed" may be traced in the press back to the 1840s and the American Party, but those were used mostly to mean honorable personal conduct. This usage had survived in 1909; see *Coeur d'Alene Evening Press*, March 13, 1909, 2; cf. Churchwell, *Behold, America*, 24–26. The modern use as a patriotic civil religion dates from World War I (1914–19).

40. John Higham, *Hanging Together: Unity and Diversity in American Culture*, ed. Carl Guarneri (New Haven, CT: Yale University Press, 2001), 222.

41. Seymour Martin Lipset finds three types, but these can be further generalized into two; see Seymour Martin Lipset, review of *American Exceptionalism*, by Deborah Madsen, *Journal of American History* 87 (December 2000): 1019.

42. Byron Shafer, ed., *Is America Different? A New Look at American Exceptionalism* (Oxford: Oxford University Press, 1991); Charles Lockhart, *The Roots of American Exceptionalism*, rev. ed. (New York: Palgrave, 2012); Frank J. Lechner, *The American Exception* (New York: Palgrave, 2017); Kevin R. Reitz, ed., *American Exceptionalism in Crime and Punishment* (New York: Oxford University Press, 2017).

43. Louise C. Keely, "American Exceptionalism," in *The New Palgrave Dictionary of Economics* (London: Palgrave Macmillan, 2018), 300–304; Lall B. Ramrattan and Michael Szenberg, "American Exceptionalism: An Appraisal—Political, Economic, Qualitative, and Quantitative," *American Economist* 62, no. 2 (2017): 222–46; Stephen Gardbaum, "The Myth and the Reality of American Constitutional Exceptionalism," *Michigan Law Review* 107, no. 3 (2008), https://repository.law.umich.edu/mlr/vol107/iss3/1; Amalia D. Kessler, *Inventing American Exceptionalism: The Origins*

of American Adversarial Legal Culture, 1800–1877 (New Haven, CT: Yale University Press, 2017), 323–25, 336–37; Matt Killingsworth, "America's Exceptionalist Tradition: From the Law of Nations to the International Criminal Court," *Journal of Global Society* 33, no. 2 (2019): 285–304.

44. Quotation from Lipset, *American Exceptionalism: Double-Edged Sword*, 19. See also Lipset, *First New Nation*, 366; Dunn, *American Exceptionalism: Origins, History, and Future*, 2; Charles Murray, *American Exceptionalism: An Experiment in History* (Washington, DC: AEI Press, 2013), 19, 22.

45. Lipset, *First New Nation*, 7–8. For a major post-Lipset example, see Peter H. Schuck and James Q. Wilson, eds., *Understanding America: The Anatomy of an Exceptional Nation* (New York: Public Affairs, 2008).

46. Dean C. Tipps, "Modernization Theory and the Comparative Study of National Societies: A Critical Perspective," *Comparative Studies in Society and History* 15, no. 2 (1973): 199–226.

47. Keith Dowding, "Australian Exceptionalism Reconsidered," *Australian Journal of Political Science* 52, no. 2 (2017): 165–82, at 178.

48. For the theory, see Jürgen Kocka, "Asymmetrical Historical Comparison: The Case of the German Sonderweg," *History and Theory* 38 (February 1999): 40–50.

49. Mircea Eliade, *Myths, Dreams and Mysteries: The Encounter between Contemporary Faiths and Archaic Realities* (New York: Harper and Row, 1975), 15. See also Ivan Strenski, *Understanding Theories of Religion: An Introduction* (Malden, MA: Wiley, 2015), 146. For appraisals, see also Cristiano Grottanelli, "Discussing Theories of Myth: Four Theories of Myth in Twentieth-Century History: Cassirer, Eliade, Lévi-Strauss and Malinowski by Ivan Strenski," *History of Religions* 30 (November 1990): 197–203; Mihaela Paraschivescu, "'We the People' and God: Religion and the Political Discourse in the United States of America," *Journal for the Study of Religions and Ideologies* 11 (Winter 2012): 21–35.

50. That Winthrop was the author of the original sermon cannot be proven, but he has been closely identified with it. Abram C. Van Engen, *City on a Hill: A History of American Exceptionalism* (New Haven, CT: Yale University Press, 2020), 25–26, 296n3; Jerome McGann, "'Christian Charity,' A Sacred American Text: Fact, Truth, Method," *Textual Cultures: Texts, Contexts, Interpretation* 12 (Spring 2019): 27–52.

51. Cf. Nicholas Guyatt, *Providence and the Invention of the United States, 1607–1876* (New York: Cambridge University Press, 2007), 304.

52. David Barton, "Is America a Christian Nation?" WallBuilders, February 14, 2017, https://wallbuilders.com/america-christian-nation/#; Michael Shea, *In God We Trust: George Washington and the Spiritual Destiny of the United States of America* (self-pub., 2012), 447.

53. Katherine Stewart, *The Power Worshippers: Inside the Dangerous Rise of Religious Nationalism* (New York: Bloomsbury, 2019), 135.

54. David P. Gushee, "America Is Not God's Chosen People," Union University Institute for Intellectual Discipleship, March 12, 2003, https://www.uu.edu/institutes/id/evangelogia/post.cfm?ID=34 (content no longer available); Jennifer Crumpton, comments on the America Dream, in David Gushee, ed., *A New Evangelical Manifesto: A Kingdom Vision for the Common Good* (St. Louis, MO: Chalice Press, 2012), 216–18.

55. Patrick Wolfe, *Settler Colonialism and the Transformation of Anthropology: The Politics and Poetics of an Ethnographic Event* (London: Cassel, 1999), 167; Patrick Wolfe, *Traces of History: Elementary Structures of Race* (London: Verso, 2016), chs. 5, 6; Lorenzo Veracini, "'Settler Colonialism': Career of a Concept," *Journal of Imperial and Commonwealth History* 41,

no. 2 (2013): 313–33. Settler colonialism theory may also be applicable to the Japanese Empire, nineteenth-century Russia, and modern-day Israel. Ramon H. Myers and Mark R. Peattie, eds., *The Japanese Colonial Empire, 1895–1945* (Princeton, NJ: Princeton University Press, 1984); Jun Uchida, *Brokers of Empire: Japanese Settler Colonialism in Korea, 1876–1945* (Cambridge, MA: Harvard University Press, 2011); Amy Kaplan, *Our American Israel: The Story of an Entangled Alliance* (Cambridge, MA: Harvard University Press, 2018); Steven Sabol, *"The Touch of Civilization": Comparing American and Russian Internal Colonization* (Boulder, CO: University of Colorado Press, 2017).

56. Jeffrey Ostler and Nancy Shoemaker, "Settler Colonialism in Early American History: Introduction," *William and Mary Quarterly* 76, no. 3 (July 2019): 361–68; Jeffrey Ostler, *The Plains Sioux and U.S. Colonialism from Lewis and Clark to Wounded Knee* (Cambridge: Cambridge University Press, 2004).

57. Elizabeth Cook-Lynn, *Anti-Indianism in Modern America: A Voice from Tatekeya's Earth* (Urbana: University of Illinois Press, 2001). On the pros and cons of settler colonialism analysis, see Margaret D. Jacobs, "Seeing Like a Settler Colonial State," *Modern American History* 1 (July 2018): 257–70; Frederick E. Hoxie, "Retrieving the Red Continent: Settler Colonialism and the History of American Indians in the US," *Ethnic and Racial Studies* 31 (September 2008): 1153–67; Allan Greer, "Settler Colonialism and Empire in Early America," *William and Mary Quarterly* 76, no. 3 (July 2019): 383–90. For a settler colonial overview, see Roxanne Dunbar-Ortiz, *An Indigenous Peoples' History of the United States* (Boston: Beacon Press, 2018). For the connections of settler societies with "empire," see esp. Gautham Rao, "The New Historiography of the Early Federal Government: Institutions, Contexts, and the Imperial State," *William and Mary Quarterly* 77, no. 1 (January 2020): 117–20; and Aziz Rana, *The Two Faces of American Freedom* (Cambridge, MA: Harvard University Press, 2010).

58. Gehmann, "Modern Myths."

59. Cf. Russel B. Nye, *This Almost Chosen People: Essays in the History of American Ideas* (East Lansing: Michigan State University Press, 1966), 164.

60. Louis R. Pondy et al., eds., *Organizational Symbolism* (Greenwich, CT: JAI Press, 1983), 273–93; Mats Alvesson and Per O. Berg, *Corporate Culture and Organizational Symbolism: An Overview* (Berlin: De Gruyter, 1992), 114.

61. A point elaborated in Roddey Reid, *Globalizing Tobacco Control: Anti-Smoking Campaigns in California, France, and Japan* (Bloomington: Indiana University Press, 2005), 11–12.

62. Restad, *American Exceptionalism: Idea That Made a Nation*, 46.

63. Iliya Harik, "Democracy, 'Arab Exceptionalism,' and Social Science," *Middle East Journal* 60 (Autumn 2006): 664–83, quotation at 680. See also Tatu Vanhanen, *The Process of Democracy: A Comparative Study of 147 States, 1980–1988* (New York: Crane Russak, 1990); M. Steven Fish, "Islam and Authoritarianism," *World Politics* 55 (October 2002): 4–37.

64. Justin Vaïsse, *Neoconservatism: The Biography of a Movement* (Cambridge, MA: Harvard University Press, 2011), 12.

65. Gerard Toal, *Near Abroad: Putin, the West, and the Contest Over Ukraine and the Caucasus* (New York: Oxford University Press, 2017), 99–100; Dan Tschirgi, "Bringing Radical Change to the Arab World: The 'Democratizing' Legacy of George W. Bush," UNISCI Discussion Papers, no. 12, October 2006, https://www.ucm.es/data/cont/media/www/pag-72529/UNISCI Tschirgi12.pdf; Elliott Abrams et al., "PNAC—Statement of Principles," Project for a New American Century, June 3, 1997, https://www.rrojasdatabank.info/pfpc/PNAC---statement%20of%20 principles.pdf.

66. Tamara Cofman Wittes, *Freedom's Unsteady March: America's Role in Building Arab Democracy* (Washington, DC: Brookings Institution, 2008), 2. For a critique, see Robert Springborg, "Freedom's Unsteady March: America's Role in Building Arab Democracy," *Middle East Policy* 15, no. 3 (2008): 157–66.

Chapter One

1. Heike Paul, *The Myths That Made America: An Introduction to American Studies* (Bielefeld, Ger.: Transcript Verlag, 2014), ch. 3.

2. Tocqueville, *Democracy in America*, 1:19. Cf. Sanford Kessler, "Tocqueville's Puritans: Christianity and the American Founding," *Journal of Politics* 54 (August 1992): 776–79.

3. Ralph Barton Perry, *Puritanism and Democracy* (New York: Vanguard Press, 1944); Joshua I. Miller, *The Rise and Fall of Democracy in Early America, 1630–1789: The Legacy for Contemporary Politics* (College Park, MD: Penn State University Press, 1991).

4. Sarah Rivett and Abram C. Van Engen, "Postexceptionalist Puritanism," *American Literature* 90 (December 2018): 675–92; Van Engen, *City on a Hill*.

5. William Cronon, *Changes in the Land: Indians, Colonists, and the Ecology of New England* (New York: Hill and Wang, 1983).

6. Alan Simpson, "How Democratic Was Roger Williams?" *William and Mary Quarterly* 13, no. 1 (January 1956): 53–67, at 59–60; B. Katherine Brown, "The Controversy over the Franchise in Puritan Massachusetts, 1954 to 1974," *William and Mary Quarterly* 33, no. 2 (April 1976): 212–41; Michael P. Winship, "Godly Republicanism and the Origins of the Massachusetts Polity," *William and Mary Quarterly* 63, no. 3 (July 2006): 427–62; Van Engen, *City on a Hill*, 33–34; Marvin Gettleman, *The Dorr Rebellion: A Study in American Radicalism, 1833–1849* (New York: Random House, 1973).

7. Lipset, *First New Nation*, 107–8.

8. Max Weber, *The Protestant Ethic and the Spirit of Capitalism* (New York: Charles Scribner's Sons, 1954).

9. Notably this intellectual culture was studied by Perry Miller, *The New England Mind: The Seventeenth Century*, vol. 1 (1939; repr., Cambridge, MA: Harvard University Press, 1983), 416. On Miller, see Robert Middlekauff, "Perry Miller," in *Pastmasters: Some Essays on American Historians*, ed. Marcus Cunliffe and Robin Winks (New York: Harper and Row, 1969), 167–90, at 186. See also E. Clinton Gardner, "Justice in the Puritan Covenantal Tradition," *Journal of Law and Religion* 6, no. 1 (1988): 39–60.

10. R. H. Tawney, *Religion and the Rise of Capitalism*, with a new introduction by Adam Seligman (New York: Transaction Books, 1998).

11. Arminianism will be discussed further in chapter 4. For the Protestant ethic in New England historiography, see Charles L. Cohen, "Mad Max (Weber) in New England," *Reviews in American History* 25 (March 1997): 19–24, at 19–20. For Puritanism's economic influence, see Stephen Innes, *Creating the Commonwealth: The Economic Culture of Puritan New England* (New York: Norton, 1995). For the work ethic's later mutation, see Daniel T. Rodgers, *The Work Ethic in Industrial America 1850–1920* (Chicago: University of Chicago Press, 1978), 4–14, 17–18, 245n15.

12. On Winthrop, see Francis J. Bremer, *John Winthrop: America's Forgotten Founding Father* (New York: Oxford University Press, 2003).

13. Richard Gamble, *In Search of the City on a Hill: The Making and Unmaking of an American Myth* (London: Continuum, 2012); Daniel T. Rodgers, *As a City on a Hill: The Story of*

America's Most Famous Lay Sermon (Princeton, NJ: Princeton University Press, 2018); Van Engen, *City on a Hill*, 3–4, 153–54.

14. Sandra M. Gustafson, *Imagining Deliberative Democracy in the Early American Republic* (Chicago: University of Chicago Press, 2011), 42–46. Webster knew that the Pilgrims were not establishing the first North American colony, rather, what he regarded as the nation's *true* beginnings. Daniel Webster, *The Speeches of Daniel Webster and His Masterpieces*, ed. Benjamin F. Tefft (Philadelphia: Coates, 1854), 62, 63, 79.

15. Paul Kengor, *God and Ronald Reagan: A Spiritual Life* (New York: Harper Collins, 2004), 92. A theological derivation for *shining* comes from Revelation 21, Authorized (King James) Version.

16. Rodgers, *As a City on a Hill*; Gamble, *In Search of the City on a Hill*, 48–50.

17. Thomas Thatcher, *A fast of Gods chusing, plainly opened, for the help of those poor in spirit, whose hearts are set to seek the Lord their God in New-England . . . Preached on a Fast called by publick Authority, on 26. 1. 74* (Boston: Printed by John Foster, 1678), 19.

18. Cotton Mather, *Magnalia Christi Americana, or the Ecclesiastical History of New England*, 2 vols. (1702; repr., Hartford, CT: Silus Andrus, 1820), 1:83–84, 92.

19. Jonathan Edwards, *A Narrative of the Revival of Religion in New England; with Thoughts on that revival, . . .* (Glasgow: William Collins, 1829), 244–52, at 244.

20. Apologists for the chosen nation as concept from the 1950s onward referred to a Judeo-Christian rather than a purely Christian tradition. K. Healan Gaston, *Imagining Judeo-Christian America* (Chicago: University of Chicago Press, 2020); Mark Silk, "Notes on the Judeo-Christian Tradition in America," *American Quarterly* 36, no. 1 (Spring 1984): 65–85; Bellah, *Broken Covenant*.

21. Richard Hughes, *Myths America Lives By* (Urbana: University of Illinois Press, 2003), ch. 1; Braden Anderson, *Chosen Nation: Scripture, Theopolitics, and the Project of National Identity* (Eugene, OR: Cascade Books, 2012).

22. A. Smith, *Chosen Peoples*, esp. 66–73, 76; Donald H. Akenson, *God's Peoples: Covenant and Land in South Africa, Israel, and Ulster* (Kingston, ON: McGill University Press, 1992); William Haller, *Foxe's Book of Martyrs and the Elect Nation* (London: Jonathan Cape, 1963).

23. Mark Thomas McNally, *Like No Other: Exceptionalism and Nativism in Early Modern Japan* (Honolulu: University of Hawaii Press, 2016); S. N. Eisenstadt, *Japanese Civilization: A Comparative View* (Chicago: University of Chicago Press, 1996), 283.

24. Albert J. Raboteau, *Fire in the Bones: Reflections on African-American Religious History* (Boston: Beacon Press, 1995), 17–36; Jacob S. Dorman, *Chosen People: The Rise of American Black Israelite Religions* (New York: Oxford University Press, 2012), 151; Jérémie Kroubo Dagnini, "Rastafari: Alternative Religion and Resistance against 'White' Christianity," *Études Caribéennes* 12 (April 2009), https://journals.openedition.org/etudescaribeennes/3665.

25. Eran Shalev, *American Zion: The Old Testament as a Political Text from the Revolution to the Civil War* (New Haven, CT: Yale University Press, 2013), 56–57.

26. David Dreisbach, "A Peculiar People in 'God's American Israel,'" in Dunn, *American Exceptionalism: Origins, History, and Future*, 54–64, at 64.

27. John Cushing, *A Discourse, Delivered at Ashburnham, July 4th, 1796, at the Request of the Militia Officers in said town . . . to celebrate the Anniversary of the Declaration of Independence of the United States of America* (Leominster, MA: John Prentis, 1796), 6, quoted in Dreisbach, "Peculiar People," 64.

28. Abiel Abbot, *Traits of Resemblance in the People of the United States of America to Ancient Israel. In a sermon, delivered at Haverhill, on the twenty-eighth of November, 1799, the day of anniversary thanksgiving* (Haverhill, MA: Moore & Stebbins, 1799), 6. For Anatol Lieven, the

roots of modern U.S. policy toward the Middle East lie in texts such as Abbot's and its claim that the United States came "nearer to a parallel with Ancient Israel, than any other nation upon the globe." Anatol Lieven, *America Right or Wrong: An Anatomy of American Nationalism* (New York: Harper Collins, 2005), 188. American studies scholar Amy Kaplan has concluded that, in this identification, Americans claimed a parallel exceptionalism "right from the start." Kaplan, *Our American Israel*, 5.

29. Solomon Aiken, *An Oration Delivered Before the Republican Citizens of Newburyport, and Its Vicinity, July 4, 1810* (Newburyport, MA: N. H. Wright, 1810).

30. Jonathan Maxcy, *An Oration, delivered in the Baptist Meeting-House in Providence, July 4, A.D. 1795, at the celebration of the nineteenth anniversary of American independence* (Providence, RI: Carter and Wilkinson, 1795), 16–17; Elias Smith, *The Clergyman's Looking-Glass*, 3rd ed. (Boston: n.p., 1804), 28.

31. Abbot, *Traits of Resemblance*; Hans Kohn, *The Idea of Nationalism: A Study in its Origins and Background* (New York: Macmillan, 1944), 665.

32. James Byrd, *Sacred Scripture, Sacred War: The Bible and the American Revolution* (New York: Oxford University Press, 2013), 8 (quote), 177n22; E. Brooks Holifield, *Theology in America: Christian Thought from the Age of the Puritans to the Civil War* (New Haven, CT: Yale University Press, 2003), 77.

33. Abbot, *Traits of Resemblance*, 6.

34. Abbot, *Traits of Resemblance*, 19 (italics in original).

35. Abbot, *Traits of Resemblance*, 20.

36. Abbot, *Traits of Resemblance*, 20–21.

37. For anxieties over the cultural position of the New England states, see John McWilliams, *New England's Crises and Cultural Memory: Literature, Politics, History, Religion, 1620–1860* (New York: Cambridge University Press, 2004), 12–13.

38. Abbot, *Traits of Resemblance*, 11 (italics in original).

39. Abbot, *Traits of Resemblance*, 24, 25.

40. Abbot, *Traits of Resemblance*, 23 ("infidel philosophy"), 6 ("indefeasible title").

41. *Twelfth Report of the American Home Missionary Society* (New York: William Osborn, 1838), 74: "Let men be selected with great care from the churches of our American Israel"; "Notices of Recent Publications," *Monthly Miscellany of Religion and Letter* (Boston), ed. Ezra Stiles Gannett, 5, no. 3 (September 1841): 167; Samuel Gilman, *Discourse Delivered in the Unitarian Church, Charleston, S.C., on the Day of National Fasting, Appointed in Consequence of the Death of President Harrison* (Charleston, SC: B. B. Hussey, 1841), 4. Gilman was a New Englander by upbringing and education.

42. Shalev, *American Zion*, 85.

43. Thomas Jefferson, "Inaugural Address," March 4, 1801, American Presidency Project, https://www.presidency.ucsb.edu/node/201948.

44. Jefferson, "Inaugural Address."

45. Myra Jehlen, *American Incarnation: The Individual, the Nation, and the Continent* (Cambridge, MA: Harvard University Press, 1988), 32.

46. Nicholas Onuf and Peter Onuf, *Nations, Markets, and War: Modern History and the American Civil War* (Charlottesville: University of Virginia Press, 2006), 221; Thomas Jefferson, "First Inaugural Address" [1801], in *Jefferson: Writings*, comp. Merrill D. Peterson (New York: Library of America, 1984), 494; Bernard W. Sheehan, "Jefferson's 'Empire for Liberty,'" *Indiana Magazine of History* 100 (December 2004): 346–63, at 354.

47. Andrew Jackson, "Farewell Address," March 4, 1837, American Presidency Project, https://www.presidency.ucsb.edu/node/201770.

48. Philip L. Barlow, "Chosen Land, Chosen People: Religious and American Exceptionalism among the Mormons," *Review of Faith and International Affairs* 10, no. 2 (2012): 51–58, at 54.

49. Shalev, *American Zion*, 116, 151–52.

50. Deborah L. Madsen, *American Exceptionalism* (Jackson: University Press of Mississippi, 1998), 81. See also Herman Melville, *White-Jacket: or the World in a Man-of-War* (London: Richard Bentley, 1850), 238–39; Paul Lyons, "Global Melville," in *A Companion to Herman Melville*, ed. Wyn Kelley (Malden, MA: Blackwell, 2006), 60–61.

51. Abraham Lincoln, "Address to the New Jersey State Senate, Trenton, New Jersey February 21, 1861," Abraham Lincoln Online, http://www.abrahamlincolnonline.org/lincoln/speeches /trenton1.htm; Ronald C. White, *Lincoln: A Biography* (New York: Random House, 2009), 377; Rodgers, *As a City on a Hill*, 151.

Chapter Two

1. G. Groenhuis, "Calvinism and National Consciousness: The Dutch Republic as the New Israel," in *Britain and The Netherlands*, vol. 6, *Church and State since the Reformation: Papers Delivered to the Seventh Anglo-Dutch Historical Conference*, ed. A. C. Duke and C. A. Tamse (Dordrecht, Neth.: Springer, 1981), 118–33, at 118.

2. J. L. Price, *Dutch Culture in the Golden Age* (London: Reaktion Books, 2011), 44–45.

3. As reflected in Lipset, *First New Nation*, 17; Charles Gibson, "Latin America and the Americas," in *The Past before Us: Contemporary Historical Writing in the United States*, ed. Michael Kammen (Ithaca, NY: Cornell University Press, 1980), 194.

4. See, e.g., Catherine L. Albanese, *Sons of the Fathers: The Civil Religion of the American Revolution* (Philadelphia: Temple University Press, 1976).

5. Lipset, *First New Nation*, 97n57. See also Louis Hartz, *The Liberal Tradition in America* (New York: Harcourt, Brace and World, 1955); Lipset, *Revolution and Counterrevolution*, 24–25.

6. Michael McDonnell, "War Stories: Remembering and Forgetting the American Revolution," in *The American Revolution Reborn*, ed. Patrick Spero and Michael Zuckerman (Philadelphia: University of Pennsylvania Press, 2016), 9–28.

7. Jack Greene, *The Intellectual Construction of America: Exceptionalism and Identity from 1492 to 1800* (Chapel Hill: University of North Carolina Press, 1993), esp. 69–70, 142.

8. See Alfred F. Young and Gregory Nobles, *Whose American Revolution Was It? Historians Interpret the Founding* (New York: New York University Press, 2011), esp. 17, 32 ("generic" quotation); John Franklin Jameson, *The American Revolution Considered as a Social Movement* (Princeton, NJ: Princeton University Press, 1926).

9. Gordon S. Wood, *The Radicalism of the American Revolution* (New York: Alfred A. Knopf, 1992), esp. 5–6. Wood claimed that he did not see this revolution as truly exceptional because he believed that most if not all nineteenth-century revolutions were also democratic revolutions. However, elsewhere Wood endorses this democracy as part of American liberal exceptionalism. See, e.g., Gordon S. Wood, *The Idea of America: Reflections on the Birth of the United States* (New York: Penguin, 2011); Gordon S. Wood, "Doing the Continental," *New York Review of Books*, November 20, 1997, 55.

10. Thomas Paine, *The Thomas Paine Reader*, ed. Michael Foot and Isaac Kramnick (Harmondsworth, UK: Penguin, 1987), 25; Woody Holton, *Unruly Americans and the Origins of the Constitution* (New York: Hill and Wang, 2007).

11. Rodgers, *As a City on a Hill*, 128–29.

12. Thomas Paine, *Common Sense* (1776), in *Thomas Paine Reader*, 90.

13. Thomas Paine, *The Rights of Man* (1791), in *Thomas Paine Reader*, 263–64.

14. Michael McDonnell, "National Identity and the American War for Independence Reconsidered," *Australasian Journal of American Studies* 20 (July 2001): 3–17, at 10.

15. Christopher Clark, *Social Change in America: From the Revolution to the Civil War* (Chicago: Ivan Dee, 2005), 80–81.

16. Lipset, *First New Nation*, 5, quotation at 110.

17. On the Tea Party, see Andrew M. Schocket, *Fighting over the Founders: How We Remember the American Revolution* (New York: New York University Press, 2015), 184–94; Ronald Formisano, *The Tea Party: A Brief History* (Baltimore: Johns Hopkins University Press, 2012), 8; Jens Rydgren and Christopher Parker, *The Oxford Handbook of the Radical Right* (New York: Oxford University Press, 2018), 13, 15.

18. Jill Lepore, *The Whites of Their Eyes: The Tea Party's Revolution and the Battle over American History* (Princeton, NJ: Princeton University Press, 2010), 11, 47, quotation at 97.

19. Beeman quoted in William H. Freivogel, "'We the People'—What Do We Really Know about the Constitution?" St. Louis Public Radio (website), May 9, 2013, http://news.stlpublicra dio.org/post/we-people-what-do-we-really-know-about-constitution#stream/0.

20. Ilya Somin, "Public Ignorance about the Constitution," *Washington Post*, September 15, 2017.

21. Ian Tyrrell, *Historians in Public: The Practice of American History, 1890–1970* (Chicago: University of Chicago Press, 2005), 132–33.

22. Lipset, *First New Nation*, 19–26. For a similar view of charisma and exceptionalism applied to the U.S. Constitution, see Bruce Ackerman, *Revolutionary Constitutions: Charismatic Leadership and the Rule of Law* (Cambridge, MA: Harvard University Press, 2019), 365.

23. Lipset, *First New Nation*, 17, 26–28, 282. For the comparative history of charisma, see David A. Bell, "Charismatic Authority in Revolutionary and Republican France," in *Rethinking the Age of Revolutions: France and the Birth of the Modern World*, ed. David A. Bell and Yair Mintzker (New York: Oxford University Press, 2018), 104–33; Ronald M. Glassman and William H. Swatos, Jr., eds., *Charisma, History and Social Structure* (New York: Greenwood, 1986), 61, 183–87, 197; Barry Schwartz, "George Washington and the Whig Conception of Heroic Leadership," *American Sociological Review* 48 (February 1983): 18–33.

24. Lipset, *First New Nation*, 27–28.

25. Clark, *Social Change in America*, 66, 75–76, 78, 110–11.

26. Michael A. McDonnell et al., eds., *Remembering the Revolution: Memory, History, and Nation Making from Independence to the Civil War* (Amherst: University of Massachusetts Press, 2013); McDonnell, "National Identity," 3–17.

27. Thomas Jefferson to Roger Weightman, June 24, 1826, in *Jefferson: Writings*, 1516–17.

28. Thomas Jefferson, "Autobiography," in *Jefferson: Writings*, 97.

29. Maurizio Valsania, *The Limits of Optimism: Thomas Jefferson's Dualistic Enlightenment* (Charlottesville: University of Virginia Press, 2011), 108–11; Hannah D. Spahn, *Thomas Jefferson, Time, and History* (Charlottesville: University of Virginia Press, 2011), 193.

30. Joel Barlow, *An Oration, delivered at the North Church in Hartford, at the meeting of the Connecticut Society of the Cincinnati, July 4th, 1787. In commemoration of the independence of the United States* (Hartford, CT: Hudson and Goodwin, [1787]), 8, quotation at 31.

31. Len Travers, *Celebrating the Fourth: Independence Day and the Rites of Nationalism in the Early Republic* (Amherst: University of Massachusetts Press, 1997), 26–27, 59–61; James A. Colaiaco, *Frederick Douglass and the Fourth of July* (New York: Palgrave, 2006), 8 ("sporadic" quotation); Simon Newman, *Parades and the Politics of the Street: Festive Culture in the Early American Republic* (Philadelphia: University of Pennsylvania Press, 1997), 149; Matthew Rainbow Hale, "Regenerating the World: The French Revolution, Civic Festivals, and the Forging of Modern American Democracy, 1793–1795," *Journal of American History* 103 (March 2017): 891–920.

32. McDonnell, "National Identity," 10; Michael A. McDonnell, "Men Out of Time: Confronting History and Myth," *William and Mary Quarterly* 68, no. 4 (October 2011): 644–48, at 647.

33. Caroline Cox, "Public Memories, Private Lives: The First Greatest Generation Remembers the Revolutionary War," in McDonnell et al., *Remembering the Revolution*, 110–24, at 122.

34. Jonathan Loring Austin, *An Oration, delivered July 4, 1786, at the request of the inhabitants of the town of Boston, in celebration of the anniversary of American independence* (Boston: Peter Edes, [1786]), 11.

35. "Rev Solomon Aiken," Find a Grave, August 23, 2012, https://www.findagrave.com/cgi-bin/fg.cgi?page=gr&GRid=95834489.

36. Aiken, *Oration*.

37. For enlistees, see Charles Patrick Neimeyer, *America Goes to War: A Social History of the Continental Army* (New York: New York University Press, 1996); for veterans, John Resch, *Suffering Soldiers: Revolutionary War Veterans, Moral Sentiment, and Political Culture in the Early Republic* (Amherst: University of Massachusetts Press, 1999).

38. Austin, *Oration*, 11; "Benjamin Rush: Observations on the Fourth of July Procession in Philadelphia," *Pennsylvania Mercury*, July 15, 1788. See also James Spear Loring, *The Hundred Boston Orators Appointed by the Municipal Authorities and Other Public Bodies, from 1770 to 1852* (Boston: John P. Jewett, 1854), 174, 179. For background, see Paul Goetsch and Gerd Hurm, *Political Oratory and Literary Reactions, 1776–1876* (Tübingen, Ger.: Gunter Narr Verlag, 1992), 47–59; Howard Martin, "Orations on the Anniversary of American Independence, 1777–1876" (PhD diss., Northwestern University, 1955); Travers, *Celebrating the Fourth*, 48, 58, 159; Michael McDonnell, "War and Nationhood: Founding Myths and Historical Realities," in McDonnell et al., *Remembering the Revolution*, 33 (quotation "forget the war").

39. Catherine Albanese, "Newness Transcending: Civil Religion and the American Revolution," *Southern Quarterly* 14 (July 1976): 307–31, quotations at 310.

40. John Hutchinson, *Nationalism and War* (Oxford: Clarendon, 2017), 84; Ken Inglis, *Sacred Places: War Memorials in the Australian Landscape* (Melbourne: Oxford University Press, 1998).

41. Maxcy, *Oration*, 9.

42. David Glassberg, "Patriotism from the Ground Up," *Reviews in American History* 22 (March 1993): 2; Austin, *Oration*, 11; Travers, *Celebrating the Fourth*, 34; Sarah J. Purcell, *Sealed with Blood: War, Sacrifice, and Memory in Revolutionary America* (Philadelphia: University of Pennsylvania Press, 2002), 8.

43. Purcell, *Sealed with Blood*, 6, 10; Angelo T. Angelis, "For God and Country: Crafting Memory and Meaning from War and Independence," *Reviews in American History* 31 (September 2003): 356–62, at 358.

44. See, e.g., Newman, *Parades and the Politics of the Street*, 96.

45. Karen O'Brien, "David Ramsay and the Delayed Americanization of American History," *Early American Literature* 29, no. 1 (1994): 1–18, at 5.

46. Harvey Kaye, *Thomas Paine and the Promise of America* (New York: Farrar and Strauss, 2007), 5; Paine, *Rights of Man*, 263–64.

47. O'Brien, "David Ramsay and Delayed Americanization," 5.

48. Samuel Thatcher, *An Oration, pronounced July 4, 1796, at the request of the inhabitants of the town of Concord, in commemoration of the twentieth anniversary of American independence* ([Boston]: Samuel Hall, 1796), 19.

49. Peter C. Messer, "From a Revolutionary History to a History of Revolution: David Ramsay and the American Revolution," *Journal of the Early Republic* 22, no. 2 (2002): 205–33, at 208.

50. Arthur H. Shaffer, *The Politics of History: Writing the History of the American Revolution* (1975; repr., New Brunswick, NJ: Transaction Publishers, 2010), 42–43; O'Brien, "David Ramsay and Delayed Americanization."

51. "[February 1765, from the Diary of John Adams]: [Fragmentary Draft of a Dissertation on Canon and Feudal Law, February 1765]," Founders Online, accessed December 28, 2020, https://founders.archives.gov/documents/Adams/01-01-02-0009-0002; "From John Adams to John Taylor, 29 July 1814," Founders Online, accessed December 28, 2020, https://founders.archives.gov/documents/Adams/99-02-02-6322.

52. Luke Mayville, *John Adams and the Fear of American Oligarchy* (Princeton, NJ: Princeton University Press, 2016), 150–51.

53. Ritchie quoted in Charlene Boyer Lewis, "Elizabeth Patterson Bonaparte: A Woman between Two Worlds," in *Old World, New World: America and Europe in the Age of Jefferson*, ed. Leonard J. Sadosky et al. (Charlottesville: University of Virginia Press, 2010), 247–77, at 247.

54. Alan Taylor, *The Civil War of 1812: American Citizens, British Subjects, Irish Rebels and Indian Allies* (Toronto: Random House, 2010).

55. "Report and Resolutions of the Hartford Convention," *Public Documents, Containing Proceedings of the Hartford Convention of Delegates* (n.p.: Published by Order of the Senate, 1815), 4.

56. Lawrence Friedman and Arthur H. Shaffer, "David Ramsay and the Quest for an American Historical Identity," *Southern Quarterly* 14 (July 1976): 351; David Ramsay, *History of South Carolina from Its First Settlement in 1670 to the Year of 1808*, vol. 1 (1809; repr., Newberry, SC, 1858), 13; Messer, "From a Revolutionary History to a History of Revolution," 205–33, examines the transition in Ramsay's republican perspective from his *History of the American Revolution* (1789) to his more conservative *History of the United States* (1816–17).

57. William C. Freehling, *Prelude to Civil War: The Nullification Controversy in South Carolina, 1816–1836* (New York: Harper and Row, 1966).

Chapter Three

1. Paul C. Nagel, *This Sacred Trust: American Nationality, 1798–1898* (New York: Oxford University Press, 1971).

2. Daniel Walker Howe, *The Political Culture of the American Whigs* (Chicago: University of Chicago Press, 1979), 212–13, quotation at 216. See also Daniel Webster, *The Completion of The Bunker Hill Monument. An address delivered on Bunker Hill, on the 17th of June, 1843* (Boston: Press of T. R. Marvin, 1843); Sarah J. Purcell, "Commemoration, Public Art, and the Changing Meaning of the Bunker Hill Monument," *Public Historian* 25 (Spring 2003): 55–71, at 66.

3. Marcus Cunliffe, *George Washington: Man and Monument*, rev. ed. (New York: Mentor, 1982).

4. John Higham, "America in Person: The Evolution of National Symbols," *Amerikastudien* 36 (Spring 1991): 474.

5. Lyman Beecher, "The Means of National Prosperity. A sermon, delivered at Litchfield, on the day of the Anniversary Thanksgiving, Dec. 2, 1819," in *Addresses of the Philadelphia Society for the Promotion of National Industry*, 5th ed. (Philadelphia: James Maxwell, 1820), 261–71, quotation at 271.

6. Daniel S. Dupree, "The Panic of 1819 and the Politics of Sectionalism," in *The Economy of Early America: Historical Perspectives & New Directions*, ed. Cathy D. Matson (University Park, PA: Penn State University Press, 2006), 268–69; Murray Newton Rothbard, *The Panic of 1819: Reactions and Policies* (New York: Columbia University Press, 1962), 2–8; Charles Sellers, *The Market Revolution: Jacksonian America, 1815–1846* (New York: Oxford University Press, 1991); Andrew H. Browning, *The Panic of 1819: The First Great Depression* (Columbia: University of Missouri Press, 2019), 4–5.

7. John C. Gray, "An Oration pronounced before the Society of Phi Beta Kappa, at Cambridge, August 30, 1821," *North American Review and Miscellaneous Journal* 13 (January 1821): 478–92, at 488, 489.

8. Sam W. Haynes, *Unfinished Revolution: The Early American Republic in a British World* (Charlottesville: University of Virginia Press, 2010), 2.

9. Haynes, *Unfinished Revolution*, 12, 59; Jennifer Clark, *The American Idea of England, 1776–1840: Transatlantic Writing* (New York: Routledge, 2013). Regarding Noah Webster, see A. G. Hopkins, *American Empire: A Global History* (Princeton, NJ: Princeton University Press, 2018), 179.

10. Russel Blaine Nye, *The Cultural Life of the New Nation, 1776–1830* (New York: Harper and Brothers, 1960), 255.

11. Emily B. Todd, "Establishing Routes for Fiction in the United States: Walter Scott's Novels and the Early Nineteenth-Century American Publishing Industry," *Book History* 12 (January 2009): 100–128; Ann Rigney, *The Afterlives of Walter Scott: Memory on the Move* (New York: Oxford University Press, 2012), 119; Haynes, *Unfinished Revolution*, 59; J. Clark, *American Idea of England*; Lawrence W. Levine, *The Opening of the American Mind: Canons, Culture, and History* (Boston: Beacon Press, 1996), 75–90.

12. Nye, *Cultural Life of the New Nation*.

13. Ralph Waldo Emerson, *The American Scholar* (New York: American Book Company, [1911]).

14. Ralph Waldo Emerson, "The Naturalist" ("Address to the Boston Natural History Society . . . 1834"), in *The Early Lectures of Ralph Waldo Emerson*, vol. 1, ed. Stephen E. Whicher and Robert Spiller (Cambridge, MA: Belknap Press of Harvard University Press, 1966), 75. On Carlyle's influence, see Barbara L. Packer, "Carlyle and the Beginnings of American Transcendentalism," in *Cambridge History of American Literature*, vol. 2, *Prose Writing 1820–1865*, ed. Sacvan Bercovitch and Cyrus R. K. Patell (New York: Cambridge University Press, 1995), 365.

15. Ralph Waldo Emerson, *English Traits*, rev. ed. (Boston: James R. Osgood, 1876). See also J. Clark, *American Idea of England*, 164n126, citing Christopher Hanlon, "'The Old Race Are All Gone': Transatlantic Bloodlines and 'English Traits,'" *American Literary History* 19 (Winter 2007): 800–823, at 802.

16. Haynes, *Unfinished Revolution*, 52–53.

17. William J. Sowder, "Emerson's Early Impact on England: A Study in British Periodicals," *Proceedings of the Modern Language Association 77* (December 1962): 561–76.

18. Edward Everett, *An Oration Pronounced at Cambridge, before the Society of Phi Beta Kappa, August 27, 1824* (New York: J. W. Palmer, 1824). On Everett, see Paul Varg, *Edward Everett: The Intellectual in the Turmoil of Politics* (Cranbury, NJ: Susquehanna University Press, 1992), 27–30; Richard A. Katula, *The Eloquence of Edward Everett: America's Greatest Orator* (New York: Peter Lang, 2010), 70–77; Matthew Mason, *Apostle of Union: A Political Biography of Edward Everett* (Chapel Hill: University of North Carolina Press, 2016).

19. Mason, *Apostle of Union*, 34.

20. *American Oratory; or, Selections from the speeches of eminent Americans* (Philadelphia: Thomas Desilver, 1836); Edward Everett, *Orations and Speeches on Various Occasions*, vol. 1, 7th ed. (Boston: Little, Brown, 1865).

21. Mason, *Apostle of Union*, 34; Varg, *Edward Everett*, 27–29; Howe, *Political Culture of American Whigs*, 210–25.

22. Kurt Mueller-Vollmer, *Transatlantic Crossings and Transformations: German-American Cultural Transfer from the 18th to the End of the 19th Century* (Frankfurt am Main: Peter Lang, 2015), 106–7, 112, 122.

23. Everett, *Oration at Cambridge*, 35.

24. Everett, *Oration at Cambridge*, 15.

25. Everett, *Oration at Cambridge*, 15.

26. Edward Everett, "The Circumstances Favorable to Literary Improvement in America," in Edward Everett, *Importance of Practical Education and Useful Knowledge: A Selection from his Orations and Other Discourses* (Boston: Wm. Crosby and H. Nichols, 1840), 11.

27. Tocqueville, *Democracy in America*, 2:42.

28. Everett, *Oration at Cambridge*, 18. See also Everett, "Circumstances," 20.

29. Everett, *Oration at Cambridge*, 11, 15 (quote).

30. Everett, *Oration at Cambridge*, 28–29.

31. Everett, *Oration at Cambridge*, 24.

32. Edward Everett, *An Oration Delivered at Plymouth, December 22, 1824* (Boston: Cummings, Hillard, 1825), 38.

33. Everett, *Oration at Plymouth*, 13, 35; J. C. D. Clark, "Providence, Predestination and Progress: Or, Did the Enlightenment Fail?" *Albion* 35 (Winter 2003): 559–60.

34. Everett, *Oration at Plymouth*, 38, 69; Everett, *Oration at Cambridge*, 25. "Futurity" is discussed further in chapter 6.

35. Everett, *Oration at Plymouth*, 38. Everett critiqued the further expropriation of Indian land in Edward Everett, *Speech of Mr. Everett, of Massachusetts, on the bill for removing the Indians from the east to the west side of the Mississippi. Delivered in the House of Representatives, on the 19th May, 1830* (Washington, DC: Gales and Seaton, 1830), esp. 28.

36. Mann quoted in James W. Fraser, *Between Church and State: Religion and Public Education in a Multicultural America* (New York: St. Martin's Griffin, 1999), 25. See also Jonathan Messerli, *Horace Mann: A Biography* (New York: Alfred A. Knopf, 1972), 281, 376, 389–91; Horace Mann, *An Oration Delivered before the Authorities of the City of Boston, July 4, 1842* (Boston: J. H. Eastburn, 1842), 2–3.

37. Emma Willard, *History of the United States, or Republic of America: exhibited in connexion with its chronology & progressive geography; by means of a series of maps* (New York: White, Gallaher and White, 1828), vi, 3, 4, 17–18. See also Van Engen, *City on a Hill*, 123–24 ("million").

38. Van Engen, *City on a Hill*, 124.

39. Samuel R. Hall and A. R. Baker, *School History of the United States: Containing Maps, a Chronological Chart and an Outline of Topics for a more extensive course of study* (Andover, MA: William Pierce, 1839), 67.

40. Hall and Baker, *School History of the United States*, 4. See also Barry Joyce, *The First U.S. History Textbooks: Constructing and Disseminating the American Tale in the Nineteenth Century* (Lanham, MD: Lexington Books, 2015), 41.

41. On school texts, see Ruth Miller Elson, *Guardians of Tradition: American Schoolbooks of the Nineteenth Century* (Lincoln: University of Nebraska Press, 1964), 59–62, 106–7, 244; J. M. England, "The Democratic Faith in American Schoolbooks, 1783–1860," *American Quarterly* 15, no. 2, part 1 (Summer 1963): 191–99; Richard Mosier, *Making the American Mind: Social and Moral Ideas in the McGuffey Readers* (New York: King's Crown Press, 1947), 25; Elliot J. Gorn, *The McGuffey Readers: Selections from the 1879 Edition* (Boston: Bedford Books, 1998), 2.

42. Quentin R. Skrabec, *William McGuffey: Mentor to American Industry* (New York: Algora Publishing, 2009), 223, 226; Jean H. Baker, *Affairs of Party: The Political Culture of Northern Democrats in the Mid-Nineteenth Century* (New York: Fordham University Press, 1998), 82–83.

43. Maxcy quoted in William H. McGuffey, *The Eclectic Fourth Reader . . .* (Cincinnati, OH: Truman and Smith, 1838), 184.

44. See, e.g., Catholic National System Readers, *The New First[-fifth] reader: by Rt. Rev. Richard Gilmour*, 5 vols. (New York: Benziger Brothers, 1886–94). See also Fraser, *Between Church and State*, 35–38, 45, 49–60; Joseph Moreau, *Schoolbook Nation: Conflicts over American History Textbooks from the Civil War to the Present* (Ann Arbor: University of Michigan Press, 2003), ch. 3; Eugene Provenzo Jr., "Catholic Textbooks and Cultural Legitimacy," in *The Textbook as Discourse: Sociocultural Dimensions of American Schoolbooks*, ed. Eugene F. Provenzo Jr., Annis N. Shaver, and Manuel Bello (New York: Routledge, 2011), 47–54.

45. Mosier, *Making the American Mind*, 34–35; cf. Gorn, *McGuffey Readers*, 16.

46. John E. Lovell, ed., *The United States Speaker . . .* (New Haven, CT: Babcock, 1843). John Epy Lovell (1795–1892) founded the New Haven Lancasterian School, running it from 1822 to 1857.

47. M. M. Mason [and Sarah Griffin], *The Southern First Class Book: Or, Exercises in Reading and Declamation* (Macon, GA: B. F. Griffin and John E. Cooper, 1839).

48. Daniel Walker Howe, *What Hath God Wrought: The Transformation of America, 1815–1848* (New York: Oxford University Press, 2007), 424–25, 696–98; David Paul Nord, "The Evangelical Origins of Mass Media in America, 1815–1835," Journalism Monographs, no. 88, Association for Education in Journalism and Mass Communication, Columbia, SC, 1984.

49. Mason [and Griffin], *Southern First Class Book*, iii; Michael O'Brien, *Intellectual Life and the American South, 1810–1860: An Abridged Edition of Conjectures of Order* (Chapel Hill: University of North Carolina Press, 2010), 136.

50. Lindal Buchanan, *Regendering Delivery: The Fifth Canon and Antebellum Women Rhetors* (Carbondale: Southern Illinois University Press, 2005), 35–37; Carl Bode, *The American Lyceum: Town Meeting of the Mind* (New York: Oxford University Press, 1956), 117, 223; James Perrin Warren, *Culture of Eloquence: Oratory and Reform in Antebellum America* (University Park, PA: Penn State University Press, 2010); Jean Ferguson Carr, Stephen L. Carr, and Lucille M. Schultz, *Archives of Instruction: Nineteenth-Century Rhetorics, Readers, and Composition Books in the United States* (Carbondale: Southern Illinois University Press, 2005).

51. Joyce, *First U.S. History Textbooks*, 120.

52. James Grant Wilson and John Fiske, eds., *Appletons' Cyclopædia of American Biography*, vol. 1 (New York: D. Appleton, 1886), 155.

53. Baker, *Affairs of Party*, 82–83; Joyce, *First U.S. History Textbooks*, 117–18, 122–23, 156n46; Elson, *Guardians of Tradition*; England, "Democratic Faith in American Schoolbooks," 191–99; John D. Wilsey, *American Exceptionalism and Civil Religion: Reassessing the History of an Idea* (Westmont, IL: InterVarsity Press, 2015), 60–62.

54. Russel B. Nye, *George Bancroft: Brahmin Rebel* (New York: Octagon Books, 1972).

55. George Bancroft, *An Oration delivered on the Fourth of July, 1826, at Northampton, Mass.* (Northampton, MA: T. Watson Shepard, 1826), 22.

56. Nye, *George Bancroft*, 86–88, 106–12.

57. Bancroft, *Oration at Northampton*, 3, 4.

58. Bancroft, *Oration at Northampton*, 9.

59. Bancroft, *Oration at Northampton*, 11.

60. Ross, "Historical Consciousness," 912.

61. George Bancroft, *History of the United States of America as Colonies*, vol. 1, rev. ed. (New York: D. Appleton, 1888), 85.

62. George Bancroft, *An Oration delivered before the democracy of Springfield and neighboring towns, July 4, 1836* (Springfield [MA]: George and Charles Merriam, 1836), 19, 20.

63. Nye, *This Almost Chosen People*, 196.

Chapter Four

1. Johann N. Neem, "American History in a Global Age," *History and Theory* 50 (February 2011): 41–70, at 65–66, 67.

2. Tocqueville, *Democracy in America*, 1:358–59.

3. Tocqueville, *Democracy in America*, 1:358.

4. G. W. Pierson, *Tocqueville and Beaumont in America* (New York: Oxford University Press, 1938), 358.

5. George M. Marsden, *The Evangelical Mind and the New School Presbyterian Experience: A Case Study of Thought and Theology in Nineteenth-Century America* (New Haven, CT: Yale University Press, 1970), ch. 1.

6. Complete disestablishment in Massachusetts came in 1833. John D. Cushing, "Notes on Disestablishment in Massachusetts, 1780–1833," *William and Mary Quarterly* 26, no. 2 (April 1969): 169–90, at 190.

7. Lyman Beecher, *A Sermon, Addressed to the Legislature of Connecticut; at New-Haven* (New Haven, CT: I. Bunce, 1826); Lyman Beecher, *The Memory of Our Fathers. A Sermon Delivered at Plymouth, on the Twenty-Second of December, 1827* (Boston: T. R. Marvin, 1828), 1.

8. L. Beecher, *Memory of Our Fathers*, 7.

9. L. Beecher, *Memory of Our Fathers*, 18.

10. Beecher announced that "the possession of the earth in fee simple by the cultivator, is the great principle of action in the moral world." L. Beecher, *Memory of Our Fathers*, 9.

11. L. Beecher, *Memory of Our Fathers*, 19.

12. Charles Beecher, ed., *Autobiography, Correspondence, Etc., of Lyman Beecher, D.D.*, 2 vols. (New York: Harper and Brothers, 1864–65), 17.

13. L. Beecher, *Memory of Our Fathers*, 17.

14. L. Beecher, *Memory of Our Fathers*, 14.

15. L. Beecher, *Memory of Our Fathers*, 16.

16. L. Beecher, *Memory of Our Fathers*, 16.

17. L. Beecher, *Memory of Our Fathers*, 24.

18. L. Beecher, *Memory of Our Fathers*, 16, 17.

19. L. Beecher, *Memory of Our Fathers*, 18.

20. L. Beecher, *Memory of Our Fathers*, 18. Unlike Beecher, Tocqueville did not use "unexampled" as characteristic of an American system. Tocqueville, *Democracy in America*, 2:49. For Beecher, see Stuart C. Henry, *Unvanquished Puritan: A Portrait of Lyman Beecher* (Grand Rapids, MI: William B. Eerdmans, 1973); James W. Fraser, *Pedagogue for God's Kingdom: Lyman Beecher and the Second Great Awakening* (Lanham, MD: University Press of America, 1985); Vincent Harding, *A Certain Magnificence: Lyman Beecher and the Transformation of American Protestantism, 1775–1863* (Brooklyn, NY: Carlson, 1991); Marsden, *Evangelical Mind*, ch. 1.

21. L. Beecher, *Memory of Our Fathers*, 20.

22. Obbie Tyler Todd, "Baptist Federalism: Religious Liberty and Public Virtue in the Early Republic," *Journal of Church and State*, csaa035, June 28, 2020, https://doi.org/10.1093/jcs/csaa035.

23. Jonathan D. Sassi, "The First Party Competition and Southern New England's Public Christianity," *Journal of the Early Republic* 21 (Summer 2001): 261–99, quotation at 298; Whitney Cross, *The Burned-Over District: The Social and Intellectual History of Enthusiastic Religion in Western New York, 1800–1850* (Ithaca, NY: Cornell University Press, 1950); John L. Thomas, *Romantic Reform in America, 1815–1865* (Indianapolis, IN: Bobbs-Merrill, 1965); Paul E. Johnson, *A Shopkeeper's Millennium: Society and Revivals in Rochester, New York, 1815–1837* (New York: Hill and Wang, 1978); Judith Wellman, "Crossing Over Cross," *Reviews in American History* 17 (March 1989): 159–74.

24. Richard Carwardine, *Evangelicals and Politics in Antebellum America* (New Haven, CT: Yale University Press, 1993), 44.

25. Mark Noll, *America's God: From Jonathan Edwards to Abraham Lincoln* (New York: Oxford University Press, 2002), 197.

26. Hughes Oliphant Old, *The Modern Age, 1789–1889* (Grand Rapids, MI: William B. Eerdmans, 2007), 168. See also Lyman Beecher, *The Faith once delivered to the Saints: A sermon delivered at Worcester, Mass., Oct. 15, 1823 . . .* (Boston: Crocker and Brewster, 1824).

27. Carwardine, *Evangelicals and Politics*.

28. *Address of the Managers of the American Bible Society to its Auxiliaries, Members, and Friends, in regard to a General Supply of the United States: The Sacred Scriptures; together with Resolutions as to the Details of the Work* (New York: American Bible Society's Press, 1856); *Proceedings of the First Ten Years of the American Tract Society . . .* (New York: Flagg and Gould, 1824), 8; American Society for the Promotion of Temperance, "Fourth Annual Report" [1831], in *Permanent Documents of the American Temperance Society* (Boston: Seth Bliss, 1835), hereafter cited as *PTD*. See also Clifford S. Griffin, *Their Brothers' Keepers: Moral Stewardship in the United States, 1800–1865* (New Brunswick, NJ: Rutgers University Press, 1960); Charles I. Foster, *An Errand of Mercy: The Evangelical United Front, 1790–1837* (Chapel Hill: University of North Carolina Press, 1960); Bertram Wyatt-Brown, *Lewis Tappan and the Evangelical War against Slavery* (Cleveland, OH: Case Western Reserve University Press, 1969); Anne M. Boylan, *The Origins of Women's Activism: New York and Boston, 1797–1840* (Chapel Hill: University of North Carolina Press, 2002).

29. Michael Young, *Bearing Witness against Sin: The Evangelical Birth of the American Social Movement* (Chicago: University of Chicago Press, 2006), ch. 3; Clifford S. Griffin, *The Ferment*

of Reform, 1830–1860 (New York: Thomas Y. Crowell, 1967); Thomas, *Romantic Reform in America*; Cross, *Burned-Over District*; Johnson, *Shopkeeper's Millennium*; Wellman, "Crossing Over Cross," 159–74; Ronald G. Walters, *American Reformers 1815–1860* (New York: Hill and Wang, 1978). Cf. Johann N. Neem, "Taking Modernity's Wager: Tocqueville, Social Capital, and the American Civil War," *Journal of Interdisciplinary History* 41 (Spring 2011): 591–618.

30. L. Beecher, *Memory of Our Fathers*, 18.

31. L. Beecher, *Memory of Our Fathers*, 19.

32. Emily Conroy-Krutz, *Christian Imperialism: Converting the World in the Early American Republic* (Ithaca, NY: Cornell University Press, 2015), 10–12; [Hannah Lyman Willard], *The Martyr of Sumatra: A Memoir of Henry Lyman* (New York: R. Carter and Brothers, 1856); Henry Lyman, *Condition and Character of Females in Pagan and Mohammedan Countries* (Boston: Perkins and Marvin, 1831); John Angell James, *Female Piety: Or the Young Woman's Friend and Guide through Life to Immortality* (New York: Robert Carter and Brothers, 1854), 12.

33. Phillip S. Paludan, "The Civil War as a Crisis of Law and Order," *American Historical Review* 77 (October 1972): 1016–17, 1021, 1026; Rush Welter, *The Mind of America, 1820–1860* (New York: Columbia University Press, 1975), 396.

34. M. Young, *Bearing Witness against Sin*, 10, 56–58.

35. Lyman Beecher, *A Plea for the West*, 2nd ed. (New York: Leavitt, Lord, 1835), 32; Jon Gjerde, *The Minds of the West: Ethnocultural Evolution in the Rural Middle West* (Chapel Hill: University of North Carolina Press, 1997), 47.

36. Bryant M. Kirkland, "Albert Barnes and Doctrinal Freedom," *Journal of the Presbyterian Historical Society* 29 (June 1951): 97–106; Albert Barnes, *Essays on Intemperance* (Morristown, NJ: J. Mann, 1828); Albert Barnes, *The Church and Slavery* (Philadelphia: Parry and McMillan, 1857); Bruce Dorsey, *Reforming Men and Women: Gender in the Antebellum City* (Ithaca, NY: Cornell University Press, 2002), 122; Albert Barnes, *American Enterprise; or, Christianity adapted to the active powers of American youth: A discourse, delivered before the Philadelphia Institute in the first Presbyterian Church, Philadelphia, December 2, 1832* (Philadelphia: George, Latimer, 1832).

37. L. Beecher, *Plea for the West*, 17.

38. L. Beecher, *Plea for the West*, 17. See also Gjerde, *Minds of the West*, 47.

39. L. Beecher, *Plea for the West*, 10.

40. L. Beecher, *Plea for the West*, 30. Conrad Cherry, ed., *God's New Israel: Religious Interpretations of American Destiny*, rev. ed. (Chapel Hill, NC: University of North Carolina Press, 1998), 127–28.

41. For a revealing exposition of this mentality, see Lucien B. Woolfolk, *"Influence of the Baptists": A Centennial Oration* (Louisville, KY: Western Recorder, 1876).

42. Lyman Beecher, *Six Sermons on the Nature, Occasions, Signs, Evils, and Remedy of Intemperance* (Boston: T. R. Marvin, 1827); American Society for the Promotion of Temperance, "Fourth Annual Report," 16, 18, 69–70.

43. Pierson, *Tocqueville and Beaumont in America*, 177–78, 479–80; Tocqueville, *Democracy in America*, 1:217; 2:132–33.

44. Tocqueville, *Democracy in America*, 1:217; Kevin Butterfield, *The Making of Tocqueville's America: Law and Association in the Early United States* (Chicago: University of Chicago Press, 2015), 237; cf. Neem, "Taking Modernity's Wager," 591–618.

45. Felix Grundy quoted in American Society for the Promotion of Temperance, "Seventh Annual Report," [1834], in *PTD*, 103. See also Keith L. Sprunger, "Cold Water Congressmen: The Congressional Temperance Society before the Civil War," *Historian* 27 (August 1965): 498–515.

46. Jonas Platt, quoted in American Society for the Promotion of Temperance, "Sixth Annual Report" [1833], in *PTD*, 79.

47. American Society for the Promotion of Temperance, "Fourth Annual Report," 42, 50; American Society for the Promotion of Temperance, "Fifth Annual Report" [1832], in *PTD*, 107.

48. Ian Tyrrell, *Sobering Up: From Temperance to Prohibition in Antebellum America, 1800–1860* (Westport, CT: Greenwood Press, 1979), 228–29.

49. American Society for the Promotion of Temperance, "Fourth Annual Report," 14.

50. Daggett quoted in American Society for the Promotion of Temperance, "Seventh Annual Report," 52.

51. *The Sons of Temperance Offering for 1851* (New York: Cornish, Lamport, 1851), iii, 38, facing 38 (illus.), 297, 302; American Temperance Union, *Report of the Executive Committee, 1840* (New York: S. W. Benedict, 1840), appendix, 40 (regarding Faneuil Hall); *National Temperance Offering and Sons of Temperance Gift* (New York: R. Vanian, 1850), 319–20.

52. *Sons of Temperance Offering for 1851*, 302. The Temple of Sobriety situated on a hill in the John McKee illustration (facing 38) presented a generic design, similar to Charles Bullfinch's Boston State House. This image reflected the still decentralized nature of American patriotism, with the states retaining the primary loyalties. See also T. S. Arthur, ed., *The Temperance Gift* (New York: Leavitt and Allen, 1854).

53. Cf. Butterfield, *Making of Tocqueville's America*, 237–38, 242–45.

54. Abraham Lincoln, "An Address, Delivered before the Springfield Washington Temperance Society, on the 22d February, 1842," in *Collected Works of Abraham Lincoln*, ed. Roy Basler et al., 8 vols. (New Brunswick, NJ: Rutgers University Press, 1953), 1:271–79; cf. Abraham Lincoln, "The Perpetuation of Our Political Institutions," [January 27, 1838], in *Collected Works*, 108–15.

55. Cf. Butterfield, *Making of Tocqueville's America*; Tyrrell, *Sobering Up*, chs. 2, 5.

56. Sam Haselby, *The Origins of American Religious Nationalism* (New York: Oxford University Press, 2015).

57. Joshua Lawrence, *A Patriotic Discourse: Delivered by the Rev. Joshua Lawrence, at the Old Church in Tarborough, North Carolina, on Sunday, the 4th of July, 1830* (Tarboro, NC: Free Press, 1830), 8; Randy K. Mills, "The Struggle for the Soul of Frontier Baptists: The Anti-Mission Controversy in the Lower Wabash Valley," *Indiana Magazine of History* 94 (December 1998): 303–22, at 321.

58. Haselby, *Origins of American Religious Nationalism*; Lawrence, *Patriotic Discourse*, 16 (quotation), 18.

59. Lawrence, *Patriotic Discourse*, 2, 11 ("missionary establishment" quotation).

60. Joseph S. Moore, *Founding Sins: How a Group of Antislavery Radicals Fought to Put Christ into the Constitution* (New York: Oxford University Press, 2016), 80.

61. Ezra Stiles Ely, *The Duty of Christian Freemen to Elect Christian Rulers: A Discourse Delivered on the Fourth of July, 1827* (Philadelphia: William F. Geddes, 1828), 7, 9, 10, quotation at 13. For reactions, see William Morse, *An Oration Delivered Before the Citizens of Nantucket, July 4, 1829, Being the 53rd Anniversary of the Declaration of Independence* (Boston: Putnam and Hunt, 1829); Zelotes Fuller, "The Tree of Liberty: An Address in Celebration of the Birth of Washington" [1830], in *Cornerstones of Religious Freedom in America*, rev. ed., ed. Joseph Blau (New York: Harper and Row, 1964), esp. 134–36; Blau, *Cornerstones*, 126.

62. Morse, *Oration*, 11. See also Moore, *Founding Sins*, 80.

63. David Moulton and Mordecai Myers, "Report of the Select Committee of the New York State Assembly" [1832], in Blau, *Cornerstones*, 157.

64. Timothy Verhoeven, *Secularists, Religion and Government in Nineteenth-Century America* (New York: Palgrave Macmillan, 2019), 57–58.

65. Moore, *Founding Sins*, 80, 82.

66. Lawrence, *Patriotic Discourse*, 20.

67. Fraser, *Between Church and State*, 44, 54–57.

68. Godfrey Hodgson, *The Myth of American Exceptionalism* (New Haven, CT: Yale University Press, 2009), 48; John T. McGreevy, *Catholicism and American Freedom: A History* (New York: Norton, 2003), 58, 80; Verhoeven, *Secularists, Religion and Government*, ch. 7.

69. John Hughes, "Catholicity and American Liberty," in *The New Fifth Reader*, Catholic National Series (New York: Benziger Brothers, 1894), 55–58; Timothy Roberts, ed., *American Exceptionalism*, vol. 2, *The American Revolution* (London: Chatto and Windus, 2013), 140.

70. Roberts, *American Revolution*, 140.

71. Michael G. Kenny, *The Perfect Law of Liberty: Elias Smith and the Providential History of America* (Washington, DC: Smithsonian Institution, 1994).

72. Alexander Campbell, "An Oration in Honor of the Fourth of July" [1830], in *Popular Lectures and Addresses: Alexander Campbell, President of Bethany College Virginia* (Philadelphia: James Challen and Son, 1863), 377, 378.

73. Alexander Campbell, "Baccalaureate Address to the Graduates of Bethany College," [1847] in *Popular Lectures*, 494.

74. Campbell, "Baccalaureate Address," 497.

75. Holifield, *Theology in America*, 301.

76. Henry M. Baird, *The Life of the Rev. Robert Baird, D.D.* (New York: A. D. F. Randolph, 1866); Robert Baird, *Religion in America* (New York: Harper and Brothers, 1844); Robert Baird, *The Progress and Prospects of Christianity in the United States of America* (London: Partridge and Oakey, 1851), 6, 45; Noll, *America's God*, 166–69.

Chapter Five

1. See, e.g., the writings reviewed in J. S. Mill, "State of Society in America," *London Review* 2 (January 1836): 365–89.

2. Linda Kerber, *Women of the Republic: Intellect and Ideology in the American Republic* (Chapel Hill: University of North Carolina Press, 1980).

3. Mary Wollstonecraft, *A Vindication of the Rights of Woman* (London: J. Johnson, 1792).

4. Linda Kerber, *Toward an Intellectual History of Women: Essays by Linda K. Kerber* (Chapel Hill: University of North Carolina Press, 1997), esp. 35–36.

5. Barbara Welter, *Dimity Convictions: The American Woman in the Nineteenth Century* (Athens: Ohio University Press, 1976); Barbara Welter, "The Feminization of American Religion: 1800–1860," in *Clio's Consciousness Raised: New Perspectives on the History of Women*, ed. Mary S. Hartman and Lois W. Banner (New York: Harper and Row, 1974), 137–57.

6. Kathryn Sklar, *Catharine Beecher: A Study in American Domesticity* (New Haven, CT: Yale University Press, 1973).

7. Catharine Beecher, *A Treatise on Domestic Economy*, 3rd ed. (New York: Harper and Brothers, 1848), 33–34.

8. C. Beecher, *Treatise on Domestic Economy*, 28–32. The original 1841 edition also had Tocqueville's material and argument.

9. C. Beecher, *Treatise on Domestic Economy*, 33–34.

10. C. Beecher, *Treatise on Domestic Economy*, 42.

11. Lisa Pace Vetter, "Sympathy, Equality, and Consent: Tocqueville and Harriet Martineau on Women and Democracy in America," in *Feminist Interpretations of Alexis de Tocqueville*, ed. Jill Locke and Eileen Hunt Botting (University Park, PA: Penn State University Press, 2008), 171-72.

12. C. Beecher, *Treatise on Domestic Economy*, 43.

13. C. Beecher, *Treatise on Domestic Economy*, 44.

14. Lydia Child, *The Frugal Housewife, dedicated to those who are not ashamed of economy*, 22nd ed. (New York: Samuel S. and William L. Wood, 1838), 99.

15. C. Beecher, *Treatise on Domestic Economy*, 47.

16. C. Beecher, *Treatise on Domestic Economy*, 42.

17. C. Beecher, *Treatise on Domestic Economy*, 45.

18. C. Beecher, *Treatise on Domestic Economy*, 44.

19. C. Beecher, *Treatise on Domestic Economy*, 44.

20. C. Beecher, *Treatise on Domestic Economy*, 56, 57 (quotations), 61.

21. C. Beecher, *Treatise on Domestic Economy*, 44.

22. C. Beecher, *Treatise on Domestic Economy*, 61.

23. C. Beecher, *Treatise on Domestic Economy*, 259.

24. Catharine E. Beecher and Harriet Beecher Stowe, *The American Woman's Home: Or, Principles of Domestic Science* (New York: J. B. Ford, 1869), 311.

25. Sklar, *Catharine Beecher*, 151.

26. Susan Levine, "Labor's True Woman: Domesticity and Equal Rights in the Knights of Labor," *Journal of American History* 70 (September 1983): 323-39, at 338.

27. Beecher and Stowe, *American Woman's Home*, 15, 53-54, 140-46, 148.

28. Beecher and Stowe, *American Woman's Home*. Cf. Sarah A. Leavitt, *From Catharine Beecher to Martha Stewart: A Cultural History of Domestic Advice* (Chapel Hill: University of North Carolina Press, 2002), 41.

29. Timothy Roberts, *Distant Revolutions: 1848 and the Challenge to American Exceptionalism* (Charlottesville: University of Virginia Press, 2009), 92 (quotation); Patrick J. Kelly, "The European Revolutions of 1848 and the Transnational Turn in Civil War History," *Journal of the Civil War Era* 4 (September 2014): 436.

30. Elizabeth Cady Stanton, *A History of Woman Suffrage*, vol. 1 (Rochester, NY: Fowler and Wells, 1889), 67-74. Louise Michele Newman, *White Women's Rights: The Racial Origins of Feminism in the United States* (New York: Oxford University Press, 1999), 22. On the association of women with civilization, see Sylvana Tomaselli, "The Enlightenment Debate on Women," *History Workshop Journal* 20 (October 1985): 101-24.

31. James Bryce, *The American Commonwealth*, vol. 3 (London: Macmillan, 1888), 690, 735.

32. S. Levine, "Labor's True Woman," 323-24; Stowe and Beecher, *American Woman's Home*.

33. Dexter C. Bloomer, *The Life and Writings of Amelia Bloomer* (Boston: Arena Publishing, 1895), 59; Ian Tyrrell, "Women and Temperance in Antebellum America, 1830-1860," *Civil War History* 28 (Summer 1982): 128-52.

34. Melanie J. Kisthardt, "Flirting with Patriarchy: Feminist Dialogics," in *The Stowe Debate: Rhetorical Strategies in "Uncle Tom's Cabin,"* ed. Mason I. Lowance, Ellen E. Westbrook and Robert Prospero (Amherst: University of Massachusetts Press, 1994), 45, 55.

35. Harriet Beecher Stowe, *Uncle Tom's Cabin: Or, Life among the Lowly* (Boston: John Jewett, 1852), 624.

36. John L. Thomas, "Romantic Reform in America, 1815–1865," *American Quarterly* 17, no. 4 (Winter 1965): 656–81.

37. Mary Kelley, "Feeling Right: Harriet Beecher Stowe, *Uncle Tom's Cabin*, and the Power of Sympathy" (paper presented at *Uncle Tom's Cabin* and the Web of Culture conference, June 2007), http://utc.iath.virginia.edu/interpret/exhibits/kelley/kelley.html.

38. See, e.g., McGuffey, *Eclectic Fourth Reader*, 184–85.

39. Harriet Beecher Stowe, *Sunny Memories of Foreign Lands*, vol. 1 (Boston: Phillips, Sampson, and Company, 1854), 18.

40. Stowe, *Sunny Memories of Foreign Lands*, 18. See also Frank Prochaska, *Eminent Victorians on American Democracy: The View from Albion* (New York: Oxford University Press, 2012), 127.

41. Stowe, *Sunny Memories of Foreign Lands*, 18.

42. Stowe, *Sunny Memories of Foreign Lands*, 18.

Chapter Six

1. Anders Stephanson, *Manifest Destiny: American Expansion and the Empire of Right* (New York: Hill and Wang, 1995), ch. 2; Frederick Merk, *Manifest Destiny and Mission in American History: A Reinterpretation* (New York: Alfred A. Knopf, 1963). See also Albert K. Weinberg, *Manifest Destiny: A Study of Nationalist Expansionism in American History* (Baltimore: Johns Hopkins University Press, 1935). For the contingencies of Manifest Destiny as history, see Andrew C. Isenberg and Thomas Richards Jr., "Alternative Wests: Rethinking Manifest Destiny," *Pacific Historical Review* 86 (February 2017): 4–17.

2. Reginald Horsman, *Race and Manifest Destiny: The Origins of American Racial Anglo-Saxonism* (Cambridge, MA: Harvard University Press, 1981), 208–9. For an indication of the spikes in usage, I conducted a series of Google Ngram searches for the term *Anglo-Saxon* in books in American English published in the years 1800–1860.

3. M. O'Brien, *Intellectual Life and the American South*, 60–61.

4. Daniel Walker Howe, *The Political Culture of the American Whigs* (Chicago: University of Chicago Press, 1979), 39.

5. American Home Missionary Society, *Our Country: Its Capabilities, Its Perils, and Its Hope; Being a Plea for the Early Establishment of Gospel Institutions in the Destitute Portions of the United States* (New York: American Home Missionary Society, 1842), 12.

6. Josiah Strong, *Our Country: Its Possible Future and Its Present Crisis* (New York: Baker and Taylor, 1885); Wendy J. Deichmann Edwards, "Forging an Ideology for American Missions: Josiah Strong and Manifest Destiny," Currents in World Christianity Position Paper Number 59, 1999, Centre for Advanced Religious and Theological Studies, University of Cambridge, 9.

7. "Campbellism," *Home Missionary* 14 (December 1841): 193–94.

8. Alexander Campbell, *Popular Lectures and Addresses. . . .* (Philadelphia: James Challen and Son, 1863), quotations at 35, 44.

9. American Home Missionary Society, *Our Country*, 12.

10. Campbell, *Popular Lectures*, 42.

11. John L. O'Sullivan, "The Great Nation of Futurity," *United States Magazine and Democratic Review* 6 (November 1839): 426–30.

12. John L. O'Sullivan, "Annexation (1845)," *United States Magazine and Democratic Review* 17 (July-August 1845): 5–10, at 9. See also Horsman, *Race and Manifest Destiny*, 63; Michael

Modarelli, *The Transatlantic Genealogy of American Anglo-Saxonism* (New York: Routledge, 2019).

13. Modarelli, *Transatlantic Genealogy*; Eric Gerald Stanley, *Imagining the Anglo-Saxon Past: The Search for Anglo-Saxon Paganism and Anglo-Saxon Trial by Jury* (1975; repr., Woodbridge, UK: Boydell and Brewer, 2000), 26; Horsman, *Race and Manifest Destiny*, ch. 4.

14. Michael Michie, *An Enlightenment Tory in Victorian Scotland: The Career of Sir Archibald Alison* (Montreal: McGill University Press; Kingston, ON: Queen's University Press, 1997), 153; Leslie Stephen, "Alison, Sir Archibald (1792–1867)," in *Dictionary of National Biography*, vol. 1 (New York: Macmillan, 1885), 287–89.

15. "European History," *Blackwood's Magazine*, October 1842, 419–45, in *Home Missionary* 16 (January 1843): 194–95.

16. Samuel F. Smith, review of *History of Europe from the Commencement of the French Revolution in 1789, to the restoration of the Bourbons in 1815*, by Archibald Alison, *Christian Review* 8 (March 1843): 97.

17. Alexander Campbell, "Address on the Anglo-Saxon Language: Its Origin, Character, and Destiny" [Cincinnati, 1849], in Campbell, *Popular Lectures*, 420.

18. Campbell, *Popular Lectures*, 44–45.

19. Frederick Douglass, "The Future of the Negro People of the Slave States" [1862], in *Frederick Douglass: Selected Speeches and Writings*, ed. Philip Foner and Yuval Taylor (Chicago: Chicago Review Press, 1999), 485; Frederick Douglass, "The Claims of the Negro Ethologically Considered" [1854], in Douglass, *Selected Speeches*, 297. See also Modarelli, *Transatlantic Genealogy*; David Blight, *Frederick Douglass: Prophet of Freedom* (New York: Simon and Schuster, 2018), 447.

20. Martin R. Delany, *The Condition, Elevation, Emigration, and Destiny of the Colored People of the United States, Politically Considered* (Philadelphia: printed by the author, 1852), 203, 209; Frank A. Hollin, *The Life and Public Services of Martin R. Delany* (Boston: Lee and Shepard, 1883); M. R. Delaney and Robert Campbell, *Search for a Place: Black Separatism and Africa, 1860* (Ann Arbor: University of Michigan Press, 1969); Mia Bay, *The White Image in the Black Mind: African-American Ideas about White People, 1830–1925* (New York: Oxford University Press, 2000), 65–66, 106–10.

21. Haselby, *Origins of American Religious Nationalism*.

22. L. Beecher, *Plea for the West*.

23. Jeremiah Evarts, *Essays on the present crisis in the condition of the American Indians* (Philadelphia: T. Kite, 1830), 4. See also Charles Maxfield, "The Legacy of Jeremiah Evarts," *International Bureau of Missions Research* 22, no. 4 (1998): 174; John A. Andrews III, *From Revivals to Removal: Jeremiah Evarts, the Cherokee Nation, and the Search for the Soul of America* (Athens: University of Georgia Press, 1992), 267–68.

24. Evarts, *Essays on the present crisis*, 5. Cf. Francis Paul Prucha, "Protest by Petition: Jeremiah Evarts and the Cherokee Indians," *Proceedings of the Massachusetts Historical Society*, 3rd ser., 97 (1985): 42–58.

25. This argument missed the point that the expansion of Christian republicanism itself was founded on the expectation of further Indian removal and hence implicated in the moral disgrace. Cf. Claudio Saunt, *Unworthy Republic: The Dispossession of Native Americans and the Road to Indian Territory* (New York: W. W. Norton, 2020), 66.

26. William G. McLoughlin, *Cherokee Renascence in the New Republic* (Princeton, NJ: Princeton University Press, 1986), 448.

27. John Demos, *The Heathen School: A Story of Hope and Betrayal in the Age of the Early Republic* (New York: Alfred A. Knopf, 2004); McLoughlin, *Cherokee Renascence*, 367–68.

28. Howard A. Barnes, *Horace Bushnell and the Virtuous Republic* (Metuchen, NJ: Scarecrow Press, 1991), 129.

29. Beecher quoted in Cherry, *God's New Israel*, 11–12.

30. L. Beecher, *Plea for the West*, 51.

31. L. Beecher, *Plea for the West*, 62, 63, quotation at 78.

32. L. Beecher, *Plea for the West*, 11.

33. John C. Pinheiro, *Missionaries of Republicanism: A Religious History of the Mexican-American War* (New York: Oxford University Press, 2015), 137, 141, 166–67.

34. Juan Francisco Martínez, *Sea la Luz: The Making of Mexican Protestantism in the American Southwest, 1829–1900* (Denton: University of North Texas Press, 2006), 11–13. Some evangelical missionaries continued to proselytize among the removed tribes in the Indian Territory of present-day Oklahoma.

35. Horace Bushnell, *Barbarism the First Danger: A Discourse for Home Missions* (New York: American Home Missionary Society, 1847), 27.

36. For an image of this striking lithograph, see Martha A. Sandweiss, "John Gast, American Progress, 1872," Picturing United States History, accessed January 5, 2021, http://picturinghistory .gc.cuny.edu/john-gast-american-progress-1872/.

37. The conflict within the Lane Seminary in 1832–33 over Beecher's tepid attitude toward the abolition question showed how northern evangelical opinion was changing. J. Earl Thompson Jr., "Lyman Beecher's Long Road to Conservative Abolitionism," *Church History* 42 (March 1973): 89–109.

38. *History of Dodge County Wisconsin* (Chicago: Western Historical, 1880), 590–91, at 591; Frank N. Dexter, *A Hundred Years of Congregational History in Wisconsin* (n.p.: Wisconsin Congregational Conference, 1933), 256–57.

39. J. J. Miter, "Address of the Rev. J. J. Miter, Milwaukee, Wisconsin . . ." *Home Missionary* 19 (July 1846): 61–65, at 65 (italics added).

40. Bushnell, *Barbarism*, 31.

41. Cf. Pinheiro, *Missionaries of Republicanism*; Thomas Hietala, *Manifest Design: American Exceptionalism and Empire*, rev. ed. (Ithaca, NY: Cornell University Press, 2003), 167.

42. Robert Sampson, *John L. O'Sullivan and His Times* (Kent, OH: Kent State University Press, 2003), 247. For O'Sullivan's thought, see Adam Gomez, "Deus Vult: John L. O'Sullivan, Manifest Destiny, and American Democratic Messianism," *American Political Thought* 1 (Fall 2012): 236–62, at 237; John D. Wilsey, " 'Our Country Is Destined to be the Great Nation of Futurity': John L. O'Sullivan's Manifest Destiny and Christian Nationalism, 1837–1846," *Religions* 8 (April 2017): 45–61.

43. O'Sullivan, "Great Nation of Futurity," 426–29; Bancroft, *History of the United States*, 9.

44. O'Sullivan, "Great Nation of Futurity," 426.

45. O'Sullivan, "Great Nation of Futurity," 430 (italics added).

46. Wilsey, " 'Our Country Is Destined,' " 57–58.

47. Edward L. Widmer, *Young America: The Flowering of Democracy in New York City* (New York: Oxford University Press, 1999), 32–35; Brett Goodin, *From Captives to Consuls: Three Sailors in Barbary and Their Self-Making across the Early American Republic, 1770–1840* (Baltimore: Johns Hopkins University Press, 2020).

48. Guyatt, *Providence and the Invention of the United States*, 217.

49. Major L. Wilson, *Space, Time, and Freedom: The Quest for Nationality and the Irrepressible Conflict, 1815–1861* (Westport, CT: Greenwood, 1974); cf. Thomas M. Allen, *A Republic in Time: Temporality and Social Imagination in Nineteenth-Century America* (Chapel Hill: University of North Carolina Press, 2008), 17–18.

50. O'Sullivan, "Annexation (1845)," 9 (italics added). O'Sullivan had earlier referred only to "Saxon" traditions of Americans in the 1839 address.

51. O'Sullivan, "Annexation (1845)," 7, 10.

52. Isenberg and Richards, "Alternative Wests," 12, 16.

53. O'Sullivan, "Annexation (1845)," 7.

54. "Slavery, Uncle Tom's Cabin and the North American Review," *Freewill Baptist Quarterly* 1–2 (January 1854): 38.

55. Quoted in Widmer, *Young America*, 187.

56. "Slavery, Uncle Tom's Cabin and North American Review," 25–28.

57. "Address of Rev. John P. Gulliver, of Norwich, Ct.," in *Twenty-Sixth Report of the American Home Missionary Society, . . . May 12, 1852* (New York: Baker Godwin, 1852), 115; "American Home Missionary Society and Slavery," *Twenty-Seventh Report of the American Home Missionary Society, . . . May 11, 1853* (New York: Baker Godwin, 1853), 120–24; "Civilization: Helps and Hindrances," *Freewill Baptist Quarterly* 1–2 (April 1854): 206–7; American Home Missionary Society, *Thirtieth Report of the American Home Missionary Society . . . 1856* (New York: American Home Missionary Society, 1856), 86–87.

58. Tyrrell, *Sobering Up*, ch. 10.

59. Edwin Hubbell Chapin, "The Fourth of July at the Crystal Palace," *New York Times*, July 5, 1854, 2; Edwin Hubbell Chapin, *The American Idea, and what grows out of it. An oration, delivered in the New-York Crystal Palace, July 4, 1854* (Boston: A. Tompkins, 1854); Edwin Hubbell Chapin, *A Discourse Preached in the Universalist Church, Charlestown, on Sunday May 12, 1844: in reference to the recent riots in Philadelphia* (Boston: A. Tompkins, 1844).

60. Cf. Churchwell, *Behold, America*, 24–25.

61. Quotation from preface to Ryder, *Our Country*, v. See also David Paul Brown, "Naturalization of Aliens," in Ryder, *Our Country*, 38–39.

62. A. D. Challoner, "The Duties of American Women," in Ryder, *Our Country*, 218–21, at 221.

63. Eric Foner, *Free Soil, Free Labor, Free Men: The Ideology of the Republican Party before the Civil War* (New York: Oxford University Press, 1970); William E. Gienapp, "Nativism and the Creation of a Republican Majority in the North before the Civil War," *Journal of American History* 72 (December 1985): 529–59.

Chapter Seven

1. For an extended treatment of the Civil War as a crisis of exceptionalism, see Andrew F. Lang, *A Contrast of Civilizations: Exposing the Crisis of American Exceptionalism in the Civil War Era* (Chapel Hill: University of North Carolina Press, 2021).

2. [Russell], "Civil War in America."

3. John L. Thomas, *The Liberator: William Lloyd Garrison: A Biography* (Boston: Little, Brown, 1963).

4. Frederick Douglass, "The Meaning of the Fourth of July for the Negro," in Douglass, *Selected Speeches*, 188–206, at 192–92, 203–5. Originally published as Frederick Douglass, *Oration,*

Delivered in Corinthian Hall, Rochester, by Frederick Douglass, July 5th, 1852 (Rochester: Lee, Mann, 1852). See also Colaiaco, *Frederick Douglass and the Fourth of July*.

5. John R. McKivigan IV, Heather L. Kaufman, and Julie Husband, eds., *The Speeches of Frederick Douglass: A Critical Edition* (New Haven, CT: Yale University Press, 2018), 55, 68.

6. The original title was *National philanthropist and investigator and genius of temperance* (Boston, 1829–1830). See Holly Berkley Fletcher, *Gender and the American Temperance Movement of the Nineteenth Century* (New York: Routledge, 2008), 50–52.

7. William Goodell, *Views of American Constitutional Law, in its Bearing upon American Slavery* (Utica, NY: Jackson and Chaplin, 1844), 154.

8. William Goodell, *Slavery and Anti-slavery; A history of the great struggle in both hemispheres; with a view of the slavery question in the United States* (New York: William Harned, 1852), 1.

9. Goodell, *Views of American Constitutional Law*, 152.

10. Lewis Perry, *Radical Abolitionism: Anarchy and the Government of God in Antislavery Thought* (Ithaca, NY: Cornell University Press, 1973), 47, 270. Goodell, *Views of American Constitutional Law*, 10, used the "house divided against itself" phrase. On Goodell, see Rebecca E. Zietlow, *The Forgotten Emancipator: James Mitchell Ashley and the Ideological Origins of Reconstruction* (New York: Cambridge University Press, 2018), 28–32; Steve Gowler, "Radical Orthodoxy: William Goodell and the Abolition of American Slavery," *New England Quarterly* 91, no. 4 (December 2018): 592–623.

11. George B. Cheever, *God's Hand in America* (New York: Thompson and Otis, 1841), vii–viii.

12. George B. Cheever, *God against Slavery, and the Freedom and Duty of the Pulpit to Rebuke, as a Sin against God* (New York: Joseph H. Ladd, 1857), 92.

13. John Lothrop Motley, "The Polity of the Puritans," *North American Review* 69 (October 1849): 470–96, at 481; John Lothrop Motley, *The Rise of the Dutch Republic, A History*, vol. 1 (New York: Harper and Brothers, 1855), v.

14. Richard Hildreth, *Despotism in America: An inquiry into the nature, results, and legal basis of the slave-holding system in the United States* (Boston: J. P. Jewett, 1854), esp. 7–8.

15. Eileen Ka-May Cheng, *The Plain and Noble Garb of Truth: Nationalism and Impartiality in American Historical Writing, 1784–1860* (Athens: University of Georgia Press, 2008), 188–89; Richard Hildreth, *The History of the United States of America from the Adoption of the Federal Constitution . . .* 3 vols. (New York: Harper and Brothers, 1851–52).

16. Lydia Maria Child, *An Appeal in Favor of That Class of Americans Called Africans* (Boston: Allen and Ticknor, 1833), 36.

17. Arthur Simkins, *An Address Before the State Agricultural Society of South Carolina . . . November 1855 at Columbia, S. C.* (Edgefield Court House, SC, 1855), 7–8, quoted in Drew Gilpin Faust, "The Rhetoric and Ritual of Agriculture in Antebellum South Carolina," *Journal of Southern History* 45 (November 1979): 566.

18. This Atlanta speech is published in full in the *Southern Confederacy* (Atlanta, GA), March 13, 1861, 2. It predated the oft-cited "Corner-stone Speech" of March 21 in Augusta, Georgia. See *Chicago Daily Tribune*, March 23, 1861, 2; Alexander H. Stephens, "Cornerstone Address, March 21, 1861," in *The Rebellion Record: A Diary of American Events with Documents, Narratives, Illustrative Incidents, Poetry, etc.*, ed. Frank Moore, vol. 1 (New York: G. P. Putnam, 1862), 44–49. On Southern exceptionalism, see James M. McPherson, "Antebellum Southern Exceptionalism: A New Look at an Old Question," *Civil War History* 29 (September 1983): 418–33; Lang, *Contrast of Civilizations*.

19. For a Northern Unionist critique, see [John Jay], *The Great Conspiracy: An address delivered at Mt. Kisco, Westchester County, New York, on the 4th of July, 1861, the eighty-fifth anniversary*

of American independence (New York: James G. Gregory, 1861), 20–26, 48–50; *Ashtabula Weekly Telegraph* (Ashtabula, OH), November 1, 1862, 2; *Evening Telegraph* (Philadelphia), November 12, 1864, 2: "we shall then be a model nation, without the puerility of boasting of it."

20. Hollis Read, *The Coming Crisis of the World* (Columbus, OH: Follett, Foster, 1861), 228.

21. Read, *Coming Crisis of the World*, 228. African American abolitionist Frederick Douglass was less critical of the nation, retaining more hope in the Declaration of Independence. Douglass, *Selected Speeches*, 188–206.

22. Brown quoted in Stephen B. Oates, *To Purge This Land with Blood*, 2nd ed. (Amherst: University of Massachusetts Press, 1984), 245–46, 264, quotation at 351.

23. Read, *Coming Crisis of the World*, 226.

24. Read, *Coming Crisis of the World*, vi (quotation), vii.

25. David Hackett Fischer, *Liberty and Freedom: A Visual History of America's Founding Ideas* (New York: Oxford University Press, 2004), 330–31.

26. Elaine Showalter, *The Civil Wars of Julia Ward Howe: A Biography* (New York: Simon and Schuster, 2016), 166–67, 241–42.

27. Ernest L. Tuveson, *Redeemer Nation: The Idea of America's Millennial Role* (Chicago: University of Chicago Press, 1968), 187–214. See also James H. Moorhead, *American Apocalypse: Yankee Protestants and the Civil War, 1860–1869* (New Haven, CT: Yale University Press, 1978); Ronald White, "Lincoln's Sermon on the Mount: The Second Inaugural," in *Religion and the Civil War*, ed. Randall M. Miller, Harry S. Stout and Charles Reagan (New York: Oxford University Press, 1998), 208–25; George C. Rable, *God's Almost Chosen Peoples: A Religious History of the American Civil War* (Chapel Hill: University of North Carolina Press, 2010), 63–64, 68, 258–63; George Fredrickson, "The Coming of the Lord: The Northern Protestant Clergy and the Civil War Crisis," in Miller, Stout, and Reagan, *Religion and the Civil War*, 110–30.

28. Tuveson, *Redeemer Nation*, 191, 208.

29. George Fredrickson, *The Inner Civil War: Northern Intellectuals and the Crisis of the Union* (New York: Oxford University Press, 1965), 61.

30. Rable, *Almost Chosen Peoples*, 43.

31. Steven K. Green, *The Second Disestablishment: Church and State in Nineteenth-Century America* (New York: Oxford University Press, 2010); Moore, *Founding Sins*, ch. 5.

32. Moore, *Founding Sins*, 119, 131–32 (quotation); Gaines Foster, *Moral Reconstruction: Christian Lobbyists and the Federal Legislation of Morality, 1865–1920* (Chapel Hill: University of North Carolina Press, 2003), 22–23.

33. National Reform Association, *Proceedings of the National Reform Convention . . . 1874* (Philadelphia: Christian Statesman Association, 1874), 81 (hereafter cited as *NRA 1874*).

34. T. Stephenson, "The Ends We Seek," in National Reform Association, *NRA 1874*, 26, 28.

35. Alexander quoted in National Reform Association, *Proceedings of the National Convention to Secure the Religious Amendment of the Constitution of the United States. Held in New York, Feb. 26 and 27, 1873. With an Account of the Origin and Progress of the Movement* (New York: John Polhemus, 1873), 4 (hereafter cited as *NRA 1873*).

36. National Reform Association, *NRA 1873*, 4 (italics added).

37. David Kerr, "The Moral Responsibility of Nations," in National Reform Association, *NRA 1874*, 66.

38. National Reform Association, "Testimonies to the Defect of the Constitution," in *NRA 1874*, 42.

39. Solomon Pool to Rev. D. McAllister, January 29, 1874, in National Reform Association, *NRA 1874*, 37.

40. National Reform Association, *NRA 1873*, 17 (italics in original).

41. Craven quoted in National Reform Association, *NRA 1873*, 16, 17. For more on Craven, see *Princeton Alumni Weekly* 5 (January 21, 1905): 258.

42. Hagans quoted in National Reform Association, *Proceedings of the National Convention to Secure the Religious Amendment of the Constitution of the United States . . . 1872* (Philadelphia: James B. Rodgers, 1872), 10, 11 (hereafter cited as *NRA 1872*).

43. National Reform Association, *NRA 1873*, 10.

44. Hagans quoted in National Reform Association, *NRA 1872*, 10.

45. Milligan quoted in National Reform Association, *NRA 1872*, 11.

46. G. Foster, *Moral Reconstruction*, 91–102; Verhoeven, *Secularists, Religion and Government*, 209–12.

47. Foster, *Moral Reconstruction*, 81, 84–88, 115, 273.

48. Church of the Holy Trinity v. United States, 143 U.S. 457 (1892); Steven K. Green, "Justice David Josiah Brewer and the 'Christian Nation' Maxim," *Albany Law Review* 63 (1999): 427–76, at 437; Foster, *Moral Reconstruction*, 117.

49. J. Gordon Hylton, "David Josiah Brewer and the Christian Constitution," *Marquette Law Review* 81 (Winter 1998): 417.

50. Michael J. Brodhead, *David J. Brewer: The Life of a Supreme Court Justice, 1837–1910* (Carbondale: Southern Illinois University Press, 1994), 129. Cf. David Sehat, *The Myth of American Religious Freedom* (New York: Oxford University Press, 2011), 176–78.

51. *Church of the Holy Trinity*, 143 U.S. at 457.

52. Carol Chomsky, "Unlocking the Mysteries of Holy Trinity: Spirit, Letter, and History in Statutory Interpretation," *Columbia Law Review* 100 (May 2000): 901–2.

53. Phillip Muñoz, *Religious Liberty and the American Supreme Court: The Essential Cases and Documents* (Lanham, MD: Rowman and Littlefield, 2013), 20.

54. David Brewer, *The United States a Christian Nation* (Philadelphia: John C. Winston, 1905), 11. See also David Brewer, *The Mission of the United States in the Cause of Peace* (Boston: International School of Peace, 1910), 16, 12.

55. Brewer, *United States a Christian Nation*, 76.

56. Brewer, *United States a Christian Nation*, 76. See also National Reform Association, *Report of the World's Christian Citizenship Conference, held in Philadelphia, ...* (Pittsburgh, PA: National Reform Association, [1910]), 159.

57. Tisa Wenger, "The God-in-the-Constitution Controversy: American Secularisms in Historical Perspective," in *Comparative Secularisms in a Global Age*, ed. Linell E. Cady and Elizabeth Shakman Hurd (New York: Palgrave, 2010), 87–105.

58. Lilienthal quoted in Wenger, "God-in-the-Constitution Controversy," 98.

59. Verhoeven, *Secularists, Religion and Government*, 211; National Reform Association, *NRA 1873*, 9, 128, 208–9; Moore, *Founding Sins*, 141–43.

Chapter Eight

1. Grover Cleveland, *The Public Papers of Grover Cleveland: Twenty-second President of the United States* (Washington, DC: Government Printing Office, 1889), 177.

2. Isaac Parker, "Fourth of July Address," in Saunders, *Our National Centennial Jubilee*, 757–64, at 761.

3. Edward Berenson, *The Statue of Liberty: A Transatlantic Story* (New Haven, CT: Yale University Press, 2012).

4. Parsons quoted in August Spies et al., *The Accused the Accusers: Famous Speeches of the Eight Chicago Anarchists in Court* (Chicago: Socialistic Publishing Society, [1886]), 117.

5. Fabian Hilfrich, *Debating American Exceptionalism: Empire and Democracy in the Wake of the Spanish-American War* (New York: Palgrave Macmillan, 2012).

6. David Wrobel, *The End of American Exceptionalism: Frontier Anxiety from the Old West to the New Deal* (Lawrence: University Press of Kansas, 1993).

7. Frederick Jackson Turner, "The Significance of the Frontier in American History" [1893], in *The Frontier in American History* (New York: Henry Holt, 1920), 37.

8. Henry Nash Smith, *Virgin Land: The American West as Symbol and Myth* (Cambridge, MA: Harvard University Press, 1950), esp. ch. 12; Ben Wattenberg, "Seymour Martin Lipset Interview" [c. 1997], PBS (website), accessed January 7, 2021, https://www.pbs.org/fmc/interviews/lipset.htm; Seymour Martin Lipset and Richard Hofstadter, eds., *Turner and the Sociology of the Frontier* (New York: Basic Books, 1968).

9. Turner, *Frontier*, 242, 349–56, esp. "Middle-Western Pioneer Democracy" [1918]: "the creation of a new type, which was neither the sum of, all its elements, nor a complete fusion in a melting pot" (349).

10. Patricia Kelly Hall and Steven Ruggles, "'Restless in the Midst of Their Prosperity': New Evidence on the Internal Migration of Americans, 1850–2000," *Journal of American History* 91 (December 2004): 829–46; Joseph Ferrie, "Migration to the Frontier in Mid-Nineteenth Century America: A Re-Examination of Turner's 'Safety Valve,'" Department of Economics and Institute for Policy Research, Northwestern University and NBER, July 1997, http://faculty.wcas.northwestern.edu/~fe2r/papers/munich.pdf.

11. Turner, "Significance of the Frontier," 38.

12. Frederick Jackson Turner, "Pioneer Ideals and the State University: Commencement Address at the University of Indiana, 1910," in Turner, *Frontier*, 269–90, at 280 (italics added).

13. Charles Postel, *Equality: An American Dilemma, 1866–1896* (New York: Farrar, Straus and Giroux, 2019).

14. Frederick Jackson Turner, "The Problem of the West" [1896], in Turner, *Frontier*, 220–21.

15. Ian Tyrrell, *Crisis of the Wasteful Nation: Empire and Conservation in Theodore Roosevelt's America* (Chicago: University of Chicago Press, 2015); Frederick Jackson Turner, "Contributions of the West to American Democracy" [1903], in Turner, *Frontier*, 243–69, at 244; Frederick Jackson Turner, "Pioneer Ideals," 279.

16. Turner, "Contributions of the West," 266–68; Turner, "Pioneer Ideals," 282–89.

17. Merle Curti, *The Making of an American Community* (Stanford, CA: Stanford University Press, 1959).

18. See, e.g., Patricia Nelson Limerick, *Legacy of Conquest: The Unbroken Past of the American West* (New York: Norton, 1987).

19. Frederick Jackson Turner, *The Character and Influence of the Indian Trade in Wisconsin: A Study of the Trading Post as an Institution* (Baltimore: Johns Hopkins University Studies in Historical and Political Science, 1891). A strong influence on Turner was Italian economist Achille Loria, who argued for the economic determination of the stages of value in land under

social systems. Lee Benson, "Achille Loria's Influence on American Economic Thought: Including His Contributions to the Frontier Hypothesis," *Agricultural History* 24 (October 1950): 184.

20. Jon Lauck, *The Lost Region: Toward a Revival of Midwestern History* (Iowa City: University of Iowa Press, 2013), 40; Ian Tyrrell, "Making Nations/Making States: American Historians in the Context of Empire," *Journal of American History* 86 (December 1999): 1015–44.

21. Frederick Jackson Turner, *The Significance of Sections in American History* (New York: Harper and Row, 1932).

22. H. Smith, *Virgin Land*, 251.

23. Henry David Thoreau, *Walden and Other Writings*, ed. Brooks Atkinson (New York: Modern Library, 1992); Steven J. Holmes, *The Young John Muir: An Environmental Biography* (Madison: University of Wisconsin Press, 1999), ch. 1.

24. Roderick Nash, *Wilderness and the American Mind* (New Haven, CT: Yale University Press, 1967); Roderick Nash, "The American Invention of National Parks," *American Quarterly* 22, no. 3 (Autumn 1970): 726–35.

25. Alan MacEachern, "Canada's Best Idea? The Canadian and American National Park Services in the 1910s," in *National Parks Beyond the Nation: Global Perspectives on "America's Best Idea,"* ed. Adrian Howkins, Jared Orsi, and Mark Fiege (Norman: University of Oklahoma Press, 2016), 51–67; Tyrrell, *Crisis of the Wasteful Nation*, ch. 8.

26. Claudia Leal et al., eds., *Nature States: Rethinking the History of Conservation* (London: Routledge, 2017), 16–36.

27. Tyrrell, *Crisis of the Wasteful Nation*.

28. Theodore Roosevelt, "Democratic Ideals," *Outlook*, November 15, 1913, 589. See also Tyrrell, *Crisis of the Wasteful Nation*, ch. 11.

29. Phelps quoted in Strong, *Our Country*, 219.

30. Strong, *Our Country*, 218.

31. Albert J. Beveridge, "Policy Regarding the Philippines" [1900], *Congressional Record*, 56 Cong., 1st Sess., vol. 33, pt. 9, 704–12, at 704.

32. Albert J. Beveridge, "March of the Flag," September 16, 1898, Voices of Democracy, http://voicesofdemocracy.umd.edu/beveridge-march-of-the-flag-speech-text/. The speech was given at an Indiana Republican meeting in Indianapolis.

33. Ian Tyrrell, *Reforming the World: The Creation of America's Moral Empire* (Princeton, NJ: Princeton University Press, 2010), 193; Suzanne Geissler, *God and Sea Power: The Influence of Religion on Alfred Thayer Mahan* (Annapolis, MD: Naval Institute Press, 2015).

34. Alfred T. Mahan, *The Harvest Within: Thoughts on the Life of the Christian* (Boston: Little, Brown, 1909), 119–20.

35. Mahan, *Harvest Within*, 120–21.

36. Mahan, *Harvest Within*, 123.

37. Mahan, *Harvest Within*, 119.

38. Frank Ninkovich, *Global Dawn: The Cultural Foundation of American Internationalism, 1865–1890* (Cambridge, MA: Harvard University Press, 2009).

39. Michael Patrick Cullinane, *Liberty and American Anti-Imperialism, 1898–1909* (New York: Palgrave Macmillan, 2012); Hilfrich, *Debating American Exceptionalism*.

40. Ian Tyrrell, "Empire in American History," in *Colonial Crucible: Empire in the Making of the Modern American State*, ed. Alfred W. McCoy and Francisco A. Scarano (Madison: University of Wisconsin Press, 2009), 541–56.

41. Cara Lea Burnidge, *A Peaceful Conquest: Woodrow Wilson, Religion, and the New World Order* (Chicago: University of Chicago Press, 2016).

42. Malcolm D. Magee, *What the World Should Be: Woodrow Wilson and the Crafting of a Faith-Based Foreign Policy* (Waco, TX: Baylor University Press, 2008), 34, 76–77.

43. Wilson quoted in Walter McDougall, *Promised Land, Crusader State* (Boston: Houghton Mifflin, 1997), 136 (italics added). See also Guyatt, *Providence and the Invention of the United States*, 319.

44. Eric Rauchway, *Blessed among Nations: How the World Made America* (New York: Hill and Wang, 2006), 147.

45. Lloyd E. Ambrosius, *Woodrow Wilson and the American Diplomatic Tradition: The Treaty Fight in Perspective* (New York: Cambridge University Press, 1987), xii, 23. Arthur S. Link, "The Higher Realism of Woodrow Wilson," *Journal of Presbyterian History* 76 (Summer 1998): 151–58. Despite its schematic analysis, N. Gordon Levin's work remains useful for its discussion of American exceptionalism. N. Gordon Levin, *Woodrow Wilson and World Politics: America's Response to War and Revolution* (New York: Oxford University Press, 1968).

46. Burnidge, *Peaceful Conquest*, 101–2.

47. Samuel Flagg Bemis, *A Diplomatic History of the United States* (New York: Henry Holt, 1936), 463. See also Ian Tyrrell and Jay Sexton, introduction to *Empire's Twin: U.S. Anti-Imperialism from the Founding Era to the Age of Terrorism*, ed. Ian Tyrrell and Jay Sexton (Ithaca, NY: Cornell University Press, 2015), 1–18.

48. Daniel Immerwahr, *How to Hide an Empire: A History of the Greater United States* (New York: Farrar, Straus, and Giroux, 2019).

49. Tyrrell, "Empire in American History."

Chapter Nine

1. Know-Nothing leaders believed they were "entirely consistent with the ideals of the Founding Fathers." Gregg Cantrell, "Southerner and Nativist: Kenneth Rayner and the Ideology of 'Americanism,'" *North Carolina Historical Review* 69 (April 1992): 131–47, at 146; Tyler Anbinder, *Nativism and Slavery: The Northern Know Nothings and the Politics of the 1850s* (New York: Oxford University Press, 1992).

2. James T. Fisher, *Communion of Immigrants: A History of Catholics in America*, rev. ed. (New York: Oxford University Press, 2008), 82–83, 87.

3. Carl Degler, *Out of Our Past: The Forces that Shaped Modern America*, 3rd ed. (New York: Harper and Row, 1984), 325–26; Kristofer Allerfeldt, *Race, Radicalism, Religion, and Restriction: Immigration in the Pacific Northwest, 1890–1924* (Westport, CT: Greenwood, 2003), 57.

4. Katherine Benton-Cohen, *Inventing the Immigration Problem: The Dillingham Commission and Its Legacy* (Cambridge, MA: Harvard University Press, 2018).

5. Prescott Hall, *The Future of American Ideals* (New York: NAR, 1912), 1–2.

6. Prescott Hall, "The Present and Future of Immigration" [1921], repr. from *North American Review* (May 1921), in *Immigration and Other Interests of Prescott Farnsworth Hall*, comp. Mrs. Prescott F. [Lucyle Irby] Hall (New York: Knickerbocker Press, 1922), 92.

7. Madison Grant, *Conquest of a Continent: or, The Expansion of Races in America* (New York: Charles Scribner's Sons, 1933).

8. Madison Grant, *The Passing of the Great Race; or, The Racial Basis of European History*, 4th ed. (New York: Charles Scribner's Sons, 1921), 84–85.

9. Henry Fairfield Osborn, preface to Grant, *Passing of the Great Race*, viii, quotation at ix. See also Grant, *Conquest of a Continent*, ix: "America was made by Protestants of Nordic origin and that their ideas about what makes true greatness should be perpetuated."

10. Osborn, preface to Grant, *Passing of the Great Race*, ix.

11. John R. Commons, *Race and Immigrants in America* (New York: Macmillan, 1907), 5.

12. Prescott Hall, *The Case for the Literacy Test*, Publications of the Immigration Restriction League, no. 66 (1916), 3–20, at 14. See also Prescott Hall, "Brief in Favor of the Numerical Limitation Bill," Publications of the Immigration Restriction League, no. 73 (66th Congress, E. R. 10837), in [L.] Hall, *Immigration and Other Interests*, 45.

13. Prescott Hall, "The Future of American Ideals" [1912], in [L.] Hall, *Immigration and Other Interests*, 34.

14. Linda Gordon, *The Second Coming of the KKK: The Ku Klux Klan of the 1920s and the American Political Tradition* (New York: Liveright, 2017).

15. I owe this observation to David Goodman.

16. P. Hall, *Case for the Literacy Test*, 14.

17. Rogers Smith, *Civic Ideals: Conflicting Visions of Citizenship in U.S. History* (New Haven, CT: Yale University Press, 1997), 364.

18. P. Hall, "Brief in Favor of the Numerical Limitation Bill," 45.

19. P. Hall, "Brief in Favor of the Numerical Limitation Bill," 50.

20. Edwin Black, *War against the Weak: Eugenics and America's Campaign to Create a Master Race* (New York: Four Walls Eight Windows, 2003), 239–45, 259; Marilyn Lake and Henry Reynolds, *Drawing the Global Colour Line: White Men's Countries and the International Challenge of Racial Equality* (Cambridge: Cambridge University Press, 2008).

21. Grant, *Passing of the Great Race*, xxviii.

22. P. Hall, "Immigration and the World War" [1921], in [L.] Hall, *Immigration and Other Interests*, 83.

23. Osborn, preface to Grant, *Passing of the Great Race*, ix.

24. Speech by Ellison DuRant Smith, April 9, 1924, in 65 Cong. Rec. 5961 (1924).

25. Stefan Kühl, *The Nazi Connection: Eugenics, American Racism, and German National Socialism* (New York: Oxford University Press, 2002), 85.

26. Theodore Roosevelt, "What 'Americanism' Means," *Forum* 17 (April 1894): 196–206, at 196; Gary Gerstle, *American Crucible: Race and Nation in the Twentieth Century* (Princeton, NJ: Princeton University Press, 2001), 45–46.

27. T. Roosevelt, "What 'Americanism' Means," 203.

28. Gerstle, *American Crucible*, 46–47.

29. T. Roosevelt, "What 'Americanism' Means," 197.

30. Horace Kallen, "Democracy versus the Melting-Pot: A Study of American Nationality," parts 1 and 2, *Nation*, February 18, 1915, 190–94; and February 25, 1915, 217–20; Randolph Bourne, "Trans-National America," *Atlantic Monthly*, July 1916, 86–97.

31. Jonathan Hansen, "True Americanism: Progressive Era Intellectuals and the Origins of Progressive Nationalism," in *Americanism: New Perspectives on the History of an Ideal*, ed. Michael Kazin and Joseph A. McCartin (Chapel Hill: University of North Carolina Press, 2006), 73–89, at 77.

32. T. Roosevelt, "What 'Americanism' Means," 196, 199.

33. Quoted in Gerstle, *American Crucible*, 51.

34. Barbara Truesdell, " 'Exalting U.S.ness': Patriotic Rituals of the Daughters of the American Revolution," in *Bonds of Affection: Americans Define Their Patriotism*, ed. John E. Bodnar (Princeton, NJ: Princeton University Press, 1996), 285, 286.

35. The later form was "the American Creed" used by the Swedish sociologist Gunnar Myrdal. See Myrdal, *American Dilemma*, xlii, xlvii. See also Lieven, *America, Right or Wrong*, 5; Lipset, *First New Nation*, 366. Versions can be traced back to the 1840s, without the critical mass that developed in the era of World War I. See Churchwell, *Behold, America*, 25.

36. Theodore Roosevelt, "America for Americans: Afternoon Speech of Theodore Roosevelt at St Louis, 31 May 1916," in *The Progressive Party: Its Record from January to July, 1916, Including Statements and Speeches of Theodore Roosevelt*, comp. Executive Committee of the Progressive National Committee (New York: Mail and Express Job Print, [1916]), 77–85.

37. William Preston Jr., *Aliens and Dissenters: Federal Suppression of Radicals, 1903–1933*, 2nd ed. (Urbana: University of Illinois Press, 1994); William Pencak, *For God and Country: The American Legion, 1919–1941* (Boston: Northeastern University Press, 1989), ch. 3; Desmond King, *The Liberty of Strangers: Making the American Nation* (Oxford: Oxford University Press, 2005), 70.

38. The hyperbole is typified in Ole Hanson, *Americanism versus Bolshevism* (New York: Doubleday, Page, 1920).

39. Lisa McGirr, "The Passion of Sacco and Vanzetti: A Global History," *Journal of American History* 93 (March 2007): 1085–1115.

40. Tyrrell, *Historians in Public*, 115, 130–31.

41. Max Paul Friedman, *Rethinking Anti-Americanism: The History of an Exceptional Concept in American Foreign Relations* (New York: Cambridge University Press, 2012), 52.

42. Ian Tyrrell, "American Exceptionalism and Anti-Americanism," in *Anti-Americanism: History, Causes, and Themes*, vol. 2, *Historical Perspectives*, ed. Brendon O'Connor (Oxford: Greenwood World Publishing, 2007), 112–13, 114–15; McGirr, "Passion of Sacco and Vanzetti," 1088–89.

43. William T. Colyer, *Americanism: A World Menace* (London: Labour Publishing, 1922); William T. Colyer, *The Worker's Passport: A Study of Legal Restrictions on Migrant Workers* (London: Labour Research Dept., 1928); Deidre M. Moloney, *National Insecurities: Immigrants and U.S. Deportation Policy since 1882* (Chapel Hill: University of North Carolina Press, 2012), 180.

44. Tom Mann, preface to Colyer, *Americanism: A World Menace*, v–vii.

45. David Ellwood, *The Shock of America: Europe and the Challenge of the Century* (New York: Oxford University Press, 2012), esp. 96–104. This anxiety began earlier. See Frederick A. McKenzie, *The American Invaders* (London: Grant Richards, 1902).

46. Antonio Gramsci, *Selections from the Prison Notebooks of Antonio Gramsci*, ed. and trans. Quentin Hoare and Geoffrey Nowell Smith (London: Lawrence and Wishart, 1971), 279–318; Colyer, *Americanism: A World Menace*, 8, 33, 81–82.

47. On capitalist production being already well established in the mid- to late nineteenth century, see, e.g., Friedrich Engels to Friedrich Adolph Sorge, December 31, 1892, in "Marx-Engels Correspondence 1892," Marxists Internet Archive, https://www.marxists.org/archive/marx/works/1892/letters/92_12_31.htm; David Herreshoff, *American Disciples of Marx: From the Age of Jackson to the Progressive Era* (Detroit: Wayne State University Press, 1967), 181, 186.

48. Quoted in Seymour Martin Lipset, ed., *Consensus and Conflict: Essays in Political Sociology* (New Brunswick, NJ: Transaction Books, 1985), 189. British Marxist H. M. Hyndman similarly noted that "just as north America is today the most advanced country economically

and socially, so it will be the first in which socialism will find open and legal expression." Quoted in Laurie Taylor, "America's Lost Revolution," *Guardian* (UK), June 29, 2000.

49. David Shannon, *The Socialist Party of America: A History* (New York: Macmillan, 1955), 259–60.

50. Jerome Karabel, "The Failure of American Socialism Reconsidered," *Socialist Register* 16 (1979): 207.

51. On social progressivism in the transatlantic context, see Daniel T. Rodgers, *Atlantic Crossings: Social Politics in a Progressive Age* (Cambridge, MA: Belknap Press of Harvard University Press, 1998).

52. Werner Sombart, "Preface to the Original German Edition," in *Why Is There No Socialism in the United States?* by Werner Sombart, ed. Patricia Hocking and C. T. Husbands (London: Macmillan, 1976), vii. See also C. T. Husbands, "Editor's Introductory Essay," in Sombart, *Why Is There No Socialism*, xv–xxxvii; Walter McDougall, "American Exceptionalism . . . Exposed," *Foreign Policy Research Institute E-Notes*, October 2012, https://www.files.ethz.ch/isn/161931/201210.mcdougall.americanexceptionalism.pdf. Sombart was also influenced by James Bryce, who had already developed his own theory that the egalitarian social customs and symbols of the United States could account for the blunting of class enmities. Maurice Garland Fulton, ed., *Bryce on American Democracy: Selections from the American Commonwealth and the Hindrances to Good Citizenship* (New York: Macmillan, 1919), 207.

53. Husbands, "Editor's Introductory Essay," xvi; Sombart, *Why Is There No Socialism*, 118. For the place of anti-Semitism in Sombart, see Colin Loader, "Puritans and Jews: Weber, Sombart and the Transvaluators of Modern Society," *Canadian Journal of Sociology / Cahiers canadiens de sociologie* 26 (Autumn 2001): 635–53.

54. McDougall, "American Exceptionalism . . . Exposed."

55. Sombart, *Why Is There No Socialism*, 10.

56. Sombart, *Why Is There No Socialism*, 3.

57. Sombart, *Why Is There No Socialism*, 118.

58. Sombart, *Why Is There No Socialism*, 119.

59. M. C. Howard and J. E. King, "Trotsky on Uneven and Combined Development," in *A History of Marxian Economics*, ed. M. C. Howard and J. E. King (Princeton, NJ: Princeton University Press, 1989), 222–42.

60. V. I. Lenin, "The Heritage We Renounce" [1897], Marxists Internet Archive, https://www.marxists.org/archive/lenin/works/1897/dec/31c.htm. See also V. I. Lenin, "What the 'Friends of the People' Are and How They Fight the Social-Democrats" [1894], Marxists Internet Archive, https://www.marxists.org/archive/lenin/works/1894/friends/08.htm#v01zz99h-271-GUESS.

61. Theodore Draper, *American Communism and Soviet Russia* (1957; repr., Abingdon, UK: Routledge, 2017), ch. 12.

62. John Pepper and John Louis Engdahl, "An Outline for the Labour Party Policy of the Workers' (Communist) Party of America" [1928], quoted in Jacob Zumoff, *The Communist International and US Communism, 1919–1929* (Leiden, Neth.: Brill, 2014), 233; Paul Le Blanc and Tim Davenport, eds., *The "American Exceptionalism" of Jay Lovestone and His Comrades, 1929–1940: Dissident Marxism in the United States*, vol. 1 (Leiden, Neth.: Brill, 2015), ch. 2.

63. Zumoff, *Communist International and US Communism*, 232–33.

64. Zumoff, *Communist International and US Communism*, 233.

65. "Address by the Executive Committee of the Communist International, . . . 14 May 1929," in Le Blanc and Davenport, *"American Exceptionalism" of Jay Lovestone*, 118.

66. Zumoff, *Communist International and US Communism*, 232.

67. "Speech Delivered by Joseph Stalin in the American Commission of the Presidium of the Executive Committee of the Communist International 6 May 1929," in Le Blanc and Davenport, *"American Exceptionalism" of Jay Lovestone*, 106.

68. William Z. Foster, "Marxism and 'American Exceptionalism,'" *Political Affairs*, September 1947, 794; "Address by the Executive Committee of the Communist International," 118; Louis Stark, "Moscow Detains Leaders of Quarrel in Reds' Party Here," *New York Times*, July 5, 1929, 1.

69. Bertram Wolfe, *What Is the Communist Opposition?* 2nd ed. (New York: Communist Party U.S.A. [Opposition], 1933), 15.

70. Wolfe, *What Is the Communist Opposition?* 15.

71. See, e.g., Zolberg, "How Many Exceptionalisms?"

72. Le Blanc and Davenport, *"American Exceptionalism" of Jay Lovestone*, ch. 2; Robert Alexander, *The Right Opposition: The Lovestoneites and the International Communist Opposition of the 1930s* (Westport, CT: Greenwood, 1981), 114–15.

73. Robert Hessen, introduction to *Breaking with Communism: The Intellectual Odyssey of Bertram D. Wolfe*, ed. Robert Hessen (Stanford, CA: Hoover Institution, 1990), 10, 15–16; Alexander, *Right Opposition*, 124–26.

74. Will Herberg, "The New Imperialism of Stalinist Russia," in Le Blanc and Davenport, *"American Exceptionalism" of Jay Lovestone*, 361; Alexander, *Right Opposition*, 127.

75. Michael J. Denning, *Culture in the Age of Three Worlds* (London: Verso, 2004), 195–96; Hartz, *Liberal Tradition in America*, 254 (quotation), 278–80.

76. Mark Hulliung, ed., *The American Liberal Tradition Reconsidered: The Contested Legacy of Louis Hartz* (Lawrence: University Press of Kansas, 2010); James T. Kloppenberg, "In Retrospect: Louis Hartz's 'The Liberal Tradition in America,'" *Reviews in American History* 29 (September 2001): 460–78; Louis Hartz et al., *The Founding of New Societies: Studies in the History of the United States, Latin America, South Africa, Canada, and Australia* (New York: Harcourt Brace, 1964).

77. Max Lerner, *America as a Civilization: Life and Thought in the United States Today* (New York: Simon and Schuster, 1957).

78. Alan Wald, *The New York Intellectuals: The Rise and Decline of the Anti-Stalinist Left* (Chapel Hill: University of North Carolina Press, 1987), 312, 359; Malcolm Walters, *Daniel Bell* (New York: Routledge, 1996), 18; Seymour Martin Lipset, "Steady Work: An Academic Memoir," *Annual Review of Sociology* 22 (1996): 1–27.

79. For Parsons's legacy, see Renee C. Fox, Victor M. Lidz, and Harold J. Bershady, eds., *After Parsons: A Theory of Action for the Twenty-First Century* (New York: Russell Sage Foundation, 2005).

80. For economics, see the survey in Keely, "American Exceptionalism."

81. Lipset, "Steady Work," 1; Jesús Velasco, "Seymour Martin Lipset: Life and Work," *Canadian Journal of Sociology / Cahiers canadiens de sociologie* 29 (Autumn 2004): 583–601; Robin Archer, "Seymour Martin Lipset and Political Sociology," special issue, *British Journal of Sociology* 61, no. 1 (January 2010): 43–50; Jack Citron, "Political Culture," in Schuck and Wilson, *Understanding America*, 167; Peter Schuck, "James Q. Wilson and American Exceptionalism," *National Affairs* 26 (Winter 2016): 135–53; Dunn, *American Exceptionalism: Origins, History, and Future*, 2; Murray, *American Exceptionalism: Experiment in History*, 19, 22.

82. Editions of *Democracy in America* appeared in 1945 (Knopf), 1947 (Oxford University Press), 1951 (Henry Regnery), 1954 (Vintage Books), and 1956 (New American Library); Julian

Bretz, review of *Democracy in America*, ed. Phillips Bradley, *New York History* 26 (October 1945): 505–6; F. O. Matthiessen, "A Classic Study of America: Alexis de Tocqueville's Masterpiece," *New York Times*, April 15, 1945, BR1; Eileen Ka-May Cheng, review of *Tocqueville: A Biography*, by Andre Jardin, H-Net, August 1999, http://www.h-net.org/reviews/showrev.php?id=3338; Denning, *Culture in the Age of Three Worlds*, 193–94.

83. David Stoesz, *The Dynamic Welfare State* (New York: Oxford University Press, 2016), 10.

Chapter Ten

1. Jay Sexton, *A Nation Forged by Crisis: A New American History* (New York: Basic Books, 2018).

2. As Sarah Churchwell shows, casual reference to the American Dream was older, but the concept crystallized in the 1930s. See Churchwell, *Behold, America*, 23, 26, 29.

3. For "world empire," see James Burnham, *The Struggle for the World* (New York: John Day, 1947).

4. PBS, "Ken Burns's 'The Dust Bowl' Explores the Largest Manmade Ecological Disaster in History," press release, April 11, 2012, PBS (website), updated August 17, 2020, https://www.pbs .org/about/blogs/news/ken-burnss-the-dust-bowl-explores-the-largest-manmade-ecological -disaster-in-history-airing-november-18-and-19-on-pbs/.

5. Jefferson Cowie, *The Great Exception: The New Deal and the Limits of American Politics* (Princeton, NJ: Princeton University Press, 2016), 9 (quotation), 237n22, 131–32. See also Rodgers, *Atlantic Crossings*.

6. Cowie, *Great Exception*, 3, quotation at 162.

7. Kiran Klaus Patel, *The New Deal: A Global History* (Princeton, NJ: Princeton University Press, 2016), 120, 274–83.

8. See, e.g., Josiah W. Bailey, "Our Republic: It Must be Preserved," *Vital Speeches of the Day* 7 (August 1941): 633–37.

9. On the political development of the American state, Steven Skowronek, *Building a New American State: The Expansion of National Administrative Capacities, 1877–1920* (Cambridge: Cambridge University Press, 1982); Kenneth Finegold and Theda Skocpol, *State and Party in America's New Deal* (Madison: University of Wisconsin Press, 1995).

10. Cowie, *Great Exception*. For the alternative of a "long" New Deal covering 1933 to 1952, see Ira Katznelson, *Fear Itself: The New Deal and the Origins of Our Time* (New York: W. W. Norton, 2013).

11. Cf. John Fousek, *To Lead the Free World: American Nationalism and the Cultural Roots of the Cold War* (Chapel Hill: University of North Carolina Press, 2000), 10.

12. Nicholas Vincent Montalto, "The Forgotten Dream: A History of the Intercultural Education Movement, 1924–1941" (PhD diss., University of Minnesota, 1978), 165; Dan Shiffman, "A Standard for the Wise and Honest: The 'Americans All . . . Immigrants All' Radio Broadcasts," *Studies in Popular Culture* 19 (October 1996): 99–107, quotation at 99; Barbara D. Savage, *Broadcasting Freedom: Radio, War, and the Politics of Race, 1938–1948* (Chapel Hill: University of North Carolina Press, 1999), 21–37.

13. United States Office of Education and Columbia Broadcasting System, *Americans All: Immigrants All* (Washington, DC: US Department of Education, 1939).

14. Broadcast episodes have been preserved in the New York Public Radio Archive Collections, available through the New York radio station WYNC website, https://www.wnyc

.org/series/americans-all-immigrants-all. Text quotation from "No. 26: Grand Finale," *Americans All: Immigrants All*, airdate May 6, 1939, MP3 audio, 29:33, https://www.wnyc.org/story/no
-26-grand-finale.

15. Quotation from "No. 10: Germans in the United States," *Americans All: Immigrants All*, airdate January 14, 1939, MP3 audio, 29:37, https://www.wnyc.org/story/episode-10-germans-in
-the-united-states. See also Shiffman, "A Standard for the Wise and Honest," 99–107.

16. Franklin D. Roosevelt, "Remarks to the Daughters of the American Revolution, Washington, D.C.," April 21, 1938, American Presidency Project, https://www.presidency.ucsb.edu
/node/209635.

17. Oscar Handlin, *The Uprooted: The Epic Story of the Great Migrations that Made the American People*, 2nd ed. (1951; repr., Philadelphia: University of Pennsylvania Press, 2002), 3.

18. See also Louis Adamic, *A Nation of Nations* (New York: Harper and Brothers, 1945).

19. Miriam Jordan, "Is America a 'Nation of Immigrants'? Immigration Agency Says No," *New York Times*, February 22, 2018.

20. John F. Kennedy, *A Nation of Immigrants*, rev. ed. (London: Hamish Hamilton, 1964), 3. See also Ali Behdad, *A Forgetful Nation: On Immigration and Cultural Identity in the United States* (Durham, NC: Duke University Press, 2005), 97.

21. Vine Deloria, Jr., *Red Earth, White Lies: Native Americans and the Myth of Scientific Fact* (Golden, CO: Fulcrum Publishing, 1997), 68.

22. Roxanne Dunbar-Ortiz and Dina Gilio-Whitaker, *"All the Real Indians Died Off": And 20 Other Myths about Native Americans* (Boston: Beacon Press, 2016).

23. J. T. Adams, *Epic of America*, 404. See also Churchwell, *Behold, America*, 25–26, 105, 169–74; Nevins, *James Truslow Adams*, 68.

24. J. T. Adams, *Epic of America*, 360, 403, quotation at 404. See also Roland Marchand, *Advertising the American Dream: Making Way for Modernity* (Berkeley: University of California Press, 1985).

25. Wilson Carey McWilliams, *The Idea of Fraternity in America* (Berkeley: University of California Press, 1973), ch. 19.

26. Marchand, *Advertising the American Dream*; Cullen, *American Dream: Short History*, 147, 150–57.

27. David Potter, *People of Plenty: Economic Abundance and the American Character* (Chicago: University of Chicago Press, 1954); Robert M. Collins, "David Potter's People of Plenty and the Recycling of Consensus History," *Reviews in American History* 16 (June 1988): 321–35.

28. Martin Luther King Jr., "I Have a Dream . . ." [speech presented at the March on Washington], August 28, 1963, 4, http://teachtnhistory.org/file/I%20Have%20A%20Dream%20Speech
.pdf.

29. King, "I Have a Dream," 5 (italics added).

30. Martin Luther King Jr., "Address at the Freedom Rally in Cobo Hall," [Detroit], June 23, 1963(?), Martin Luther King Jr. Research and Education Institute, Stanford University, https://
kinginstitute.stanford.edu/king-papers/documents/address-freedom-rally-cobo-hall.

31. Ian Tyrrell and Jay Sexton, "Whither American Anti-Imperialism in a Post-Colonial World," in Tyrrell and Sexton, *Empire's Twin*, 223–24.

32. See, e.g., Elizabeth Borgwardt, *A New Deal for the World: America's Vision for Human Rights* (Cambridge, MA: Harvard University Press, 2005), 158–59; Robert Divine, *Second Chance: The Triumph of Internationalism in America during World War II* (New York: Atheneum, 1967), 66–66, 78, 105.

33. Henry R. Luce, "The American Century," *Life*, February 1941, 65.

34. Luce, "American Century," 65; Michael J. Hogan, ed., *The Ambiguous Legacy: U.S. Foreign Relations in the 'American Century'* (New York: Cambridge University Press, 1999); Alan Brinkley, *The Publisher: Henry Luce and His American Century* (New York: Norton, 2010), 168–69, 267–71; William O. Walker III, *The Rise and Decline of the American Century* (Ithaca, NY: Cornell University Press, 2018), 85.

35. Michael H. Hunt, "East Asia in Henry Luce's 'American Century,'" in Hogan, *Ambiguous Legacy*, 232.

36. Brinkley, *Publisher*, 270–71.

37. Luce, "American Century," 64.

38. Luce, "American Century," 65.

39. Luce, "American Century," 65.

40. Luce, "American Century," 63.

41. Luce, "American Century," 65.

42. Herbert Hoover, *Addresses upon the American Road, 1940–1941* (New York: Charles Scribner's Sons, 1941), 53.

43. Luce, "American Century," 65.

44. Wendell L. Willkie, *One World* (New York: Simon and Schuster, 1943), 133.

45. Willkie, *One World*, 2; David Reynolds, "Power and Superpower: The Impact of Two World Wars on America's International Role," in *America Unbound: World War II and the Making of a Superpower*, ed. Warren Kimball (New York: St. Martin's Press, 1992), 24.

46. Samuel Zipp, "When Wendell Willkie Went Visiting: Between Interdependency and Exceptionalism in the Public Feeling for *One World*," *American Literary History* 26 (September 2014): 484–510, at 486. See also Samuel Zipp, "Dilemmas of World-Wide Thinking: Popular Geographies and the Problem of Empire in Wendell Willkie's Search for One World," *Modern American History* 1, no. 3 (2018): 295–319; Samuel Zipp, *The Idealist: Wendell Willkie's Wartime Quest to Build One World* (Cambridge, MA: Harvard University Press, 2020).

47. Brinkley, *Publisher*, 271–73.

48. Henry Wallace, "Century of the Common Man," in *Prefaces to Peace: A Symposium . . .* (New York: Doubleday Doran, 1943), 371–72, 374.

49. Wallace, "Century of the Common Man," 371–72.

50. Wallace, "Century of the Common Man," 369.

51. Wallace, "Century of the Common Man," 372, 374.

52. Brinkley, *Publisher*, 273, noted the similarities.

53. Elizabeth Cobbs Hoffman, *All You Need Is Love: The Peace Corps and the Spirit of the 1960s* (Cambridge, MA: Harvard University Press, 1998), quotations at 22–23, see also 25. See also Tyrrell, *Crisis of the Wasteful Nation*, 247; Jenna N. Hanchey, "Constructing 'American Exceptionalism': Peace Corps Volunteer Discourses of Race, Gender, and Empowerment," in *Volunteering and Communication*, vol. 2, *Studies in International and Intercultural Contexts*, ed. Michael W. Kramer, Laurie K. Lewis, and Loril M. Gossett (New York: Peter Lang, 2015), 233–50.

54. Borgwardt, *New Deal for the World*, 263–65. See also United Nations, "History of the Document," accessed January 9, 2021, http://www.un.org/en/sections/universal-declaration/history-document/index.html; Mary Ann Glendon, "The Rule of Law in the Universal Declaration of Human Rights," *Northwestern Journal of International Human Rights* 2, no. 1 (Spring 2004): article 5, https://scholarlycommons.law.northwestern.edu/cgi/viewcontent.cgi?article=1008&context=njihr.

55. Andrew Preston, *Sword of the Spirit, Shield of Faith: Religion in American War and Diplomacy* (New York: Knopf, 2012), 476.

56. Luce, "American Century," 64.

57. Luce, "American Century," 65.

58. Clive Ponting, *A Green History of the World* (London: Penguin, 1991), 292. It should be noted that the wartime destruction of the Axis powers' industrial base (and that of some of the Allies, too) temporarily exaggerated this global imbalance in fossil fuel energy consumption, but the disparity was indeed considerable.

59. Edward A. Ackerman, "Resources for Freedom by the U. S. President's Materials Policy Commission," 288 (July 1953): 172–75, at 173.

60. *Resources for Freedom: A Report to the President by the President's Materials Policy Commission*, 5 vols. (Washington, DC: Government Printing Office, 1952); *Summary of Volume One* (Washington, DC: Government Printing Office, 1952), 61.

61. Dwight D. Eisenhower, "Remarks at the Governors' Conference, Seattle, Washington," August 4, 1953, American Presidency Project, http://www.presidency.ucsb.edu/ws/?pid=9663.

62. [George Kennan], "The Sources of Soviet Conduct," *Foreign Affairs*, March 1947, History Guide, revised April 13, 2012, http://www.historyguide.org/europe/kennan.html.

63. Fredrik Logevall, *Embers of War: The Fall of an Empire and the Making of America's Vietnam* (New York: Random House, 2012).

64. Dianne Kirby, "John Foster Dulles: Moralism and Anti-Communism," *Journal of Transatlantic Studies* 6 (December 2008): 279–89; Jonathan Herzog, *The Spiritual-Industrial Complex: America's Religious Battle against Communism in the Early Cold War* (New York: Oxford University Press, 2011). On the broader relationship between religion and foreign policy, see A. Preston, *Sword of the Spirit, Shield of Faith*.

65. John Foster Dulles, *The Challenge to Freedom: Text of Speech at the Annual Commemoration of the Virginia Resolution for American Independence and the Virginia Bill of Rights, Williamsburg, Va., May 15, 1954* (Washington, DC: Department of State, 1954), 2, quotations at 7. On Dulles, see Richard H. Immerman, *John Foster Dulles: Piety, Pragmatism, and Power in U.S. Foreign Policy* (Wilmington, DE: Scholarly Resources, 1999), 2–3.

66. Boris I. Bittker, Scott C. Idleman, and Frank S. Ravitch, eds., *Religion and the State in American Law* (New York: Cambridge University Press, 2015), 136; Kevin M. Kruse, *One Nation under God: How Corporate America Invented Christian America* (New York: Basic Books, 2015).

67. Gaston, *Imagining Judeo-Christian America*, esp. 71–76, 191–92.

68. *The Report of the President's Commission on National Goals* (Washington, DC: Government Printer, 1960), 21, 23, mentioning only "vestiges of religious prejudice."

69. Quoted in Michael J. Cohen, *Truman and Israel* (Berkeley: University of California Press, 1990), 7.

70. Walter Hixson, *The Myth of American Diplomacy: National Identity and U.S. Foreign Policy* (New Haven, CT: Yale University Press, 2008), 172–73.

71. Andrew L. Yarrow, *Measuring America: How Economic Growth Came to Define American Greatness in the Late Twentieth Century* (Amherst: University of Massachusetts Press, 2010), 2–3, 26–27, 165–71.

72. Susan E. Reid, "The Khrushchev Kitchen: Domesticating the Scientific-Technological Revolution," *Journal of Contemporary History* 40 (April 2005): 289–316, at 289, 308–9.

73. Emily S. Rosenberg, "Consuming Women: Images of Americanization in the 'American Century,'" *Diplomatic History* 23 (Summer 1999): 479–97, at 481.

74. Rosenberg, "Consuming Women," 481.

75. Rosenberg, "Consuming Women," 487.

76. Rosenberg, "Consuming Women," 487.

77. Rosenberg, "Consuming Women," 481.

78. John Kenneth Galbraith, *The Affluent Society* (Harmondsworth, UK: Penguin, 1962). See also Daniel Horowitz, *Vance Packard and American Social Criticism* (Chapel Hill: University of North Carolina Press, 1994), 3–4, 130–31, 133; Vance Packard, *The Waste Makers* (New York: David McKay, 1960); Vance Packard, *The Hidden Persuaders* (London: Longmans, 1957).

79. John Kenneth Galbraith, *The New Industrial State* (1967; repr., Princeton, NJ: Princeton University Press, 2007), 45. See also Jean Baudrillard, "The Logistic Function of the Individual," in *Reflections on Commercial Life: An Anthology of Classic Texts from Plato to the Present*, ed. Patrick Murray (New York: Routledge, 1997), 469.

80. Extension of Remarks of Hon. Alexander Wiley of Wisconsin in the Senate of the United States, Friday, June 10, 1955, in 101 Cong. Rec. A4144 (1955); David S. Bovée, *The Church and the Land: The National Catholic Rural Life Conference and American Society, 1923–2007* (Washington, DC: Catholic University of America Press, 2010), 197.

81. Extension of Remarks, 101 Cong. Rec. A4144 (1955).

82. Extension of Remarks, 101 Cong. Rec. A4144 (1955).

83. Extension of Remarks, 101 Cong. Rec. A4145 (1955).

84. Bovée, *Church and Land*, 197. See also Yarrow, *Measuring America*, 168.

85. Mark Edwards, "'God Has Chosen Us': Re-Membering Christian Realism, Rescuing Christendom, and the Contest of Responsibilities during the Cold War," *Diplomatic History* 33 (January 2009): 67–94, at 73.

86. Arthur M. Schlesinger Jr., *"The Politics of Hope" and "The Bitter Heritage": American Liberalism in the 1950s*, with a new foreword by Sean Wilentz (Princeton, NJ: Princeton University Press, 2008), 158.

87. New Yorker columnist Richard Rovere coined this phrase in a 1961 article, "The American Establishment," republished in Richard Rovere, *The American Establishment and Other Reports, Opinions, and Speculations* (New York: Harcourt, Brace, and World, 1962), 13. See also Cornel West, *The American Evasion of Philosophy: A Genealogy of Pragmatism* (Basingstoke, UK: Macmillan, 1989), 163.

88. This paragraph draws on Noam Chomsky, "Reinhold Niebuhr," *Grand Street* 6 (Winter 1987): 197.

89. Niebuhr, *Irony of American History*, 82.

90. Niebuhr, *Irony of American History*, 53.

91. Niebuhr, *Irony of American History*, 35, 37, 38; cf. Reinhold Niebuhr, *Moral Man and Immoral Society: A Study in Ethics and Politics* (Louisville, KY: Westminster Press, 1932), 100–104, 106.

92. Niebuhr, *Irony of American History*, 56.

93. Jace Weaver, "Original Simplicities and Present Complexities: Reinhold Niebuhr, Ethnocentrism, and the Myth of American Exceptionalism," *Journal of the American Academy of Religion* 63 (Summer 1995): 231–47, at 237.

94. Niebuhr, *Irony of American History*, 29; cf. Potter, *People of Plenty*.

95. Obama quoted in David Brooks, "Obama, Gospel and Verse," *New York Times*, April 26, 2007; R. Ward Holder and Peter B. Josephson, "Obama's Niebuhr Problem," *Church History* 82 (September 2013): 678–87; Ross Douthat, "Obama the Theologian," *New York Times*,

February 7, 2015, https://www.nytimes.com/2015/02/08/opinion/sunday/ross-douthat-obama
-the-theologian.html.

96. Jackson Lears, "American Oracle: The Uses and Abuses of Reinhold Niebuhr," *Commonweal* 138, no. 18 (October 11, 2011), 12–14, https://www.commonwealmagazine.org/american
-oracle. See also Richard W. Fox, *Reinhold Niebuhr: A Biography* (New York: Pantheon Books,
1985), 284–85.

Chapter Eleven

1. Harold John Ockenga, *God Save America* (Boston: John W. Schaeffer, 1939), 14, 15, 16.

2. Will Herberg, *Protestant-Catholic-Jew: An Essay in American Religious Sociology* (Garden
City, NY: Doubleday, 1955), 75; Kruse, *One Nation under God*; Matthew Avery Sutton, *American
Apocalypse: A History of Modern Evangelicalism* (Cambridge, MA: Harvard University Press,
2017), 264–66, 310, 316; Ronald Reagan, "Remarks at the Annual Convention of the National
Association of Evangelicals in Orlando, Florida," March 8, 1983, American Presidency Project,
https://www.presidency.ucsb.edu/node/262885.

3. Surveying presidential rhetoric from 1933 to 2008, David Domke and Kevin Coe found
this change manifest in the 1980s. David Domke and Kevin Coe, *The God Strategy: How Religion
Became a Political Weapon in America* (New York: Oxford University Press, 2008), 61–64.

4. Bercovitch, *American Jeremiad.*

5. Perry Miller, "Errand into the Wilderness," *William and Mary Quarterly* 10, no. 1 (January
1953): 4–32, at 7.

6. Nicholas Guyatt, "'An Instrument of National Policy': Perry Miller and the Cold
War," *Journal of American Studies* 36 (April 2002): 107–49; P. Miller, "Errand into the Wilderness," 19.

7. P. Miller, "Errand into the Wilderness," 17.

8. P. Miller, "Errand into the Wilderness," 19.

9. Perry Miller, *The Life of the Mind in America: From the Revolution to the Civil War* (New
York: Harcourt, Brace and World, 1965).

10. Harry Ritter, *Dictionary of Concepts in History* (Westport, CT: Greenwood, 1986), 290–
92; Potter, *People of Plenty*, 7; David E. Stannard, "American Historians and the Idea of National
Character: Some Problems and Prospects," *American Quarterly* 23, no. 2 (May 1971): 202–20;
Michael McGiffert, "Selected Writings on American National Character and Related Subjects to
1969," *American Quarterly* 21, Supplement (Summer 1969): 330–49.

11. Gamble, *In Search of the City on a Hill*, 133, 137.

12. Arthur M. Schlesinger Jr., *A Life in the Twentieth Century: Innocent Beginnings, 1917–1950*
(New York: Knopf, 2000), 161–63.

13. John F. Kennedy, "Remarks of Senator John F. Kennedy, Mississippi Valley Historical
Association, Minneapolis, Minnesota, April 25, 1958," John F. Kennedy Presidential Library and
Museum, https://www.jfklibrary.org/archives/other-resources/john-f-kennedy-speeches/minn
eapolis-mn-19580425; Rodgers, *As a City on a Hill*, 190, 202, 223–24.

14. John F. Kennedy, "Address of President-Elect John F. Kennedy Delivered to a Joint
Convention of the General Court of the Commonwealth of Massachusetts, January 9, 1961,"
John F. Kennedy Presidential Library and Museum, https://www.jfklibrary.org/archives/other
-resources/john-f-kennedy-speeches/massachusetts-general-court-19610109.

15. Gamble, *In Search of the City on a Hill*, 139; Lyndon B. Johnson, "Remarks in Boston at Post Office Square," October 27, 1964, American Presidency Project, https://www.presidency.ucsb.edu/node/241885.

16. Reagan, "Election Eve Address." Abram C. Van Engen mentions the "shining" addition in a footnote without interpretation: Van Engen, *City on a Hill*, 359n1; cf. Gamble, *In Search of the City on a Hill*, 144–45.

17. Seymour Martin Lipset cites only Robert Bellah's reference to Miller. See Lipset, *American Exceptionalism: Double-Edged Sword*, 64n63; Lipset, *Continental Divide*, 77, 238n13–14.

18. Kevin M. Schultz and Paul Harvey, "Everywhere and Nowhere: Recent Trends in American Religious History and Historiography," *Journal of the American Academy of Religion* 78 (March 2010): 129–62, at 133; Jon Butler, "Jack-in-the-Box Faith: The Religion Problem in Modern American History," *Journal of American History* 90 (March 2004): 1357–78.

19. Bellah, *Broken Covenant*, 13–15, 42, 46, 167n9.

20. Herbert Gans, "The American Malaise," *New York Times*, February 6, 1972, SM16–17.

21. Dispensationalists divided God's plan for the world into a series of (usually seven) "dispensations." The idea of the United States as central to the penultimate phase to save the world galvanized many conservative evangelicals. Jonathan R. Baer, "American Dispensationalism's Perpetually Imminent End Times," *Journal of Religion* 87 (April 2007): 248–64; Mark A. Noll, *A History of Christianity in the United States and Canada* (Grand Rapids, MI: William B. Eerdmans, 1992), 376–78.

22. Jerry Falwell, *Listen, America!* (1980; repr., New York: Bantam Books, 1981), 12, 88, 101. On Falwell, see Michael Sean Winters, *God's Right Hand: How Jerry Falwell Made God a Republican and Baptized the American Right* (New York: HarperCollins, 2012).

23. Kaplan, *Our American Israel*, 220, 221.

24. Gans, "American Malaise."

25. Richard J. Tofel, "The Real Issues," *New York Times*, June 24, 1980, A14.

26. Daniel Bell, "The End of American Exceptionalism," *National Affairs*, no. 41 (Fall 1975): 193–224, at 204, 222.

27. Seymour Martin Lipset, *The First New Nation*, rev. ed. (New York: Norton, 1979), vi. See also Seymour Martin Lipset and William Schneider, "The Decline of Confidence in American Institutions," *Political Science Quarterly* 98, no. 3 (Autumn 1983): 379–402.

28. Daniel Horowitz, *Jimmy Carter and the Energy Crisis of the 1970s: The "Crisis of Confidence" Speech of July 15, 1979; A Brief History with Documents* (Boston: Bedford/St. Martin's, 2005); Finis Dunaway, *Seeing Green: The Use and Abuse of American Environmental Images* (Chicago: University of Chicago Press, 2015), 171–76; Jimmy Carter, "Address to the Nation on Energy and National Goals: 'The Malaise Speech,'" July 15, 1979, American Presidency Project, https://www.presidency.ucsb.edu/node/249458.

29. Trevor B. McCrisken, "Exceptionalism: Exceptionalism and the Legacy of Vietnam," *American Foreign Relations*, accessed January 11, 2021, http://www.americanforeignrelations.com/E-N/Exceptionalism-Exceptionalism-and-the-legacy-of-vietnam.html#ixzz0kIUkB0l9. See also Trevor B. McCrisken, *American Exceptionalism and the Legacy of Vietnam: U.S. Foreign Policy Since 1974* (New York: Palgrave Macmillan, 2003), 62–65.

30. Kenneth E. Boulding, Michael Kammen, and Seymour Martin Lipset, *From Abundance to Scarcity: Implications for the American Tradition* (Columbus: Ohio State University Press, 1978).

31. Dan F. Hahn, "Flailing the Profligate: Carter's Energy Sermon of 1979," *Presidential Studies Quarterly* 10, no. 4 (1980): 583–87.

32. Carter, "Address to the Nation: 'Malaise Speech.'" See also Kevin Mattson, *What the Heck are You Up To, Mr. President? Jimmy Carter, America's "Malaise," and the Speech That Should Have Changed the Country* (New York: Bloomsbury USA, 2009).

33. Carter, "Address to the Nation: 'Malaise Speech.'"

34. For a review of the Court versus Country issue, see Alan Gibson, "'No Ordinary Historian': Lance Banning and the Founding," *American Political Thought: A Journal of Ideas, Institutions, and Culture* 5 (Fall 2016): 686–708.

35. Philip Jenkins, *Decade of Nightmares: The End of the Sixties and the Making of Eighties America* (New York: Oxford University Press, 2006), 156; Andrew Murphy, *Prodigal Nation: Moral Decline and Divine Punishment from New England to 9/11* (New York: Oxford University Press, 2008); Lipset, *First New Nation*, Norton rev. ed., vi.

36. Jenkins, *Decade of Nightmares*, 155–56, 174–75.

37. Lipset, *First New Nation*, Norton rev. ed., xl.

38. Jenkins, *Decade of Nightmares*, 175. See also Murphy, *Prodigal Nation*, 77–106; James Morton Turner and Andrew C. Isenberg, *The Republican Reversal: Conservatives and the Environment from Nixon to Trump* (Cambridge, MA: Harvard University Press, 2018), 62–64.

39. John M. Jones and Robert C. Rowland, "A Covenant-Affirming Jeremiad: The Post-Presidential Ideological Appeals of Ronald Wilson Reagan," *Communication Studies* 56, no. 2 (2005): 157–74. For the traditional jeremiad, see esp. P. Miller, "Errand into the Wilderness," 22: "A nation in covenant is systematically punished, the degree of affliction being exquisitely proportioned to the amount of depravity. While thus being chastised it is still in covenant—or, at least, as long as it has not committed the unpardonable sin which conclusively severs the covenant." For the range of "modern" jeremiads, see Mark Stephen Jendrysik, *Modern Jeremiahs: Contemporary Visions of American Decline* (Lanham, MD: Rowman and Littlefield, 2008). See also Andrew Murphy, "Longing, Nostalgia, and Golden Age Politics: The American Jeremiad and the Power of the Past," *Perspectives on Politics* 7 (March 2009): 125–41.

40. Falwell, *Listen America!* 12. See also Gillis J. Harp, *Protestants and American Conservatism: A Short History* (New York: Oxford University Press, 2019), 214; Philip Gorski, *American Covenant: A History of Civil Religion from the Puritans to the Present* (Princeton, NJ: Princeton University Press, 2017), 179–83, 272n9. Politicians, too, sometimes used a secular form of the jeremiad, as Representative Ron Paul did in the 2008 presidential primaries. But Paul received only a tiny minority of votes. Jason A. Edwards, "Debating America's Role in the World: Representative Ron Paul's Exceptionalist Jeremiad," *American Behavioral Scientist* 55, no. 3 (2011): 253–69.

41. Gil Troy, *Morning in America: How Ronald Reagan Invented the 1980s* (Princeton, NJ: Princeton University Press, 2005), 253–55.

42. Quoted in Jenkins, *Decade of Nightmares*, 176; Ronald Reagan, "Remarks at the Annual Convention of the National Religious Broadcasters," February 9, 1982, American Presidency Project, https://www.presidency.ucsb.edu/node/244759.

43. Peale's influence in Cold War America was important ideologically. Christopher J. Lane, *Surge of Piety: Norman Vincent Peale and the Remaking of American Religious Life* (New Haven, CT: Yale University Press, 2012); Donald B. Meyer, *The Positive Thinkers: Popular Religious Psychology from Mary Baker Eddy to Norman Vincent Peale and Ronald Reagan* (Middletown, CT: Wesleyan University Press, 1988); Carol V. R. George, *God's Salesman: Norman Vincent Peale and the Power of Positive Thinking*, 2nd ed. (New York: Oxford University Press, 2019), 206–7.

44. George, *God's Salesman*, x.

45. David Forsythe, "Exploring American Exceptionalism (Part I)," *Globalist*, July 17, 2007, https://www.theglobalist.com/exploring-american-exceptionalism-part-1/.

46. Francis Fukuyama, *The End of History and the Last Man* (New York: Free Press, 1992).

47. James H. Billington and Kathleen Parthé, *The Search for a New Russian National Identity: Russian Perspectives* (Washington, DC: Library of Congress, 2003), 12; Fukuyama, *End of History*.

48. Marshall I. Goldman, "The Convergence of Environmental Disruption," *Science* 170, no. 3953 (October 2, 1970): 37–42; Marion J. Levy Jr., *Modernization and the Structure of Society: A Setting of International Affairs* (Princeton, NJ: Princeton University Press, 1966); Lowell Dittmer, "Soviet Reform and the Prospect of Sino-Soviet Convergence," *Studies in Comparative Communism* 22 (Summer–Autumn 1989): 125–38; cf. Daniel Bell, *The Coming of Post-Industrial Society: A Venture in Social Forecasting*, 2nd ed. (New York: Basic Books, 1976), 112–14.

49. James Spiller, *Frontiers for the American Century: Outer Space, Antarctica, and Cold War Nationalism* (New York: Palgrave Macmillan, 2010), 21–22.

50. Neither phrase, "chosen nation" nor "chosen people," appeared in the speeches of presidents from 1948 to 1980, as measured by the American Presidency Project digital files, (https://www.presidency.ucsb.edu/advanced-search), and these ideas did not influence the platforms of the political parties. Ari L. Goldman, "God and Party Platforms," *New York Times*, October 17, 1992, sec. 1, 32.

51. McCrisken, *American Exceptionalism and the Legacy of Vietnam*, 169–80.

52. Madeleine K. Albright, "Interview on NBC-TV, *The Today Show* with Matt Lauer, Columbus, Ohio, February 19, 1998," US Department of State Archive, https://1997-2001.state.gov/statements/1998/980219a.html. On the genealogy of the indispensable nation and Donald Trump, see Jeet Heer, "Donald Trump Killed the 'Indispensable Nation.' Good!" *New Republic*, May 15, 2017, https://newrepublic.com/article/142571/donald-trump-killed-indispensable-nation-good.

53. Lipset, *Continental Divide*; Lipset, *American Exceptionalism: Double-Edged Sword*; Gary Marks and Seymour Martin Lipset, *It Didn't Happen Here: Why Socialism Failed in the United States* (New York: Norton, 2000).

54. Robert Patman, "Globalisation, the New US Exceptionalism and the War on Terror," *Third World Quarterly* 27, no. 6 (2006): 963–86, at 964.

55. Rudy Giuliani, "Remarks at The Federalist Society in Washington, DC," November 16, 2007, American Presidency Project, https://www.presidency.ucsb.edu/node/295496.

56. Jacob Heilbrunn, "Norman's Conquest," *Washington Monthly*, December 1, 2007, https://washingtonmonthly.com/2007/12/01/normans-conquest/; Norman Podhoretz, "Is America Exceptional?" *Imprimis* 41, no. 10 (October 2012), https://imprimis.hillsdale.edu/is-america-exceptional/.

57. Mark West and Chris Carey, "(Re)Enacting Frontier Justice: The Bush Administration's Tactical Narration of the Old West Fantasy after September 11," *Quarterly Journal of Speech* 92, no. 4 (2006): 379–412.

58. Barack Obama, *The Audacity of Hope: Thoughts on Reclaiming the American Dream* (New York: Random House, 2006).

59. Barbara Finlay, *George W. Bush and the War on Women: Turning Back the Clock on Progress* (London: Zed Books, 2006), 210–14; Sonali Kolhatkar, "Afghan Women: Enduring American 'Freedom,'" Institute for Policy Studies, November 1, 2002, https://ips-dc.org/afghan_women_enduring_american_freedom/; Meghan Keneally, "Why the US Got Involved in Afghanistan— and Why It's Been Difficult to Get Out," ABC News (website), August 21, 2017, https://abcnews.go.com/US/us-involved-afghanistan-difficult/story?id=49341264.

60. Andrew J. Bacevich, *The Limits of Power: The End of American Exceptionalism* (New York: Metropolitan Books, 2008).

61. Federalist Society, "2007 National Lawyers Convention: Shining City upon a Hill: American Exceptionalism," November 15–17, 2007, https://fedsoc.org/events/2007-national-lawyers -convention. For video of Giuliani's speech, see "Rudy Giuliani Address at the 2007 National Lawyers Convention," November 16, 2007, video, 48:10, https://fedsoc.org/conferences/2007-national -lawyers-convention#agenda-item-rudy-giuliani-address-at-the-2007-national-lawyers -convention.

62. Gordon Wood quoted in "Beacon of Freedom: Does America Have a Special Mission?" 2007 National Lawyers Convention, November 15, 2007, video, 2:11:00, https://fedsoc.org /conferences/2007-national-lawyers-convention#agenda-item-beacon-of-freedom-does-america -have-a-special-mission.

63. For Wood's remarks, see "Is America Different from Other Major Western Democracies?" 2007 National Lawyers Convention, November 16, 2007, video, 1:17:17, https://fedsoc.org /conferences/2007-national-lawyers-convention#agenda-item-is-america-different-from-other -major-western-democracies. See also remarks by Professor Randy Barnett in "American Exceptionalism, the War on Terror and the Rule of Law in the Islamic World," 2007 National Lawyers Convention, November 17, 2007, video, 1:58:45, https://fedsoc.org/conferences/2007-national -lawyers-convention#agenda-item-american-exceptionalism-the-war-on-terror-and-the-rule-of -law-in-the-islamic-world.

64. Obama, "President's News Conference in Strasbourg."; Patman and Southgate, "Globalization."

65. Monica Crowley, "American Exceptionalism, RIP," *Washington Times*, March 23, 2010, https://www.washingtontimes.com/news/2010/mar/23/american-exceptionalism-rip/.

66. Seymour Martin Lipset and Jason M. Lakin, *The Democratic Century* (Norman: University of Oklahoma Press, 2004), xiii–xiv, 294, 295; Seymour Martin Lipset, "Still the Exceptional Nation?" *Wilson Quarterly* 24 (Winter 2000): 31–45; Seymour Martin Lipset and Earl Raab, *The Politics of Unreason: Right-Wing Extremism* (New York: Harper and Row, 1970).

67. An updated edition was issued five years later. See Morris Berman, *Dark Ages America: The Final Phase of Empire*, rev. ed. (New York: W. W. Norton, 2011).

68. Alfred W. McCoy, *In the Shadows of the American Century: The Rise and Decline of US Global Power* (Chicago: Haymarket Books, 2017). See also Julian Go, *Patterns of Empire: The British and American Empires, 1688 to the Present* (New York: Cambridge University Press, 2011).

69. Uri Friedman, "Why America Resists Learning from Other Countries," *Atlantic*, May 14, 2020.

70. Charles I. Jones, "The Facts of Economic Growth," in *Handbook of Macroeconomics*, vol. 2A, published 2016, p. 6, https://web.stanford.edu/~chadj/facts.pdf; Robert J. Gordon, "The Demise of U. S. Economic Growth: Restatement, Rebuttal, and Reflections," Northwestern University and NBER, January 20, 2014, http://economics.weinberg.northwestern.edu/robert-gordon /files/RescPapers/DemiseUSEconGrowth.pdf.

71. U. Friedman, "Why America Resists Learning"; Martha Lincoln, "Study the Role of Hubris in Nations' COVID-19 Response," *Nature* 585 (September 17, 2020): 325, https://doi.org /10.1038/d41586-020-02596-8.

72. See, e.g., Newt Gingrich, *Trump's America: The Truth about Our Nation's Great Comeback* (London: Hachette, 2018), 9–12, 67; J. Turner and Isenberg, *Republican Reversal*, esp. 187, 197, 211.

73. "#OurAmerica," American Exceptionalism: A Project of the Heartland Institute (website), accessed January 11, 2021, http://american-exceptionalism.org/.

74. Partners included the Center for Security Policy, the National Association of Scholars, and the Center for Urban Renewal and Education.

75. "What Is American Exceptionalism?" American Exceptionalism: A Project of the Heartland Institute (website), accessed January 11, 2021, http://american-exceptionalism.org/.

Afterword

1. Ellwood, *Shock of America*; Victoria de Grazia, *Irresistible Empire: America's Advance through 20th-Century Europe* (Cambridge, MA: Harvard University Press, 2005).

2. Even in those United Nations trusteeships gained from Japan after World War II that retain an associated status, de facto and strategic control remains with the United States.

3. Immerwahr, *How to Hide an Empire*; Chalmers Johnson, "Empire of Bases," *New York Times*, July 13, 2009; Chalmers Johnson, *The Sorrows of Empire: Militarism, Secrecy, and the End of the Republic* (London: Verso, 2004), 8; David Vine, *Base Nation: How U.S. Military Bases Abroad Harm America and the World* (New York: Henry Holt, 2015). Cf. Hopkins, *American Empire*.

4. Jacobs, "Seeing Like a Settler Colonial State"; Ostler, *Plains Sioux and U.S. Colonialism*; Tyrrell, *Crisis of the Wasteful Nation*, esp. 108–12.

5. Peter Onuf, "Imperialism and Nationalism in the Early Republic," in Tyrrell and Sexton, *Empire's Twin*, 25–26.

6. Esmond Wright, "The Revolution and the Constitution: Models of What and for Whom?" *Annals of the American Academy of Political and Social Science* 428 (November 1976): 1–21; Fred Halliday, *Revolution and World Politics: The Rise and Fall of the Sixth Great Power* (Basingstoke, UK: Macmillan, 1999), 69, 99, 181.

7. Mila Versteeg and Emily Zackin, "American Constitutional Exceptionalism Revisited," *University of Chicago Law Review* 81 (Fall 2014): 1641. See also Wright, "Revolution and the Constitution."

8. Eric Foner, *The Second Founding: How the Civil War and Reconstruction Remade the Constitution* (New York: W.W. Norton, 2019).

9. Lipset, *First New Nation*, 97–98.

10. See, e.g., Donald J. Maletz, "Tocqueville on Mores and the Preservation of Republics," *American Journal of Political Science* 49 (January 2005): 1–15.

11. Lipset, *First New Nation*, 2.

12. Alex Keyssar, *The Right to Vote: The Contested History of Democracy in the United States*, rev. ed. (New York: Basic Books, 2009), 44, Tables A2 and A3.

13. Keyssar, *Right to Vote*, 70, 71.

14. Tocqueville, *Democracy in America*, 1:455.

15. Michael Omi and Howard Winant, *Racial Formation in the United States: From the 1960s to the 1990s*, 2nd ed. (New York: Routledge, 1994); cf. Joe Feagin and Sean Elias, "Rethinking Racial Formation Theory: A Systemic Racism Critique," *Ethnic and Racial Studies* 36, no. 6 (2013): 931–36; "#BlackLivesMatter: The Birth of a New Civil Rights Movement," *Guardian* (UK), July 19, 2015, https://www.theguardian.com/world/2015/jul/19/blacklivesmatter-birth-civil-rights-movement.

16. Philip Nord, "The Origins of the Third Republic in France, 1860–1885," in *The Social Construction of Democracy, 1870–1990*, ed. G. R. Andrews and H. Chapman (London: Palgrave Macmillan, 1995), 31.

17. Paul Pickering, "A Wider Field in a New Country: Chartism in Colonial Australia," in *Elections: Full, Free and Fair*, ed. Marian Sawer (Annandale, NSW: Federation Press, 2001), 28–44.

18. Jad Adams, *Women and the Vote: A World History* (New York: Oxford University Press, 2014), 131–32.

19. Marian Sawer, "Pacemakers of the World," in Sawer, *Elections: Full, Free and Fair*, 1–27; Judith Brett, *From Secret Ballot to Democracy Sausage: How Australia Got Compulsory Voting* (Melbourne: Text, 2019), 23–25; Keyssar, *Right to Vote*, 115.

20. Albert Métin, *Le Socialisme sans doctrines: La question agraire et la question ouvriere en Australie et Nouvelle-Zelande* (Paris: F. Alcan, 1901).

21. Victor Selden Clark, *The Labour Movement in Australasia: A Study in Social Democracy* (New York: Henry Holt, 1906); Ian Tyrrell, "Victor Selden Clark's *The Labour Movement in Australasia*: Comparative Colonialism and American Exceptionalism," in *Contesting Australian History: Essays in Honour of Marilyn Lake*, ed. Joy Damousi and Judith Smart (Melbourne: Monash University Publishing, 2019), 190–203; Arthur C. Veatch, *Mining Laws of Australia and New Zealand* (Washington, DC: Government Printing Office, 1911), 7.

22. Senator Hugh de Largie, *Commonwealth of Australia Parliamentary Debates* 59, no. 17 (November 1910): 6305, quoted in Sawer, "Pacemakers of the World," 1.

23. For New Zealand's role, see Peter J. Coleman, *Progressivism and the World of Reform: New Zealand and the Origins of the American Welfare State* (Lawrence: University Press of Kansas, 1987).

24. Dowding, "Australian Exceptionalism Reconsidered," 178. Cf. William O. Coleman, ed., *Only in Australia: The History, Politics, and Economics of Australian Exceptionalism* (Melbourne: Oxford University Press, 2016).

25. Halliday, *Revolution and World Politics*, 99–103.

26. David Armitage, *The Declaration of Independence: A Global History* (Cambridge, MA: Harvard University Press, 2007), esp. 133–35.

27. See, e.g., Dunn, *American Exceptionalism: Origins, History, and Future*, 3.

28. Ian Tyrrell, *Transnational Nation: United States History in Global Perspective since 1789*, rev. ed. (Basingstoke, UK: Palgrave Macmillan, 2015), 62.

29. For a summary of migration as a transnational system, see Tyrrell, *Transnational Nation*, ch. 4. For American-bound migration's attractions, see Philip A. M. Taylor, *The Distant Magnet: European Emigration to the U.S.A.* (New York: Harper and Row, 1971), 8–11, 14–16, 44–45, 47, 86. On repatriation, see, e.g., Mark Wyman, *Round-Trip to America: The Immigrants Return to Europe, 1880–1930* (Ithaca, NY: Cornell University Press, 1993).

30. International Organization for Migration, *World Migration Report 2020* (Geneva, Switz.: International Organization for Migration, 2019), 25–26, 97–98, 102, 103.

31. Mark Hugo Lopez, Anna Gonzalez-Barrera, and Jens Manuel Krogstad, "Latinos Are More Likely to Believe in the American Dream, but Most Say It Is Hard to Achieve," Pew Research Center, September 11, 2018, https://www.pewresearch.org/fact-tank/2018/09/11/latinos-are-more-likely-to-believe-in-the-american-dream-but-most-say-it-is-hard-to-achieve/.

32. Jacob Poushter, "How People Around the World See the U.S. and Donald Trump in 10 Charts," Pew Research Center, January 8, 2020, https://www.pewresearch.org/fact-tank/2020/01/08/how-people-around-the-world-see-the-u-s-and-donald-trump-in-10-charts/; Richard Wike et al., "Trump Ratings Remain Low around Globe while Views of U.S. Stay Mostly

Favorable," Pew Research Center, January 8, 2020, https://www.pewresearch.org/global/2020/01/08/trump-ratings-remain-low-around-globe-while-views-of-u-s-stay-mostly-favorable/.

33. Evan Osnos, *Joe Biden: American Dreamer* (London: Bloomsbury, 2021). On the wider difficulties of the Trump legacy, see David Frum, *Trumpocalypse: Restoring American Democracy* (New York: HarperCollins, 2020). For a critical analysis of Biden's record and suitability, see Branco Marcetic, *Yesterday's Man: The Case against Joe Biden* (London: Verso, 2020). For an illuminating commentary on "success" and "defeat," see C. Vann Woodward, "The Irony of Southern History," *Journal of Southern History* 19 (February 1953): 3–19.

Index